BACK IN THE DAY

The Education of an Oklahoma Boy

A MEMOIR

KENNETH R. YOUNG

Copyright © 2020 by Kenneth R. Young

All rights reserved. No part of this book may be reproduced, distributed, or transmitted in any form or by any means, including photocopying, recording, or other electronic or mechanical methods, without the prior written permission of the author.

Cover design & formatting by Damonza.com

Publisher's Cataloging-In-Publication Data
(Prepared by The Donohue Group, Inc.)

Names: Young, Kenneth Ray, author.
Title: Back in the day : the education of an Oklahoma boy (a memoir) / by Kenneth R. Young.
Description: Mills River, NC : Ray Hill Publishing, [2020]
Identifiers: ISBN 9780578586625 | ISBN 9780578586632 (ebook)
Subjects: LCSH: Young, Kenneth Ray--Knowledge and learning. | College teachers--Connecticut--Biography. | Scholars--United States--Biography. | Connecticut--Biography. | Oklahoma--Biography. | LCGFT: Autobiographies.
Classification: LCC LA2317.Y68 A3 2020 (print) | LCC LA2317.Y68 (ebook) | DDC 371.20092--dc23

Library of Congress Control Number: 2020903922

Ray Hill Publishing
236 Ray Hill Road
Mills River, NC 28759

Printed in the United States of America

I wrote this book for my wife, Midge, my brother, Charlie, and my children, Cathy, Susie, and James. I told them to read only the sections they enjoy and skim through the chapters that bore them. I recommend all readers follow that advice.

The book is also dedicated to my mother and Uncle Bunk.

On a beautiful spring day, the eighty-year-old master Chuang-tzu was hoeing his flower garden. A disciple came to him for advice, seeking Chuang-tzu's words of wisdom. As the disciple watched the great philosopher weeding he wondered why his mentor wasted his time on such a menial task when he might die before the flowers bloomed. When Chuang-tzu paused, his disciple asked, "Master Chuang, if you knew you were going to die tomorrow, what would you do to prepare for your death?" Master Chuang thought for only a moment and said, "I would cultivate my garden," and returned to tilling the ground. And those were the Master's words of wisdom.

—*Ancient Chinese proverb*

Chapter 1

In the Beginning

Some of my earliest memories revolve around the desire to learn, and school was where learning happened. In early September 1945, when I was five years old, I desperately wanted to go to school. Alas, my dream would have to wait. On the day Roosevelt Elementary School opened, my brother Corky, who was two years older, entered the second grade. But I was ordered to stay home. I did not understand why I could not also go to school, and I cried when he left the house.

I snuck out later that morning and crossed a dirt road, hiding in a large open field covered with high grass almost as tall as I was. I wandered over to an old red metal oil drum that lay on its side with a bow in the middle. Kids often mounted it and pretended the barrel was a horse, but there were no kids around that early September day, just me.

I heard yelling in the distance, and I stood on the barrel to take a look. A quarter of a mile away, kids were enjoying their morning recess on their first day of school. Some were playing on two small merry-go-rounds and several were horsing around on the playground's four seesaws; other kids were on the six swings. The swing poles rose twenty feet high, and the boys and girls screamed as they reached the top and dropped back down. Another group of boys, including my brother, were even closer, yelling at each other as they played "Red Rover, Red Rover, Come Over" in the open field between me and the school. In the distance to the east and south, there were a few scattered trees and houses; to the north and west, there was nothing but pastureland for miles. Roosevelt was on the edge of the city limits of Lawton, Oklahoma.

I envied my brother and dreamed of going to school to be with the other kids, but I was stuck at home. I felt like a martyr condemned by an accident of birth. A child had to be six years old to attend grammar school, and I was five years and ten months. This meant I would not be allowed to go to school until September 1946. There were no public kindergartens in Lawton, and if there had been private ones, my parents could not have afforded them.

The "six-year-old" policy had been instituted in 1943 because of World War II. By 1945 Lawton was the third-largest city in Oklahoma, with 20,000 people and growing. Officially established in 1901, Lawton had been a service town for nearby Fort Sill for many years. The older buildings at Fort Sill were constructed in 1869 during the Indian Wars with stone obtained from the nearby Wichita Mountains, whose granite peaks rose to almost 2,500 feet. A lake in the mountains supplied plentiful water.

Soldiers based at the fort in 1869 included various infantry and cavalry regiments including the Tenth Cavalry, composed of white officers and black enlisted men called "Buffalo Soldiers" by Indian scouts. Buffalo Bill, the famous bison hunter and showman, was often on post alongside other army scouts. The Indian Wars ended in the 1880s with the surrender of the Chiricahua Apaches. The Apache chief Geronimo lived his last days in jail at Fort Sill.

Through the 1890s, the troops stationed at Fort Sill—officially considered to be in "Indian Territory"—enforced the law in nearby towns and chased Indian renegades, outlaws, whiskey runners, and cattle rustlers until Oklahoma became a state in 1901.

During World War I, Fort Sill became a training base for the army's artillery and infantry and became one of the largest army bases in the United States, encompassing over 94,000 acres. Base personnel declined dramatically in the 1920s but exploded in size in the late 1930s as World War II appeared on the horizon. The fort became the headquarters for the U.S. Army Field Artillery and a basic training camp for both the army and marines. More soldiers stationed at Fort Sill meant more jobs for civilians both on the post and in the city.

As people moved to Lawton for jobs, developers built new homes and houses, and the city expanded its sewage and water lines. New grammar schools such as Roosevelt were built on the edge of the developments but were soon overwhelmed with new students. There was a shortage of teachers because better-paying jobs were available. Most commercial and residential development stopped with Pearl Harbor and the outbreak of World War II, but the population continued to grow.

Roosevelt Elementary was on the edge of town where sewage and water lines had been laid. My home, at 1511 I Street, was three blocks away from the new lines.

As I stood staring from my post that September day, bells rang and children playing on the school's playground returned to class. With a hangdog look, I crossed the field back toward home, watching out for stickers that were very painful on my bare feet; Momma only allowed me to wear shoes in the wintertime or when we went to town. I headed for the small house consisting of two rooms without indoor plumbing. There was a two-seat outhouse and a well with one pump in the backyard and another in the kitchen.

My grandma was waiting for me at the front door. She was a short, heavy woman, obese by modern standards. In later years she was confined to a wheelchair, but in 1945 she was still mobile. Around sixty years old, she wore "granny" dresses that reached the ground and covered her heavy frame. The cloth came from the local bakery. She made her dresses from their flour sacks, usually white with blue polka dots, purchased for pennies. She changed to her "good" clothes only for funerals, church, or to go downtown. She smelled faintly of sweat and overwhelmingly of snuff, a powdered tobacco popular with older women who were not supposed to smoke. In movies of the era, wealthy men sniffed a pinch of snuff, but Grandma used it much like it was chewing tobacco. She put a pinch in her mouth and every few minutes spit tobacco juice into an empty tin can—not an appealing sight to look at but one no worse than chewing tobacco.

"Where you been, child?" she asked as she hugged me. "Time for your lessons." Since I was not allowed in school, she had decided to tutor me at home. She always told me I was her favorite grandchild, no small honor considering she had many grandchildren. We called her Grandma Bell; I assumed this was because some earlier grandmother had the family name of Young when Grandma Bell first became one. I don't know whether Bell was her maiden name or given name, but technically she was Grandma Young, my father's mother. At any rate, she had five children, four boys and one girl. The boys all bore family names: William (Bill), Curly (I don't know his true first name), Charles (Charlie, my father), and Hubert (Hoot). The girl, Nadine, was the youngest of the bunch.

The oldest, Uncle Bill, a deputy sheriff, lived in Wichita Falls, Texas, about sixty miles southwest of Lawton. He had seven kids; Curly had two; my dad two; and Aunt Nadine, who lived in California, had three girls. I was the only boy of my generation without a traditional family name: Charles, William, Hubert, Walter, and James. Charles was the most popular and was given to my brother, Charles W. Young, Jr. Because so many people had the same given name, all the younger children except me carried nicknames: Corky, Jimmie Jo, Billy Ross, etc. My mother selected my name for me because the Youngs had "too many damn children" with the same names.

Grandpa Charles Young died many years before I was born. He had worked for the railroad, and Grandma Bell received a small pension after his death. Before World War II, she moved from son to son, usually for a year or two at a time. When my father was drafted in late 1943, she moved in with us to help Mom raise two small children. My mother took a job as a waitress, and Grandma Bell took care of me and my brother.

My father did not believe women should work outside the home, but with him in the navy fighting the "dirty Japs," Mom, a twenty-three-year-old blonde-haired, blue-eyed beauty, decided to work at a diner in downtown Lawton about a mile away. I was not allowed to go to the restaurant. She enjoyed the work, since it was her first job. For the first time she was free of Dad's rules, and often went to parties with her brother, Uncle Red, who was in the army and stationed at Fort Sill.

By modern standards, Grandma Bell, with her ninth-grade education, was not qualified to teach school. At the time, though, she had more schooling than most women in Oklahoma. When her family moved to Lawton, sometime after 1901, she even got a teaching job at a grammar school. She was qualified enough to teach me to read and write when I was denied enrollment at Roosevelt.

At first, she used comic books, which I loved. She asked me what the stories were about, having me interpret them not by reading the words but by analyzing the drawings. That is, she taught me sight-reading rather than phonetics. She obtained old copies of reading books for the first through third grades. I did not learn to pronounce the "a" in cat or the "ou" in house; instead, I memorized the words associated with color drawings of a cat or house. At the time, Lawton grammar schools also taught sight-reading.

Later in life I realized that sight-reading had major disadvantages. I can't sound out words—I visualize them. It was hard to learn to pronounce or spell complicated new words; that required memorization. The dictionary became my constant companion over the years; it aided my spelling but did not help my pronunciation. Sight-reading proved a real, perhaps insurmountable, problem when I attempted to learn a foreign language.

That said, I do not regret learning sight-reading, because it does have a major advantage: it helped me learn to love reading, a passion I've had my entire life. Since I read images rather than words, reading is like going to the movies. That creates problems as well, though: since I don't read words, I am a speed-reader who often has problems with grammatical rules and sentence construction. When reading nonfiction books, I write comments in the margins to force myself to read slowly.

Grandma would sit at the kitchen table for a few hours each day as she taught me the alphabet, basic arithmetic, and writing. Writing was her worst subject, and much like hers, my penmanship is atrocious. She was proud of my studiousness, though, bragging that I could read better than my brother.

My brother's nickname was Corky, from a character in *Gasoline Alley,* a once-popular comic strip. Published in newspapers around the country from 1918 through the early 1960s, the strip depicted the life of a lower-middle-class family. The male members of the family had tufts of front hair that were uncontrollable. Apparently, my brother had such hair when he was a baby. *Gasoline Alley* is often compared to *Dagwood* and *Blondie,* another notable American comic.

When he would come home from school that year, Corky and I seldom played together. He had new friends. When I tried to join them, he threw stones at me, yelling, "Go home!" I did not like playing with him anyway. Like many older brothers, he tried to tell—or in his words, "teach"—me how to do everything, insisting it must be done his way. He picked on me constantly, not only physically but also psychologically. When no grown-ups were around, his favorite sport was to hit me or twist my arm behind my back, and often threatened to break it, calling me stupid when I refused to do things his way. If I screamed, he laughed and called me a crybaby.

If I complained to my mother, she would look at me and say, "Take care of yourself."

"But he's bigger than me."

She'd laugh and say, "That's why they made tools—pick up a stick and fight back." I once picked up a hammer and chased him around the house, but he was faster and simply laughed at me.

Sympathy was not my mother's strong suit. "Be a man," she would say. "I ain't raising no sissies." She liked alpha men and boys. "He's a handful," my mother would say when talking about my brother, but in a tone of voice that indicated she was proud of him.

Even at eight, my brother was much like my father—he wanted to be the boss. He even bossed my mother around when my father was gone. Conversely, I grew to dislike dominant personalities and dreamed of a day when no one could tell me what to do. Living alone in Alaska in a log cabin sounded ideal. Today, my wife tells our friends, "He's my cave man." I smile and return to my office to write.

Thus, I learned early some basic lessons in life: I should not expect sympathy; the only person I could depend on to take care of me was me; and I should stay away from people with dominating personalities.

My mother loved me, but she loved my father and brother more. She liked and respected feisty men. I was quiet, laid-back, and generally easygoing. I loved my mother and accepted, without bitterness, that my brother, as the firstborn, had a legitimate right to be loved more than me, the right to more attention, and the right to get his way more often. I did not resent my brother. I loved him too, more than anyone except Mom.

Although my mother admired my brother's feisty nature, she relied on me to help her and in many ways showed that she enjoyed my company and considered me an ally. I assisted her with most of the household chores, from washing the clothes to mopping the floors. She taught me an important lesson. Unlike my brother and father, I learned I was not the center of the universe.

My brother had many good traits. He was a happy kid who enjoyed playing with other boys in the neighborhood. He was smart and confident, and very good at sports, particularly baseball. He never allowed any older boys to pick on me; only he could do that. His constant attacks on me also proved valuable. Big boys did not scare me, and verbal attacks meant nothing to me. My willingness to fight meant few boys picked on me. Anyone who threatened me was a lesser threat than my brother who often bloodied my nose, bruised my arms and legs, and even gave me black eyes. However, he needed to be careful. I got in my licks if he didn't stop, and there was always the hammer. Later in life, whenever I met a man who admitted to being the older child, I would hit him (gently) and say, "I know you deserved that blow." Generally, they admitted they did and laughed.

My mother's lack of sympathy, or perhaps her dislike of whining little boys, was based on the realities of life. She was truly a beautiful woman who at twenty-three looked like Ingrid Bergman, the Swedish blonde-haired movie star. Her name was Mildred, and her friends called her Milly. But her family nickname was Toad because of her big, beautiful blue eyes.

Socially, though, she had a number of liabilities. For one, she was a Bass. Many people in Lawton considered the Basses to be "Okies" or ignorant "rednecks" who worked in the fields picking cotton, wore dirty clothes, and drove broken-down cars, if they could even afford a car. Rednecks were generally considered to be stupid, lazy, and untrustworthy. "Basses were poor," Mom said. "We wore faded and patched clothes, but when we went to town, we wore clean clothes. We were poor but we were not white trash."

The Bass family was "down-to-earth," and they lived a hard life. Like most of Mom's extended family, the Basses were subsistence farmers who owned small plots of land but earned their money as sharecroppers. When cotton-picking time arrived, the family, including the children, worked twelve-hour days bent over in the blazing sun picking the infamous crop for a few dollars. Although the educated city dwellers looked down on them as poor white trash, the Basses were hard workers who never looked for handouts and did not accept insults. They felt comfortable with friends who said "shit" rather than "number two," said "piss" for "urinate," and knew how to wipe their asses with buffalo grass or a corn cobb. Most could not read or write and had never been to school. Perhaps one or two could read, but certainly none of them quoted Socrates or Shakespeare.

That does not mean they were stupid. The educated city dwellers were more prosperous than the Basses, but, as they often said, having an IQ of 160 doesn't mean a person knows how to pour piss out of a boot with directions written on the heel. They knew things city dwellers did not: how to plow a field with a mule team, build a house, drill a well, or string barbwire. They were hardworking men and women, proud and realistic. "Too poor to spit," they admitted, but they shared their food and prepared sleeping pallets for visiting family or friends.

Mom was nearly illiterate. Until she was fourteen, she lived on different farms miles from the nearest school and often worked in the fields, so her attendance record was horrendous. When she was fifteen, she was in the fifth grade but read at a third-grade level, and her math skills were practically nonexistent. Her skills improved over the years, and in her sixties, she became a reader. Her math skills improved with every job. I learned from her that illiterate did not mean stupid, for she was an intelligent woman who happened to be born in poverty.

Living in tar-paper shacks, working in the cotton fields, and often going to bed hungry and cold made her extremely practical and less sympathetic to what she saw as my insignificant childhood problems. The word "I want" was a bright red flag to her. "I want to go to the movies, I want ice cream, I want a new pair of shoes, I want a bicycle," I would say. Her response: "Yeah, and people in hell want ice water. Lots of luck." Cut yourself? "Stop crying, stupid. That'll make you more careful," she'd say as she poured iodine on the wound and covered it with a piece of white tape. Burn yourself on the stove? You'd get a dash of lard, and that's it. A doctor? Are you crazy—doctors cost money. If you played cards with her and lost a few pennies, she kept the pennies. "Don't cry, stupid. I cheated," she'd say. To her, to expect sympathy was stupid—you'd be a whole lot better off accepting the real world.

Mom's paternal grandfather, John Holland Bass, was born in Texas in 1863. He worked as a blacksmith and a mule skinner delivering supplies to army posts. In the 1880s, he began delivering to Indian reservations and moved his family to Indian Territory in Oklahoma. Four of his six children were born there, including my mother's father, Papa Joe, in 1888. Papa Joe's mother was an Indian.[1]

What tribe? The extended Bass family disagreed and often named different tribes: some said Choctaw, some said Comanche, some said Pawnee, but most said Cherokee. Although three of John Holland's sons and one of his daughters were born in Indian Territory, the Basses never lived on any Indian reservation. When Oklahoma was opened to white settlers in 1901, John Holland did not register his children with the Indian Bureau. After his death in 1910, his children refused to acknowledge they were "half-breeds." In Oklahoma, many considered half-breeds to be on the same level as Mexicans and "Negroes." Prejudices were strong on the frontier, where many had lost family members during the Indian Wars.

No one dared call Papa Joe a half-breed to his face. He was of

---

[1] "Indian Territory Records," Chickasaw Nation, Vol.6, No. 125.

medium height, skinny, and considered to be a dangerous man. He carried a gun in one boot and a knife in the other. Papa Joe followed in his father's footsteps. He made his living as a mule skinner driving freight wagons often hauling supplies, including whiskey, to Indian reservations, as a cowboy, and as an adroit cattle rustler, among many other activities that put him on the edge of being an outlaw and a renegade. Around 1910 he married Effie Long, the sixteen-year-old daughter of a farmer who had been selling his crops to Fort Sill since the 1880s. Effie was a half-breed, too, but her father also refused to register his children with the Indian Bureau. Her Grandpa Ward was a cattle rancher in Texas near the Oklahoma border who provided beef to Fort Sill. He and Grandpa Long were the family patriarchs.

Why Effie married Papa Joe remains a mystery, but for nineteen years she was the heart of the Bass family. She had five children, two sons and three daughters. They all looked like their mother: the girls were blonde and blue-eyed, while the sons were tall, red-headed, and freckle-faced. Hazel, called Dobber, was the first, born in 1913 and at fifteen married to a half-breed Choctaw. She had two children, Jimmie Joe and Billy Katherine. Her sister Hester, called Nig, was next to marry and had one child, named Charles, then divorced and remarried an army sergeant named Ted. Effie and Joe's third child was a boy, named Clint but called Red. He was six feet, two inches tall, and in his prime weighed 180 pounds. No one, not even Papa Joe, messed with Red. He had one daughter, Caroline. My mother was the fourth child, born in 1921. The last, a boy named Marvin but called Bunky, was born in 1929, and became an integral part of my mother's life.

The Basses were a prideful family and took any insult personally. Like their extended family, which included the Longs and Wards, they were clannish. In a fight, they stood together. In hard times, every person was expected to take care of themselves.

As his four children were born, Joe continued to work as a mule skinner distributing goods to most of the Indian reservations, but in the early 1920s trucks were quickly replacing wagons. His wife and children tried to get him to register with the Indian Bureau. Being half-Indian, he was entitled to 160 acres of land, but he refused. "Ain't no damn Indian," he said. He wandered around Oklahoma smuggling whiskey to the reservations, doing odd jobs, and getting drunk. In Lawton, he often got into saloon fights and went to jail. He was so familiar to police that when the judges sentenced him to a week or month in jail, the sheriff seldom put him in a locked cell. In the daytime he sat on a bench on the large tree-lined lawn in front of the courthouse, the most impressive building in Lawton.

In February 1929 a major crisis struck the Bass family. Effie Long Bass died giving birth to her fifth child, Marvin (who we called "Bunk"). In Bunk's telling, his mother died not because she couldn't be saved, but because she was a true believer. After he was born, she bled, and bled, and bled. Papa Joe wasn't there and Hazel, the oldest daughter, called a doctor. The doctor recommended medicine to stop the bleeding. But Effie's minister, and a number of members of her church, told her not to take the medicine, saying it was "God's will whether she lived or died." Hazel, Hester, and Toad watched their mother bleed to death.

Thereafter, every member of the Bass family hated established churches of any variety, particularly Baptist ones in Oklahoma. Say the word "minister" or "preacher" and my mother's face would harden. "Shit on all preachers," she would mutter. She never attended church, not even for funerals. If I mentioned going to church, she'd roll her eyes. "Not me," she'd say. "Go if you want, but not me." In Baptist country, that made her even more of an outsider. "What do you mean you don't believe in Jesus Christ!" they gasped. "Didn't say that," she answered. "I said, 'I don't believe in churches.'"

Fortunately for her, my father and his family agreed with this view, but for different reasons. The Youngs were several steps up the social ladder from the Basses. Very few were farmers; most specialized in clerical areas such as bank telling and grocery clerking. A number were whiskey runners while others were preachers, deputy sheriffs, or local policemen. They seldom worked at jobs that required hard, physical labor. Born salesmen, they considered preaching simply another salesman's job—preach on Sundays and fleece the gullible the rest of the week. "Thank you, Jesus," sprang from their mouths with the best of them, but they never stepped inside a church unless it meant they could make money. A few of my father's drinking buddies in Lawton were preachers, and in his mind they were scam artists and "fake sons of bitches."

In almost any social group, my father's charisma was obvious. Charlie Young was the life of the party, a good old boy with lots of drinking buddies. I often wondered why my father married my mother, a serious, no-nonsense woman who seldom drank or enjoyed parties. When I was older, Bunk told me the story of how it happened.

When my father met my mother in 1936, Oklahoma was in a severe depression. (John Steinbeck's novel *The Grapes of Wrath* offers a vivid account of life at the time.) To make matters worse, Northwest Oklahoma had been suffering through a major drought for several years; even into the early '40s, dust storms erupted as far south as Lawton. My mother often screamed at us boys to close the windows and sweep the floors. Some mornings, we had to shovel piles of sand off the front porch before the door could be opened.

Lawton, located in southwestern Oklahoma, suffered less than the northwestern part of the state, but it was still in the grip of deep economic crisis. After World War I, the army contingent at Fort Sill declined dramatically, with major repercussions for the local economy. By the time the drought came, the local water shortage was not as great as it was in the northwest because the Army Corps of Engineers had built reservoirs in the Wichita Mountains in the early 1900s to supply Fort Sill and Lawton, but the farms around the city were in desperate straits. The Basses, the Longs, and the Wards suffered as farmers and ranchers. The drought hit them hard.

When my mother's mother, Effie Long Bass, died in February 1929, Red, who was eleven years old, continued to live with Papa Joe. Hazel was married with a new baby, and Hester, only fourteen years old, moved in with her boyfriend, got pregnant, and married.

My mother, who was eight, and Bunk, the newborn, were shuffled off to relatives who lived on farms near Lawton. Aunt Lomer, one of Effie Long's sisters, took them for a few months before they were moved to Aunt Molly's farm near Duncan. The farm was in rough shape. The barn, sheds, corrals, and fences badly needed repairs. Broken farm machinery was scattered around the area. The house had no inside plumbing or electricity. The outhouse was about a hundred yards from the back door. Water was hand-pumped from a well in the front yard that was nothing but hard-packed dirt. Because of the drought, the land barely produced enough food and water for the extended family.

Nevertheless, Mom and Bunk were happy on the farms and always praised Aunt Lomer and Aunt Molly for their kindness. Money was scarce but the Aunts gave them a roof over their heads and food for their bellies. Mom (and when he was old enough, Bunk) helped with the chores, slept on quilted pallets on the floor, wore hand-me-down clothes, and often went barefoot. They had cousins to play with. Times were hard, and some nights they went to bed hungry.

By 1935, Aunt Molly's farm was not producing enough food to feed so many mouths. So, Aunt Molly moved to Lawton to live with one of her daughters. My mother was fourteen and Bunk was six, and they were forced to search for another place to live.

Papa Joe refused to help. He had remarried, and his new wife—according to Bunk, "the meanest woman" he ever knew—had two children from a previous marriage, and she did not want any of Papa Joe's children living with them. Papa Joe remained Papa Joe. He ignored his children, with the exception of Hazel, his oldest daughter, and Red, who was seventeen. As Bunk later explained to me, "Papa Joe had one son, and that was Red, and one daughter, and that was Hazel." I nodded. My father had one son, and that was Corky.

Mom and Bunk moved to a small, isolated, tar-paper shack near Lawton in the fall of 1936. When winter came, they were in desperate straits. They had no heat, no running water, and very little to eat. The sisters helped, slipping Mom a few dollars here and there, but they had very limited resources themselves.

With the few dollars, Mom, dressed in a "flour dress," towed Bunk into town to shop at Dewey Shaw's General Store. Dewey Shaw's covered more than two city blocks; the grocery section alone employed over thirty people, from stock boys to butchers to clerks. Large wooden barrels full of beans, rice, pickles, candy, and a myriad of other items lined the aisles. A clothing section sold jeans, suits, dresses, shoes, boots, and many other goods. Farm equipment and hardware were sold in the yard outside the store.

Although only twenty-one years old, my father was one of the assistant managers in the grocery section. He earned twelve dollars a week, a good salary in Depression times. In the evenings, he was allowed to drive home one of Shaw's delivery trucks, a converted Model A. He was the sole breadwinner for his family, which included Grandma Bell and his two younger brothers and sister.

The first time Mom and Bunk came to Shaw's they were frightened—they had never been to town alone and the store was huge. My father, on the other hand, was mesmerized, and he immediately went over to assist her. I am sure my mother was a dazzlingly beautiful fifteen-year-old girl. Dad guided her to the best buys, then offered to drive them home. They accepted.

The obvious happened. For the next several months, he came over two or three nights a week with groceries and firewood. My mom loved being courted. She giggled when she told me the story about how they took rides at night in the truck. She proclaimed she loved it when he shifted gears. She would sit as close to Dad as possible, and when he shifted into fourth gear his hand always went up her skirt. She was barely fifteen, but she was world-wise. And she knew she had him. He had a good job, and was handsome, funny, and extremely self-confident. He knew more than her about most things. He could read, knew his arithmetic, and had beautiful penmanship. She did not know how to write a check until after he died. I can visualize the fear Mom felt before Dad "saved" her. She was strong on the inside but feared the outside world. Dad fought the world while she fought for survival.

Of course, she got pregnant. They married three months later.

My mother loved my father for being a strong, dominant man who protected her. He was the boss; his position on any topic was the only acceptable opinion. She followed his whims without complaint, and over the years, she had many reasons to complain. But she seldom said a critical word about him. After his death, she continued to defend him.

My brother was born six months after the wedding, in November 1937. Dad bought a small house on 1511 I Street on the outskirts of

Lawton with a few acres of land. Land was cheap during the Depression. The sandstorms were strong enough to force many farmers to sell their land. Much of Oklahoma gradually became ranching country, turning over from farm country.

When Mom and Dad married, Bunk spent his teenage years being passed back and forth among the family members. He usually lived with Hazel, his oldest sister, who had two small children, Jimmy Joe and Billy Katherine, both near his age. They became his brother and sister while his older siblings were more like aunts, with Red serving as the mean uncle. If he made trouble or messes around Hazel's house, she kicked him out for a few days but always welcomed him back. He often stayed a few days with Toad and Charlie (Mom and Dad), and he was welcome to stay a few days with many of his other relatives who lived in Lawton.

As a young boy I saw Bunk hanging around relatives' houses, but he was ten years older than me and we paid little attention to each other. In my forties, however, he became my favorite uncle. His view of the world was much like my mother's, a view that was different from most people's. To my delight, I came to realize that in public he played a role that partially hid his true self, much like my mother. In her later years, she acted around bosses and bureaucrats as if she were a frightened, ignorant, old woman. Similarly, Bunk played the good old country boy, a man who wore cowboy boots, jeans, and a cowboy hat in public and maintained an Oklahoma accent that disappeared when we talked. He liked cowboy duds; when I gave him a Stetson hat, he was delighted. Although he was not rich later in life, he was no longer poor, but while he was in town he enjoyed acting as if he were still a genuine Oklahoma cowboy.

Dad felt he had married beneath his station. He enjoyed telling stories about how unsophisticated my mom was at the time. One favorite was the bean story. Nearly every day, mom cooked red beans and potatoes for the evening meal. The beans came in bulk from Shaw's. Before going to work one Saturday morning, Dad decided he wanted white beans for Sunday dinner. He gave Mom a silver dollar to buy some white beans at the local market. She came back with twenty pounds of white beans. She didn't know their price and had bought enough to last several months.

In return, Mom would tell a funny story about Dad. One Saturday night in the deep of winter, Dad got drunk. He woke up during the middle of the night and, not wishing to walk the hundred yards to the outhouse in the cold weather, attempted to piss out the bedroom window. Drunk, he missed the window and accidentally peed in a chest full of clean clothes. Most women would scream at such an event. The clothes had been handwashed on a washboard and took considerable time and energy to clean. My mother laughed instead, always hugging my father after telling the story. She loved him, and I loved her for laughing about it. He smiled at the story because it proved he was the boss. She was his wife, but she was not his equal.

When I think of home, I think of the house on I Street. It's where my earliest memories begin, from late 1943 to the summer of 1946, while my father was in the navy. For the first time in seven years, Mom was outside Dad's control. Within months, she broke one of his rules: "No woman of mine is going to work at any manual job. No, sir!" Perhaps to make a little extra money, but just as likely to escape from us kids and Grandma, she took a job as a waitress, leaving Grandma Bell home to take care of the boys. For Mom, it was one of her happiest times. During the war there were constant parties at the house with family and friends dancing and drinking beer. Her brothers and sisters came and had a grand old time. My brother and I were never chased from the room.

The house on I Street was small even by Depression standards. And it did not have indoor plumbing, since the city lines stopped about a quarter mile south at Roosevelt Elementary School, usually called either grade or grammar school. Most of the kids lived in homes east and south of Roosevelt with indoor bathrooms, but the city stopped extending plumbing lines in December 1941, when the war erupted. For my mother, though, it was the best place she had ever lived.

The dirt road in front of the house was sometimes impassable in the rainy season. The house was about fifty yards east of the road and was covered in clapboard siding, painted white but peeling in several places. The front door had screens, as did two windows in front, to keep the flies out in the summertime. The roof leaked in spots. When it rained, pots and pans covered the floor to catch the dripping water. Fortunately, it didn't rain often in Lawton.

The house had only two rooms. When you entered the front door, you arrived in a large room that served as a living room, kitchen, and bedroom. To the left of the front door, there was a small bedroom with a window and another window into the living room/kitchen. The floors in the house were linoleum, worn in several spots in the larger room. There were no closets. In the bedroom, there were hooks and two chests. I slept with my grandmother and my brother in a large bed in the living room. If guests stayed over, my brother and I slept on the floor on a layer of quilts sewed by my mother and grandmother over the years. A couple of hope chests were used to store clothes, and they also served as stools; a couple of wooden chairs completed the furnishings.

At the back of the large room was the kitchen, with a door exiting onto a large field. A pathway through it led to the outhouse, located three or four hundred feet away—far enough away to prevent contamination of the well or send unwanted smells into the house. We boys never used the outhouse for peeing, though; anywhere outside was good enough. But number two required a trip to the hated shack. It had two seats, although in my memory, only one person at a time used the facility. It was a scary place for a young boy. In the summertime, horse flies, mosquitoes, and ants were everywhere. I was always afraid that spiders might bite me on the ass. The inside smelled nasty, and was especially overwhelming in the summer heat. Old newspapers or pages torn from Sears or "Monkey Ward" (Montgomery Ward) catalogs served as toilet paper. The commandment "Don't use the gun section" was drummed into my mind. Several bags of lye were poured into the hole every year.

The kitchen area was the social center of the house. It consisted of a sink with a water pump, an old iron gas stove with an oven, and a linoleum countertop that covered a quarter of one outer wall. A wooden table and several wooden chairs separated the kitchen from the living room area. Surprisingly, gas and electrical lines had been installed. But the stove heated the house in the wintertime. On laundry days, water was heated in two large tin washtubs. Using a washboard and homemade lye soap, my mother or grandmother scrubbed the clothes and then placed them in the other tub to rinse. The wrung-out clothes were dumped into a basket, taken outside, and pinned on the clothesline, a duty I often performed by standing on a stool. I needed help to pin the sheets on the line. Meanwhile, wooden-handled flatirons heated up on the stove to press the clothes.

Saturday night baths, which were given "whether we needed them or not," in the words of Grandma Bell, followed the same ritual. My brother always went first, to my irritation, dipping into a tin washtub full of clean hot water. He scrubbed and shampooed himself, then transferred to the rinse tub full of warm water.

Then it was my turn. I bathed in the same water, now soapy from my brother's bath. Mother and Grandma Bell insisted I was too young to bathe myself until I became a defiant six years old. They scrubbed me with harsh lye soap until my skin turned red. Worse was shampooing my hair. Invariably, the soapy water got into my eyes and I screamed. "Stop it," my mother would say. "A little soap ain't going to kill you. Stop being such a big baby." To this day, I take extreme caution not to get shampoo in my eyes when I shower. Saturday night was not the only time we washed ourselves. We took "whores' baths" every night to wash our arms, feet, and private parts before going to bed.

The kitchen also had an icebox, the best-constructed piece of furniture in the house. Made of hardwood with an interior lined with sheet metal, the door closed tightly and locked with two large steel handles. There was no such thing as a freezer back then; the icebox kept food for a few days, not a few weeks or months. An ice man delivered ice twice a week. A cardboard sign with the numbers 5, 10, 15, and 20, placed in the window, told the ice man how many pounds of ice to bring into the house. A similar sign informed the milk man. Milk was delivered to the door twice a week and quickly placed in the icebox. Farm-fresh milk, not pasteurized, came in half-gallon bottles with two or three inches of cream on the top. Although local farms provided the milk, we seldom had butter during the war and used the cream as substitute butter. Other times we used Crisco (lard) mixed with yellow coloring. At the bottom of the icebox, a drawer held a pan to catch the melting ice water intermixed with sour milk and a myriad of other food waste that had dropped down from above.

The ice man typically delivered ten to fifteen pounds of ice at a time. The slabs were too large to fit in the icebox, so first we put them in a washtub. Mom and I usually spent a few minutes using icepicks to chop the slabs into smaller sections and dumped them into the ice section of the icebox.

That wasn't the end of our ice adventures. Mother always looked for opportunities to teach me "life's lessons," and some of them involved our ice deliveries. She did not want me to be naïve, and often played tricks on me that, from today's perspective, seem almost sadistic.

One day when I was around six years old I helped Mom chop the ice. Chopping ice is hard work, and it took some time to split the block into smaller pieces. At one point she stopped and put her ice pick on the table.

"Damn," she said, waving her hands, "that ice is cold."

"I like it," I said, as I wiped the back of my neck with my cold hand. It was a hot summer day. I dumped another handful of ice in the box and wiped my neck again.

My mother laughed. "Feels good in the summer, but in the winter, when your hands get really cold, the ice can burn you if you hold it in your hands more than five minutes."

I didn't believe her. She smiled. "Betcha."

I stopped and looked at her.

"Betcha a nickel you can't hold one of those chips of ice in your hand for five minutes without dropping it."

"Betcha I could," I said.

"Get your nickel."

A nickel was a lot of money when I was six years old. At the grocery store, a nickel bought five pieces of bubble gum, a big chocolate candy bar, or a soda pop.

I got five of my nine pennies from my secret hiding place and placed them on the table next to my mother's nickel.

"To win, you have to keep your closed fist over the ice for five minutes," she said. Then she picked up a small piece of ice and a box of Morton's salt. She sprinkled salt on my palm and placed the ice on top of it. "Close your fist," she said, "and squeeze tightly." I squeezed my fist around the ice, certain I would win the bet.

Within two minutes, my palm began to burn. I held on for another minute then dropped the ice. I looked down at my palm, which was bright red; blisters appeared to be forming. I started whimpering.

Mom placed a spoonful of Crisco in my hand. "Stop your crying. Rub that grease in your hand."

She picked up the pennies and placed them her pocket. "Betcha remember that lesson," she said.

I did. I learned to watch out for cheaters who always want to "betcha" because they usually have an ace up their sleeve. Like knowing that ice and salt don't mix, and that when they're combined, they lower the temperature at which water freezes. She was simply trying to help me understand the real world. She played the same trick on all her grandchildren. My mother loved me, but she was not raising any stupid, naïve children. "It's a hard world out there. Don't trust anybody, not even me," she would say.

With the exception of baked goods, such as pies and biscuits, most of the food she made was fried. Pan-fried potatoes and okra, fried chicken, and occasionally chicken-fried steaks. A small piece of meat pounded with a meat cleaver stretched the steak enough to feed the four of us. Bacon grease and fried oil were strained and used again until the oil turned rancid. Mother bought Crisco in five-gallon cans.

Besides potatoes and biscuits, the other staple at every meal was pinto beans bought in ten-pound bags. A pot of beans was always on the stove with another pot of "stew" where leftovers were dumped after every meal. Fresh vegetables, if available, were boiled. Mother tried to grow carrots, tomatoes, and squash but they seldom survived the hot, dry Southwest Oklahoma summer. The only water available for the crops was from an outside pump, but mother was afraid if she used too much the well might go dry. Only one crop survived the late-summer heat: okra, which she fried with cornmeal. Giant wild sunflowers also grew in the garden but no one ate the seeds. Why not? I don't know. Canned vegetables, such as peas, were boiled so long they became pea soup.

There was plenty of food, but if you didn't like pea soup, tough luck. You ate what was served or you went hungry. When I whined about the pea soup, Grandma would remind me of the story about a cowboy who often grumbled about the crummy chow the cook served him on the trail. If the cowboy bitched too often, the boss made him the cook. One evening, he came into camp, crammed beans on his tin plate, and took a bite. He spit them out. "These beans are too damn salty," he sputtered. He looked up at the cook and foreman, took another bite, and said, "Damn tasty." He took another bite, grinned, picked up a biscuit and sat down. Do you want to cook supper? Complain and the job is yours.

Were we poor? Poor is a relative word. We were poor, but we weren't dirt-poor. We had a house, although a small one that needed repairs but was basically sound. There was not a single day during my childhood in which there was not enough food on the table, including pies and cakes. Occasionally, there was money for movies, candy, ice cream, and bubble gum. We did not have the material things that the middle class accumulated—a car, a refrigerator, a washing machine, a radio, or a telephone. But those were unnecessary material things. Our family owed no one money.

Actually, my memories of these early years are happy memories. But, of course, the times they were a-changing.

Chapter 2

After the War:
1945 to 1950

Church bells rang for hours throughout Lawton on May 8, 1945, to celebrate the end of World War II in Europe, and again on September 2 to mark its end in Asia. Parties erupted all over the city because, as Grandma Bell informed me, my father and the other "boys" were coming home. I was so young when he left, I didn't remember him. But with the news of his impending arrival, things changed almost immediately around home.

Knowing my father's attitude about women working, my mother quickly quit her job and returned to being a full-time mom. Within a few months, Grandma Bell moved to a tiny cottage in the small town of Medicine Park in the Wichita Mountains. Medicine Park was near a wildlife reserve for buffalo and Texas longhorn cattle. (Years later, when I visited the reserve, I smiled; only in Oklahoma would the pile of barren rocks be called mountains.) Besides the buffalo and longhorn cattle, the area's major attractions were several lakes built as reservoirs to serve Fort Sill, and a gigantic statue of Jesus nailed to a cross placed on top of one of the mountains. Each Easter, a sunrise ceremony attracted hundreds to honor Jesus. Although she lived less than thirty miles from Lawton, Grandma Bell slowly faded out of my life for the next few years.

In September 1946, I started school at Roosevelt Elementary. I loved it. In the classroom, I was in my element. After missing a few days with the chicken pox in my first year I did not miss another day for eight and a half years. Grandma Bell's teaching gave me a head start, and I immediately shined in the first grade. Since I could already read and write, I finished classroom assignments faster than any other student. The teacher assigned me to be a monitor to assist other students, who often took thirty minutes for a reading assignment I finished in five minutes. As a monitor, I walked around the room and helped students having trouble reading certain words.

By the second grade, I was feeling cocky. My reading skills had improved even more, and I remained the class monitor. A few weeks into the year, though, an incident occurred that reminded me to be humble. The teacher gave the class a writing assignment. Pick any topic and write at least two paragraphs, she directed. I wrote about my dog chasing cats. But for the life of me, I could not remember how to spell cat. I had learned sight-reading, not phonetics, and single-syllable words were dragged out in the South. C… A… T sounded like a long word to me. Finally, I raised my hand and asked the teacher how to spell cat.

Giggles erupted in the classroom. *The monitor did not know how to spell cat.* This incident taught me to be humble about my accomplishments, because as great as I might've thought I was, there were still gaps in my ability and knowledge. It also taught me that superiority was temporary. To remain the best student, I needed to apply myself, a lesson I remembered for the rest of my life.

My father arrived home in the fall of 1946. I do not remember the family reunion, although years later my mother told me a story about it that saddened me. Apparently my father brought home gifts from Hawaii and San Diego. He had many presents for my mother and brother but not a single present for me. When he left for the navy in '43, I was a toddler that he barely remembered. My mother was embarrassed for me, but he never apologized. He didn't care that he had hurt my feelings, an attitude he would display many times over the years. I remember asking my mother on several occasions if he was really my father. She always smiled and said, "It's a wise man that knows his own father," and giggled. "It could be your father is the ice man or the milk man."

My first memory of my father registered shortly thereafter. My father and I were in a car. I must have been about six or seven, because I was standing next to him in the front bench seat—back in the day, bucket seats were not installed in family cars. I was rubbing his day-old beard, fascinated by the rough stubble. "Stop that," he snapped. "Set down in the damn seat."

Another early incident with my family that I vividly remember occurred on a return trip from visiting my father's brother, Uncle Bill, in Wichita Falls. I was asleep in the car when my father stopped at a small diner. He, my mother, and brother went inside to get something to eat. When they returned, I woke up. They hadn't brought me any food, and, emotionally hurt, I pouted. "Don't cry. Don't be a baby," was a constant refrain in my life.

There's another example from around the same time, when I was perhaps eight years old. On Saturday nights, my family often went to the Austin Drive-in movie theater. One day when I returned home from playing with friends, around 6:30, no one was home. They had gone to the movies without me.

Today it would be unusual for a family to leave an eight-year-old home alone for several hours. My mother asked Dad to wait, but his response was, "Boy should have been home for supper at six. His own damn fault." Remember, my mother always obeyed my father. But she had absolute confidence in my ability to take care of myself. She wasn't raising any "sissies." She had stayed home alone many times before she was eight. "Don't Cry. Don't be a baby."

Something happened before then that made me glad I was not my father's favorite son. One evening we went to see my Uncle Red in a fast-pitch softball game. His team had reached the finals in the city's softball league. The night we went, the game was under the lights in a ballpark near downtown with about five hundred people in attendance. Uncle Red was the pitcher. I watched in awe as he mowed down batter after batter, throwing harder than anyone I had ever seen.

It was soon after Dad returned from the navy, and he had gone back to work at his old job at Dewey Shaw's General Store. Well, not exactly his old job as an assistant manager, but as just another clerk in the store at lower pay without use of a truck after work. Although he was promoted six months later, he never forgave Dewey Shaw. Because of the pay cut, money was tight that first summer, and we only went out for free entertainment, like watching Uncle Red play.

Popcorn and soda pop vendors roamed the stands. Dad bought a box of popcorn for us to share. With such a close game, the stands remained crowded to the very end. In one of the later innings a popcorn vendor came by, and Corky begged my father to buy some more.

Dad said no.

Corky continued to whine about wanting more popcorn.

Angry as hell, my father stood up and motioned to my mother. "We are leaving. Now!"

So, we left and headed for home about mile away.

The moment we were beyond the eyes and ears of the crowd at the baseball park, Dad took off his belt and whacked my brother on the ass and back.

Corky screamed and jumped away.

"Boy," Dad said in a controlled but angry voice. "Don't you ever embarrass me that way again. When I say no, I mean no."

He whacked my brother again. Corky yelped and ran a few yards ahead. My father followed him. Whack! A yelp, a run, a whack, always with my father saying, "Do you hear me, son?" "Yes, Dad." Whack.

"Do you hear me, son?"

My mother whispered in my ear as we continued up the rear. "Corky was wrong, baby. Don't be scared."

My father finally stopped and hugged my brother. Corky did not cry, nor did he apologize. I heard my father say, "Son, I love you very much but don't ever embarrass me in public. Do you understand?"

"Yessir."

Later, my mother told me the reason Dad was so furious. He didn't have twenty-five cents, or even a nickel, in his pocket for another box of popcorn. He did not want anybody to know he was that broke—it would have been a loss of face. We were dirt-poor, but we still had our pride.

After that incident, I was glad I was not my father's favorite son. He never whipped me, but he occasionally punished my brother, who often defied his orders. My father preferred using verbal abuse on me. In comparison to my brother, I was a disappointment because I never fought back; instead, I learned to ignore his criticism. And my heart hardened over the years. One particular example illustrates both my Dad's attitude toward me and my attitude toward him. When I was in the fourth grade, I brought my report card home for my father to sign. When my father signed Corky's card, he praised him. I was proud of my grades and expected him to be equally pleased with me. I had As in every single subject except penmanship, where I made a B. Dad looked at the card and said, "B in penmanship. Hell, you made a B in the easiest course in school." He signed the card without another word.

My reaction was to never show my report cards to the family again. I signed them myself, and no questions were asked. Every year, I was on the honor roll, an honor shared only by about 10 percent of the students in Lawton, and the names were published in the newspaper. Grandma Bell always noted this and said how proud she was. My father did not.

Going to school kicked off a new phase in my life and is among my fondest memories. It also helped me realize certain things about myself. No longer did I have to follow my brother and his friends hoping I would be allowed to play in their games. They always picked me last in team sports because I was the worst player, and it stung. So, I made a promise to myself that if I were ever the one who got to choose sides, I'd pick the worst player first (well, on occasion). Later I realized I had learned empathy that became part of my character. It was not sympathy nor was it pity. Empathy means I feel someone else's pain because I have been in a similar situation. It does not mean I am a bleeding-heart liberal. I give but not until it hurts. My experiences led me to formulate my number one rule for life: "Take care of yourself, first and foremost, then your family, then your friends, and finally mere acquaintances."

Thanks to school, now I had my own friends. Among the group,

I was the oldest, although we were still too young to be very good at team sports. Baseball was the game we played the most. We were too young to play in the city-sponsored Little League, which was for boys ten to fourteen, but that did not matter to us. We played pickup games nearly every afternoon. Of course, we played other games, such as "Kick the Can," football, and marbles.

We also played games that would have horrified our mothers, such as War. Until we got BB guns, our favorite weapon was the homemade slingshot. The materials cost little (or nothing) and were widely available: Take a small tree limb in the shape of a Y, rubber from an old car or bicycle tire, and a piece of leather from the tongue of an old shoe. Shoot small stones or marbles at mailboxes, and shoot at each other—boom, you had a game of War. When a stone hit you, you were dead. It was hard to deny you had been hit.

The game escalated when we got air rifles, usually Red Rider BB guns. An air rifle's power was awesome; at close range, a BB could go through a tin mailbox. Given this, we quickly stopped playing War to become hunters of water moccasins. One time a boy in our group brought a small pistol, and down at the creek we took turns shooting at the snakes and later at tin cans.

One summer we built a stockade to fight off "the Indians" and dug hidden tunnels in the open fields. We often took walks on the railroad tracks outside of town, including a stretch across a trestle bridge that crossed Cache Creek. Since we never knew when a train might be coming down the tracks, the game was meant to prove who was brave enough, or fast enough, to walk across the trestle.

Halloween was the second-best holiday of the year; only Christmas was better. I couldn't believe people gave you candy for simply knocking on the door and screaming "Trick or treat"!" People foolish enough not to be home got their screens covered with soap. Since my brother liked Halloween as much as me, we dressed in homemade costumes to hit the bigger developments south and east of our house. Using separate bags, we collected a bonanza of goodies. Even during Halloween, I was able to pick up on an important life lesson. To maximize my bounty, I rationed the candy in my bag, eating only a small amount each day for two or three weeks. My brother, on the other hand, ate all his candy in two days. After this the hunt began, and my mother joined my brother in search of the goody bag—aka my stash. Eventually, they always found it. I learned that it's difficult for rational people to hide their goodies from villains.

⁂

In the spring of 1947, when I was seven years old, Bunk came to our house late one afternoon carrying a three-month-old puppy in a small basket. He came over often to socialize with Mom and Dad but still lived with his older sister, Aunt Hazel. Mom always claimed she had raised him. Bunk's response was typical Bunk. "Bullshit," he'd say, "I raised myself." Although only seventeen years old, Bunk took no bullshit from anyone. Even my Dad treated him with the respect he usually reserved for full-grown men.

By the time he was nine, Bunk had learned the rule that my mother pounded into my head: *Take care of yourself—sure as shit, no one else is going to do it.* If he wanted new clothes, a soda pop, or a bicycle, he earned the money. Uncle Curly, one of my father's brothers, was a short-order cook in a downtown diner and offered to pay Bunk ten cents an hour to come to the diner and sweep and mop the floor after school. He accepted and worked two hours a day, earning $1.00 to $1.50 a week. Not much in today's money, but movies only cost a dime back then. He saved his money and bought a used bicycle for ten dollars. When he was twelve, he got a job delivering papers for the *Lawton Constitution*, an afternoon paper. Each afternoon, delivery vans picked up the papers and delivered them to spots around town. The newspaper boys then carried the papers to the homes in Lawton. Bunk's route was different: Each day, he and a half dozen boys rode a delivery van to Fort Sill, about twelve miles from downtown Lawton. The base was one of the largest army posts in the United States, with thousands of soldiers who lived on base, including many officers, and each boy had a route within the complex. When they were finished, a van picked up the boys and returned them to Lawton. He made about seven dollars a week.

In the summertime, Bunk didn't play baseball like most of the boys his age. Instead, he rode his bicycle around Lawton looking for items to pick up and sell, from soda pop bottles to recently weaned puppies. He sold a baby goat to my brother for fifty cents. "When he's older," he said to my brother, "He'll be worth ten dollars."

That was true, but the goat did not last long at our place. Goats eat almost anything, from clothes on the line to paper labels off tin cans. Eventually my mother insisted Corky get rid of the goat. Dad and Corky sold the goat for seventy-five cents to one of the local farmers.

When Bunk was fifteen, he got a summer job on a ranch, and for the rest of his life he wore cowboy boots. Despite his enthusiasm for cowboy-style clothes, after working on the ranch for the next two summers he realized the cowboy's life was not for him. The pay was lousy, the work hard, and the horses mean. When he was in town, he switched to dress boots because they had low heels, which were better for walking. After he left the ranch, he never rode a horse again. "Most working horses are mean," he later told me. "They're not pets—they bite and kick you in the head if you aren't careful."

In the spring of 1947, Bunk was on the verge of graduating from high school and still squeezing out a living. Although he was often around, we usually ignored each other after a brief greeting. He was seventeen and I was only seven. He wrestled with Corky, but he mainly came over to see Toad and Charlie.

One day he came to our house carrying a puppy in a basket. I ran over. Bunk motioned that I could pick up the puppy, and I did. The pup licked my face, happy to be alive, and so enthusiastic it was impossible to hold him. I sat down on the grass and played with him; just holding and looking at him made me happy. Someone had cut off his tail, so he wagged his entire rear end. He looked like a small bulldog but with a longer snout. His hair was black, very short, with a white spot on his nose and white stocking on his four legs. Mom, who had been around many dogs on farms, said he was a beautiful puppy who would grow up to be the perfect size for a house pet, neither too big nor too small. Obviously a feisty dog, he would be able to take care of himself. Mom loved feisty men and feisty dogs, and later in life, feisty cats.

I pleaded with Bunky to give me the dog if Daddy agreed when he came home. "Nope," said Bunk. "Bought three of these pups and have already sold two for three dollars apiece." Then he smiled. "You got three dollars, Skinny?" he said, teasing me; Skinny was his nickname for me, and he meant it to be affectionate.

"No," I said, "but I got fifty cents." Money was more valuable back in the day. A Coke cost a nickel and a penny got you a bag of candy. When I was seven years old, fifty cents was a small fortune. Seeing my face, Bunk relented. When Dad came home, he agreed I could have the dog. I gave Bunk my fifty cents and I named the puppy Butch—why, I don't remember.

That night, my brother, Butch, and I slept in the bed of my father's delivery pickup truck. A few quilts, a couple of pillows, and full moonlight with a sky full of stars overhead. What more could a pair of boys need?

Butch won over my father and mother's hearts. He became the family pet and a good guard dog. No one came near our house without him giving a warning. If he was outside, he barked; if he was inside, he growled when anyone approached the house. Strangers were advised to stand still until a family member gave them the okay to proceed. A family rule, like most folks had, was that strangers should not pet a dog without permission. Butch growled at strangers until we said "Hush." Extended family members and close friends could pet him, and from then on, he recognized their smell and never growled at them again. Mom even trained him to look after the little kids who visited the house. If a small child who could barely walk wandered toward the road, Butch yipped. Not barked but yipped until the mother came running. "Best damn dog in the county," my father proclaimed with pride.

Butch had one bad habit: he chased cars and tried to bite their rear tires. Most cars came down the dirt road rather slowly, and Butch had a ball, triumphantly returning to us having chased the car away. We tried, unsuccessfully, to break Butch of the habit, as dogs that chase cars can get run over. And a car eventually struck Butch.

The blow did not kill him, but it did break one of his back legs. Holding Butch in my arms, I sobbed. I believed he was a dead dog, given a recent incident.

Butch was three years old when he was injured. In those three years our family had adopted another dog, a happy but not very smart Cocker Spaniel. Dad put up with the dog because she was friendly and never got into fights with other dogs, like Butch did. "Scared to death," Dad proclaimed. "Stupid dog."

The neighbors about a mile away did not like dogs. They hated Butch because he chased their cats if they wandered onto our property. The neighbor, who Dad called "that damn son-of-bitch," apparently decided to do something to protect his cats. He got some hamburger meat, laced it with ground-up glass, and threw it on our property. Butch was the target, but it was the Cocker Spaniel who ate the meat. There was snow on the ground and blood dripped from her mouth, staining it. Dad was home that day, and he saw the dog bleeding. He went outside, picked up the remaining meat, saw the glass, and muttered, "Stupid dog." He grabbed a hammer and put the dog out of its misery.

Now Butch had a broken leg, and I was sure Dad would kill him with his hammer. It never occurred to me that a vet could fix the leg. Neither I nor my brother had ever been to a doctor or a dentist. "If you are dying," my father would say, "maybe." But for a little bruise or cut or broken finger, forget it. Doctors cost money. When I was around nine years old, my mother sent me to the local store to buy a gallon of milk. As I was walking home, I fell and dropped the milk bottle. My right knee hit the glass and the cut went down to the bone. I limped home, bleeding badly and crying, not because of the cut but because I broke the bottle of milk. Mom examined the cut, stopped the bleeding, then drenched it with iodine and covered it with a large butterfly bandage with some white tape. When I healed, I had a sizeable scar on my left knee, but as predicted, I was still alive.

This time Dad surprised me. He loved Butch, as did every member of the family and most of our friends. He took Butch to the vet, who set the broken leg and put on a plaster cast. Butch hobbled around for a few weeks with a metal brace on his right rear leg. He lived twelve more years and never chased another car. Then again, it's possible my interpretation is wrong. Perhaps my Dad knew how much Butch meant to me and took the dog to the vet for my benefit.

After Bunk sold me Butch, I did not see him for several years. In later years he became my favorite relative, and he told me many stories about his growing up in Lawton in the 1930s and 1940s. Bunk's earlier years in Oklahoma were tougher but similar to mine. In our later years, our lives were vastly different but in some ways much the same. The core beliefs we learned in our youth were quite comparable.

Bunk graduated from high school in June 1947 and had no idea what to do with his life except survive. That summer he took a job at a local concrete plant that produced foundation blocks. After the war, construction in Lawton had slowed, but by 1947 the army was expanding again, and more soldiers poured into Fort Sill. The population of Lawton exploded over the next few years from 20,000 to 34,000, and it remained the third-largest city in Oklahoma. This stimulated new building projects, and the cement factory hired Bunk to load concrete blocks onto the trucks delivering them to construction sites. By today's standards, the factory was archaic. The cement blocks were stacked in a yard covering several acres. A dozen men split up into two-man teams to hand-load the blocks onto delivery trucks.

Unfortunately for Bunk, one of the older workers disliked him. Bunk called him Bubba.

Bubba was Bunk's boss and teammate. Bubba stood on the truck bed, and his job was to stack the blocks front to rear. Bunk had the harder job of lifting the thirty-pound concrete blocks and tossing them onto the truck bed.

Bunk tossed hundreds of blocks a day onto the bed. Occasionally, he threw one too far, barely missing Bubba, who would scream out, "Damn it! Bunk, are you trying to kill me? Stupid-ass kid."

Under his breath, Bunk said, "Stop sitting on your ass, shithead." He described Bubba as a big fat good old boy, a despicable bully.

One day the inevitable happened. Bunk threw a block that struck Bubba in the ankle. Bubba screamed out, "Asshole. I'm coming down to beat the shit out of you."

Bubba screamed at Bunk so often he ignored the warning. He tossed a new brick onto the truck bed and bent over to pick up another.

"Wham!"

Bubba had picked up a thirty-pound block and thrown it at Bunk. It hit him in the back and glanced off his head. Dazed, he rose to his feet. Blood dripped down from his head and his shoulder was numb.

Bubba jumped off the bed. Bunk staggered to the opposite side of the truck and ran for the cab. He stepped on the running board, and instead of opening the cab door, he swung onto the bed of the truck. When Bubba looked back, Bunk charged down the bed and jumped feet-first, striking Bubba in the head. Both fell to the ground.

And this is when I realized Bunk's rules for fighting were the same as mine: Avoid if possible. Walk away if you can. If they are bigger than you, run if you can. But, if you must fight, fight. "If you are going to take a whipping," Bunk said, "bite the son-of-bitch or give him a few bruises to remember you."

Bubba rolled over and grabbed Bunk and started hammering his face into the ground. Bubba weighed over 225 pounds to Bunk's 140. Bunk had no chance, but humanity intervened. Other teams ran over and saw this big fat man beating the shit out of the skinny kid. Using a shovel, one of the men knocked Bubba off Bunk, who rolled over and nodded at his savior.

The supervisor called the cops before running over to question the men. The cops arrived and listened to the story. Bunk's savior was fired on the spot. "No damn nigger can hit a white man."

Bunk and Bubba were arrested for fighting. At the county jail, Bunk identified himself as Marvin Bass. The jailer looked up, stared at Bunk for a second, and asked, "You one of Joe Bass's kids?"

As mentioned earlier, Joe Bass was a well-known figure in the local police department. At sixty, Papa Joe was still a mean man when he was drunk, and the police arrested him with care. Usually, the judge imposed a fine or three or four nights in jail. He would refuse to pay the fine. His first night in jail, he stayed in his cell and sobered up. The rest of the time he could leave the premises, so long as he stayed on the courthouse's manicured lawn, nearby, where he sat on tree-shaded benches. The courthouse was the grandest building in all of Lawton, and during the day, people wandered the lawn paths as Papa

Joe smoked hand-rolled cigarettes and watched the crowds. When not drunk, Papa Joe had better control of his temper.

Bunk had no such luck, however. To get out of jail, he had to pay a fine. He went down a list of relatives and decided there were two possibilities: his sister Hazel and his sister Toad (Mother). He contacted Toad and Charlie. "Hell," Bunk told me, "I knew Hazel would say, 'Let the kid stay in jail for a few days. Teach him a lesson.'" My mother loved him. Dad teased him but paid the fine. Bunk later repaid him, but Dad thought the whole incident was funny.

Bunk knew the fight wasn't over. He did not return to work at the cement factory, but he knew that Bubba would not forget the incident. Bunk looked around for a weapon he could carry that technically did not break the law. He found a rubber fan belt in the garbage of an auto-repair shop. He could use it as a whip if attacked.

A few days later, Bubba jumped him. Bunk kept him at bay with his whip as a few cars passed down the road. Bigger and stronger, Bubba charged Bunk then tossed him to the ground, but before he could stomp him to death, a sheriff's car arrived, and Bubba and Bunk again found themselves in jail.

When he was released Bunk left town and enlisted in the air force, and after that I did not see him for a few years.

Over the years, I came to realize that much of my personality came from my Mother and Bunk. They taught me that I was expected to take care of myself and deal with bullies. Bullies are everywhere, even in our families. My brother picked on me, but Bunk had a harder time with his brother Red, who was eleven years older. Bunk learned to avoid Red, saying Red always hustled him. "Tried to whoop me," Bunk would say. "Fortunately, I could run faster."

Uncle Red looked like a German-Swede with his short, reddish-blonde hair. He was over six feet tall, with broad shoulders and a muscular physique. In other words, he was a handsome alpha male. In the family's evaluation, he was much like his father, Papa Joe.

Red lived on the line between legal and illegal. He worked hard and owned a small gravel truck company, but he also spent more than he earned on wine, women, and poker. Thus, he had illegal sidelines, the biggest being a whiskey-running operation. He used two identical Hudsons, large, powerful automobiles much faster than any cop car. He bought his whiskey from a warehouse in Wichita Falls, Texas, where whiskey was legal.

Red and Bunk couldn't have been more unalike. One incident in particular illustrates their different personalities. One night, Bunk, on leave from the air force, was sleeping at Red's on the couch in his living room. When Red came home drunk, he saw Bunk sleeping peacefully.

What an opportunity to tease his brother. Red quietly eased himself into the kitchen, opened the icebox, and removed a large carrot. He snuck back into the living room, unzipped his pants, pulled out his pecker, straddled Bunk, and pushed the carrot into Bunk's mouth, slowly moving it in and out. Bunk woke up gagging. Red tossed the carrot aside and said, "Damn fine blow job, Bunk."

Bunk pushed him off, and Red dashed to the door and ran for his car laughing his head off. Bunk yelled curses at Red as his car sped into the night.

Bunk was up before dawn the next day. He packed his bag and got ready to escape town, but not before planning his revenge.

Coincidentally, a couple of days before the carrot caper, Bunk had spotted a small black snake in the barn. Black snakes are not poisonous, and farmers did not kill them. Like cats, they eat rats.

This offered Bunk a great opportunity to exact revenge. Red had a phobia of snakes. In Southwest Oklahoma, rattlesnakes are plentiful, and when Red picked cotton as a young boy, he was frightened of being bitten. Several times it almost happened, and it scared the shit out of him. He loved hunting and killing snakes.

Bunk went to the barn and captured the snake while Red was sleeping. He carried the snake to Red's big gravel truck and carefully placed it over the driver's visor in the cab, where Red kept his keys. Then he got the hell out of town.

According to my mother, who years later told me what happened, early the next morning Red stumbled into the cab and settled into his seat drinking his coffee, hungover from partying the night away. Then he reached for the keys. The snake dropped into his lap, wiggling frantically in attempt to get away.

Red went "apeshit," according to Mom. He fell out of the truck door screaming, with hot coffee burning him through his shirt. Mom said he shit his pants—probably an exaggeration, but he might have pissed them. He grabbed a stick and chased the snake, caught it, saw it was a black snake, and beat it to death—he hated all snakes.

Red threatened to kill Bunk, then declared he would merely beat the shit out of him, and finally accepted that Bunk had simply paid him back for the carrot caper.

Bunk stayed away for a few months. By the time he returned, Red had fled Oklahoma.

Red's problem was threefold: greed, the syndicate, and Oklahoma cops. Although it was a dry state, Oklahoma was overflowing with whiskey. A syndicate in Oklahoma City controlled all the bootlegging in the state. They paid off state politicians, state police, local politicians, sheriffs, police chiefs, and judges. The system worked, and the politicians, the preachers, the cops, and the syndicate all loved Oklahoma's Prohibition era.

Red loved it too, but he refused to pay the syndicate. He sold his whiskey to friends and family and saw no reason to give "the mob" a cut. When it came time to transport it from Wichita Falls, he had a specific plan. He would start by loading up one of his two Hudsons with whiskey. The highway patrol and local cops on the roads all the way to Lawton were always looking for the many whiskey runners avoiding the "law," so Red would send the other Hudson, empty of booze, up ahead a couple of miles. If cops were around, the Hudson running interference took off like a whiskey runner, sending the cops chasing after it. The loaded Hudson would then take an alternate route through Walters and down to Lawton. Sometimes both cars were chased, but neither were ever caught.

The syndicate had representatives throughout the state. Red was more an irritant than a problem, but he was still competition, which meant he had to be eliminated. The syndicate sent several enforcers to

Lawton to do just that. Realizing he was outgunned, Red fled the state to save his life.

※

The fifty cents I paid for Butch made me more aware of money. Mother constantly asked my father for money. He gave her a weekly allowance for groceries and to pay the milk and ice men. But she also needed money for school lunches, supplies, and clothes.

The beginning of school each year was money crunch time. First, we needed to buy the required schoolbooks. Back in the day, the city provided the buildings and the teachers, but books and supplies were the parents' responsibility. New books were expensive; used books were available but often in bad shape. Notebooks, paper, ink pens, and pencils added to the list.

Just like my father, Mother felt compelled to maintain the family image. New school clothes were essential. My brother and I needed a minimum of two pairs of jeans. The old jeans were patched for after school, and often as my brother grew, his clothes became my after-school clothes. Thus the rule: "Don't play in your school clothes." After classes, we changed clothes before we went out to play.

Mother took us downtown for school shopping trips. Back then there were no malls, and as a result businesses downtown were vibrant and full of customers. All the major department stores were downtown. The town was laid out with letters for avenues running east to west, and numbers for streets running north to south. First Street was in the east end of town and the bus depot was located between Avenues B and C. The public bus system was excellent, carrying workers, schoolchildren, and soldiers to their jobs and schools. Many people did not have cars. Downtown extended west to the City Hall lawn on Ninth Street, and north to south from Avenues B to E. We lived at 1511 I, six to nine (as I recall) long country blocks from downtown. Most of the businesses were located on Avenues B and C between First and Sixth Street. From First to Third Street, Avenue B was the "red-light" district catering to the young army recruits searching for a good time. Bars, pool halls, tattoo parlors, cheap cafes, and dirty movie theaters lined the street and were off-limits to the kids of the city. Most of the retail businesses were located on Avenue C: department stores such as Sears, Penney's, and Montgomery Ward; Five-and-ten-cent stores such as Woolworth and McClellan's; chain stores such as Buster Brown's; many independent, expensive retail stores selling men's clothing, hats, ties, and shoes; and four or five movie theaters.

I realize that map descriptions are confusing. Who cares?—streets, highways, avenues, boulevards, and the like are simply other names for roads. When I was ten, I could not have told you whether I lived east or west or north or south of downtown Lawton. The locals didn't bother with avenues and streets; thus, our house was on 1511 I Street, and the department stores were on C Street. Some of the highways did not follow the official pattern, e.g., Gore Blvd. and Sheridan Rd. The motivation here is to say that Lawton was a much smaller "city" than it is today. In 1948, the business district in downtown was the center of a small city whose prosperity was based on the soldiers stationed at Fort Sill.

Mother shopped mostly at Penney's. The store was crowded in the days before school started, and clerks were plentiful. Unlike today, in both small and large stores clerks greeted customers at the door, and often escorted them to a fellow clerk working in specific department. The shoe clerk sat down with you, measured your foot, and retrieved the shoes from storage. If a man was in the suit department, a clerk measured him, helped him pick out a suit, and arranged for the in-house tailor to cut the pants to the right length.

There were no credit cards, and cash was king. When it was time to pay, clerks checked your purchases and sent your money through pneumatic tubes to a cash room; change and receipts came back the same way. At the time, the smallest currency was a "mill"—one-tenth of a penny and about the size of a nickel but made of hard cardboard with a hole in the center. Thus, a bill might be five dollars, twenty cents, and five mills. With inflation, mills were discontinued sometime in 1948.

The department stores had separate bathrooms and drinking fountains for whites and "coloreds," although there were few black people shopping in downtown Lawton; the area's black population lived in a separate town that I never saw. Black residents went to separate schools, sat in the rear seats on buses, used balconies at the movie theaters, and did not go to white restaurants. I never knew a single black kid all the time I lived in Lawton, and truthfully, did not even know that "nigger" was a derogatory word. Although I realized later that both the Youngs and Basses were prejudiced, neither I nor my brother realized it at the time. When Uncle Red's daughter Caroline married a black man, she was expelled from the family. Later, when my brother married a second-generation Mexican American, my father belittled my brother's children.

But, like I said, the times were a-changing.

Chapter 3
Bathrooms & Chickens

My father changed jobs in fall of 1948. He quit Dewey Shaw's and went to work as a salesman for Wertz Wholesale Fruit Company. The company sold fruit and vegetables in the forty or so smaller towns around Lawton. He traveled a different route every day and stopped at grocery stores. The pay was two or three times more than he earned at Shaw's, and the money propelled the family from the lower-wage working class to a state of modest prosperity.

From previous comments, it should be obvious I had issues with my father, but I never denigrated his abilities. He was an ambitious man, determined to be successful. He believed—and I never doubted—he had the charm and ability to accomplish great things as a salesman with Wertz Wholesale Fruit Company, merely a stepping-stone to even greater successes.

His new job did not come to him out of the blue. He worked diligently to obtain it. With the help of the G. I. Bill, he attended night courses at Oklahoma City Community College, a two-hour drive from Lawton. Although he only had a ninth-grade formal education, even that was more than most working men in Oklahoma. The college accepted his application because he had passed GRE exams while in the navy.

He took sales and management courses. He was smart and motivated. He was not interested in a diploma and the status it offered; he just wanted to be able to get a better job. Because he worked at Shaw's, he knew a number of Wertz's salesmen, and having some college under his belt, he was an attractive prospect. He proved to be an excellent sales rep and before long he was making even more money. To him, that equaled success, and he expected to be even more successful in the future.

In later years, while a college student and a future university teacher, I heard many middle-class students and professors proclaim, in a tone etched with moral superiority, that money was not the most essential thing in life. More important was the development of *character*. In my opinion, they were wealthy, disillusioned snobs who knew little about life without money. When you have no money, it's the most important thing in the world. Money does not guarantee a happy life, but it sure as hell improves the possibility that you will have a better life than those without money. Perhaps it's true that money does not make you a better person, but poverty certainly makes it harder to be a better person. Poverty has no morality. For the poor, survival is the goal.

The university courses taught Dad that successful salesmen dressed the part, something that took me many years to learn. Clothes make a good impression and give a salesman confidence. Accordingly, he purchased several dress suits, an overcoat, shirts, ties, shoes, and hats, a typical dress requirement back in the day.

Wertz's reimbursed him for travel expenses, but since he was a traveling salesman, a respectable car was essential for his job, and he purchased a new Plymouth or Ford with a small down payment. His sales routes took him to independent grocery stores in the small towns surrounding Lawton. None were as large as Dewey Shaw's, but some were the size of modern supermarkets, with large produce departments. His job was to convince the owners to purchase fresh fruit and vegetables from Wertz rather than their competitors.

Dad was good at his job. He knew that selling was more than offering a superior product at a lower price. A salesman forms a friendship with the buyers, making each one believe they are special. Never in a hurry, Dad took them out for lunch or a beer and talked family, hunting, fishing, and other hobbies. In the terms of the time, he acted like a "good old boy."

His new car did not last long. To celebrate his new job, one night he decided to take Mom "honky-tonking." Mom dressed up in high heels, hose, and makeup. Daddy invited Curly, one of his younger brothers, his wife, and even Grandma Bell along. He picked up his mother, and off they went to the bars playing Country–Western music with a dance floor. Oklahoma was a dry state, but beer was available in all the bars. In the parking lot, local whiskey dealers sold their wares in small paper bags that lovers of hard liquor took into the bar and mixed with their beers.

When the bars closed, Dad drove back toward Grandma's home in the Wichita Mountains. Moving at about sixty miles an hour, disaster struck. In the back seat, Grandma needed to spit—remember the snuff—and opened the rear door. It blew right off. The car had "suicide doors" that opened backward instead of forward. The car spun, hit the gravel apron, and flipped over several times. No one was seriously injured, but the car was a total wreck. For years, Dad mumbled about the incident, blaming Grandma Bell and her stupid snuff. Insurance covered the car, and within weeks he had another one—without suicide doors.

Home life changed in 1949. The city renewed construction on the sewage and water lines. In the spring, the lines extended down the center of the dirt road in front of our house. The ground was no longer frozen, but it was cold and rainy out. On good days, a dozen men shoveled dirt out of a trench about four feet deep and three feet wide. Slowed by the rain, the project took longer than expected. During the night, small oil-burning pots lined both sides of the trench as a warning to motorists. The pots looked like bowling balls spewing out smoke as well as light. Corky and I bought Big Daddy caramel candy bars that came on a stick. We held the bars over the flames, pulled the hot candy away, and ate it.

Dad paid to connect the house to the new water and sewage lines. While he was at it, he updated the kitchen and built a new bathroom. Inside plumbing was a step up in the world. When the project was completed, Mom wanted to have a party to show off her new bathroom and kitchen to the aunts, uncles, and cousins she had lived with on the farm.

Why have a party over a bathroom? Mom knew the elders would be proud of her. Dad, however, was not enthusiastic. The Youngs and Basses seldom threw parties. Relatives dropped in to play cards or dominoes on Sundays and usually went home before suppertime. Not to mention, children were not encouraged to participate in grown-up conversations; a good kid was a quiet kid. My brother often broke the rule. I did not. I was always the first to sneak out the back door and play with my cousins until the guests went home.

The party took a few weeks to arrange. The invitations were delivered by word of mouth. Like most families, we did not yet have a telephone. Few homes, and almost no farmers, had them.

The Basses who came to see my mother's new bathroom were from the older generation. She invited her sisters, but not Red or Papa Joe. Bunk was in the air force and out of town. My father's family was not invited. The Youngs thought they were superior to the Basses, and the Basses considered the Youngs slick salesmen who could not be trusted.

Mom's aunts, uncles, and cousins, plus Grandpa Long, came to see "Toad's" new bathroom. A few lived in town but most remained farmers. They were the last of the small farmers who lived through the Depression and the dust storms. Many others had fled to California, Oregon, and Washington.

Our guests shared rides from their farms in several old, rusted trucks and cars that needed constant repairs. They parked in the fields surrounding our house. The women carried covered bowls of food. The men wore their Sunday-best overalls (blue jeans with suspenders), flannel shirts, and brogans. Grandpa Long walked with a cane. The women's dresses reached to their ankles and their shoes were black lace-up half-boots. The men were tall and rugged-looking. The women were sturdy, used to a hard life. They were poor but had an air of dignity—they were the hardworking farmers in the arid land of southwest

Oklahoma. All had some Indian blood from families that lived in Oklahoma before it was opened to white settlers. Their lot had not changed since the Depression years.

They came after supper as the blazing prairie sun eased down on the distant horizon. They chose this time to preempt Toad from the burden of feeding them. In a Bass home, if friends or family stopped by around supper time, new places were set. All shared the meal—no exceptions. Guests were expected to pull up a chair and eat. It was considered impolite to eat in front of people during hard times. The family would not eat until guests sat down at the table or left the house. After I grew up and left home, I had trouble eating if unexpected guests refused food offered to them at suppertime. If they said, "No, thanks," I did not eat.

Good guests that they were, the women carried pies, cakes, cornbread, biscuits, and cookies. The men brought moonshine from their stills. Dad bought a couple cases of beer to help get the party started.

Mother spent two days preparing for her company. She cleaned the house, and ordered Corky and me to scrub ourselves and put on clean clothes. She made me promise not to disappear when her family arrived. After a brief "Hi," I should sit quietly, listen, and respect my elders.

Snacks included red beans, pan-fried potatoes, and biscuits, all placed on the kitchen table. Bowls, cups, glasses, and plates were set near the sink. No one noticed that the dishes did not match, the cups were chipped, and the glasses were small mason jars. Several wooden kitchen chairs and a few sturdy wooden milk crates were placed around the room, and the bed, shoved against the wall, provided another place to sit.

With great pride, Mom showed them the new kitchen and bathroom. The women were thrilled. Most lived on farms without indoor plumbing, and they particularly appreciated my mom's new bathroom. They laughed and enjoyed her earthy sense of humor. She had placed two small wooden plaques in the bathroom that remained in every place she lived for the rest of her life. The first plaque said, "Sure do love my new bathroom, but it cost a pretty penny. Any contribution would be appreciated." A small wooden bank was attached below the inscription, and above it in small letters read, "A nickel will do."

The second plaque had hung in our outhouse for years. Hung on the wall just in front of the toilet, it read, "Here I sat brokenhearted, came to shit but only farted." Anyone who has trudged to an outhouse on a cold winter night can truly appreciate the sentiment. Mom was an earthy woman who seldom used cuss words, but she had no problem referring to basic human functions with down-to-earth language. "Shit is shit," she said. "Ain't no snooty smarty-pants going to tell me otherwise."

The guests sat in the scattered chairs and on the bed. Corky and I sat on the floor. A light remained on in the kitchen, and the guests piled food on their plates. Mom opened a couple of jars of her canned strawberry jam and the guests filled their glasses with beer or sweet iced tea. They talked about the old times and told family jokes.

I liked them—they were down-to-earth people, and I decided I must be a Bass rather than a Young. Mom and Bunk always said I was a Bass.

When they finished snacking, the men passed around their jugs of homemade whiskey, and most of the women took small sips during the evening.

The greatest laugh came when Grandpa Long stood and started for the back door, obviously heading for the outhouse. Grandpa Long was the oldest Bass in the extended family, around eighty-five and the father of Effie Bass, my mother's mother. He refused rides and walked miles every day using a cane. My mother stopped him with a laugh. "Grandpa Long, you don't have to go to the outhouse anymore. We have an inside bathroom now."

Grandpa Long stopped, turned, and looked at his granddaughter. "I don't shit in my house, and I ain't gonna to shit in yours."

A chorus of laughter erupted. A couple of the older gentlemen rose and followed Grandpa Long out the back door. "Got to go see a man about a dog," one with a jug of moonshine in his hand shouted back, and laughter erupted again.

Some of the older folks stayed late into the night, drinking, telling family stories, and smoking. In my youth, nearly every adult member of the extended Bass and Young families smoked or chewed tobacco.

(Except for Grandma Bell, of course, who preferred snuff.) All had home radios, and tobacco companies were prime advertisers on the shows they listened to, which included popular programs such as *The Lone Ranger*, *Terry and the Pirates*, *Amos 'n' Andy*, and Bob Hope. Slogans such as "Call for Philip Morris";" "LSMFT is Lucky Strike Means Fine Tobacco";" and "I'd walk a mile for a Camel" were sprinkled throughout the programs. The Youngs bought rolled cigarettes but the Basses rolled their own. "What fool would pay twenty cents a pack for Lucky Strikes?" Grandfather Long asked. "You can get a sack of Bull Durham, including rolling papers, for ten cents. Better tobacco. Only fools believe those damn advertisements."

Even as the years have passed, I vividly remember the stories and jokes they told that night. My mother joined in and told several stories that are embedded in my mind even though I did not fully understand at the time why everyone laughed at them.

"Why did the rooster cross the road?"

Answer: "That's where his pecker led him."

The women laughed, and the men snorted. Today, I realize that the joke was that males of all species are controlled by their "peckers," as every woman in the room surely knew.

The second joke she told was even cruder but representative of the world she lived in as a young girl. My mother and Bunk lived with these people until she was fifteen. They were the salt of the earth.

The joke: "Do you remember those Indians who used to camp outside Fort Sill?" she asked.

They all nodded. Grandpa Long, the patriarch of the family, asked, "Do you mean the whores?"

His question was not meant to be belittling. It was the lot of reservation Indians back in the day. Every Bass in the room was part Indian and did not judge the Indian prostitutes. Money was scarce, and many "squaws" did tricks for a little money to feed their families. Immoral perhaps to Christians, but like I said, "poverty trumps morality."

Mom nodded and continued her story.

A pretty squaw sat outside her tent.

A young Union solder approached and asked her price.

Her response: "Five dollars."

That does not seem like much today. But at the time, a private made $19 a month, cowboys made $40, and an Indian brave, if he found work, made about $5 a week.

The private stumbled away. He had fifty cents but no takers among the squaws.

A couple of weeks passed, and the private returned to the pretty squaw's tent with a bushel basket of corn. He offered the corn to her for a "piece of ass." The bushel of corn was worth about $2.50.

She looked at the corn, nodded her head, and went into the tent. He followed with a grin on his face. She pulled off her dress and lay face down on her blanket.

He dropped his trousers, got behind her on his knees and tried to turn her over. Remaining face down, she turned her head and pointed to her pussy, declaring, "This is the money hole." Then she pointed to her ass and said, "This is the corn hole."

The room erupted in laughter. The women giggled and the men took another snort of whiskey. I did not understand why they thought the joke was so funny.

When I was older, I finally understood the context. When my mother lived on the farm, many people, including most Indians, did not even have an outhouse. Men pissed anywhere and went out into the fields to defecate (or, if you like, shit). The women used another field. Horses grazed in the fields. There was plenty of manure to spread around. There was a problem, though: the farmers and Indians had no toilet paper. So how did they wipe their asses? The farmers used Sears catalogs or old newspapers. With no papers, the Indians could use a small wet towel, but more often they used buffalo grass, which was scratchy. The perfect wipe, widely used, was corn cobs; they were soft, effective, and plentiful. Thus the "corn hole."

Today, I would be embarrassed to tell such a joke at parties, particularly in the presence of a nine-year-old boy. Today's society shutters at the image of corn cobbs as a wiping agent—or crude metaphors for sexual acts. My mother never had trouble with reality. Of course, she hid toilet paper for her personal use when we had an outhouse. Women did have a few "rights" acknowledged by all.

When people ask about my Indian heritage, they expect me to say my great-grandmother was an Indian princess, the daughter of a famous Cherokee or Choctaw Chief. I smile at them. My Indian great-grandmother was more likely the squaw who sold sex to the young Union soldier who paid her with a bushel of corn.

As people search their ancestry, they sometimes discover knights, lords, princesses, famous men and women in their expanded genealogy charts. This is true of all of us; if you go back far enough and examine all the various branches of a family, there are inevitably saints—and devils. I am sure there is Irish, Scottish, Swedish, German, African, and Indian blood in my distant past, some of it good and some of it bad. My distant male relatives were comparable to horny young men of all generations that would fuck a goat if it were the only thing available. Just as some family members were role models, I am sure many were also thieves, bootleggers, embezzlers, and charlatans.

One rumor in the Young family held that they were distant relatives of the Younger Brothers, an outlaw gang who often went on raids with the James gang. The Bass family claimed Sam Bass, a somewhat notorious outlaw in southwest Texas in the 1890s. As a young cowboy, Sam, like many of the Basses, loved saloons, prostitutes, and poker games. One day the foreman assigned him and another young cowboy to take several steers to the butcher in town. The butcher paid them, but Sam and his friend went to a saloon for a drink and to spend time with the prostitutes. Later, Sam sat down at a poker table to win back the money they had spent. Naturally, he lost it all. They robbed a bank and took off for Oklahoma where he had kin. The law never caught him, but he was eventually killed in Little Rock, Arkansas, and buried in Texas. Papa Joe claimed his father, John Holland Bass, was Sam's cousin.

When I ask Bunk about Sam Bass, he snorted. "Don't doubt it. Sounds like something a Bass would do. Of course, Papa Joe did tell a few tall tales."

For me, all this talk of ancestry is irrelevant. It does not matter if one of my distant relatives was a wealthy Scottish Lord or a bank robber in the 1890s. My identity began at my birth in 1939. My mother was from a redneck family of poor farmers. My father was from a family of crooked sheriffs, clerks, phony preachers, and salesmen.

I am from working-class families, not from the elite families of the best and the brightest who gleefully trace their powerful relatives back generations. In my youth, I lived in the last years of the Great Depression. My elders struggled to put food on the table, a roof over their heads, and provide education for their children. Our family distrusted the government, banks, and wealthy owners of factories. My grandmother buried her money in the backyard in mason jars because her family lost their savings when the banks collapsed in the early 1930s. None of this was lost on me. As I worked to get off the bottom, I never lost the "Depression mindset": hard times will return, prepare for it, and expect no help.

❧

A big change occurred in the summer of 1950—Dad sold the house and surrounding property. The property's value had exploded with the new city water and sewage lines. A real estate developer offered Dad a new house, valued at $7,000, plus an undisclosed (to me) amount of money. Unfortunately, the new house was in a different school district, requiring me to move from Roosevelt Elementary School to McKinley Elementary School. For my brother, this was no problem. He had graduated from Roosevelt and was headed for junior high in downtown Lawton.

Before the move could happen, there was one major problem that had to be resolved. In the spring, my mother had decided to raise chickens to supplement her household budget. Dad was still tight with money, and she wanted to buy a few nonessentials that she wanted. Not clothes for herself, but some modern appliances such as an electric iron, a refrigerator, and a washing machine.

At the time Bunk was on leave from the air force and was staying with us. He helped my brother and me built a small chicken coop near the old outhouse and enclosed it with a chicken wire fence. Bantam chickens already roamed the vacant fields behind our house. Occasionally Dad shot one for dinner, but it was impossible to find their nests and retrieve the eggs. It was the eggs that Mom planned to sell.

Mom bought four dozen chicks that came in two yellow boxes. The chicks were cute, but very vulnerable. She hoped at least ten to fifteen would survive to become laying hens. When they grew up, all but one or two of the roosters would become chicken dinner.

Mom's plan worked. When fifteen hens begin to lay, she sold eggs to the neighbors. I personally grew to hate those damn chickens. They constantly escaped from their pen and had to be rounded up, and any new chicks had to be separated and protected or the older chickens would peck them to death. It didn't matter if they were injured or bleeding; they'd still be attacked. The chickens were fed twice a day, and each week the pen and coop had to be cleaned. Few things smell as bad as chicken shit. Then the eggs needed to be collected. Mom did it with ease, but when I got eggs the hens pecked me hard enough to draw blood.

So, with the house sold, what do you do with fifteen laying hens and two roosters? Mom wanted to sell them to one of the neighbors. Dad said he had a better idea. "Let's throw a backyard party."

Family and friends came over with chairs and side dishes including potato salad, chili, hot dogs, sausages, and a large variety of pies, cakes, and puddings. Daddy provided the chickens and beer.

Party time!

Cars and trucks crowded the back fields. In an area near the house, sawhorse tables were stacked with dishes of food. Ice-cold beer lay in nearby buckets. The older men met behind the old outhouse to share their jars of moonshine or store-bought liquor. Several fires burned in pits covered with iron grills. The women prepared pans with breading for Southern-fried chicken. Washtubs were placed over the fires to heat up water for defeathering the chickens.

Dad and his three brothers—Hoot, Curly, and Bill from Texas—were in charge of killing the fifteen hens and two roosters. Most of the guests were members of the extended Young family, with only a few Basses present. The men and some of the older boys gathered around

Dad, waiting expectantly. The women and younger children stopped to watch.

Dad, or one of his brothers, took a chicken from the pen. Each of the men took a turn killing a chicken as their wives and kids watched. The method was simple: A chicken was taken by the neck, and with a bullwhip throw, its head snapped off. The headless chicken ran around the yard for two or three minutes before dropping over dead. Scared the hell out of me. If someone chopped my head off, would I run around for three minutes like a dead chicken? Hopefully I'll never find out.

After allowing the dead chicken to bleed out for a few minutes, one of the women grabbed the carcass and dumped it into a washtub full of heated water. The younger boys, including me, helped remove the feathers. I hated the job. The water in the tub turned red, and the smell of heated blood flew up and hit me in the nose.

Some of the women degutted the now-featherless chickens at a nearby table and passed them on to another group of women, who cut it into parts and threw the breaded pieces into pans bubbling with lard on one of the several grills. I ate a piece, along with some taters, pinto beans, and baked bread. Homemade ice cream with several different desserts came next. I grabbed a piece of cherry pie and a scoop of ice cream.

Dad was in his element, joking with the men and flirting with the young girls. Mom gossiped with the other women, who shooed the men away. The men drank their whiskey and beer, joking and telling stories. Everybody had a grand time.

A few weeks later, we moved to 2405 E Street about a mile north and east of the old house.

Chapter 4

The New House:
2405 E Street

Although an upgrade from our old house, the house on E Street had little character. The developer used three or four different designs for the fifty to sixty houses placed next to each other on relatively small lots. Inside, each had two bedrooms, one bathroom, a combined living-dining room, and in the back, a small kitchen. The floors were hardwood except in the small kitchen, where they were linoleum. The kitchen had a gas stove, an electric refrigerator—always called "the icebox"—and the normal cabinets and sink. A gas furnace in the living room served the whole house, and outside there was an attached single-car garage. At the time some families did not own a car, and fewer still owned two cars.

My brother and I shared the smaller bedroom. He slept on a queen-size bed while I slept on a cot near a corner window. I opened the window at bedtime even in the wintertime, to the annoyance of my brother, mother, and father. "It's freezing in here," my brother would yell. "Shut the damn window." "Close the damn door," my mother shouted. "You're freezing us out in here." "Close that damn window," Dad yelled. "It costs a lot of money to heat this house." I ignored them—I loved fresh air, particularly in the wintertime. When I wasn't home, they closed the damn window, and I opened it when I went to bed.

My behavior with the open window seemed irrational to my family, but later in life I discovered there was a medical reason for my actions. During the summer and fall I had allergies—or as Mom said, "hay fever"." In the winter, breathing the cool, fresh air alleviated the problem. When it snowed, I woke up with the upper part of my blanket covered in snowflakes. Feeling warm under the blanket, breathing the clean, fresh air soothed my soul. I felt safe.

The front yard was small, as were the side yards near the neighboring houses. The backyard was the same width but at least twice as long as the front yard, and extended to a dirt lane, or alley, in the rear. Mom placed her new washing machine on the small covered back porch, near an electrical outlet. By modern standards, the machine was primitive. We heated hot water on the kitchen stove and poured it into the machine, which churned the clothes for thirty minutes. The machine was then drained of the soapy water, and a hose connected it to an outside water line to rinse the clothes. Once the machine drained, hand-powered rollers squeezed the water out of the clothes, which were then hung on the line to dry. Still, it beat using the washboard.

Over the next few years, I spent as little time in the house as possible. I came home to eat, do my homework, and sleep. I spent my time outside playing with neighborhood kids.

We moved in mid-August. It was then that I suddenly realized I would not be attending Roosevelt for the fifth grade but a different school near downtown. Another school was scheduled to be built across the road from our house but would not be completed for two years. In the meantime, elementary school kids in the area rode buses to two old elementary schools near downtown, Washington, and in my case, McKinley. The schools had lost students as families moved out of downtown to new suburban areas. For his part, my brother took a bus to the only junior high in Lawton, which was attached to the city's only high school and located on the edge of downtown.

The city did not have designated school buses but its excellent public bus system was good enough. Service was not free, but students bought tokens at discounted prices. The bus cost about five cents a ride. Fortunately, there was a bus stop less than a quarter of a block from our house, and on school days buses came by every morning in thirty-minute intervals.

McKinley Elementary School was an imposing building, probably built sometime in the 1920s or earlier, copying the look of prestigious universities such as Harvard and Yale. The front entry had pillars and a porch overhang. Constructed with granite from the Wichita Mountains, the building was two stories, and inside the wooden floors were beautifully maintained. Equally impressive, ten acres of sports fields surrounded the main building. Its sister school, Washington, looked like a twin. The nearby Carnegie Library was smaller but built in the same Victorian style.

Students of all grades, first through sixth, were separated into two classes each according to academic performance, attendance, age, and behavior. Students who skipped school too often, had poor grades, or lots of disciplinary problems were placed in the "dumbbell" class (not the technical term). In Oklahoma at the time, going to school was considered a privilege, not a requirement. Social workers were not sent to households that failed to send their children to school. That said, poor grades were generally caused by lack of attendance. Students who had discipline problems were expelled, sometimes for an entire year.

I was placed in the "upper" fifth-grade class with around thirty students. Normally, forcing young boys or girls to change schools is potentially traumatic. For me, it was simply moving to a new world, and I fit in easily. My two years at McKinley are among the most formative years of my life, years when I gained more independence.

As always, I enjoyed school and stood above most of my peers in academic achievement. I did not feel superior or more intelligent; I simply worked harder and more diligently than most other students.

The teachers were excellent, but they did not pamper the students. The teacher I remember most vividly was Mrs. Ferguson. She was around sixty, and matronly in appearance, but a strict disciplinarian. She often reminded the students that she was their teacher, not their mother. Like most grade-school teachers, she hammered into our minds the three Rs. We had twenty spelling words a week as well as weekly homework assignments in math and reading. Failure to do your homework could mean a paddling, which was allowed. Mrs. Ferguson preferred tongue-lashings. She got me two different times.

About two weeks after the beginning of school, she announced that she wanted to see me after class. Naturally, I feared the worst, even though I did not know what I had done.

After the bell rung and my classmates left, I came up to Mrs. Ferguson's desk. She frowned, stood up, and said, "Follow me."

She marched me back to my desk and looked down. The desk was an antique, made of hardwood, highly varnished, and with the bottom legs screwed to the floor. Each year maintenance crews sanded the desks and applied new coats of lacquer. Many desks had carved initials of past occupants that were too deep to sand out. Opening the desktop revealed a twelve-inch-high storage area for books, pencils, pens, ink, crayons, and notebooks. To me, the desk was a thing of beauty.

"See that," Mrs. Ferguson said, pointing at the scratches on the desk's seat. She gestured at my work boots. "You're scratching the seat."

My new boots were my prized possession. When we went to buy school clothes, my brother wanted loafers and I wanted work boots instead of the high-top sneakers we had been buying for years. My brother and I had made some money mowing lawns that summer, and Mom said if we paid the difference between the cheaper sneakers, we could have the shoes of our choice. We agreed, even though for me it meant spending most of the money I had saved.

I loved the boots. They laced up past my ankles and had steel protection for the toes. Incredible metal horseshoe plates covered the rubber heels. When I walked down the school hallways, I sounded like the tap dancers in the movies. Because I was still small, in class I folded my feet under me, and the steel cleats were cutting deep groves into the wooden seat.

"Don't wear those boots to school," Mrs. Ferguson said. "You're damaging school property."

"Yes, Ma'am."

The only other pair of shoes I owned were high-top sneakers I wore the previous year. They were too small and torn in several places from a long summer playing baseball and marbles.

When I told my mother the story, she asked Dad for money to buy me a new pair of sneakers.

"Hell no!" Dad said. "He wanted those damn boots. Let him learn from his mistakes."

I wore my old sneakers to school.

The situation taught me that it was foolish to spend my money for frivolous things I wanted but did not need. Better to save it for a rainy day—and in my opinion, it was raining. My old shoes wouldn't cut it.

While I was licking my wounds, fate intervened.

It happened a few weeks later, when I was near downtown and passed the fuel depot where my Uncle Hoot worked. He drove a truck that supplied gasoline to stations in the area. He was filling up his tanks when he saw me walking past and waved me over. Apparently, my father had told him the story about the boots. Uncle Hoot offered to buy me a new pair of shoes but requested a favor in return. Two years earlier, he had married Kate, my favorite aunt, and bought a home a couple of blocks from our new house. It needed some yard work, and he asked me if I wanted the job. He would deduct the cost of my new shoes from my pay. I immediately accepted his offer.

He had another request as well. Grandma Bell had recently moved in with Hoot and Kate, as it was Hoot's turn to take care of his mother for a year. She was now in a wheelchair and demanded a great deal of attention, leaving him and his wife little alone time. Grandma was lonely, Uncle Hoot said, and she talked about me all the time. This was before TV offered some solace to older people stuck home alone. Before she moved in, Hoot and Kate went out on Wednesday nights for dinner and a movie, but now he was worried about leaving his mother alone. He asked me to come over on Wednesday nights and keep her company from seven to nine-thirty. I immediately agreed, feeling guilty for not visiting my grandmother more often.

I spent many Wednesday nights with my grandmother that school year. I did not see it as a burden. Each week, Mrs. Ferguson gave the class twenty words, testing us not only on the spelling of the words but their definitions too. Grandma Bell and I returned to our lessons; I brought my spelling words, and we studied them for two hours. It was like old times.

My lowest score on a spelling test that year was 95 percent, and usually I correctly spelled and defined every word. It was a tremendous feat for a sight-reader. Thanks again, Grandma.

My second clash with Mrs. Ferguson came in the spring, near the end of the school year, when she severely reprimanded me in front of the class and then sent me to the principal's office.

My offense was unforgivable to her. That morning I had arrived early to class and opened a book to read before the other students arrived. I had gotten it from the Carnegie Library, which I visited nearly every week. The class began with the pledge of allegiance to the flag. Students then took their seats, and Mrs. Ferguson read a selection from the Bible. She was a devout Baptist and demanded absolute silence during the reading. I closed my eyes and rested my head on my shoulder. My family did not believe in churches, but they did read the Bible.

After the reading, Mrs. Ferguson walked down the aisle, saw my open book, and exploded. Loudly condemning me in front of the class, she declared I had shown disrespect for God and the Holy Book. Defending myself was impossible. I was sent to the office.

The principal took the note from my hand, read it, and placed it on her desk. She was a kindly woman who obviously knew Mrs. Ferguson's religious beliefs. Her secretary retrieved my records, and I waited to hear the punishment. She looked at the records, smiled, and asked: "Were you reading a book while Mrs. Ferguson read her Bible selection?"

"No, Ma'am," I said.

To my surprise, she said, "Very well, young man. You can return to class. I will talk to Mrs. Ferguson later." I never heard anything more about the embarrassing moment, but I also never told my family of the reprimand.

The same day I went to the principal's office, Mrs. Ferguson informed the class that local American Legion posts were going to present a special award to the two best students in the fifth and sixth grades throughout all elementary schools in Lawton, one for a boy and one for a girl. Being in a military town, the American Legion had many active posts engaged in social and community activity. She told us the "best" students in each class would be chosen not by the teacher but by the students in their classroom. The awards would be announced at the end-of-year ceremonies in the auditorium.

I knew my grades were the "best," but I also knew it was a popularity contest, not an academic one. Several boys were good students, and, since it was my first year at McKinley, more popular than me. I voted for the one I liked best and assumed he would win.

Imagine my surprise when I received the award, a high point in my life. I was thrilled but also humbled. At eleven, I realized I did not need to be an alpha male at school but could be myself. My empathy was not a liability but an asset.

I received an embellished blue cardboard plaque with the American Legion emblem signed by the commander of Post 22. Obviously, the plaque was meant to be framed and hung at home. When I told my mom and brother, they congratulated me—and then turned to another topic. The plaque never hung on the wall. The next year, when I graduated from McKinley, I again received the American Legion award but did not tell my parents or brother about it.

Surprisingly, I did not care about their lack of interest. The real struggle in families is to discover your rank. As the second son, I was last on the list, and that was okay with me. I had my own list: me, Mom, then Corky. My father was last.

꘎

After we moved to E Street, I looked forward to Saturdays because my father would drive my brother and me downtown to see a movie. That is, my brother and I went to the movies. Saturday night was Mom and Dad's "romance" night, so we were left alone to make our own fun. One Saturday Bunk, home on leave from the air force, hitched a ride and sat in the front seat while Corky and I shared the back seat. When we got to the theater, my father turned, reached over the front seat and handed a dollar bill to my brother.

Annoyed, I spoke up and said, "I want my own money. You promised."

Every week we had the same argument. My father gave my brother the money, and my brother acted like I was a junior partner. I asked my father several times to give me the money, and every week he said, "Okay, next week I will." He never kept his promise.

Today, a dollar is not a lot of money, but back then it bought our movie tickets with money left over to buy popcorn and candy. After buying the tickets, my brother had fifty cents to spend at the refreshment stand. Every week he bought a box of popcorn and two candies. He knew I didn't like Good & Plenty, so he'd buy it and eat the whole box. He also ate most of the chocolate bar and popcorn. No matter how much I complained, he did the same thing every week. It taught me a rule: "Never let my brother cut the cake—he always takes the biggest piece."

Apparently, my demand to control the dollar was stronger than I remember. In later years, Bunk recounted a different version of the story. According to him, I threw a tantrum the night he was with us, screaming that it was my turn to buy the treats *I* enjoyed.

"What's that all about?" he asked after my fit.

"I want my half because my brother doesn't share with me," I responded.

Bunk laughed. "Give me the dollar; I'll split it for you."

Bunk was a wiseass. My brother hesitated, reluctant to give up the money.

"Come on," Bunk said. "Give me the money. I'll split it in half. Promise."

My brother gave him the dollar.

Bunk looked at the dollar, carefully examining the bill as if it might be counterfeit. He then tore the dollar in half, handing half to Corky and half to me.

"You went ballistic," Bunk remembered. "Only time I ever I saw you go over the top," he said, laughing.

I'm sure Bunk exaggerated. I don't remember losing my cool, although I was more assertive than usual. Apparently I thought the torn dollar bill was worthless. I knew Daddy certainly wouldn't give us another dollar to go the movies.

Bunk tried to calm me down. "The money is still good. The theater cashier will accept the two halves and give you change."

Maybe he was right, but my father—who had observed the whole sad scene—took the two halves and gave my brother another dollar bill.

I did not say another word, but the incident meant something to me. If you want chocolate candy, earn the money and buy it. If you need a new pair of shoes, earn the money and buy them. I vowed to avoid asking my father for money because it was degrading. In my quest for independence from my father, I realized money was the key.

Up to this point in my life I had earned small amounts of money in various ways, but earning enough to become independent seemed impossible when I was eleven years old. My thirteen-year-old brother showed me the way. He wanted his independence from Dad as much as I did, and he had thought of a way we could achieve our shared goal. Corky was persuasive, much like Dad, and extremely confident in his abilities. He wanted Dad to buy him a gasoline-powered lawn mower. Corky assured Dad he and I, the junior partner, could mow enough lawns in two months to pay for the mower and even have money left over. They argued over figures, but Corky had done his homework. After listening to my brother for weeks, Dad reluctantly agreed to buy a powered lawn mower.

My brother was persistent and persuasive, but Dad had no intention of giving up complete control. After looking at mowers at Sears, we went to Monkey Ward to look at cheaper models. Dad and Corky got into a heated argument over the type of lawn mower "we" wanted. Corky wanted a self-propelled rotary mower that was easier to use and better in high grass. Dad insisted on a traditional mower, with a gasoline-powered engine that was half the price. If the grass was short, it made a better cut, like on golf greens. But it was not good in tall grass, which we would have to hand-sickle before mowing. Dad bought the cheaper mower.

In early spring and summer of 1951, my brother and I rose early in the cool of the morning to mow lawns. My brother was the boss and I accepted his orders because he had earned that right. In the afternoons, he scouted the neighborhoods and found the jobs. While mowing, he was bigger and stronger than me. He also decided how much I was paid. Again, I accepted his decision because it was more consistent money than I had ever earned in my life. We paid for the first lawn mower in six weeks; three weeks later my brother bought the lawn mower he had wanted. Suddenly, we could cut twice as many lawns. My pay didn't increase, but it was steady. From then on, I bought my own movie tickets and candy. My dream of independence was slowly becoming reality.

Over the next two years, I earned a good share of my income mowing lawns, but I wanted more. I wanted to be independent from my father and brother. I looked for other opportunities to make money.

I started with the bowling alley. Bowling was popular, but at the time there were no automatic pinsetters. Men and older boys typically set the pins, a dangerous job that required dodging bowling balls and resetting the pins. If a setter was slow, bowlers shouted out abuse in coarse language. If all twelve lanes were in play when the balls crashed into the pins, the noise was horrendous. When I applied for the job, though, the manager said I was too small to set pins—in retrospect, a fortunate turn of events.

Somewhere I had heard that players at the local golf course hired boys to carry their golf clubs. Few clubs had motorized golf carts, and most members did not want to carry a twenty-to-fifty-pound bag of clubs for four to six hours.

Golf as a sport was not on my horizon. Golf was for the rich and prosperous, not for the working class. The course was private and expensive. The public could play if they could afford the price of a round, an amount higher than what most men made in a day.

I had no knowledge of golf but went to the course one Saturday morning to scout for a job. There was no caddy shack; the caddies congregated near a supply shed about seventy yards from the first tee. About twelve boys were there waiting to pick up jobs. All were older than me, but not by much. Neither the club nor the players expected the caddies to be much more than a boy who carried their bags. A professional caddy would die before coming to Lawton to caddy at a nine-hole golf course where the pay was seventy-five cents for nine holes and $1.50 for eighteen, with a possibility of a fifty-cent tip. But two bucks for four to five hours of work sounded okay to me.

I saw a member talk to the starter, who called out for a caddy, usually by name. Some members carried their own bags, and others used pull carts. Enough used caddies, though, that by late morning, only a few boys were left. To signal that our services were wanted, the starter simply waved at one of us. Finally, he waved at me.

For the next few months I went to the golf course on Saturday and Sunday mornings, when the course was busiest. I caddied for good and bad players in the first few weeks. After a while, the caddy master called me by name. On normal weekends, I caddied thirty-six holes a day.

I got lucky three months later. I found myself caddying in a group that included Wayne, the best caddy at the club. He was sixteen and caddied for the pro. If he was available, every good player wanted him as his caddy. On Monday afternoons, caddies could play the course for free, and over the years Wayne took advantage of the opportunity to become a scratch golfer—giving him terrific appeal as a caddy. He was paid three times the regular caddy fee, plus tips. For the first time, working with Wayne, I saw a player ask a caddy's advice, not once but on nearly every shot.

After the round, Wayne and I walked down the road toward home. The course was on the outskirts of Lawton, and we lived in the same direction, although he lived in a poorer part of town.

I came to admire and respect Wayne. He could barely read or write, but he had natural talent, and the pro became his mentor. He was doing his best with a hard life, and although we never became close friends, he became my adviser on how to be a good caddy even if I didn't know much about the game. Anytime you can get a mentor or adviser when entering a new endeavor, jump at the chance. This was something I forgot time and time again, but it is a truism.

If I agreed to practice a few basic rules, Wayne said, he would recommend me as a caddy for the pro group, made up of the best golfers at the course. "Tell me more," I said, my eyes open wide.

Wayne explained that it was difficult to be a professional caddy unless you were a golfer, and at our course, he was the closest thing to a professional caddy. Most caddies at the course did not play golf; they were young, and often did not pay enough attention to the game. To be a good caddy, certain rules had to be followed. The first and most important rule was to be quiet and not distract the players; ideally, only the player you are assisting should notice you. The second rule was to keep your focus on your player and his ball. Follow his ball in flight and find it if possible after it lands. Get his bag to his ball as fast as possible but never get in front of any other player. Refrain from saying anything to other players unless they initiate the conversation. If you're a caddy that does not play golf (as I was), you should avoid giving advice. If a player asks a question about yardage, club selection, or the break on the green, and you don't know the answer, say you don't know. Hold, remove, and replace the pin. Don't place your feet in any player's putting line. Always have a clean ball to give to your player. And never forget Rule No. 1—be quiet and don't distract the players.

For a few weeks I followed Wayne's suggestions, and the next time I caddied in a group with him, he gave me a thumbs-up. When one of the pro group's normal caddies wasn't available, Wayne recommended me.

I became the replacement caddy for the group, and soon after good players started requesting me by name. On a normal day, I was paid $1.25 to $1.50 per nine.

Amazingly, I made enough money that summer to buy my own school clothes, books, and supplies. I went to the movies anytime I wanted and still saved money for a rainy day. Still, I continued looking for opportunities to make even more money.

My love of baseball gave me another opportunity to do just that.

Few homes had TVs in 1950 and Lawton received only one snowy channel. People attended more local sporting events, many of them free. Football games, from high school down to the Pop Warner league, were popular, as were baseball games at all levels, from the American Legion League to Little League. The local paper carried stories about the Oklahoma Sooners and Major League Baseball teams but also covered local teams, including the only professional game in town, the Lawton Giants.

Major League Baseball had farm teams in the small towns and cities in Oklahoma and nearby Texas. The Giants were in the Sooner Class D league, the lowest level in professional baseball (and one which doesn't exist today). The stadium was small, holding about six hundred people. Loyal fans came to the night games, and if the home team was leading the league, the stadium was often packed to capacity on weekends. The league had sixteen teams, but the Giants never won a pennant. People came because the tickets were inexpensive, it was a good family outing, and, perhaps, they might see a future Major Leaguer.

I saw many of their games, although I never bought a ticket. The park encouraged boys from ten to sixteen to climb on the outside fences along the first- and third-base sides of the park. The reason was economics. The boys were expected to chase foul balls, and if they recovered a ball, the park superintendent paid twenty-five cents for its return. Baseballs were expensive back then, and a Class D-level umpire seldom threw one out of play. When a foul ball was hit over the fences, a dozen kids dropped down to chase after it. On a good night, I might get two balls. Although it was against the rules, I kept some of the balls to use in the games I played with my friends after school. Fifty cents a night wasn't much money, but I also saw the games for free.

One night I learned that a few kids had arrived a couple hours early for jobs inside the park. I went early myself the next night and saw around twelve boys waiting near the concession stand, where the manager picked them for different jobs. I wasn't picked, but I came back the next night and the night after that. The manager kept selecting the same bunch of kids; apparently if you were drafted once and did a good job, your odds of being picked again increased. When I was finally picked, I was given the lowest-level position: renting pillows for fifteen cents. The stands were wood and hard on the behind. Regular fans usually brought their own pillows, but a few fans rented them. I was paid five cents a pillow. The job required more work than simply renting pillows. After the game, considerate customers tossed their rentals into buckets near the gates. Others left them in the bleachers, and it was my job to retrieve them. On a good night, I made around $1.25.

When I kept showing up, the manager moved me up a notch to popcorn vender. In the concession stand, hot popcorn sold for ten cents. Fans coming into the stadium heard the corn popping, and the smell percolated around the front entrance. At the time, movie theaters and concession stands in parks and stadiums cooked fresh popcorn onsite. Popcorn vendors wandered the stands yelling out, "Get your hot butter popcorn. Right Here!" Well, I sang this very song. Usually, four or five popcorn vendors roamed through the stands until after the seventh inning. The vendor's price was fifteen cents, and I made five cents a box. If the stands were crowded, I made about $2.50; on a slow night, perhaps $1.25.

Then the boss gave me the best vendor's job—selling "ice-cold soda pop! Right here!" At the concession stand, Cokes, Double Colas, 7-Up, and orange and strawberry sodas sold for a dime, but vendors waltzing through the stands sold them for fifteen cents. During a hot Oklahoma summer night, soda vendors sold more cold soft drinks and made between $2.50 and $3.50 a night. We worked for the money; being a soda vendor was more physically demanding than being a popcorn vendor. The vendors got their pop at the concession stand, loading up twelve bottles of different brands into a tin carrying box topped with crushed ice. Then the vendor lugged the soda pop up and down the wooden stands for two or three hours. I was always tired when the night was over, but money is money.

After all the hours I spent making money between the ages of ten and fourteen, I still had time to play marbles, baseball, and football, among other outside games. Although I have no idea what girls were doing at that age, boys were outside playing. Before the age of the television and the computer, boys usually did not play inside games until the evening. I mowed lawns in the morning, worked at the ballpark about fifty nights a year, and caddied on weekends. But I still had plenty of time to play organized sports.

One thing in particular improved my ability to do all of the above activities. On Christmas day of 1950, when I was eleven years old, I received the biggest surprise present of my life: a new Schwinn bicycle. I had wanted a bicycle for three years and was saving my money to buy a secondhand one. The Schwinn was top-of-the-line, the most luxurious bicycle at Sears. The bike was equipped with a battery-operated horn and light. It was the most expensive present I ever received from my parents. Initially, I was in shock, and then I was delighted. The bicycle allowed me more freedom than I had ever imagined.

What enticed my father to fork over thirty dollars? I really don't know. Perhaps he felt guilty. Three years earlier he had given the same model of bike to my brother for Christmas. More likely, my mother persuaded him.

Within a few months, I stripped the bike down to the essentials: no lights because I did not ride at night, and no horn because the batteries cost more than the horn or lights were worth. I learned how to repair flat tires, straighten spokes, and get up from bad falls.

For several years I rode my bike all over Lawton except to school, where bikes were not allowed. I rode it to movies, baseball practice, and the Carnegie Library downtown. My mom's only rule was that I had to be home for supper if I wanted to eat. If I was late, the food would be in the fridge we called the icebox. She encouraged her boys to be independent. Remember, she wasn't raising any sissies. She wanted us to take care of ourselves, and only on rare occasions showed any worry or concern over our behavior.

For a few months after we moved from I Street to E Street, I returned to my old Roosevelt neighborhood to play baseball and football with friends, but I quickly formed friends in my new neighborhood. These friendships were centered around a new passion: marbles. I was the best marble shooter in my neighborhood, and we played for keeps.

Although there are many marbles games, the main one we played was "circles." It worked like this: The previous game's loser used his pocketknife to draw a circle in the dirt. The circle could be as large as he could reach or as small as he desired. Each player placed five or ten marbles in the center of the circle and racked them into a triangle much like pool balls in a game of 8 ball. Each player took a turn and tried to knock the marbles out of the circle using his strongest marble, the "shooter." From outside the circle, he took his shooter and hit the rack of marbles. If he knocked a marble out of the circle, it was his. If his shooter remained in the circle, he got another shot. A good player—and I was one—could knock five to ten marbles out of the circle before his shooter careened outside it. The secret was to play for position, much as in 8 ball. The winners did not return the marbles to the losers, who were constantly running to the store to buy another bag. A sack of twenty marbles cost fifteen cents in most grocery and drug stores. After a couple of weeks, I never bought another bag of marbles.

I played marbles on many afternoons in the summer months. My mother was less thrilled about my new hobby. She screamed at me for wearing holes in the knees of my patched blue jeans. When I came home for lunch, she made me wash my hands, which I disliked because soap made the marbles slippery. She also made me tuck in my shirt, take off my baseball hat, and get rid of my bubble gum before I could eat.

I used my earnings from marbles to finance my comic book passion. When a player lost his marbles (no pun intended), I traded marbles from my large stash for comic books. That summer I accumulated several hundred comic books, including *GI Joe* (in the Korean War), history stories from Ivanhoe to Davy Crockett to Westerns, *Donald Duck*, and *Superman*. I stored my marbles and comic books, along with my collection of Indian head pennies, in the attic. It was in the garage and accessible by ladder. When Dad learned of my collections, he shook his head. He wasn't impressed.

―

In the summer of 1950, I had joined the Roosevelt Little League baseball team that my brother had played for the previous two years. I was the youngest player on the team, which was composed primarily of eleven-to-thirteen-year-old players. My abilities were still limited, and my playing time occurred in the late innings. I was a lousy batter but a good third baseman. The coach nicknamed me "Stopper." In Little League, a hard-hit ground ball, particularly to third base, usually meant a hit—often a double or a triple. When I played, though, there were no doubles and triples. If I did not catch the ball, it hit me in the chest, or even the face, but it never got by me. I often came home with bruises.

Corky was the star player on the team. He nearly always hit the ball hard and had a good batting average. Even more impressive was his play in right field. He was fast and played a very shallow right field, almost like a deep second baseman. Over the course of the season, when opponents hit a hard ground ball past the second baseman, my brother scooped it and fired a strike to first for an out.

Roosevelt reached the city Little League finals but lost the championship game. Over four hundred fans attended the game including my mother and father. After it ended, there was a ceremony naming the Little League All-Stars.

My brother was the All-Star right fielder. For a couple of years after this, my father would remind friends and family members of his son's accomplishment. Although proud of my brother for his achievement, I also envied him. The All-Stars received a special plastic baseball that unscrewed to display a beautiful wristwatch with a clock face decorated with the text "1950 Lawton Little League All-Star." I decided that in my next two years as a Little Leaguer, I would win one of those plastic baseballs.

My work caddying, playing marbles, and earning money had shifted my main focus away from baseball, but in the summer after completing the fifth grade, I returned to my true passion, joining McKinley's Little League baseball team. Over the previous year, my skills had improved dramatically. In practice, and later, in all the games that season', I was no longer "Stopper" but a slick-fielding third baseman. I easily caught all the hard-hit grounders and foul ball pop-ups. At the plate, I seldom struck out, although I was not a slugger but more of a Punch-and-Judy hitter. That said, if you hit the ball in Little League, you often got on base. The following year, I was even better.

The McKinley team was average. We lost about as many games as we won but never got close to being in the city playoffs in late August. I did not care. Winning is always nice, but I loved playing the game. We lost—so what? Deal the cards and let's play another game. I wished the season lasted all year.

My family never came to my McKinley games, and it did not bother me. I was playing for the joy of playing. My father worked late hours, my mother didn't have a car nor could she drive, and my brother had moved on to being interested in girls.

When not working or playing baseball, I went to the movies, sometimes with friends, but usually by myself. With money in my pocket, movies became a passion. In downtown Lawton there were six movie theaters, and all except one were relatively inexpensive, averaging between fifteen and twenty-five cents a movie. The expensive theater had plush seats and showed the latest top-rated movies. The others had double features and included at least one serial and several cartoons before and between movies. Some even had the *March of Time* newsreels. On hot summer afternoons, before most homes had air-conditioning, movie theaters were the coolest places in town. Popcorn, hot dogs, and soda pop were relatively inexpensive, or one could stock up on candy at the cheaper five-and-ten cent stores.

Saturday at the movies was a special day. Mother would wave me out of the house mid-morning, expecting me not to return until after 9:00 p.m. Although Dad no longer bought the tickets, Saturday remained "romance night" at home. She was confident I could take care of myself.

One theater had a Saturday-morning movie club for kids between six and sixteen. Hundreds of screaming kids packed the theater and the noise, on occasion, was overpowering. Before a dozen cartoons and a double feature were shown, live entertainers performed to the delighted crowd. Comics, magicians, and best of all, professional yo-yo players, demonstrated their skills. The yo-yo players performed the classics, from around the horn, to walking the dog, to swinging the baby. Nearly all the boys played marbles and had a yo-yo, constantly replacing the broken strings that often snapped. The theater had a lottery and some lucky kid won a Schwinn bicycle every summer. One of my cousins won, and every boy in the audience was envious, including me.

Amazingly, admittance was only fifteen cents or ten Double Cola bottle caps, part of cross-promotion between the theater and Double Cola. My favorite movies were action films, particularly Westerns with stars such as Hopalong Cassidy, Buster Crabbe, Tom Mix, Tim Holt, Johnny Mack Brown, and John Wayne. Westerns with country music were not my favorite, although I tolerated Gene Autry and Gabby Hayes. Roy Rogers's movies seemed silly—a Western with station wagons and telephones? Ridiculous. War movies were popular, particularly John Wayne movies, but I liked any action movie where the hero was always heroic. Sports movies were also popular, as were Tarzan movies, and comedies with actors like the Marx Brothers, Abbott and Costello, or the new (at the time) comics Dean Martin and Jerry Lewis. I didn't like romance movies or classical musicals. Opera or ballet movies were seldom shown in Oklahoma.

By 1951, our family had two radios: an expensive cabinet model with a record player that sat in the living room and was primarily listened to when the family was together, and a smaller radio Corky and I kept in our room. Every night my brother and I listened to programs before we went to sleep. Among our favorites were *The Lone Ranger*, *Terry and the Pirates*, and *Dick Tracy*, plus comedy programs such as *Amos 'n' Andy* and *Burns and Allen*.

I liked the movies and radio, but thought reading was the best form of entertainment. I was the reader in the house; as my Grandma Bell said, "Kenny will read anything, even the back of cereal boxes, if nothing else is available." My father enjoyed reading Westerns, particularly Zane Grey novels; I read them too. From the library, I picked up historical fiction about the early American frontiersmen, books by James Fenimore Cooper, but also stories about Daniel Boone, Davy Crocket, and Kit Carson. I always enjoyed Mark Twain books, particularly *Tom Sawyer* and *Huckleberry Finn*. I read schoolbooks to learn, but I read other books simply for pleasure, the same reason I went to movies.

When I wasn't playing baseball or shut inside a movie theater, I often went swimming at Doe Doe Park, less than a half a mile from our house. The park covered several acres and was a commercial enterprise. There were lots of activities at Doe Doe, but swimming was perhaps the most popular. Their pool was two or three times the size of an Olympic pool, and on a hot summer day, a crowd of a couple hundred swimmers were in or around it. The admission price was thirty-five cents, which included a basket to hold your clothes in a secure area. My friends and I generally arrived mid-morning and stayed to late afternoon.

I was not a good swimmer. A swimming experience several years earlier did not endear me to water. When I was about seven, I was in a rowboat on a lake in the Wichita Mountains with my father, his brother Hoot, and Corky. When I admitted to my uncle I could not swim, he looked at Dad and said, "The old-fashioned way?"

Dad nodded, and then picked me up and threw me into the lake. I was lucky I didn't drown, although I thought the three in the boat hoped I would. They laughed as I kept trying to keep my head above water. I did not think it was funny and didn't trust my father, uncle, or brother to pull me out. They watched as I finally dragged myself back into the boat.

When we returned to where the women were cooking, my mother did not think it was so funny. She had learned to swim, badly, the same way. I never saw her in the water.

Fortunately for me, Doe Doe Park gave free swimming lessons in the pool's kiddie section, where the water was less than four feet deep. It took me over two weeks of lessons to accomplish my goal of being allowed in the deep end, where the diving boards were located. There were five- and ten-foot diving boards, and, for the really brave kids, a twenty-five-foot one. The boys mostly cannonballed from the high board. Only a few were brave enough, or good enough, to try to dive from that height. Many a diver wound up doing a belly flop that scared the other boys.

To get access to the deep end and the diving boards, the lifeguard monitoring the boys and girls required them to swim back and forth across the pool at least twice. For good swimmers, this was easy. It took me several attempts to pass the first time, and every time I went swimming that year, I had to again prove I could pass the test. After all this, I would come home late in the day, red-eyed and sunburnt. I don't know if sunscreen even existed back in the day; I never saw anyone using it at Doe Doe Park.

Doe Doe also had a roller-skating rink. There was another rink in downtown Lawton, but it was a magnet for young soldiers and wild local teenagers. Doe Doe Park's attracted local kids, as well as noncoms and officers with their wives and children—no rowdy recruits allowed. Unfortunately, I was a lousy skater and seldom made it around the rink without falling or grabbing the safety bars on the walls. Meanwhile, attractive girls and their boyfriends danced backward with twirls and turns in time with the music. They used their own skates rather than rented ones.

    I decided to stick to baseball in the summer months.

Chapter 5

A Thinking Boy's Game

Something unusual happened in the early fall of 1951. One day after baseball season but before I entered the sixth grade at McKinley, I biked to Carnegie Library, as I did weekly, to return books and select new ones. Since it was still early, I went over to the McKinley baseball field to see if anyone was around for a pickup game. There was no one on the diamond, but beyond left field there was a crowd of boys. I rode over to see what they were up to.

Kids in football gear were lined up in formation. A boy in the crowd told me it was tryouts for the football team. I hadn't even known McKinley had a football team. The football I played the previous fall simply involved neighborhood boys getting together. Normally, there were about five players on each side, and we played tackle, not touch, games. The only equipment we had was a football. Several times I came home limping but had lots of fun.

Resting on the bike seat with one foot on the ground, I watched for a few minutes. It was obviously a practice session; the defensive squad was slaughtering the offensive one. Several running backs were tackled for a loss, and a couple got up slowly, not hurt but bruised. Some boys in the crowd jeered the running backs, probably their friends. "My grandma runs faster than you!" Screaming and laughing, the boys yelled out, "That's a cow, get a bull!" The belittling remarks angered the coach.

In my eleven-year-old eyes, the coach—Coach Waco, I would eventually learn—was a large, heavyset man older than my father, perhaps a former high school or university football player, perhaps a former Oklahoma Sooner. After a few minutes, he grew irritated at the boys harassing his players. He came over and shouted out at the crowd, scaring some of them.

"Any of you wiseass crackers got enough guts to show us how it's done?"

Absolute silence.

Then, from way in back, someone shouted out, "Get Kenny, he'll show you how it's done."

I turned to look. It was Mickey, the second baseman on the baseball team, a wiseass but funny kid. He grinned at me and waved.

"So," the coach shouted out, "who is this Kenny?"

Mickey pointed at me and yelled back, "The boy on the bike."

The coach came over, looked at me, and grinned. I was eleven years old, perhaps five feet tall, and weighed about a hundred pounds. I thought the coach was going to laugh, but instead he said, "Well, boy? Got the guts?"

I lowered my bike to the ground and placed my bag of books near the seat. Guts had nothing to do with it. Around my neighborhood, when the boys played football, we played tackle with no padding. One of my favorite games after school was "Rover, Rover, Come Over!" a tackling game no primary school or high school would allow today. Point being, I was not afraid of being tackled. Football was a game, and I loved playing games. I assumed the coach would keep me in the practice for a few plays, and then turn to a larger boy. I would learn to never assume anything with Coach Waco.

I suited up.

Then the coach waved the quarterback over for a brief talk. Later, I realized Coach Waco was telling him to run a few plays before calling my number. I was placed in the left halfback position in a T formation. For a few plays I blocked for the other runners or the quarterback when he passed the ball. And then my number was called.

What happened next may seem stranger than fiction, but it really happened.

First though, some quick background: I am not a fast runner. Players on the baseball team often said I had trouble getting out of second gear in the run to first base. In fact, I was only faster than our fat catcher. On the other hand, I played third base because I had quicker reflexes than any other kid. When a hard-hit ground ball screamed down the third-base line, I grabbed anything within ten feet of either side of my position. In a race, I was fastest over the first ten yards. I just didn't have a third gear.

Back to the football game. The play called for me to take the ball from the quarterback's left side and hit the line between the right tackle and guard about ten yards in front of me. I hit the hole, and in a flash, I was through the defensive line and running down the field. I was twenty yards down the field before I glanced back. A giant was on the verge of slaughtering me. I stopped and jerked left; he flew past me and stumbled. I trotted back as the crowd cheered.

I stayed in for the rest of the practice but never ran another play. After several practice sessions, Coach Waco selected me to play left halfback for the team. But guess what? I never carried the ball in any of the sixteen games we played.

Only in retrospect can I understand Coach Waco's reasons for picking me. In practice, he saw I was not a good candidate as a runner, but he saw something else, too: I was an excellent blocker and not afraid to take on the biggest defensive player. Running backs blocked for the quarterback on passing plays, but in the Pop Warner league, the running game was king. When I blocked for a runner, I saw the opening in the defensive line faster than most. When a right halfback ran, it was my job to hit the hole first and block any defensive player before the actual runner came through.

Back in the day, football coaches did not call the plays during a game. At team practices, Coach Waco taught us the plays and supervised the learning process. In actual games, the quarterback called the plays. The McKinley quarterback was a good one. He was a fast runner, an adequate passer, and an experienced play-caller.

During the season, he never called my number for a running play. He praised my blocking abilities and was always pleasant but we were not close friends. His friends were team members who played for McKinley the previous two seasons. The quarterback, right halfback, and fullback had graduated from McKinley and, when school opened, were going to junior high. The Pop Warner age limit was set at thirteen at the start of the school year, which meant most seventh-grade students could play a final year for their elementary schools. They were friends in school as well as on the football team. Several linemen were also holdovers who had stuck with the other players on the team in previous years.

McKinley only had an average team but the parents took the games seriously. Although the crowds were not large, they were still sizeable, particularly when the games were at night under the lights. My parents knew I was on the football team, but they took little interest in my sports activities—or really, any of my hobbies. Their attitude did not bother me; I knew I was not the center of the universe. Besides, I played for the fun of playing and needed no encouragement to do my best.

The McKinley school administrators considered football an important after-school activity. In January, after the football season, the school held an assembly to honor the team and to present the players with their "varsity" letters.

The school auditorium was large enough to hold about 250 students and guests. The lower floor had about 150 seats for grades one through four and guests. The balcony had another hundred for the fifth and sixth graders. Throughout the year there was an assembly every week, usually on Friday afternoons. The teachers marched students to the auditorium in the same order as they sat in each classroom. Normally, the principal would address the students, discuss any problems, and encourage the students to work hard at their studies. Teachers came to the podium to announce upcoming events and remind us of the rules in the hall and on the stairs. After other adults spoke, the assembly turned into an entertainment hall. A student played the piano, a chorus sang songs, students did skits, or one of the teachers performed.

On letter day, the football coaches and team (except for the seventh graders) stood on the stage as our fellow students poured into the auditorium. After it quieted down, the principal introduced Coach Waco. He called the players to the podium in alphabetical order, handing each the letter "M" to be worn on their school jackets. I was called last.

Then something happened that remains a magical moment in my life. When I reached the podium, Coach Waco stepped out and put his arm around my shoulder. He looked at the audience, and in his booming voice, he shouted, "Here is a very special player." He paused, and then continued: "Not once all season did he complain. Not once."

Was I embarrassed? You bet! I didn't know the coach liked me that much. I wore my football letter to school for the rest of the year.

The next year I did not play football for McKinley. Instead, I played for the new grade school across the street from my house (Taft Elementary, I think?), which opened that fall. Fortunately for me, Coach Waco was the coach of Taft's football team. He contacted me and a number of other former McKinley players now in the seventh grade and asked us to come out to form the nucleus of the new team. Naturally, I went out for it. I assumed I was a shoo-in for my old position of left halfback. To my later surprise, I was not.

The team had different assistant coaches who did not know me. In practice drills they noticed I was a small, slow runner and asked Coach Waco, "Why in the world did you select him as a running back last year?"

Coach Waco responded, much to the annoyance of one of the assistants, "Wait and see." The coach's main problem was that he had no quarterback. In retrospect, I believe he planned what happened next.

He selected six boys including me and the other potential running backs to try out for quarterback. During the trials, he chose a player to be the QB and then assigned the rest of us to play running backs. Just like old times, I was always the left halfback. Each boy was allowed to run about ten plays. The first five boys followed almost the same routine. They assumed the quarterback would be chosen for his running skills. Two were good runners. Each ran quarterback option plays and kept the ball every time. The other backs were stage dressing, and the defensive players knew what to expect. Once in a while, the runner broke through and ran downfield. Mostly, they were tackled immediately. Coach Waco ordered them to throw a few passes before he called in the next contender.

With some breaks, the trials took most of the afternoon. Finally, it was my turn. I knew what the others were doing wrong, and I had a major advantage: I had played for Coach Waco the previous year and knew all the plays. (Remember, back then the quarterback called the plays.) I also knew my limitations.

I ran ten plays, explaining in the huddle exactly what every player's role was for each particular play. *Right halfback through left tackle*—the boy went through the line like it was butter. The next play was a quarterback option-right. I explained the play and informed the fullback I intended to toss him the ball and act as his forward blocker. I ran right down the line, saw an opening, tossed the ball to the fullback, and hit the line. The fullback broke through with ease. Then I called a pass play. Because of baseball, I was an adequate passer.

Coach Waco did not stop me after ten plays. For the rest of afternoon practice, I ran play after play, going through the plays the coach taught me. I passed or ran the ball occasionally. I knew then, as the coaches knew, and the other players knew, I was the quarterback.

Later on, after the last game of the season, an assistant coach came over to talk with me. He was a middle-aged man who had supported me during the season. "We were lucky"," he said.

"Yessir," I said, thinking he was talking about the game. We *were* lucky to tie the best team in the league, the team that later won the city championship. We were in fourth place in a league of sixteen teams; in each game I passed the ball often enough to keep the defense on its toes and carried the ball no more than a half dozen times. My running and pass plays were usually successful because they surprised the opposing team.

"Lucky not only in this game," the coach said. "I mean the entire season. Remember those drills we had at the beginning of the season?" I nodded yes.

"Well," he said, grinning, "I'll tell you something you don't know.

After the drills, I wanted the coach to replace you as left halfback. You were too small and too slow."

My stomach turned. The thought that I might not have made the team had never occurred to me. I realized Coach Waco must have remembered and protected me.

"Coach said no!" the assistant coach continued. "Why? I asked. Coach looked at me and said, 'You'll see why when he plays in real practice games.'"

The assistant smiled at me. "And I did see. Without you, we would have been a last-place team."

Years later, I met two cousins in Oklahoma who played on the Taft football team. Billy Ross was the oldest and was in some of my classes in junior high. He was a big boy and played tackle on the team. His younger brother, Hubert, a type A personality, played end. It had been one of my jobs to keep him toned down.

During one conversation, Hubert sneered, "You were important then." I had not felt important. I was simply a boy who recognized his own shortcomings, and that my strength was not physical but lay with my willingness to learn.

The Taft team lost the first playoff game. I went to the All-Star game as an alternate and sat on the bench throughout the game. I never played football again. And perhaps it was just as well. Small and slow, I was not meant to be a football player, but I have many pleasant memories of playing on a football team.

Chapter 6

Be an Alpha or Be a Wimp

My life changed gradually but I barely noticed. School, marbles, baseball, football, caddying, mowing yards, and working at the ballpark took up much of my time. Mother remained the primary caregiver and did most of the work around the house. I helped when asked, but my brother and father assumed it was my mother's job to clean the bathroom, wash and iron their clothes, mop the floors, and change the sheets and towels. We boys washed the supper dishes, but usually my brother avoided doing his turn on any assigned chores, from taking out the garbage to mowing the yard. I was my mother's helper, particularly on laundry days. She did not complain. As a stay-at-home mom, she assumed these chores were her job.

Mom wanted to get a driver's license to obtain more independence, but my father was not enthusiastic. When he tried to teach her to drive, he was extremely impatient and yelled at her for every minor mistake. She failed the written test twice, but she persisted and got her beginner's permit. She failed the driving test the first time because she could not parallel park. She cried but remained determined. She finally got her license, but Dad seldom allowed her to drive. "She's a lousy driver," he said. "Get us all killed one of these days." In reality, he was the one more likely to kill us. He was an aggressive driver, tailgating cars, passing in the no-passing lane, exceeding the speed limit, and often driving drunk.

Mom rarely drove if he was in the car because he constantly yelled at her. She never complained and simply said, "Yes, Charlie."

Though my brother and I lived in the same house, we seldom saw each other except when we mowed lawns. He still picked on me, verbally and physically, but I did not get irritated much anymore. His problem, in retrospect, was hormones. At fourteen, newly interested in how he appeared to girls, he insisted he would no longer wear blue jeans, T-shirts, or high-top tennis shoes to school. With his own money, he bought khaki pants, dress shirts, and dress shoes. Mom ironed his pants and shirts as she ironed Dad's clothes. Every night, he exercised before going to bed, which drove me crazy since we shared the same bedroom. He did a hundred push-ups, switched to a hundred sit-ups, and then a hundred pull-ups, counting out every rep in the process. He became so proud of his body he walked around the house without a shirt and often flexed his muscles in front of the bathroom mirror. He tried to come to dinner shirtless, but Mom said no. He pouted and said, "You let Dad come to the table in his underwear, why can't I come with no shirt?" Mom simply laughed at him.

As he went through puberty, he couldn't restrain himself in his desire to show me, and his friends, who was the "boss." To that end, two incidents with my brother from around this time stand out. One summer afternoon, I saw him walking down the sidewalk from the opposite direction with two of his friends from junior high school. I was on my way to the store to get something for Mom. I stopped to say hello and nodded to his friends. "This is my younger brother," Corky said. He turned, looked at me for a second, and in the same motion slammed his right fist into my stomach.

I dropped to my knees, gasping for breath. My brother and his grinning friends looked on. I stood up slowly, holding my stomach and catching my breath. "Why did you do that?" I asked.

"Because I could."

The times, though, were changing, for I was also growing. Although I was not in as perfect shape as my brother, I was almost as large as him. My brother would learn this soon enough.

When school started in the fall of 1952, my brother and I got ready in the small bathroom we shared. He kept shoving me around, hogging the mirror to comb his hair or admire himself in all his beauty. One morning, as I was leaving the bathroom, he stepped behind me and shoved me hard into the wall.

My reaction surprised me and shocked him.

I whipped around and instinctively defended myself—I popped him right in the mouth. Then I stepped back, expecting an instantaneous response; that is, I expected him to kick my ass.

His response blindsided me harder than any punch could have. He ran back into the bathroom, shouting out, "Oh, my God! Oh, my God!"

My mother hurried in from the kitchen and shoved me aside. "What's wrong?" she asked. "Are you badly hurt?"

"Do you see what he did?" my brother said, holding his hand to his face and glancing angrily in my direction.

"What?" Mom asked again, thinking I might have broken his nose.

He pointed to his bleeding lip where my blow had struck. It had begun to swell. "I can't go to school looking like this," he moaned as he examined the lip.

Mom looked at my brother, then turned and smiled at me. "Well, son," she said, "guess you don't need a hammer anymore." Chuckling, she walked back down the hall toward the kitchen.

My brother stayed home for almost a week. And he never picked on me again. Times were changing.

As my relations with my brother improved, my negative attitude toward my father increased. When I talk about my attitude toward him, one of my current friends believes I am being unfair and should remember my father with more respect. As a father of three grown sons and a daughter, and a grandfather of many children, my friend believes fathers deserve their family's respect, even if members believe they have good reasons not to give it. Without his hard work and constant support, he says, none of his children could have gone to college. Without his moral guidance, they might have fallen under bad influences. As the patriarch, the family should honor him, and most fathers deserve respect rather than the nitpicking of their flaws. Although he reluctantly admits some fathers do not deserve to be respected, he believes the majority do. It hurts him to think his sons and daughter might harbor any animosity toward him.

Perhaps he is right. I should be grateful my father never beat me. Food was always on the table and shelter over my head. Yet, I cannot forgive him for a lifetime of verbal abuse and constant illustrations that he had no concern for my feelings. He often implied I was a pansy, or in later years, an "educated idiot." Never once did he applaud my successes, but he always noted my failures.

By the time I was in middle school, I never expected praise from him nor expected him to show me the same love he showed my brother. I never talked to him about my life or asked him for advice. In many ways, his neglectful attitude made me stronger. I did not need his support to succeed. I was not mad at him and never impolite—he was my father.

An incident in the fall of 1952 offers an instructive example of the differences in our characters. I came home from school one day to find my father waiting by his car. This was unusual, and I assumed he was about to assign me a chore.

Much to my surprise, he said he had a present for me. He opened the door of his car and handed me a shotgun. I examined it: a single-shot .410-gauge shotgun used for hunting small game such as squirrels or ducks. It was a gun meant for boys my age.

"What's this for?" I asked.

"I bought this gun for you," he said. "We're going hunting tonight."

"Hunting? Is Corky coming?"

"No. Go change your clothes and get your ass back out here."

Scampering into the house, I couldn't figure things out. He knew I did not like camping or fishing. I had no interest in going hunting and neither did Corky. He was interested in girls, a different kind of hunting.

Corky told me later Dad had bought the gun for him. When asked to go hunting, Corky laughed and said, "No way." He considered Dad's hunting friends "a bunch of old drunks."

Corky's response angered my father. So instead, he decided to give me the opportunity to go hunting. It's likely he told the other men his son was coming along, without specifying which one. Well, I guessed I qualified.

The hunting party included eight men and me in two pickup trucks equipped with high-powered search lights. The men drank cold beer and whiskey. In reality it was not a hunting trip but a killing expedition; jackrabbits were overrunning a nearby rancher's land, eating too much of his grass and crops, and he offered the "boys" a dollar for each dead rabbit.

Dirt roads crisscrossed the large ranch. The trucks drove up and down the roads with searchlights blazing. When rabbits ran across the roads, the lights blinded them, stopping them in their tracks.

Bang! Dead rabbit.

The shooters took turns, shouting gleefully when they killed a rabbit. When it was my turn, I shot and hit the rabbit but did not kill it, though I blew off one of its hind legs. My father motioned me out of the truck bed, and we walked to the collect the body. The rabbit was not dead, and its big eyes stared at me, seemingly pleading for its life.

I was horrified. I reloaded the gun, intending to put the rabbit out of its misery. "Don't shoot it," my father said. "Those cartridges cost a dime. Just bang it in the head."

I looked at the begging rabbit, and I could not do it. Shooting it seemed more humane.

Father shook his head in disgust. He took the shotgun from my hand, popped out the cartridge, then used the gun butt to smash the rabbit in the head a couple of times. He picked up the rabbit and headed back to the truck. He did not speak to me for the rest of the night nor did he return the gun.

The hunters killed fifty rabbits that night, and the rancher paid them fifty dollars. He fed the carcasses to his pigs and chickens and used some of them to fertilize his fields.

The shouts and joy the drunken men had that night appalled me and I never went hunting again.

A word of explanation: I did not then, nor do I now, condemn hunting to put food on the table. My motto is, "If you kill it, eat it." If you are going hunting for fun, take a camera instead of a gun. Fish and release if you are not hungry. People who kill for fun are immoral in my mind.

My reaction to shooting the rabbit was colored by another experience years earlier. When I was around eight years old, I had a homemade slingshot, as did most of my friends. As a redundant reminder, we made our slingshots with easily obtained and free materials. Find a Y-shaped tree branch, some rubber from a car or bike tube, and some leather for a tongue, and you had yourself a good-enough contraption. Then go hunting, or at least pepper some tin mailboxes.

One day I went out alone with my slingshot and went to Cache Creek, the small stream just outside town near the railroad tracks. As I walked through the trees, a beautiful bluebird landed on a lower branch. I took aim and let loose a shot. To my surprise, I hit the bird and it fell to the ground. It was still alive, fluttering its wings, and then it died. The bird had been so beautiful, and I killed it. I had no desire to kill the bird; I was just practicing my skills with the slingshot. My empathy was with the bird, and later, the rabbit. I cried on the way home. I was a wimp, not a killer. I should have taken the bird home so the family could eat it. When I got a BB gun, I never shot at a living thing except snakes and other boys when we were playing War.

※

When I was thirteen, my father was not home much during the week. As a traveling sales representative, he spent his days on the roads circling Lawton and taking orders for Wertz's Fruit Company. National supermarkets, such as A&P and Safeway, now had stores in Lawton, but the smaller surrounding towns remained in the hands of local stores. Dad's ability to make friends with the owners made him Wertz's top salesman. Every couple of years he bought a new car as a "business" expense and kept it in tip-top condition. He considered himself a vastly superior driver to "those country bumpkins" who drove the backroads. No freeways existed near Lawton in the 1950s.

In his first couple of years on the job, Dad usually made it home around six or seven o'clock. Gradually his arrival became more unpredictable, and he often appeared much later in the evening. He preferred drinking with his many friends in the towns he serviced rather than his mundane family life at home. He often came home drunk. If Mother did not wait supper for him, he became angry. "I make the goddamn money for this family. The least you can do is wait dinner for me," was a common argument on those nights.

At first, Mom made us wait even if Dad did not make it home until nine or ten. Naturally, we complained, and Mom worked out a compromise. Dinner for us would be no later than seven o'clock, but she would wait for Dad no matter how late he came home.

His job allowed him to bring home cases of fruits and vegetables for the family. A full bunch of bananas, crates of apples, oranges, and pears that, he declared, with a smile, were the perks of his job. When Mom's grocery money was low, usually every Thursday before payday, we snacked on the fruits. "I'm hungry" was greeted with "Have a banana. They're good for you." Perhaps for a few days, but a crate of apples or a bunch of bananas could last a month.

On Saturdays, Dad wandered around the house in his underwear ordering us boys to do chores. *Mow the yard, clean the garage, paint the house, take out the garbage, go the store,* and a myriad of other commands were often accompanied with threats. "Pick up that damn baseball mitt or I'll throw it in the trash," he'd say. If I failed to obey immediately, he threw the glove in the garbage. Understand, I bought the glove with my own money, but in his mind anything in the house belonged to him. Naturally, my brother and I slipped out of the house on Sundays before Dad got out of bed.

Dad never did anything around the house except cook Sunday dinner when company was expected. He considered himself to be a vastly superior cook to Mom and did not want to be embarrassed. He baked ham, turkey, or roast beef, a nice change from my mother's fried food. She made all the desserts, and her pies, cakes, rolls, and biscuits were fantastic. No meal was complete without dessert. When Dad cooked, he used every pan in the kitchen, and after the meal Corky and I had to clean them all. My brother, much like my father, usually had an excuse not to help. After washing the dishes, I eased out of the house, leaving the adults sitting around the table drinking whiskey or beer and telling tall tales.

My father was a gregarious, fun-loving man who told great stories and jokes. He was a good host. The family constantly told me I was damn lucky to have a father like Charlie. "Yessir" or "Yes, ma'am" was the only proper response as I headed out the back door to play with my cousins. When the company left, he reverted back to "boss."

Dad had always enjoyed his whiskey, but his job as a traveling salesman led him to increase his consumption, and over several years he became an alcoholic. Discarded liquor bottles were scattered around the house, garage, and his car. Although Oklahoma was a dry state, whiskey was easy to obtain. In fact, as I mentioned in earlier chapters, selling whiskey was a source of income for both the Bass and Young families. My Uncle Curly sold the whiskey Uncle Red ran across state lines from nearby Wichita Falls, Texas, where my Uncle Bill was a deputy sheriff. His supply of whiskey was confiscated stock from dealers who had not paid for "protection." As with the sale of illegal marijuana today, true bootleggers sold to local dealers who sold to the public. So long as the sheriff's department received its cut, the dealers were ignored.

Like many alcoholics, my father was a good-time Charlie at social events. Around my mother, brother, and me, however, he was always the boss and demanded obedience. I avoided him as much as possible. Still, try though I might to stay out of his hair, trouble was brewing between us.

Although my brother had moved on to other ways of making money, I kept up my odd jobs of mowing lawns, caddying, and working at the baseball stadium. "Do not ask Mom or Dad for money" became a hard, fast rule. Spending my own money made me a happy boy.

Eventually my job at the ballpark changed. I became the scoreboard operator. I clicked on the lights that displayed the number of balls, strikes, and outs, and at the end of each half-inning I placed large metal sheets on the board indicating the number of runs scored. This wasn't exactly advanced technology, even for that time. But the job was simple and paid two dollars a night—easy money.

It helped me in other ways, too. In the beginning of my job, I could barely see the umpire's signals for balls and strikes from of a distance around 150 yards. I had often wondered why advertising signs covered the outfield fences. If they couldn't be read, why would businesses pay to put up the signs? When I mentioned this to a friend at the park, he laughed and said, "You need glasses if you can't read the signs." I went to the doctor to have my eyes examined and discovered I was nearsighted.

Getting glasses also helped in school. For years I had always requested seats in the front row because I could not read the blackboard. No teacher mentioned the possibility I needed glasses. The glasses also improved my baseball skills. Being able to see the ball more clearly certainly didn't hurt.

I was now in my last year of Little League eligibility. The preseason began with a rocky start. When Taft Elementary opened, I and many of my friends were assigned to play for them rather than McKinley, our old school. But it turned out Taft did not have enough players to form a team, so we were reassigned to play for Roosevelt.

At first glance, the assignment appeared to be a stroke of good luck. I had attended Roosevelt two years earlier, and several players on the team were old playmates and friends. Then again, for young boys, two years is a long time, and most of those friends were now more like friendly acquaintances more attached to other players on the team. Additionally, Roosevelt had won the city championship the previous year and did not need a new third baseman who might replace their current one. He was a good player, and his brother, an All-Star, played centerfield.

One afternoon the coach scheduled a practice game with another team for one o'clock. He knew I was a good player because he saw me play on the McKinley team a number of times the previous year. He assured me I was to be his third baseman. The players were to meet at his house, and he would drive us in the bed of his pickup truck to the practice fields near downtown, a couple miles away.

When I arrived around noon with three other players from McKinley, the older Roosevelt players ignored us and played catch or cards. I, and the other McKinley players, sat together and waited for the coach to arrive.

One o'clock came and went; then two o'clock. Still no sign of the coach.

Sitting around doing nothing was not my cup of tea, particularly when I needed to be at the ballpark by seven for scoreboard duty. I asked the coach's son, a player on the team, if the game was still on. He looked at his watch and said, "No, probably not. The game must have been canceled."

I decided to leave, and the other three players from the former McKinley team followed my lead. No one said a word as we left.

Later, I learned the game had not been canceled, and the team—"our" team—had played. When I found out about this I confronted the coach's son. He said his father had arrived a few minutes after I left. His answer and attitude reinforced what I already suspected: the other Roosevelt players were not thrilled to have me and the other McKinley players as new competitors.

I understood their loyalty, but it wasn't going to keep me from playing. I knew I was a better player than their current third baseman, but I did not want to play on a team that resented me. The next day I went with the other McKinley players to the practice fields, where a dozen teams were playing games. I discovered that McKinley students living in the downtown area had been assigned to play for Washington, another nearby elementary school. Fortunately for me, and the other former McKinley players assigned to Roosevelt, Washington was short of players. Their coach was happy to see me, and he invited us to join the Washington team. We accepted.

I telephoned the Roosevelt coach later to explain. He was not happy about losing four players. When I told him my story, he got angry with me and his players, but assured me if I returned to the Roosevelt team I would be his third baseman. In my opinion, he did not understand the level of animosity among his other players. I refused to return; my friends were now on the Washington team.

I played fantastic baseball that season. My fielding and hitting improved with my new glasses. I expected to be an All-Star and receive a watch as my brother had three years earlier. Both Washington and Roosevelt reached the playoffs, each winning their first two games and making it all the way to the city championship game. It was played under the lights in Lawton's main baseball field—the same one where I witnessed Uncle Red pitch his softball game and my brother receive his watch.

Several hundred people were in the stands on game night. During the warm-up practice, the Roosevelt coach watched me field ground balls and glared at me. He knew what I knew: Roosevelt's batters were notorious pull hitters and hit many balls down the third-base line. He knew I was an excellent third baseman, and it was unlikely that many ground balls would get pass me.

A few minutes later, I saw him talking to my coach. Suddenly, I had the awful feeling they were talking about me. I was right: the Roosevelt coach informed my coach I was ineligible. He threatened to lodge a protest if Washington won the game, and demanded I be replaced. The Roosevelt coach was a member of the league's board; my coach was a nice, much-younger man. Easily intimidated, he was afraid to confront the Roosevelt manager.

I was replaced at third base. Two other players, the second baseman and centerfielder—also former McKinley players technically assigned to Roosevelt—were allowed to play.

My coach's younger brother, the backup catcher, replaced me at third base. He made seven errors, never caught or stopped a single ball hit down the line, and missed two easy pop-ups. The Roosevelt coach's plan had gone perfectly.

I sat on the bench holding back tears and hoping the other Washington players would protest. I knew, though, that if my team walked off the field, the Roosevelt coach would have hell to pay with several hundred spectators in the stands.

None of my friends stood up for me. In fact, the other players on my team avoided looking at me during the game. Perhaps they were sympathetic, but it was not their problem. In my heart, I felt abandoned by the team but blamed myself more. I expected someone else to fight my fight.

I visualized what my brother might have done in the same situation. He would have exploded, first at my coach for being a pansy, and then he would have charged across the field to confront the Roosevelt coach. Everyone in the stands would know what had happened.

In fact, any player in the league had the right to play for any team in the city. My assignment to Roosevelt had been arbitrary, and no official, certainly not an opposing coach, had the power to disqualify me. If I had fought the decision, I am certain several Washington players, and probably even a few Roosevelt players, would have supported me.

If my father or brother had known about the incident, they would have teased me for being a wimp. I never told them about the championship game. In retrospect, their lack of interest was normal family behavior.

The irony was that after the game, won by Roosevelt, the two coaches agreed to combine teams to improve their chances of winning the state championship in Oklahoma City. I refused to play. I had learned that most coaches, at any level, are more concerned about winning than being fair.

I had a trait, and still have it after seventy years: my anger is cold not hot, and my memory is long.

I never played for another formally organized baseball team again. When I saw the other Washington and Roosevelt players, I was polite but not warm. After all, they were friendly acquaintances, not loyal friends, as I learned that night.

I couldn't mourn the end of my baseball career for long, however. A few weeks later another problem arose that made the baseball incident pale by comparison.

Chapter 7

Family Crisis

In the fall of that year, 1953, my father lost his job. Neither he, my mother, nor brother told me the reason; I was just told money was tight, and everyone needed to pitch in to help. I turned over all the money I earned from my various jobs to my mother except for four dollars, which I needed for school lunches and bus fare, with a dollar left over for movies and treats. My brother did the same, but he was allowed to keep six dollars. It was also decided that to save money we would not celebrate Christmas and birthdays. That decision never changed over the following years.

We were told to go job hunting. My brother got a bag-boy gig at Dewey Shaw's working twenty-five hours a week at sixty cents an hour. My mother, who had wanted to work for some time, also got a job. Aunt Kate, Uncle Hoot's wife, worked as a meat wrapper at Safeway. At the time, supermarkets employed several butchers. After they cut a portion of meat to a shopper's specifications, women would wrap it in cellophane and weigh it. My mother got an apprentice job at a dollar an hour, increased after six months to $1.25. On good weeks I made $10.00, but caddying, lawn mowing, and the job at the baseball stadium were seasonal. In the winter, I often made less than $4.00 a week. Finding a job at thirteen was a difficult task.

Gradually, I learned why my father had lost his job. The Wertz

Wholesale Fruit Company accused him of embezzlement and fired him. Over the years, they claimed, he developed a scheme to siphon money with the help of various grocery store owners. Wertz policy was to compensate grocery stores for fruit and vegetable spoilage. At the end of the week, Dad was charged with confirming the amount of spoilage and discounting its value on the next order. That provided the opening for the scheme: He might write off fifteen heads of lettuce, but in reality, only five heads had spoiled. One item didn't amount to much, but multiply false claims on items from tomatoes to apples to bananas by the forty grocery stores he covered, and the sum rose to a considerable amount over his five years at Wertz. The grocery store owners took their share, of course.

Wertz claimed my father embezzled over $100,000, a fortune at the time. The sum was preposterous. Even if the scam provided my father with $20.00 a week over a five-year period, that would have been less than $6,000 dollars. My father claimed he was being used as a scapegoat to cover all the losses Wertz's suffered from product spoilage. Besides, according to Dad, all the other salesmen at Wertz were involved in comparable schemes.

No one informed me of the charges, no one told me of the lawsuit, and no one told me where the money for his lawyer came from. I assumed the family thought it best for a boy of thirteen not to be burdened with such problems. Perhaps they were right.

Because of the embezzlement charge, my father found it difficult to find any job while waiting for his trial. On top of that, his family refused to help him. Uncle Curly, Uncle Hoot, and Uncle Bill avoided contact with him, afraid he might ask for money. Most men in the Young family were involved in illegal scams, but the rule was don't get caught.

Perhaps another reason was that some relatives had silently resented Dad for years. Since returning from the navy, he and everyone in the family assumed he was the best and the brightest of all the boys of his generation. He was handsome, smart, and alpha. When he became successful at Wertz, he bought a new car, a new house, and rounds at the bar. He was sure Wertz was simply a stopover with greater successes in the future. It seems unlikely to me that this couldn't have bred some level of resentment, especially among the less-successful people in his orbit. Thus, in his downfall, friends and family believed he was a damn fool for getting caught. No one expressed the idea he might be innocent.

The timing was not good, either. In Dad's time of trouble, Bunk was in the air force, Red was on the run, Hazel did not like Dad, and the Basses seldom lent money to anyone. Dad's brothers had their own problems. Curly was a drunk, and Hoot was on the verge of a divorce. His wife, Kate, found out he had committed adultery with Curly's wife, Louise. Perhaps unsurprisingly, Curly also was seeking a divorce. Uncle Bill had seven kids and many grandchildren.

Hester, one of my mother's sisters, was more sympathetic. Her second husband, Uncle Ted, a retired army sergeant, had obtained a job at Fort Sill as manager of the civilian maintenance services. He obtained a low-paying job for Dad as a painter at one of the civilian contract companies and loaned him an old Model A truck. Dad accepted the job but believed it was beneath his station. I have no idea what Dad was paid, but he spent most of the money on alcohol because he always came home drunk. It's also possible Uncle Ted lent him money. He was a prosperous member of the extended family with an army pension and a good job.

Uncle Ted and Aunt Hester offered to help in another way, one that my mother bitterly resented: they offered to let me live with them to lower our family expenses.

Hester's son (and Ted's stepson) had moved to Chicago several years earlier, and Aunt Hester was suffering from empty-nest syndrome. I had stayed with them on several occasions for a week or two over the years, and Uncle Ted was particularly fond of me. Their house was not a mansion, but it had three bedrooms and two baths on about five acres, making it quite luxurious compared to our home. He had a gigantic steel shed capable of holding trucks, tractors, and other construction equipment. He was a handyman, a welder, a plumber, and a mechanic. When I stayed over, I spent many days following him around and helping him do minor jobs. His stepson had shown absolutely no interest in Ted's work and did not like his stepfather. I, on the other hand, enjoyed my many hours with Uncle Ted as he taught me how to use a few of his tools.

Uncle Ted was a fat man who loved food and his homebrewed beer. He raised purebred bulldogs and sold a few but kept several for pets. His dogs looked fierce, but they were extremely playful and friendly. He was the only family member who ever attended a few of my baseball games. I knew when he was in the stands because if I made a good play or got a hit, he yelled out my name and clapped his hands, proclaiming to everyone that it was a great play.

The idea of my moving to Uncle Ted's house appalled Mother. "Wasn't going to give up one of my boys," she later told me. (At the time, I didn't even know of the offer.) She told them "No way!" I may have been an outsider in the family, but it was still my family. My mother appreciated Hester' and Ted's offer to help in other ways, and many years later when Mom and Dad visited Lawton, they usually stayed at Uncle Ted's house.

Despite my father's problems and the tensions at home, my life remained normal. I was not informed as to the real source of the family's crisis and thus had no emotional response. I continued to caddy when the weather allowed, but I did not make enough money to much offset the family's economic problems. School began, and as in the previous six years, I never missed a single day. The charges against my father were not a news item in the local paper, and I never mentioned family problems to teachers or school friends.

Contrary to the image often presented in the media about Southern schools, Lawton Junior High was the equal of most middle schools in the United States and certainly superior to urban schools in deprived areas. Sixty years later, I still remember some of my teachers who influenced me, particularly my history and English teachers.

Mrs. Hoffman, my eighth-grade English teacher, made a lasting impression on me. She had a passion for sentence structure and taught us to diagram sentences. Under her instruction, for the first time I understood adjectives, passive and active verbs, prepositions, and conjunctions, and how they fit together. She did not tolerate disturbances in class. And, in fact, she used corporal punishment to embarrass students. If a student failed to turn in homework on time, he or she marched to the front of the class, bent over Mrs. Hoffman's desk, and received one firm blow. On some days, students lined up for their punishment. The blow didn't hurt much and was geared more toward embarrassing the delinquent students into doing their homework. Boisterous behavior resulted in three to five blows. Even I, the "best" boy in class, once received three deserved blows when I had a friendly tussle with a couple of other boys while Mrs. Hoffman was out of the room. Surprisingly, students—certainly I—respected her and enjoyed her classes.

In the ninth grade I had Miss West, a pretty young woman, for my literature class. We read some classics, and I particularly remember reading Shakespeare's *The Merchant of Venice*. One assignment was to write a short story of three to five pages. To my delight, my story was read to the class, and for the first time, I began to dream of becoming a writer.

In the lower grades I had no problem with basic math, but in junior high algebra and trigonometry were required courses, potentially causing me trouble. I made As on tests because I was good at memorization, but I never truly understood the concepts or used them in real life. How do you solve the train question? A train leaves New York City at thirty miles an hour heading for Chicago 1,200 miles away; at the same time, a train leaves Chicago going twenty miles an hour heading for New York City. When will the two trains meet? A version of this question was on most state and national exams. I used logic rather than algebra and made a guess. On most standardized exams I scored in the top two percent, but on math tests I was lucky to score in the top ten.

I dreamed of going to college and took an elective course in typing. There were thirty students in the class. I was the only boy, and the girls teased me as did the boys in other classes. I never became a good typist, but the decision later proved valuable when I went to college.

Around this time I slowly became interested in girls. One particular girl caught my eye for the first time. A fellow student from McKinley, Judy was attractive and always said hello to me in the hallways. Accordingly, I decided to ask her for a date. The idea scared me, and before I called her, I wrote down exactly what I planned to say. I went to the neighbor who had the only telephone and made my call. Her mother answered the phone, throwing me for a loop; that scenario was not in my notes. I asked to speak to Judy. She asked, "Who is calling?" That wasn't in the notes either. I told her my name, and she called out. "Judy! Some boy named Kenneth wants to talk to you?" *Jesus—that definitely wasn't in the notes!* When Judy came to the phone, I asked her if she would like to go the movies Wednesday night. "My parents won't let me go out on weekday nights," she informed me. "Thank you," I said, and hung up. I avoided Judy at school for weeks. And I did not ask another girl for a date until I was a senior in high school, several years later.

⁂

One afternoon in October 1953, Mom sent me to Connor's, the local grocery store. She bought most of her groceries at Safeway where she worked, but for small items such as milk, bread, and cigarettes, Connor's was more convenient. Less than three blocks from the house, it was a well-stocked store that catered to local needs much like convenience stores at gas stations today.

Connor's main customers were lower-ranking army officers and noncoms who lived off-base with their families. The store offered credit to military personnel. On the first of the month, they came in to pay their bills, and, out of loyalty, immediately purchased groceries with cash. By the end of the month, they needed the credit Connor's provided.

Connor was about fifty years old, a stocky man, always busy, who drank a bit when his wife was not around. She, also about fifty, neither fat nor thin, was pleasant and efficient.

When I came up to the counter with the milk and bread and asked for cigarettes, Mr. Connor asked what kind.

"Kools," I answered, my mother's brand. At that time there was no law against selling cigarettes to minors. Cigarette machine were everywhere, in bars, bowling alleys, gas stations, and restaurants. A pack of cigarettes was twenty cents.

After collecting my money, Conner eyed me for a few seconds. Finally, he said, "Heard you are looking for an after-school job."

"Yessir."

After a pause, he said, "I'm in need of a boy. You interested?"

"Yessir."

"Pays thirty-five cents an hour. Not much I know, but it's what I can afford."

"Yessir."

"Okay. You're hired. Come in next Tuesday after school."

I went home dancing. I had a job.

It wasn't good money, but it was steady money. The hours I worked depended on the time of month and the time of year. Mid-month, I worked about sixteen hours a week, but near the military's monthly payday week I worked about forty hours. My time also ramped up near holidays, such as Christmas, when I worked eighty-one hours. In the summer months, I worked forty hours a week. There were no strict child labor laws in Oklahoma at the time. The money I earned went into the family pot except for my four-dollar-a-week allowance.

The year and a half I worked at Connor's was a real learning experience. When I was at work, I worked. As time passed, I did everything in the market except cut meat. I stocked the shelves, greeted customers, took their money at the cash register, swept the floors, took care of vegetable bins, and bagged and carried groceries to the car. Connor acknowledged I was a good, hard worker, but I needed to constantly remember who was boss. *Yessir*. I was paid to obediently do my job. I never came late, and I never missed a day's work. Connor raised my salary after six months to fifty cents an hour.

As a nice side perk, Connor allowed me to take scrap meat from the butcher shop home to my dog Butch. After work, when I was a block away from home, I whistled, and Butch came running, jumping with excitement. It was the best of times.

My grades at school remained superior despite my working. I no longer played baseball. My boyhood days were over.

When I wasn't working after school, I spent much of my time wandering downtown Lawton. If there was a good movie showing, I went to it. Some afternoons I went to the library. After work on Saturdays, I never went straight home—the tradition of being out of the house continued. On Sundays, if it was a nice day, I went to the country club to caddy. If not, I went to the movies. I seldom stayed home.

Home life remained tense. I still didn't know about Dad's legal problems. Everyone in the family worked long hours. I ate alone, did my homework, and went to bed. Being alone did not bother me.

Mother worked forty-eight hours a week at Safeway, but the housework still had to be done. Corky and I jumped up on Sunday mornings to help her while Dad remained in bed. Corky finally recognized that Mother needed help around the house. We were a team now. She usually assigned him the physical stuff while I helped her clean the house and do the laundry. Mom did all the ironing except mine. I didn't wear any clothes that needed ironing.

Mother cooked Sunday dinners since company was rare those days. We boys took turns cleaning up the kitchen. Usually I ended up doing the chore because my brother was dating someone, and seeing her was his prime goal on weekends.

One Sunday night, I left the dinner table first, easing toward the front door to go to the movies. I had done the dishes the last three times, and it was my brother's turn. Just as I opened the door, I heard yelling behind me. I turned and saw my brother and father engaged in a shouting match.

Mom stood up, picked up some dishes, and started for the kitchen. My brother followed her, heading for the back door.

"Where the hell you think you're going?" my father shouted at him.

"Got a date," my brother said over his shoulder as he continued toward the door.

"Get your ass back here, now, and help your mother with those dishes," my father yelled. Corky ignored him. My father chased after him and shoved him into the kitchen door, breaking the upper glass and sending my brother tumbling to the floor. My brother got up and pushed my father, who stumbled back and yelled, "Damn you, boy! Do what I tell you to do!"

I saw my brother leave through the back door with my father still shouting at him. I eased out the front door and headed for the bus stop.

No one in the family ever discussed the fight. The next day my father and brother were friendly, almost chummy, acting as if my brother was a real man. Fighting had made their relationship stronger. Mother was proud of them. She loved feisty men.

My solution to family strife was different than my brother's. I did not fight with my father; I avoided him. He believed his word was law in the family, and there was no reason to argue with him on any topic because he would not change his mind. He was boss. Why bother to argue with him if you could not win or change his mind? I don't fight with people like my father—I stay away from them. I know the hidden violence within me. I cannot afford to get angry. I am not good at little fights, but I am good when it becomes ugly. I'll get a hammer, a verbal one, yes, but it will hurt worse.

Chapter 8

The Boss Goes to Jail

The charges against my father slowly proceeded through the courts or through the offices of the lawyers. It also took a personal turn. In the early winter of 1953, the owner of Wertz's visited our house. He arrived in a big blue Buick convertible with the top up and his wife wearing a fur coat. I left the house as the car drove up.

Wertz offered Dad a deal. He would drop the embezzlement charges if Dad returned to work at Wertz for a few years and slowly paid back the embezzled money.

"Hell no," my father said. "I'm not going to be any man's slave."

Wertz had a problem. If the case came to trial, the grocery store owners involved in the scam might be called to testify. Dad had already declared that he was not the only person involved in the scheme, and the store owners might be brought up on charges as well. That would not be good for Wertz's business.

As I mentioned, the family did not discuss my father's legal problems in my presence. I knew he had been fired from his job but did not ask for any details. I simply ignored him as he ignored me. When I asked Mom, her answer was "Don't worry, everything will be all right." I did not know he had been charged with a crime that might lead to a long prison sentence.

Truthfully, I did not care—I seldom saw my family except on Sundays. School and my job at Connor's took up most of my time. I did not have any close friends and became a loner. I actually enjoyed doing things by myself.

Sometime in April 1954 Dad pleaded guilty and was sentenced to one year to be served at McAlester State Penitentiary about three hours from Lawton.

I assume a plea deal was reached. If he was convicted of embezzling $100,000, the penalty would have been harsher. A hundred thousand dollars was a tremendous amount of money in 1954.

For me, it felt like he was home one day and gone the next. I did not miss him and my life remained much the same. Apparently, my empathy did not extend to my father and his problems.

The family visited him once, in the late summer of 1954. Uncle Hoot and Aunt Kate drove us to the prison. (Only much later did I know they were going through a divorce at the time. Adults in the family never talked about their problems in front of the "kids.") Having seen James Cagney and Humphrey Bogart in prison movies, I expected high stone walls with steel gates, guard towers, and wire fences.

My father was not in the main prison. He was a nonviolent short-term prisoner assigned to a turkey farm. There were no gates or wire fences and only a few guards and trustees. The short-term prisoners could walk off the farm, but if they were caught, their sentences were extended, and they were placed in the harsher main prison. Dad and the other short-term prisoners slept in clean dormitories and ate in a cafeteria. His duties on the farm were to clean the pens, feed the turkeys, and slaughter them around Thanksgiving. It sounded gruesome to me.

My father looked like he was in great shape. Denied alcohol, eating a decent diet, and working a physical job outside for a few months agreed with him. He was a handsome man, about thirty-eight years old, and appeared humble in his attitude. He was paid two dollars a day for his work and sent half the money home. For our visit, the only thing he requested was a carton of cigarettes.

Mom packed a picnic lunch. The prisoners and guests used benches in a wooded picnic area to eat and socialize. Several small buildings had rooms for conjugal visits, but my father rejected that out of hand. He sat at the table and talked with my mother, his brother, and Corky. Ignored, Aunt Kate and I walked around the picnic area.

Dad must have discussed money matters with Corky, the temporary head of the family. My mother had never written a check or had a bank account. Men in suits scared her, and when she was around authority figures, she adopted her poor redneck character and played ignorant. My brother was a different breed. He was excellent at drawing up a budget and tracking every cent—it later became his specialty. He knew how every penny was earned and paid the bills. I willingly accepted his decisions because I knew little about accounting or paying light and gas bills. The two years of age difference between us was significant, plus the fact that I was not interested in business but in history and literature.

To my surprise, with Dad in prison we actually saved money. Within three months we had saved enough money for Corky to buy a family car, a 1950 Buick. Well built and maintained, the Buick remained in the family for seven years. Although my mother had a driver's license, she was too scared to drive the car. My brother took her to work at Safeway, went to his job at Dewey Shaw's, and later picked her up and drove her home. My job at Connor's market was within walking distance from home, so I had no use for it. Naturally, my brother used the car on dates, the dream of every seventeen-year-old boy.

Around this time my brother and I became close. We did not socialize much, but there was a different feeling in the air around the house. We were in this crisis together, and from this time on, we talked as equals. I was no longer his junior partner. We both knew that in hard times, we had each other's back. Mother was Mother. Life was hard, but she expected life to be hard, and she was proud of her two sons.

Dad was released from prison in January 1955 after serving only nine months. Released for good behavior, he was on probation for the final three months of his sentence. A bus transported him from McAlester to Lawton, where Corky picked him up at the station. Later that day, a Saturday, my brother waited outside the house for me until I came home from work. He suggested I go to the movies to give Mom and Dad time alone. I agreed, and he drove me downtown, dropped me off, and sped away to see his girl. I ate and went to the movies, just like the Saturday nights of old. When I caught a late bus home, the car was in the driveway and the house was dark. I didn't see Dad until the next evening after I got off work. There were no hugs and kisses.

Dad never talked to me about his time in prison nor explained why he had been sent there. The extended family held no party to celebrate his return. It's possible he and Mother visited some relatives over the next few days, but there was no rallying around the flag. I worked at Connor's, ate dinner, did my homework, and snuck out of the house.

Dad's returns caused some changes. The boss was back in town. For starters, he demanded the keys to "his" car so he could look for a job. After negotiations with my brother, now the assistant boss, the demand evolved into a request. They compromised. Duplicating the keys, Dad drove Mom and Corky to work and picked them up later. In the evening the car belonged to my brother.

Dad wanted the checkbook back. Again, I assume my brother negotiated to retain some control over the family finances. While my father considered me a naïve boy, he treated my brother as a young man. Regardless, I continued to give Mom my paycheck while keeping my $4.00 a week allowance. I wasn't saving money, but I was doing my part.

During his three months on probation, Dad was not a happy camper, and for good reason. He limited his drinking and diligently searched for a job. His old chums greeted him with a pat on the back and offered him a drink, but none offered him a job.

Today, after many years, I empathize with him. All his life he had been the smartest, the funniest, and the most ambitious of all his friends. He assumed great things were in store for him. Then, with one mistake, the world collapsed around him. He was a con artist who had made an error before amassing the wealth he expected to protect him.

He eventually found a job as a commission-based salesman at a used car lot. Prison changed his ambitions but not his personality, so it was a good fit. He had been a con man all his life, but now his cons became smaller. In subsequent years, he scammed me many times.

As a car salesman, if a car on the lot was worth $200, he listed it at $400. When it came to his marks, he preferred older widows looking for a safe, dependable car. He turned on his charm and slowly lowered the price to $300 and made the customer think they were getting a bargain from "good old Charlie." To my amazement over the years, my father was a sucker for a deal. He always wanted a bargain and seldom bought anything at list price. Thus, the con even worked on him. "I stole that car," he would say, believing it.

Unfortunately, Lawton was in a recession when he got out of prison and few people were buying cars. He continued looking for a better job but was constantly reminded that he was an ex-felon and could not be bonded. When his three months of probation ended, he decided he needed to leave Lawton. Like so many Oklahomans before him, he decided he was going to find a job in California.

Mom, of course, always followed Dad's orders, and at fifteen I had no vote. But this required negotiating with my brother, whose power in the family had remained intact. My brother's response was "No way."

He was a junior in high school, where he had many friends, and he did not want to go to California for his senior year. He had also left Dewey Shaw's for a better-paying job at another supermarket. Simply put, he could take care of himself. "You can go," he told us, "but I'm staying in Lawton."

Dad treated him respectfully. Rather than force him to go to California, he explained his reasons, hoping to persuade Corky to come with us. "Man-to-man," my father said, he needed to leave Lawton to regain his dignity and obtain an acceptable job. A simple truth he knew my brother would have respected.

My father surely told Corky he also needed to leave to realize *his* dreams, which were much like my father's before going to prison. My brother intended to be somebody, to be a grand success in life. He was handsome, smarter than most, and certainly as charismatic as anyone. "I'll be a millionaire by the time I'm thirty" was his motto. My brother was not a con artist and never tried to scam anyone, to my knowledge. But with my father's crime hanging over my brother's head, what chance did he have of achieving his goals in Lawton? Did he want to spend his whole life as a grocery clerk? My brother agreed to move.

I was pulled out of school in mid-May. The house was sold, and a small trailer was hitched to the back of the Buick. Many things a boy might save for a lifetime were left behind. Two-bushel bags of marbles, four hundred or five hundred comic books, baseball gloves, and my bicycle were all left. My mother saved a few photographs but left many things she loved, such as the quilts she and Grandma Bell had made over many years. Only necessities, like clothes, were put in the trailer. The dogs came with us.

I took several books to read on the journey Dad said would take at least a couple of days. Though romanticized many years later, Route 66 was a long, boring drive through the flatlands and desert to California.

The car was hot—few cars had air-conditioning back then. Every hundred miles or so, a small town appeared with a few gas stations, motels, and diners, and a place to buy groceries. There were no McDonald's or Burger Kings at that time. As I studied the desert, I wondered why anyone would live in such a place.

For most of the trip, I read books in the backseat as my father and brother argued about the radio station: Dad wanted Hank Williams and my brother wanted Frank Sinatra. My farther drove most of the way, only occasionally allowing my brother to drive. The boss was back in town.

Finally, we arrived in Bakersfield.

Chapter 9

Bakersfield to Belmont

If you visit Bakersfield, California, one question inevitably comes to mind: Why would anyone move here? The city is ugly and located in a semiarid area east of the Sierra Nevada Mountains. In the summer the temperature normally exceeds 100 degrees, and in 1955 most homes had no air-conditioning.

Three industries drove Bakersfield's economy in 1955: oil drilling, oil refining, and agriculture. Railroads surrounded the city, and the smell of oil and fertilizer was strong in the summertime air. The area could be classified as desert, but clever irrigation systems allowed farms to grow an abundance of crops including oranges, lettuce, avocados, and potatoes. The water came from the Kern River, groundwater, and other sources.

Dad selected Bakersfield because his younger sister, Nadine Armstrong, lived in the city with her husband Ed and three daughters. He hoped Nadine's home could serve as a base camp for a few weeks while he searched for a job. Her house was constructed in Spanish-style stucco and sat in a development surrounded by comparable houses. It had three bedrooms and two baths.

Aunt Nadine was a roly-poly woman with a pretty face and hair dyed brown. Her youngest daughter, Susan, was an attractive thirteen-year-old just entering puberty and flirted outrageously with me and my brother. Her second daughter, Norma, fifteen, was a little heavier and fully developed. Imogene, seventeen, was well-endowed and worldly.

I hadn't been aware that my father had a sister or I had three female cousins. I certainly did not expect to live, even temporarily, with three young girls near my own age. At fifteen, I had never been around girls, and they teased me constantly. I stuttered but my brother flirted with them. He was not nervous around girls, and soon they became "kissing cousins."

Aggressive males win the girls. The shy boy is considered insecure, which I certainly was around my cousins. I was naïve. Despite the girl's flirtations, I did not realize they expected me to charge, not give them an embarrassed smile. Shy boys sit on the sidelines as the alpha males get all the dances.

Our presence created tension in the house. Nadine's husband was not happy to be inundated with poor relatives from Oklahoma. Within two weeks, though, Dad found an old house in the dilapidated section of downtown Bakersfield and rented it on a weekly basis. Although relatively large, it was a rundown place, smelled, and had no air-conditioning.

Money was tight, and our prime goal was to find jobs. Dad interviewed for several, but the only ones available were selling Fuller Brush products, vacuum cleaners, or encyclopedias, so that's what he did. He also concentrated on finding jobs for mother, Corky, and me. Hard physical labor was available but dominated by undocumented Mexican laborers.

One early morning Dad dropped me and Corky off at a farm to pick oranges. It was the worst job I ever had. Using ladders, pickers climbed into the trees, picked the oranges, and put them in bushel baskets. The pay was ten cents a bushel. Sounds easy, but it was pure hell. The temperature in the sandy groves rose to over 110 degrees, and to keep us from dehydrating the grower provided salt tablets that we swallowed constantly. After working all day under horrible conditions, my brother and I together had picked a total of thirty bushels of oranges and made $3.00. The experienced Mexican pickers averaged seventy-five bushels and made $7.50. It felt like slave labor. When Dad picked us up, I was dead-tired. "I will never pick another orange," I proclaimed. My brother echoed my sentiments and complained all the way home about the brutal conditions and lousy pay.

It was potato harvesting season, and within days, Dad found us—Mom included—another job. Thankfully, this one was not in the brutally hot fields but in one of several sheds where the potatoes were washed and separated. The shed was huge, perhaps a hundred yards long and seventy yards wide, with several separating stations. Trucks dumped the harvested potatoes into large bins at the back of the shed. The potatoes were washed then dropped onto a three-foot-wide rubber conveyor belt that stretched fifty to eighty feet down to the front of the shed. On each side of the conveyor, twenty workers, mostly Mexican women, separated the partially rotted potatoes from the good ones. The conveyor belt moved at a constant speed, and pickers on each side grabbed rotten potatoes and threw them into bins behind them. Those potatoes were used as animal feed.

Corky and I were stationed on opposite sides at the start of the line. As potatoes flew past, we grabbed rotten ones and threw them behind us into large tin bins. Mother was stationed near the end of the line and had an easier time. The hours were eight to five with a fifteen-minute break in the morning and another in the afternoon, as well as a thirty-minute lunch break. It was hard work, but it was inside, out of the brutal heat. The potato job ended after two weeks at the end of harvesting season.

I don't know how much we were paid. My father collected the money at the end of each day. My brother was not as silent as me, and Dad probably gave him some money. Corky took the car out every evening for joyrides with the Armstrong girls. I wasn't invited.

During this time, Corky met several young men, and a new friend told him of a farmer looking for a hand who could drive farm machinery. The pay was eighty dollars a month with room and board. My brother took the job and moved out to the farm. I assumed he kept his paycheck and was delighted to be away from my father's control. Meanwhile, my mother obtained a temporary meat-wrapping job at the local Safeway.

With Dad out selling vacuum cleaners or encyclopedias, I was left alone in the house. Being alone didn't bother me but being broke and bored did. There was no radio, no television, and no books. I did not have any money to go to the movies or even buy a Coke. In the mornings, I wandered around downtown in the poorest section of a city with a population of about 40,000. Many stores were closed and boarded up. I asked the few open businesses if they needed any help, but when they learned I was fifteen, none of them would even accept my application. California's child labor laws were strict, except when it came to farm work, and the owners refused to consider any boy under the legal age of sixteen. Around noon, I returned to the house to get out of the heat; even without air-conditioning, it was cooler inside.

In the weeks that followed, I saw my brother a few times. He was in wonderful shape with a magnificent tan. He enjoyed working on the farm; running machinery was right up his alley. He made friends and went to parties with Imogene. Although my brother did not turn his paycheck over to my father, one weekend he slipped me ten dollars. The money lifted my spirits, and I have remained grateful for his kindness to this day.

The family stayed in Bakersfield until early August. "Ain't no jobs in Bakersfield," my father declared. *He* certainly wasn't going to pick oranges or separate potatoes. So, he decided to move to Los Angeles, a gigantic city where plenty of jobs were available. My brother stayed on the farm until the first week in September.

On the way over we made a detour to Washington State to visit Uncle Bunk. At the time he lived in a small coastal town about a hundred miles north of Seattle. He had left the air force in late 1952 and married an older woman with two children.

My memory of Bunk was as a teenage boy; now he was a grown man with responsibilities. I said hello, he gave me a hug, and then devoted his attention to Mom and Dad. After supper, the folks sat around the table gossiping about old times. I slipped out the door to explore the area.

That night changed my image of the world. Unlike the flat, arid lands of Oklahoma and Bakersfield, the land along the coast of northern Washington State glowed, even in the dark, with trees, bushes, and grasses. From the movies, I knew such places existed, but I had never seen them in color because most films were still black and white. A light fog blew in from the ocean, and I walked along the cliffs and looked down on the water. Far below the waves crashed into the rocks, spewing water high in the air. I knew then I wanted to live in a green land, not in the burnt-out land of Oklahoma. Many years passed before I found my place, but I always remembered the coastline of northern Washington.

Strangely, I remember nothing about the long drive down to Los Angeles. All I know is that we arrived in the late afternoon, at rush hour. Dad found downtown L.A. on a map and drove to Broadway, the main drag downtown.

People packed both sides of the street for blocks. I gaped. I had never seen so many people in one place in my life. The crowd was thick, block after block, as we traveled up Broadway.

Broadway was the retail and business center of the city in the age before suburban malls. High-rise buildings lined the street and stretched upward twenty or thirty stories. Business offices were on the upper floors. At street level, specialized retail stores sold a myriad of products, including shoes, hats, ties, and more. Women and men's clothing were sold in separate stores. Dozens of restaurants, cafeterias, bars, and movie theaters lined both sides of the street. Department stores, such as Sears, Penney's, and Macy's, occupied full city blocks.

Cars, buses, and trucks crammed the road. Streetcars ran along double tracks in the center of the street. Driving up Broadway for twenty to thirty blocks, we saw several streetcars rumble past in both directions more quickly than the cars. Near the end of the long business district, many of the streetcars turned off Broadway onto Pico Boulevard. My father followed them.

Dad had a talent, perhaps learned while he was in the navy, for finding the low-income districts where manual workers lived, areas with adequate but rundown apartments and boardinghouses. A few blocks down Pico and about a half mile from the University of Southern California, he turned off on a side road and drove slowly down the street until he discovered an old boardinghouse. He rented a room for a week. The room had two beds and a small kitchen, but the bathroom was down the hall and shared with other rooms.

As soon as we settled in, he pulled me aside and handed me a five-dollar bill. "Get something to eat and take in a movie," he said.

I knew why. It was Saturday night.

"How?" I asked.

He gave me a hard look, letting me know that was a stupid question. "Go back to Pico Boulevard," he said. It was about a five-block walk. "Catch a streetcar to downtown. Eat and see a movie. Then come back the same way."

I nodded and left. A father sending a fifteen-year-old country boy out in a rough urban neighborhood after dark in a strange city seems strange and inconceivable today. But that was back then.

I wasn't scared, but I was cautious. I realized I fit in. I was poor and did not fear the working class. The poor knew I had no money. No one even noticed me. I ate in a cafeteria on Broadway and saw a movie starring Burt Lancaster, *The Kentuckian*. I arrived back at the boardinghouse around eleven o'clock. My parents were in bed, my father asleep, but Mother awake. After I came in, she rolled over and went to sleep.

Things moved quickly after that first night. Almost immediately my mother found a job at a nearby Safeway—experienced meat-wrappers were in demand. With her first week's paycheck, we moved to a nearby one-bedroom apartment. Shortly afterward, Corky joined us from Bakersfield. For the next six to seven months, my brother and I slept on a couch in the living room. Meals were basic, usually cereal for breakfast, a school lunch, and a sandwich for dinner.

We registered to enroll at Belmont High School about a mile away. Our school records from Oklahoma arrived before school started two weeks later. California separated students according to their academic records, and I was placed in the tenth grade "star" classes. My brother was placed in the senior star classes. He would get his high school diploma at Belmont, but he had no desire to form friends at the school. He intended to get an after-school job.

Before he started looking for a job, he made a number of decisions. He did not want another job bagging groceries and stocking shelves.

He knew at heart he was a salesman, and that is where he could make more money. I assumed Dad gave him advice on this front. Adopting an axiom it took me forever to learn, he realized he needed to dress the part for the job he wanted. Salesman did not wear khaki pants and short-sleeve shirts. He used part of the money he earned from the farm job to buy a new wardrobe of dress shirts, jackets, pants, belts, neckties, and dress shoes. Hats were no longer in style.

A week later he found a job at Roy Logan's shoe store located at Sixth and Broadway. In the heart of downtown L.A. The store was a quick trolley or bus ride from Belmont High. In the mid-1950s, Los Angeles had an excellent public transportation system. From downtown hubs, buses and streetcars radiated out twenty miles in all directions. At the time, if you can believe it, many urban working families did not own a car. On main routes, such as Pico Boulevard, streetcars and buses came by every fifteen minutes during the day and after that every thirty minutes until midnight.

Because of my age, I could not find a job and was dependent on Mom to give me money for school. Belmont High was four or five times larger than the high school in Lawton, but I made the transition easily. Cliques had not yet formed in freshman classes because students came from many different middle schools and were as new to the class as I was.

I enjoyed my freshman year. The students in star classes were different than at other schools I had attended. In later years, I thought of Belmont as the International High School. The school was near Chinatown, and several students in the star classes were third- or fourth-generation Americans. Their parents and grandparents supported Chinese social values of consideration and respect, and education was considered essential to achieving success. The students were talented and competitive but always polite. Alpha behavior violated the code of social behavior, a trait common to people of European descent, at least in my experience.

I felt like I belonged. Academics was my domain, the place where I excelled, and even in star classes I was near the top. I enjoyed competition at school. The other students admired me for my hard work.

I still could not legally get a job, so I often stayed in the library after school rather than returning to the crowded apartment.

My dream was to go to college. My father, brother, and mother did not understand how much that dream meant to me. My brother intended to earn his millions through business, but I intended to get off the bottom by obtaining an education. Millions sounded great, but reality said an education was a better choice for me.

From September to mid-November, my mother and brother were the breadwinners in the family. Dad had trouble finding a job primarily because he had been applying for sales jobs in large businesses higher up the food chain than my brother's job as a shoe salesman. Unfortunately for him, these companies' application forms invariably asked the question, "Have you ever been convicted of a felony?" A "yes" answer destroyed Dad's chances.

Dad decided to learn a trade where employers did not ask that question. In all my years, I had never seen my father do any manual labor. He didn't dig ditches or get under the kitchen sink to unclog the drain. He did not want to be a plumber, an electrician, or a bricklayer. He disliked hard physical labor. But he enrolled in a trade school to learn tool and die making. Dressed in work clothes and carrying a lunch pail, he attended the school for three weeks before dropping out.

"Hated it," he said.

Next, he enrolled in a bartender's school. In retrospect, this wasn't an ideal choice for a former and future alcoholic. Bartender did fit his personality, however. He made people feel as if they were real friends and told great jokes. Bartending also offered him chances to skim money.

Before anti-smoking laws and harsh drunk-driving laws, there were hundreds of working man's bars in the Los Angeles area, and few did background checks on their employees. Two weeks after graduating from bartender's school, Dad obtained a job at a bar near Alhambra and Pasadena.

My brother was a hard worker, learned fast, and had a charismatic personality. It did not take him long to realize working at Roy Logan's was not his dream job. At Logan's, salesmen were paid by the hour, meaning the best salesman was paid the same wage as the most mediocre one. He wanted a job where he earned a commission on every sale. Before and after work, Corky wandered downtown and checked out other shoe stores, looking for a better opportunity.

He settled on the most expensive shoe store on Broadway, a place where salesmen worked on commission with a guaranteed minimum weekly wage. Roy Logan's was a working man's shoe store; this place was for the middle class. Logan's shoes cost $6.99 to $12.99; the least-expensive shoe at the new store was $29.99, and some cost over $100.00. (For these prices in 2020 dollars, multiple by five.)

Corky observed the dress of the salesmen, styled himself accordingly, and applied for a job. The owner asked him if he was willing to be a stock boy for a month or two until he showed he could be a good worker and salesman. My brother agreed. To be the best salesman, he needed to know the stock better than any other salesman. For the next three weeks, he moved the stock and examined every shoe for price and quality. Then he went on the floor. Within a few days he earned more money than he had earned at Logan's for a month's work.

On off days, he wandered down to Logan's to show off his new $35.00 shoes. The manager was friendly and admitted he had been unable to fill Corky's old job. Both the boys he hired came in late and then did as little work as possible. He asked my brother if he knew a good kid looking for a job.

"Yep, sure do," my grinning brother said.

Guess who?

Chapter 10

Roy Logan's Shoe Store

The first six months in California were hard for me because I couldn't work a normal, non-farming job. I felt like I lost my independence when I had to ask Mom for money. When I turned sixteen, my brother told me of the opening at Roy Logan's shoe store. He loaned me the money to buy appropriate clothes for the job before he took me down to Logan's. I got the job. I was back in the saddle again. I did not want a repeat of those six months, so I made a decision to not turn my pay over to Mother to help the family.

I worked at Roy Logan's for four years, first as a part-time clerk, and later as the assistant manager. Roy Logan's sold men's dress shoes only; they did not carry tennis shoes, sandals, boots, or bedroom slippers. The store was comparable to chains such as Thom McAn. Although the quality of their shoes did not compare to those in my brother's store, Logan's shoes were vastly superior to any shoes available today at Walmart. The store had the same styles as more expensive stores but catered to a clientele that needed budget-friendly dress shoes for church, weddings, and funerals. As the shoes aged, they became work shoes and new dress shoes were purchased.

Unlike today, back then when a man went to a shoe store, he expected to be helped by a clerk who measured his feet, got the merchandise, and used a shoe spoon to place the shoes on his feet. When he bought a suit off the rack, he expected a tailor to alter the pants and coat. This held true of many retail establishments—service was an integral part of the business.

Logan's prime liability was in sizing. Expensive dress shoes came in widths from AAA to EEE that fit their customers almost as well as handmade shoes. At Logan's, a few styles came in widths from B to EE, but most styles came only in C widths. This model hasn't changed much, and most of the shoes sold today in warehouse discount stores have even more limited widths.

The store was part of a national shoe conglomerate that manufactured shoes and distributed them to their retail outlets under many different names. Each Monday morning trucks arrived with new stock to be unpacked and placed in appropriate areas so clerks could find the merchandise.

Logan's was approximately sixty feet wide and 150 feet long. Quality carpet covered the floor, and two dozen chairs were arranged in the center facing back-to-back, with walking corridors on the sides. The shoeboxes lined the walls, extending from the floor to a fifteen-foot-high ceiling. Six library ladders mounted on rollers allowed clerks to reach the boxes near the ceiling. Stocking the merchandise often took a day or two until the boxes were shifted to the right spots. The store had the highest sales in their division because of its location on Broadway where foot traffic was high. The store remained open until 9 p.m. on Mondays and Fridays.

When I finally started work in November of 1955, my hours were Mondays and Fridays, from 3 p.m. to 9 p.m. and Saturdays from 9 a.m. to 6 p.m. On holidays, I worked more hours. The pay was $1.25 per hour.

Within a couple of months, I knew the stock better than anyone in the store, and everyone, including the manager, would ask me for help in finding a particular style or size. Then, and always, if I had a job, my goal was to be the best at it. The manager and assistant manager avoided chores, but I preferred working to sitting around doing nothing.

The rule was that a customer was to be greeted as he entered the store, escorted to a seat, his right shoe removed, and his foot measured—the thought being he was much less likely to jump up and leave in his socks. On busy Saturdays, I helped several customers at the same time. The shoes were on display in two large windows on the street. Customers looked at the shoes outside, came in, and usually requested to see a style they liked. No shoes were displayed inside.

For some reason, most customers vainly believed their shoe size was much smaller than their measured size, so sizes were in code. Often, a person who measured size nine thought his size was seven. If asked, the small lie was to tell the customer the shoe was one size smaller. They often rejected a shoe because it made their feet look larger.

The store may have thought that a sale was more important than the truth, but I believed it was essential the customer receive the correct-sized shoe. I was uncomfortable with lying, and shoes too small for the feet can cause medical problems. I usually explained shoe size varied according to style and the width of the shoe, which is the absolute truth.

Within a few months I realized I did not want to be a shoe clerk the rest of my life. But it beat picking oranges, separating potatoes, or mowing yards. I had money in my pocket even if it was slightly tainted.

⁌

At this point we were living in a predominantly black section near the University of Southern California in a small one-bedroom apartment. In January 1956, Dad decided to move us again. Our apartment was around twenty miles from his job at a bar in Pasadena, and he wanted a shorter commute. He rented a house on Ford Boulevard in East Los Angeles in the Montebello area, where the dominant racial group was Mexican. The house had two bedrooms, one bath, and an enclosed porch that became my bedroom as well as the laundry room. It was something of a ghetto area, but a nicer one than where we last lived.

The rent was within our budget and my father's commute became easier, but the location wasn't ideal for anyone else in the family. Mom worked on Pico Boulevard west of downtown, a fifty-minute bus ride from Montebello. It was also a fifty-minute bus trip to Belmont High for Corky and me. My father suggested we transfer to another high school in East L.A. My brother's response: "No way!" He was not going to change schools in his senior year. I agreed with Corky. I decided to remain at Belmont High until the end of the year.

Since Corky and I worked in downtown L.A., it was only another fifteen minutes to Belmont. So, my brother and I were only inconvenienced for a few months. The inconvenience? We had to get out of bed at 6 a.m. with a fifty-minute bus ride to Belmont. It was another forty-minute ride home after work. Mom applied for a transfer to East Los Angeles that she obtained a few weeks later.

In September, I transferred to Garfield High School in East Los Angeles. It was located near Whittier and Atlantic Boulevards, a mile from our house on Ford. I applied for the school-work program that allowed me to leave school and go to my job around 12:30. The program exempted me from all elective courses. In the two years at Garfield, I socialized with none of the other students and engaged in zero extracurricular activities. I made no friends at school. My life revolved around my job and exploring life in a large city.

Over sixty percent of the students at Garfield were from Mexican American families. Administrators considered it a rough school. For several reasons, I had no problems with other students. Mainly, since I was on the school-work program, I was at school for only four hours and left long before the other students. The commute to work was about forty minutes, and on the ride, I read fun books and class assignments, completing my written work on Sundays.

The star classes included less than 5 percent of the student body and excluded any disruptive students. Although most of the students at Garfield were of Mexican descent, only a few were in these classes. Like the poorer students in Lawton, the majority of students at Garfield thought the liberal arts courses, such as U.S. history, social studies, and literature, were boring and a waste of time. Survival was the goal. Studying philosophers such as Socrates and Aristotle, or writers such Shakespeare or Dickens, or history such as the U.S. Constitutional Convention or World War II, did not put a single penny in your pocket.

Few students in the star classes worked after-school jobs; most were from prosperous families. Students from poorer families, usually in "lower" ranked classes (the vast majority of students), were often on the work-study program.

Students in the star classes assumed they would go to college either through a scholarship or with parental support. I did not expect to get a scholarship, nor did I expect any parental support.

I walked a mile to school each day, and I wore my work clothes instead of returning home to change. I usually put my dress jacket and tie in a school locker but wore my dress pants, shoes, and button-down dress shirts to class. In the halls, students mistook me for a student teacher and treated me accordingly. One of my favorite history teachers suggested I wear different clothes to school if I wanted to form any friendships. I ignored his suggestion simply because work took up so much of my time. The inconvenience wasn't worth it.

My hours at Roy Logan's increased. In busy times I worked thirty to thirty-five hours a week. Mondays and Fridays I was there from 2 to 9; Tuesday through Thursday afternoons from 2 to 6; Saturday from 9 a.m. to 6 p.m. I stayed after work to clean up the store although I was paid only for the hours when the store was open.

With more money coming in, I began to save for college. My father offered to bank the money for me. East Los Angeles had problems with break-ins, so his suggestion seemed logical. For the next eighteen months I gave him around a $100 a month, relieved to know the money was safe in a bank. Of course, as always, I kept a secret stash for emergencies.

My classes at Garfield included the same thirty to thirty-five students in my four daily required classes. As usual, literature and history classes were my favorites. The oldest and best teachers claimed the right as senior teachers to teach star classes, where the students were interested in learning and the lowest grade was usually a C-minus. In my two years at Garfield, no student disrupted any of my classes.

My worst subject was Spanish. French and Spanish were available to students aspiring to attend college. I had never taken a foreign-language course and opted for Spanish, a pragmatic decision while living in Los Angeles, where "hablar Español" appeared almost essential.

Thirty-five students were in the class, an impractical number for learning a foreign language. Computers and portable tape recorders did not exist, and reel-to-reel tape recorders were huge and expensive. Most of the students in the class considered Spanish an easy course because they spoke it at home. They enjoyed the class, trading quips with the teacher, who corrected their grammar. Five of us were in deep trouble, particularly me, an Oklahoma boy who did not understand phonetics. In two years of Spanish with the same teacher, I was called on to read aloud in class no more than a dozen times. Visualize, if you can, a boy who spoke Spanish with a Southern accent. To my ears, my pronunciation was excellent. But the entire class held their ears and groaned. Apparently, my pronunciation was worse than fingernails dragged across the blackboard. At any rate, I learned to read Spanish and made As on the written tests. Averaging things together, the teacher was kind enough to give me a B-minus.

The Spanish story reminds me of another incident related to language tones—or rather, off-tones. When my sixth-grade class at McKinley Elementary School had graduation practice, the music teacher wanted us to sing a few songs. One of them was "Onward Christian Soldiers." After a practice session, the teacher called a break. She walked around quietly talking to individual students. When she came to me, she leaned over and whispered in my ear. "Please just mouth the words," she pleaded. Apparently, I could not carry a tune nor could I maintain the beat. Many years later, my mother, ten-year-old daughter, and I could clear a room singing "Onward Christian Soldiers." The family pleaded with us not to sing.

One semester, I skipped work one afternoon a week for six weeks to take Garfield's driver's education course. Dad offered to teach me, but I ignored his offer. I remembered when he taught Mom to drive and his constant screaming at her. I wanted a teacher, not a dictator. The driver's ed class was two hours long and limited to three students. The teacher assigned homework and usually spent about thirty minutes going over the material for the written test required to obtain a license. Then we went to the car. It was stick shift, as most cars were back in the day. Each student drove for thirty minutes, and then spent an hour watching the two other students drive under the teacher's direction. The course ended at the Motor Vehicle Department where the driving test was held. Most of the students passed with ease, me included.

My father and brother dominated use of the car. When I was allowed to use it, it was often for running errands that wound up costing me money, like picking up the cleaning. Mom refused to iron shirts, and dress clothes were dry-cleaned rather than washed. On Sunday mornings, when the cleaner was open, my father often tossed me the keys to the car and said, "Go get my cleaning." If my brother heard, he shouted out, "Get mine too." We all wore dress clothes to work, so the load was significant. Each of us usually sent three or four white dress shirts, two pair of pants, and a jacket to the cleaner. To my irritation, my father seldom paid me when I returned. If I asked for the money, he had an excuse and promised to pay me later. Sometimes he paid me and sometimes he conveniently "forgot." I realized he was scamming me but continued to pick up his clothes. I was irritated, sure, but he was my father. It seemed petty to do otherwise since I earned enough money and it was not a burden.

I seldom saw my other family members except on Sundays. All of us worked different hours and expected take to expect to take care of ourselves. Of course, my brother and father continued to believe the housework belonged to mother. They did not know how to turn on the washing machine, change sheets, or find the tools to mop the floors. I did my own laundry because my goal, as always, was to be independent.

∽

While in the eleventh and twelfth grades, I was friendly with the other students in my classes, but none were personal friends. I did not participate in any extracurricular activities, never asked a girl for a date, and was never invited to parties. I was treated as if I were a student teacher.

Social psychologists might suggest I was insecure and lonely, but I was relatively content with my life and focused on my plans to go to college. I had a job and was paying my own way. Occasionally, though, being an outsider at school backfired.

Take the following example. In my junior-year English class, I received the highest grades on every test and a B-plus or better on every paper. So, when I received a B-plus for my final grade, I didn't understand. I met my teacher, a nice older woman, and asked her why.

Her answer was enlightening. Like most teachers at the time, she was an adviser to several extracurricular groups, including the drama club. In her English class, she awarded grades on a strict bell curve. In her star class of thirty-five students, she felt she could give no more than five As. The average grade was B; a C-minus was almost a failing grade. Although I had the highest test scores, I had not participated in any after-school activities. Other students in my class, however, included the class president and vice president, the editor of the school newspaper, a student who lettered in tennis, and the star of a school play. For their efforts, all earned additional credits and were awarded As. I nodded when I heard this explanation, but I felt mistreated. I had failed to recognize a truism: who you know helps. She had more exposure and commitment to those students. It was my fault, not hers. My failure to obtain useful mentors would dog me the rest of my life.

Back at the shoe store, I interacted with coworkers but seldom socialized with them after work. The turnover in managers and assistant managers was rapid. In my four years at the store, I worked under four different managers and six different assistant managers. Initially, the managers believed the company propaganda: If they were loyal to the company and worked hard, if they increased sales and followed orders, they would be promoted to manage larger stores, become a district manager, and perhaps even a vice president; maybe even president. Reality was much different. Of the four managers, two were promoted but later fired. Two were fired without advancing, one for incompetence and the other for requesting a raise. The assistant managers were fired or quit when they found better jobs.

Some I liked, some I disliked, but they all had one thing in common: They were older than me, and several were married with children. And after working with them for thirty to sixty hours a week, I had enough of their fellowship.

I listened to the company's cheerleading but did not believe the propaganda. I didn't much matter, however, as I had no interest in being promoted. The job was a means to make money and eventually pay my way through college. My brother made twice as much at his job as I did, but he had many more wants than me. I simply wanted stability.

I seldom went home after work. I had no curfew, and, as I mentioned, I rarely saw my family except briefly on Sundays. Between sixteen and eighteen, I was content with being alone. I wandered the streets of downtown Los Angeles, from the gigantic bus depot several blocks east of Broadway, to the Biltmore Hotel several blocks west. The entire area remained active until late in the evening. On or near Broadway, a dozen movie theaters showed older films and the tickets were cheap. A few theaters showed first-run movies at higher prices.

Although television was now common, cable TV was still many years away, and there were less than thirteen channels. Few homes had colored sets because they remained expensive. Although some movies were shown on TV, the national channels primarily showed the news, variety shows (*Your Hit Parade*), comedies (*I Love Lucy*), and thirty-minute dramas (*Dragnet*). I certainly did not want to watch TV with the family—Dad chose the shows and ordered me to change channels, as remotes were also years away from being a reality. The cheaper downtown theaters showed older movies, often triple features, and changed movies twice a week. It was hard to beat that.

On the evenings I did not go to the movies, I wandered the streets observing the constant activity. I bought ice cream and watched the crowds. I also enjoyed playing pool. One pool hall was devoted strictly to the game, with dozens of tables and hundreds of pool cues in holders lining the walls. Both the tables and cues were top-of-the-line and well maintained. Patrons over twenty-one could get beer at the desk but no hard liquor. For the patrons aged sixteen to twenty, a variety of brands of soda pop were available.

The tables were rented in thirty-minute blocks. Usually, players joined each other and split the cost of a table. If you were alone, you could opt to just practice by yourself. My rule was not to bet on any games I played, usually 8 or 9 ball. In comparison to most people I was a good player, but compared to the pros and hustlers, I was an amateur, a potential sucker. The hustlers played with me for practice if the pool hall was deserted. Knowing I wouldn't be tempted to bet them, they did not hide their talent, and on many occasions, I got no more than one shot per rack in a game of 8 ball. I ran the table occasionally, but usually I just watched and admired their skills.

I enjoyed playing pool. I learned quickly that the game was much like marbles. As in marbles, good players excelled at making a shot and positioning the cue ball for the next one. I enjoyed practicing and learning how to position my cue ball. For me, winning was not the point; the point was to play good pool, and to do that, practice was required.

I began smoking at the pool hall. I proceeded to enjoy the habit for over sixty years, smoking cigarettes, cigars, and pipes. I do not regret it. Nearly every adult I knew smoked, and there were few anti-smoking groups back then. Smoking was allowed in most places, including movie theaters, restaurants, hotels, airplanes, and college classrooms. The concept of smoking bans did not exist, and the possibility anti-smoking groups would win was not even on the horizon. Cigarettes were still relatively inexpensive.

I occasionally wandered down to the red-light district near the bus station in the early evening. The streets were crowded for blocks, with working men and women going to and from the station, much like Grand Central in New York. There were dozens of bars, cheap diners, and rundown hotels. Pornography shops were interspersed with the legitimate businesses. Prostitutes and beggars accosted people as they passed. Occasionally, I went to one of the dance halls where hostesses danced with customers. Tickets were twenty-five cents a dance; a dollar was the minimum purchase. I wanted to learn to dance waltzes, but even slow dances were difficult for a tone-deaf person who did not feel the beat. I bought tickets, but usually, to the delight of the hostesses, I stopped after two dances and used my remaining tickets simply to sit and talk.

I wanted to learn how to talk to women, and the hostesses were women, not girls. I did not understand girls and often envied the boys who had sisters. At the time, all women were Doris Day and all girls were Debbie Reynolds. I had never dated a girl and wouldn't have known it if a girl was flirting with me.

I was living my life insulated from the trials and tribulations of the other members of my family. They knew nothing of my successes, failures, or insecurities, and I was no longer interested in their lives. Three or four years earlier, when my father was in trouble, the family was more important than my desire to be independent and self-sufficient. My mother, brother, and I sacrificed for the good of the group. After the family moved to California, our group feeling quickly disappeared. "Take care of yourself" was again the rule.

The pull of family, however, always returns. But this time, two family incidents illustrated how much we had all changed—how much I had changed—and how my shield of independence was hardening.

In the spring of 1957, Dad decided to honor a Young family commitment. Now that he was working again and had recovered from his time in prison, he invited his mother, Grandma Bell—now in her seventies and obese, and still in a wheelchair—to come to California to live with us. Her other three sons were having family and money problems. The scandal of Uncle Hoot's affair with Uncle Curly's wife Louise, the mother of my cousins Billy Ross and Herbert, had torn the extended family apart. Aunt Kate divorced Hoot and Curly divorced Louise. With seven kids, Uncle Bill had no room for Grandma Bell.

The thought of Grandma Bell coming to live with us did not thrill me. She supported and loved me when I was a boy, but as a teenager nearing adulthood, the idea of spending many hours with her did not fit into my plans. When she arrived, I knew the burden of taking care of her would fall on my mother and me. Dad expected applause for his actions, but neither he nor my brother would be her caretakers. I doubt my mother was thrilled with the arrangement, but she always supported my father. The situation was never discussed.

Corky volunteered to drive to Oklahoma to pick up Grandma Bell. He wanted to return to Lawton and hang out with his buddies from high school. He took my dog Butch with him. Confined mostly to the house, Butch was unhappy in Los Angeles. Several family members in Lawton remembered him as the dream dog and offered to take him in. I was sad but also relieved.

Corky drove from L.A. to Lawton in less than twenty-four hours, an impressive feat. I-40 was yet to be completed and Route 66 was still the main road. It was a hard drive, and he needed several days to recuperate and carouse with his old friends before picking up Grandma Bell. He intended to drive the 1,300 miles back to Los Angeles with no overnight stop, like how he had come.

Corky drove twelve hours before pulling off for a needed sleep break. When he woke at sunrise, he started the car. Grandma Bell was awake in the front seat. As he pulled onto the two-lane highway and picked up speed, his right front tire hit a patch of gravel, and the car spun off the road into a farmer's field. In 1957, cars did not have seatbelts.

Corky slammed on the brakes and brought the car to a controlled stop, breathing a sigh of relief. Then he heard Grandma Bell moaning. She had slid off the front seat onto the floorboard. He stopped the car, leaped out of the driver's seat, ran around the side, and opened the passenger-side door. He attempted to lift her back on the seat, but she weighed almost three hundred pounds and he struggled.

He drove to the nearest small town, about thirty miles away. Cell phones did not exist back in 1957, obviously, and nearby gas stations on Route 66 had no payphones. She was alive when an emergency crew rolled her into the hospital. She died a couple of hours later.

The house was full of family and friends when I arrived home around seven o'clock that evening. I heard the story and looked for my brother. He was in the bathroom taking a hot bath as he attempted to recover. He waved me in and told me to close the door. On the verge of tears, he recounted what happened. It pained me to see his hurt, and I came close to crying for him. Even when my brother told me Grandma Bell talked constantly about how much she wanted to see me, my pain remained for my brother, not her.

The death of our grandmother is one of my brother's most painful memories, and when he told the story to me, it made me sad to think about how little thought I had given my grandmother who loved me. I don't feel guilty about it now, but it reminds me that at the time I was a teenager focused on my own life, with less time to worry about other problems within the family.

Another family incident that summer also highlighted my changing character, but in an entirely different way.

That summer Papa Joe came to visit. Papa Joe, just to remind you, was mother's "half-breed" father who deserted his children after his wife died when Bunk was born. The Bass children acknowledged him as "Papa" but usually avoided him. In his old age, none of his children allowed him to live with them for more than a month.

In 1957 Papa Joe was a vague memory for me, a person I saw occasionally at family picnics in Oklahoma. He was a small, thin man with stooped shoulders. The family knew him as a man with a violent temper who came ready to fight and carried a small pistol and a knife hidden in his boots.

My main memory of him is from when I was around twelve years old. I was alone in downtown Lawton on a summer afternoon and on my way to see a cowboy-themed triple feature at the Ritz Theater in the red-light district.

"Hey, boy!" someone shouted as I passed a bar. As I turned, I heard the clacking of pool balls. A thin, stooped-shouldered older man dressed in jeans and cowboy boots (though no hat) stood near the bar's entrance. He was smoking a Bull Durham cigarette.

"You're one of Toad's kids?"

I recognized him, nodded, and said, "Yessir."

Papa Joe stared at me for a few seconds and tossed his cigarette away. He reached into his jeans, pulled out a coin, and flipped it to me. A silver dollar.

Surprised, I stared at him but did not respond.

"Have some fun," he said, then turned around and entered the bar.

And now, in the summer of 1957, Papa Joe was in our house on Ford street in East Los Angeles. My mom was frosty-cold toward him. "Keep your hands on your wallet around the old bastard," she warned me.

Bunk had delivered Papa Joe to us, and years later, he told me the story of their trip. Earlier in the summer Bunk and his wife were in Lawton visiting the family. While they were there, Aunt Hazel persuaded him to take Papa Joe to Los Angeles to live with Toad for a few weeks. According to Bunk, Papa Joe was a demanding pain in the ass on the trip. He was a grouchy alcoholic and wanted some wine. Bunk refused to give it to him. "Wasn't gonna drive a thousand miles with a wild, drunk Indian in the car," he said.

As Bunk passed the many small towns on Route 66, Papa Joe would shout at him to stop and buy some wine. After hours of listening to Papa Joe's whining, Bunk stopped at an all-night grocery store and got a bottle of wine. Waiting out front, Papa Joe jumped out of the car and grabbed the bag. He looked at the wine bottle and shouted, "Goddamn white wine!" He turned and threw the bottle against the store's wall. "I drink red wine," he yelled.

Though normally easygoing, Bunk could turn on the Bass temper when things got hot. "Get your ass in the car," he said to the old man. "Do it now or die here."

Bunk got in the car and started backing up. Papa Joe stumbled to the passenger side and got in. Neither said another word until they reached Toad's house.

Having Papa Joe in the house for a month was not a pleasant experience. Mom fed him but did not talk to him nor did she get him a bottle of red wine. Like everyone else in the family, I ignored him.

In retrospect, it must have been an awful time for Papa Joe. He had no money, and damn it, he wanted a bottle of wine and some cigarettes. He searched the house, but Mother had forewarned us to hide our valuables. I had hidden stashes around the house. Remember Halloween?

Unfortunately for me, Papa Joe found one of them. When I was around six years old, I began saving American Indian Head pennies. Over the years, I taped a couple hundred in an Indian Chief school notebook. In my years in California, I simply forgot about its existence. The value in 1957 was perhaps ten cents per penny, about twenty dollars for the entire notebook. Papa Joe found the pennies and disappeared. Mom learned later that he had returned to Lawton.

Then and now, the incident left me with two feelings. I was annoyed at Papa Joe, but I also felt a twinge of guilt because of his sad state. When we briefly lived in Bakersfield, I felt miserable because I had no money. By the summer of 1957, I had money in my pocket—and felt a lot better about my life. I should have slipped the old man ten bucks, repayment for his silver dollar. Papa Joe died the next year in Lawton. Shortly thereafter, Red, his eldest son, died too.

Chapter 11

Senior Year at Garfield High

My senior year at Garfield High was the best of times. Free of family obligations, I had a job, a nice nest egg in the bank, and was doing well in school. My plan to go to college appeared to be right on schedule. I believed I had the ability and the perseverance to achieve my goals.

I understood the working man's world better than most adults. I knew life was not a bed of roses, and when trouble arrived, it was every man for himself. To become independent, I needed to take care of myself. And to do that, it was necessary to earn money. The money I earned would not be spent on frivolous, material things—at least until I had established a nest egg to provide security in hard times.

Alas, for my all worldly knowledge, I did not know everything. I knew absolutely nothing about the opposite sex.

And I forgot that my father definitely needed watching.

In early November 1957, I asked my father for money. Not his money but my money. Over the previous eighteen months, you may remember, I gave him $100 to $150 a month to put in the bank. He knew I was saving the money for college and had convinced me it was safer in the bank than hiding it around the house. We lived in an area where home break-ins were common.

I wanted a portable typewriter for school. My penmanship had become harder to read over the years. Also, college professors required typed reports, and I wanted to practice typing my papers while a senior in high school. Besides, I turned eighteen on November 6, and wanted to give myself a typewriter as my present. (I doubt my father remembered the day I was born. By family tradition, we did not celebrate holidays or birthdays.) I had an emergency hoard of cash, but I did not want to tap into it. So, I asked my father for my money.

"How much?" he asked.

"$80."

In those days $80 was a lot of money, but a typewriter was as essential for college students as computers are today.

"What kind of typewriter?" Dad asked.

I didn't know anything about typewriters. I just wanted a portable model. "Remington" popped into my head.

"Okay," he said. "I'll look into it."

And he did. A week later I came home and discovered a new Remington portable in a carry case. I wore out dozens of ribbons on this typewriter over the next twenty years.

Dad did great. Dad was good.

Five months later, in April 1958, I told him I wanted to buy a new suit for my upcoming high school graduation.

"How much?" he asked in an annoyed mutter.

"$80," I said. That was a lot of money for a suit, but I estimated I had almost $2,400 in the bank and could afford to splurge. My work clothes were jackets with dress pants, and I did not own a suit.

My father laughed. "Why the hell do you need an $80 suit for graduation. No one will see the suit under your graduation gown."

I knew that. I never told my father the real reason I wanted a new suit, and he did not ask. Instead, he said, "No way. Ain't spending $80 for a damn suit."

"It's my money," I said.

"What do you mean 'your' money?"

"I gave you at least a $100 a month for two years to bank for me."

"What the hell are you talking about," he snapped. "That money paid for your room and board. It's your share of the rent. It's not free, you know."

With that he walked out of the room.

I felt like crying. He had scammed me again. Arguing with my father simply was not possible, and his argument held a certain amount of truth. Except I was damn sure he wasn't charging my brother $100 a month, and besides, I never ate at home and could have rented my own place for $50 a month.

In the back of my mind I had planned for the possibility he would scam me, so my secret stash was fairly large—about $1,000. Movies, cigarettes, and pool halls were my only vices.

Before I bought the suit from my stash, my mother intervened, one of the few times in my life she did so. She persuaded Dad to give me the $80, but I knew I would never recover another cent. I had had it, though. From now on he could pick up his own damn clothes at the cleaners. Unfortunately, this wasn't the end of the scamming. For the rest of his life he figured out ways to chisel a few dollars from me. He couldn't help himself.

What I didn't tell him was that I wanted the suit for a Judges Association luncheon, where I was to receive a small scholarship of $75 to cover my first year's tuition at East Los Angeles Community College. On the morning of the luncheon, a judge picked me up at school and took me to his courtroom. I sat near him on the bench wearing my new suit during the morning hearings. Then we went to a Judicial Club for lunch where I gave a brief speech.

I received a comparable award of $75 at an American Legion dinner—not much, perhaps, but multiply it by six or seven to get the inflation-adjusted amount in today's money and it sounds better.

~

In mid-May 1958, a few weeks before graduation, a crisis at school developed that eventually threatened to destroy my dream of attending college. The senior class at Garfield numbered around three hundred students. But from the administration's perspective, only the thirty-five students in the star class were important. As you might expect, the star class contained every senior class officer, from the school newspaper editor to the senior class president. Although a member of the star class,

I remained an outsider. I did not socialize outside class, attend dances, or picnics. I was an honorary member of the group.

The trouble began with the preparations for the graduation ceremonies, which were to be decided in Dr. Flynn's English class. After April 1, his class hours were extended to two hours to allow for planning. Flynn was the most honored and respected teacher at Garfield. Around fifty-five years old, he dressed and acted like a college professor. The administration loved him, and he chaired several school committees. The star class considered him a mentor. I liked him because he was a good teacher and an excellent discussion leader.

One day after lunch, Dr. Flynn divided the class into committees. I was excused; I was on the work-study program and left school before lunch every day. Fine with me. Truth be told, I would not have enjoyed being on any graduation committee or part of the preparations for any event. I felt no kinship with the members of the senior class and certainly wasn't interested in the class yearbook.

In early May, I heard Dr. Flynn praise the achievements of the student committees in one of his morning classes. Not all was well, however. A major problem had developed with the speaker's committee. Three of the four students selected to deliver speeches on graduation day had turned in drafts to the School Committee to be edited. This was an administration committee which included the principal, vice principal, chairs of every department, and Dr. Flynn. Speakers were expected to praise the school for providing them with a great education. That morning, Dr. Flynn informed the class that the fourth speaker, although reminded numerous times, had missed several deadlines and had failed to submit a draft of her speech.

Charlene Evans was the fourth speaker.

Over the previous two years Charlene had been in many of my classes, where she acted intellectually superior. She loved quoting poetry, citing some obscure author, or displaying her linguistic abilities. She was fluent in aristocratic Spanish, which was unusual even at Garfield. She spoke French and was studying Russian and Japanese. She was editor of the school newspaper.

A few days earlier she had been the star of the senior assembly, an event the entertainment committee scheduled to celebrate our graduation. The entire senior class marched into the auditorium as the school band, onstage, performed as if we were at a football game.

With a blast of trumpets, Charlene parted the curtains and marched to the podium. She was a tall, Swedish-looking girl who, if I belonged to the Freudian school of psychology, would say looked much as my mother must have looked at eighteen. The audience erupted in approval. Catcalls and whistles erupted throughout the auditorium. She was dressed in the shortest white shorts I had ever seen. She was the last person I would have expected to come on stage in short-shorts.

She stood at the podium, calm and confident until the crowd quieted down. Then she shouted into the microphone: "Who likes short- shorts?" The audience roared, "We like short-shorts"!" I stood in amazement. I assumed she was alluding to a current hit song.

She repeated the phrase. The crowd shouted back, stomping their feet and clapping their hands.

The band joined in as the curtains opened, and a dozen girls danced onstage shouting out "Who likes short-shorts"?"

And that was how Charlene caught my attention for the first time.

In retrospect her failure to submit a draft wasn't a huge surprise. She was notorious for being late with her papers. The school newspaper seldom came out on time, and her classroom assignments were often ignored for weeks. She believed she was smarter than anyone else, and thus, should be allowed all the time she needed. Every paper had to be perfect. Her lateness irritated Dr. Flynn, who was one of the advisers on the newspaper committee.

After mentioning the problems he was having with Charlene, Dr. Flynn made a suggestion that shocked me and the rest of the class: He recommended Charlene's removal as speaker and suggested she be replaced by Ken.

I was the only Ken in the class.

Flynn explained his reasoning: I had the next-highest GPA in the graduating senior class, ranking fourth. He also pointed out that during the entire school year, I had turned all my papers in on time.

I was not asked, but appointed, and I did not want the job. I looked at Charlene. Showing no emotion, she stared at Dr. Flynn.

I had not realized my GPA was the fourth highest in the senior class. I knew it was good enough to get me my first choice of classes at East Los Angeles Community College, but that was it. No matter what my GPA was, my failure to be involved in extracurricular activities assured I would never be rewarded a scholarship, and I never applied for one, much less for enrollment in one of the big-name universities. That was okay, though; I knew I could work my way through the public system, and California State University in Los Angeles was excellent. All I wanted from Garfield was a diploma. I certainly did not want to spend hours of my time writing and preparing to be a speaker.

While this was still being resolved, the speaker's committee chairman pointed out a problem: The graduation program was at the printer, and Charlene was listed as a speaker. It was too late to change the program.

Obviously, Dr. Flynn knew this, and suddenly I knew what was coming. He suggested Charlene's removal simply to force her to accept a compromise.

I was the compromise.

Flynn suggested I assist Charlene in finishing her speech within a week. He looked at Charlene, who nodded, said nothing, and refused to look at me.

He turned to me. "Do you accept this assignment?" he asked, as if this were an episode of *Mission: Impossible*.

Sometimes you have no choice. Truthfully, I had no interest in helping Charlene write some platitudes about the greatness of Garfield High. But the obvious answer was "yessir."

Charlene and I were excused from attending Flynn's morning class, and we met in a small room in the library. I did not write her speech. We discussed and changed a few paragraphs each day, and then I took it home and typed it into a new draft. The next day, we went over the draft, made more changes, and after work, I typed up another draft.

Naturally, her being an attractive girl and me being a teenage boy, our meeting had a flirtatious atmosphere. During our morning meetings we often got sidetracked discussing books and other activities we enjoyed. She was smart as well as attractive. I learned she was an only child in a working-class family. She came to school wearing blue jeans or practical dresses, and I felt comfortable in her presence.

On Friday of that week, I handed Charlene the draft with additional changes and said, "That's it." I intended to deliver the paper to Dr. Flynn that day.

She grabbed the paper, reading it carefully before making more changes. She was a perfectionist to the end, and the revisions meant I needed to retype the speech yet again. Before I left school that day, Charlene and I informed Dr. Flynn I would deliver a typed copy of the speech Monday morning, giving me two days to retype the final draft.

"Great," he said. Then he thought for a second and looked at Charlene. "What are you doing on Sunday?" he asked, barely glancing at me. "How about bringing the paper to my house Sunday after church? Say around one o'clock. I will read the speech before our committee meeting Monday."

Charlene nodded.

I wasn't asked but nodded anyway. Saturday night after work, I typed up the draft. I am not a great typist; it took me several hours.

I met Charlene in front of the school at 12:30 p.m. Dr. Flynn's house was only a few blocks away. I refused to show her the draft, which I carried in a manila folder. To paraphrase T. S. Eliot, "A million times she changed her mind, and now there was no more time for revisions." Thank God.

Dr. Flynn ushered us into his impressive office lined with books, took the manila folder, offered us seats, and sat behind his desk to read the draft.

When he finished, he held the paper up and read it aloud, stopping several times to praise the speech. He placed it on his desk and said, "Good speech. I am sure the School Committee will accept it with a few minor changes."

As we left his house, Dr. Flynn stood on his porch and said, "You two make a good team."

A couple weeks later I received my final grade. Flynn gave me a B-plus. Guess who got the A.

Graduation came. The auditorium was packed with families, friends, and local dignitaries. My family was not there. They were working, and I had not bothered to tell them the date. The ceremonies began in typical fashion with a local politician acting as the keynote speaker uttering long, boring platitudes repeated at thousands of graduations before and after.

Student speeches followed with their own unending platitudes. Speakers included (in order): the class president, the vice president, the valedictorian, and finally Charlene.

Then the principal announced the various awarded scholarships. The class president received a scholarship to University of Southern California; the valedictorian got one to a less-impressive university; and Charlene received a $75 scholarship to East Los Angeles Community College. My American Legion and Judges Association scholarships, as well as a number of other student awards, were not noted in the printed program. Meanwhile, the graduating class sat in the front rows in ridiculous gowns and funny hats. The room was hot and crowded. Several hundred people were in the auditorium, and I was boiling in my new suit underneath the gown. The ordeal seemed like it would never end. I felt like a stage prop sitting in the audience with the other seniors waiting for the end of the ceremonies.

After the student speakers were awarded their diplomas, the rest of the graduating students marched across the stage to accept theirs.

When I walked off the school grounds through the crowd of families and well-wishers, I vowed to never again put myself through such a façade.

Chapter 12

The Girl in the Red Dress

In May 1958, just before my graduation, there was a crisis at Roy Logan's. The manager quit. Although he was the best of the four managers I had during my tenure, he had a problem: After his transfer from Dallas to Los Angeles with his family, he realized the cost of living in L.A. was more than he could afford. He asked for a raise. The front office was upset by his request and said no. So, he quit. The assistant manager also quit. More honorable than the company, both agreed to stay on at Logan's for two weeks until another manager could be transferred to Los Angeles.

When the new manager arrived from Oklahoma, he realized he desperately needed help. After talking with the previous manager, he offered me the job as assistant manager. I knew the ins and outs at Logan's after working part-time at the store for two years. The pay was $72.80 for a forty-eight-hour week. Back in the day, that was good pay for an eighteen-year-old boy. I accepted the job for the summer. My plan was to return to part-time in the fall and enroll in courses at East L.A. Community College.

As they say, though, the best-laid plans of mice and men often go astray. Mine went astray because of a girl in a tight red dress.

A couple of weeks after graduation, Charlene reappeared. She stood in the front entrance of Roy Logan's in a red dress about an hour before closing time. For the previous two years when I had seen her at school, she was dressed in casual clothes with no regard for style. (Later I learned most of her clothes came from consignment stores or Goodwill.) That afternoon, though, she was dressed for a dinner party. She had long blonde hair down to her waist.

I hurried over to greet her. It was a slow afternoon and no customers were in the store. She appeared insecure as we said our hellos. Then, she surprised me. She said she had two tickets for a play at the L.A. Auditorium. She hoped I would come with her to the show.

And the dance began.

During our time writing her speech, I enjoyed her company because she had several attributes I respected. She was pretty, sure, but that wasn't her most attractive trait. She was extremely intelligent, and on many subjects, vastly more knowledgeable than me. She did not "waste" her time reading modern fiction by authors such as Hemingway, Steinbeck, or Faulkner. In her opinion Zane Grey books were trash. She concentrated on the classics such as Shakespeare and Chaucer, Montesquieu and Voltaire, Tolstoy and Pushkin. She could recite an impressive number of poets from memory. She preferred French, Swedish, and Japanese films over Hollywood blockbusters.

For a small-town Oklahoma boy yearning to be cultured and educated, her intellectual interests were a strong pull.

I did not know many things about her, and my understanding of girls at the time was limited; I was a virgin in every sense. This wasn't the case with her. As I learned later, this was not her first rodeo.

The summer of 1958 with Charlene is among my happiest memories. I saw her several days a week for the next three months. To my surprise, despite her involvements at school, she had no girlfriends.

When I would walk her home at night, we did not kiss, hug, or hold hands. In retrospect, it was my fault. I am not an aggressive male. I needed encouragement; the few times I touched her, she quickly pulled away. I assumed she was a good girl who was not ready for a sexual relationship.

On Saturdays, Charlene came downtown to meet me after work. Some evenings we went to the Los Angeles Public Library, one of the best public libraries in the country. We wandered the stacks and usually checked out six books each. Charlene recommended many books. On my bus rides to and from work I read Shakespeare, Tolstoy, Mann, Joyce, Gide, Beckett, and Albee. She smirked if I talked about recent novels, biographies, or history books.

On Sundays we went to museums and lectures at USC and UCLA on topics she was deeply interested in such as poetry, Shakespeare, and Chaucer. She disliked anything having to do with history, except literature and the arts, and was completely uninterested in politics.

We went to many Japanese movies. Her big dream in life was to become a sensei in the Nichiren Buddhist sect, and she loved all things Japanese. She took private Japanese lessons and attended the Buddhist temple in L.A. for several years; I accompanied her on numerous occasions. She was particularly fond of Akira Kurosawa's movies. Many of his films were rewritten and reproduced for American audiences. *The Magnificent Seven* was based on Kurosawa's *Seven Ronin*, and several of his samurai movies became the basis for Clint Eastwood's Western movies. *Roshomon* is another prime example of a movie whose theme has been frequently copied—three different characters tell a story about the same incident. Each character is a hero from his point of view while the other two are villains.

Other times we rode racing bikes to theaters showing foreign films in Alhambra and Pasadena. At the time a Swedish director, Ingmar Bergman (*The Seventh Seal*, etc.), was all the rage among the intellectual community.

Mother had a small Nash I borrowed occasionally, but mostly we rode public buses or our bicycles. The bikes had no gears, but we rode them from Montebello to Alhambra to Pasadena.

We also went to operas, ballets, and plays. In the Los Angeles area, many small theaters seated less than a hundred people. Aspiring actors were widely available. On several occasions, B-movie actors played the lead role. To my surprise, tickets to these circle theaters were less expensive than tickets at first-run movie theaters.

Through it all, Charlene was frugal with money. We ate at inexpensive local restaurants or cafeterias.

I was hooked. Charlene exposed me to many adventures, and I enjoyed her company. Our relationship seemed platonic, primarily because she displayed little sexual interest. We did not hold hands, nor did we ever kiss goodnight. (I later learned she did not enjoy being touched and thought kissing was dangerous. For her, exchanging saliva was a definite health hazard.)

The first indication she was interested in something more occurred in early August, on her eighteenth birthday. For some reason, I thought she was older. She never mentioned she was a year younger than most students in our high school graduating class.

Her birthday was on a Friday, a day we seldom saw each other because it was a thirteen-hour day for me. I worked at Logan's from 8:30 a.m. to 9:30 p.m., and the Saturday that followed was the busiest day of the week. But it was her birthday, and though I was tired, I was determined to give her a small present. After a forty-minute public bus ride and a fifteen-minute walk, I arrived at her house.

Her house was smaller but not much different than the one I lived in, about a mile away. Around eleven o'clock, I knocked on her door for the first time in our three-month relationship. Her mother answered. She was a skinny woman who looked nothing like Charlene. Motioning me to enter, she seemed meek and nervous.

What I saw should have been a warning bell. The room was crammed full of cardboard boxes stacked from floor to ceiling, with a narrow path leading to the kitchen. Charlene's parents were hoarders. Except for the kitchen and bathroom, every room in the house bulged with boxes full of newspapers, magazines, books, clothing, and trinkets. A one-car garage was also crammed full of junk. According to her parents, all these things were valuable and could not be thrown away.

Charlene's mother escorted me to the kitchen. "Charlene's resting. I'll get her."

I had always picked Charlene up outside the house. Letting me inside meant she trusted me to keep the family secret. Her mother, Inez, treated me pleasantly. When she returned, she offered me a cup of tea, but I declined. Charlene's father, Charles Evans, was not home.

Over the next three years I came to know him, I always called him Evans. He was a gifted man, but many might have called him strange.

Charlene hurried into the kitchen, grabbed my arm, and pulled me out the back door. I handed her the gift, and she placed it, unopened, on the back steps. She walked down the driveway and I followed. Without saying anything, we walked two blocks to Garfield High, deserted at that time of night. An outside stairway led to a second-floor walkway between two school buildings. I assumed she had been there many times since she lived a couple of blocks away.

We stood on the passageway admiring the night. Silence all around, apart from the distant sound of traffic on a nearby street. A big moon and clear sky full of stars hovered over us. Charlene walked over to a waist-high concrete wall, turned, and leaned back. Then she motioned for me to come closer.

What she did next shocked me.

She lifted her dress and was naked from the waist down.

I stared, speechless. She pulled me forward, unzipped my pants, and pulled out my penis.

Needless to say, it was limp. Even then, I needed some encouragement before sex became foremost in my mind. I always assumed kissing and hugging came before the actual event of penetration.

She pulled me forward as my penis touched her. I realized she was wet and ready to go. Apparently, sex in semi-public places aroused her. She must have imagined this scene all day. She was ready to perform and expected me to become an aggressive male, a tiger who could not be restrained.

Unfortunately, I was the exact opposite. During the day I seldom thought about sex, but many nights I had erotic wet dreams. In my dreams, the sex always involved kissing, hugging, and loving. I needed fifteen-minute warm-ups, and even then, a macho, aggressive male did not appear in my visions. I'm after a little loving, not a battle of the sexes to see who is more dominant or can scream louder in wild passion.

I pulled away, apologizing and feeling embarrassed. My excuse to myself was I had just finished a thirteen-hour workday and was tired. My excuse to Charlene was that I did not have a rubber. The last thing

I wanted was to get her pregnant. When a good girl got pregnant, the boy had to marry her. I wanted to go to college. Being married with children certainly was not part of my current life's plan, which was to get a college education, find a good, secure job, and then think about marrying and becoming a father.

She dropped her dress and acted as if nothing had happened. We talked about college for a few minutes. I walked her home and agreed to pick her up the next night as I had done for weeks. We never mentioned that night. Much later, I learned she had already had several sexual relationships. Although I could tell Charlene liked me, we seemed sexually incompatible; I felt more like a brother than a lover. But she had plans for me.

Our second sexual attempt was only two weeks later. In mid-August my father, mother, and brother planned a trip to visit Lawton. They missed the family and their friends. Organized to be a ten-day trip, they planned, as usual, to drive straight through to Lawton in twenty-four hours and return on the same schedule. My brother and father talked about the possibility of breaking their old record times with two drivers now at the wheel. Of course, mother was too conservative to be a race car driver.

When the trip was suggested, my answer was an emphatic no. I had no friends or family in Lawton I wanted to see badly enough to spend forty-eight hours in the car with Dad.

Besides, Charlene and I considered the absence of my family to be an ideal time for us to consummate our relationship. The idea of having sex in my parent's bedroom excited her.

Charlene and I made plans. I waited nervously and with anticipation for my parents to leave the following Sunday.

We spent Sunday afternoon at a local park that had a large pond. We fed the ducks but avoided talking about sex. With night near, we went to the apartment. Charlene went to the bathroom and removed her skirt and panties. She kept on her top, explaining she would be too cold without it. She lay on the bed staring at the ceiling as I removed my clothes.

When I started to put on a condom, she stopped me. She said she had obtained a birth control cream and applied it in the bathroom. "Totally safe," she said.

When I tried to kiss her, she put a hand over her mouth. "I don't feel comfortable kissing," she said. "Germs."

I told you I wasn't knowledgeable about women or sex. My penis was hard with anticipation, and my mind certainly did not scream at me to stop. Charlene spread her legs and I did the nasty deed. After ejaculation, Charlene held me tightly with her legs. "Just a few minutes," she whispered. "I love feeling you inside me."

When I withdrew, I felt moisture between my legs. Charlene turned on a table light.

I was horrified. The sheet was covered in blood. Charlene saw the blood, leaped out of bed, and shoved me aside. She pulled the sheets off the bed, ran into the bathroom, threw the sheets in the bathtub, and turned on the cold water.

Still recovering from the shock in the bedroom, I looked down and realized I was dripping blood on the floor. I hurried to the kitchen and found a couple of dish towels.

I had assumed it was Charlene's blood. It was normal when you had sex with a virgin, right?

But no, my love, it was *my* blood. I was the one who bled when I lost my virginity. A sinew attaches the underside of the foreskin to the penis. My sinew had snapped, and I was bleeding. I leaned over the sink and pressed a towel on my penis. The flow of blood slowed but did not stop.

Charlene came out of the bathroom for a few minutes later, saw the bleeding was slowing, and returned to the bathroom to wash the sheets. She did not smile, hug me in sympathy, or say a word. I wrapped the "poor boy" in cotton gauzes for a few days. It remained sensitive for the next couple of weeks.

Today, when I think back on the incident, I crack a big smile. You must admit it's funny. I was embarrassed, but even then, I realized some things are beyond my control. I bought new sheets the next day.

Charlene and I returned to our normal routine for the next few weeks. She never mentioned the bloody night. She remained aloof and disliked touching, even holding hands.

In early September Charlene enrolled in five courses at East L.A. I enrolled in a night course, intending to earn enough money to enroll full-time in the spring. We saw less of each other.

In late September, she came to Logan's one Saturday night and we went to a cafeteria for dinner. Smiling happily, she informed me she was pregnant.

Chapter 13

Married Life Is No Bed of Roses

I was in disbelief. We had sex one time and she used birth control cream. How could she be pregnant?

In retrospect, I assume Charlene never used the birth control cream—she got pregnant intentionally. She was smart and must have known her cycle. She wanted a place of her own near her parents. She needed a man with a job, and I was that man. She could have a baby, go to college, and not have to work, all on my dime. Indeed, soon after we got married, I realized getting a job was not in her plans. She briefly had a job decorating cakes at a local bakery but quit after a few weeks.

At the time, I saw no way out. Like I said, if you got a "good" girl pregnant, you were obligated to marry her. Good boys were honorable boys. Abortion was never mentioned or considered back in the day, at least in my world. I saw my dreams disappearing, but when I found myself in such situations, I usually accepted the consequences of my actions.

My conditions were that the wedding be simple. I had a great dislike for pomp and ceremony, and I had promised myself that I would avoid them when possible. Charlene arranged the wedding at her Buddhist temple. She later admitted it was a little awkward because the young sensei who married us had been one of her former lovers who escaped my fate. Her parents attended the wedding. I did not know the names of the other witnesses. I did not invite my family. They knew I got married but were not interested in attending a wedding conducted in a Buddhist church. I did not take any time off from work.

Thus I entered the unbelievable world of Charlene Evans. We moved into a small one-bedroom detached house about a half mile from her parents, and in the opposite direction, a half mile from my parents.

Since I was working forty-eight to sixty hours a week, Charlene found the apartment and purchased a sparse set of furniture at yard sales, except for a new mattress (for obvious reasons—some things you don't want secondhand). She did not want a bedframe but wanted to sleep on the floor, Japanese-style.

Okay, I said. I had slept on the floor on quilts many times in my life; a soft mattress should be no problem. The kicker was that she wanted to follow the Japanese custom of removing your shoes before entering a house. Shoes were filthy and carried nasty germs. Again, it sounded logical, but removing your shoes seemed like a lot of trouble to me.

On our wedding night we had sex, but it would be a rare event over the next two years. There's a popular joke that goes like this: Newlyweds should place a penny in a jar for every time they have sex in the first year of marriage. Beginning with the second year, they should remove a penny from the jar each time they have sex. The joke was that it would take forty years to remove the pennies. Well, in the first few months I would have placed six pennies in the jar. Over the next year, four pennies still remained. In the last three months of her pregnancy she decided to refrain from sexual relations completely, arguing that it might harm the baby. I realized we were sexually incompatible, but it was a topic that Charlene refused to discuss. I checked out library books in an attempt to figure out the problem. Advice from the "experts" was often ridiculous.

She attended college full-time, and I was enrolled in an evening course, so we seldom saw each other except on Sundays. Since I left the house for work while she was in bed, I often didn't see her until I picked her up from her mother's in the evening. She never cooked, changed the sheets, swept the floors, or cleaned the bathroom. I noticed but said nothing, simply doing the chores myself. In many ways she was like my father and brother.

She left most of her clothes at her mother's house where she went every day. She used only small towels in our bathroom, and I never saw her take a bath or shower.

I did my own laundry every Sunday. Charlene brought home food from her parents' house that could be consumed without cooking, such as yogurt, fruit, bread, and cereal. I noticed but it was not important. We often went out for supper at diners, and I ate most of my other meals at work. Sunday mornings we went out for breakfast.

During Charlene's pregnancy I convinced myself I was in love and the situation was not as bad as it seemed. One thing we had in common was frugality. She had little interest in material things. On Saturday nights I often borrowed one of my parent's cars, and Charlene was great at finding inexpensive restaurants that served good food. Although she was willing to pay for cultural events, she preferred free lectures, college plays, and no-charge museums. We never argued about money; in fact, we actually saved money.

I continued to admire her interest in cultural areas I had previously ignored. Once a week we went to the library and checked out novels and philosophy books by Russian, Japanese, and French authors who expanded my interests and influenced my beliefs for the rest of my life. Her involvement in Buddhism stimulated my interest in Asian philosophy, and her interest in poetry and Shakespeare encouraged me to read many British poets as well as many of Shakespeare's plays.

Charlene often irritated me as she constantly tried to show off her intellectual superiority. As a basic fact of life, most people, particularly the intelligentsia, enjoy talking about and dominating conversations around subjects they know. Charlene insisted we read poems aloud, and constantly cited her favorite literary authors. She showed no interest in my preferred fields of history, politics, and diplomacy. Her eyes rolled if I talked about Alexander Hamilton, Andrew Jackson, or Teddy Roosevelt. She talked about Japanese culture but refused to discuss Japanese cruelty during World War II in the Pacific. She particularly irritated me when she said, "Today we will speak only Spanish" or "Today we will speak only French." Her dream was to be a professor of linguistics, perhaps my worst subject.

Charlene was also convinced she was smarter than everyone she met and her great intellect gave her the right to demand special treatment. She thought of herself as a tsarina, a Catherine the Great, who should have been born with power and money, surrounded by intellectuals who admired her greatness, and with servants to satisfy her every whim. I eventually learned she was much like her father in this regard.

In the first few months, we ate at Charlene's parents' house once a week. I always came in the back door straight into a small kitchen with a tiny attached bathroom. I was discouraged from entering the living room and the only bedroom. I knew the living room was packed floor-to-ceiling with boxes and stacks of newspapers. Some of the boxes held her father's clothes. I learned later he was not allowed to enter the bedroom, where Charlene and her mother slept. I assumed it was jammed full of her mother's and Charlene's clothes. Charlene had not transferred many of her clothes to our house—mostly a few long nightshirts, since she went to her mother's every day. Sometimes she wore the same clothes for a few days. Her mother did the laundry and also most of the grocery shopping.

I had met her father briefly at the wedding, but for some reason when I came for dinner he was never home. Her mother, Inez, looked nothing like Charlene. She was skinny, always wore "granny" dresses and, even in the summer, usually two or three blouses and sometimes a sweater. I learned quickly that the Evans' family was always cold. Inez was pleasant but seldom said anything to me. When not at school, Charlene spent most of her time at her mother's house, coming home to sleep. I never thought of it as her parents' house because her father was never home.

It was fairly obvious that her mother did all the chores around the house. Charlene was expected to remain in her chair while her mother served us dinner, usually pot roast, and then cleaned up. Her mother believed her daughter was a princess.

We went to my parents' place for dinner less frequently because Charlene disliked my father. They were amazingly impolite to each other. When we arrived, she pulled a chair in front of the television and became absorbed in a program. We did not have a TV because we agreed that it was a waste of time. Yet, at my parents' house, she was a fanatic and often hissed at us to be quiet. She never offered to help my mother cook, set the table, or wash the dishes. While I helped my Mom, Dad and Charlene watched TV, seldom saying a word to each other.

On one of our visits, Charlene pointed out something I had seldom noticed. My parents moved often over the years because my father always got into verbal arguments with the neighbors. In every apartment or house there was one constant: a portrait of my brother hanging in the living room. When Corky graduated from high school in 1956, my father was so proud he took him to a professional photographer. The color photograph was enlarged to two-and-a-half by three-and-half feet, framed, and forever after hung over the living room couch in every place they lived for the rest of their lives. It was a flattering but accurate portrait of my brother at eighteen. I seldom noticed it.

The first time Charlene saw the photograph hanging on the wall, she asked, sarcastically, "Where's Ken's?" She liked my brother, who now insisted everyone call him Charles, but felt my parents were insulting me. There were no photographs of me in the house, but that was as much my own fault as my parents'. I did not allow people to take my picture. Why? It is difficult to explain, but I didn't know anyone who might be interested in me, plus, deep down, I did not want to look at a photograph of myself as a handsome, young man when I was eighty years old.

My brother was one of the few people that my father loved, but he was about to love someone else even more.

In April 1959 my daughter Catherine was born. My parents were thrilled. She was named after my mother, whose middle name was Catherine, and as she grew, looked a lot like her grandmother. By the time she was two months old, my parents were babysitting every Saturday night through Sunday afternoon. Our house became crowded with presents from my parents including baby clothes, a highchair, a crib, and a baby carriage. They grew to love the baby and showed that love for the rest of their lives. Cathy had the good grace to love them in return. My mother claimed the baby's first words, "Ga-Ga," referred to her, and thereafter everyone in the family called mom Ga-Ga. Cathy also gave the same love to my father. Over the years she has disliked when I criticize him, and I love her for her loyalty to family.

Charlene's parents were also instrumental in Cathy's life. Every day before going to school, Charlene dropped the baby off with her mother. Saturday and Sunday were Grandma Inez's only days off.

The baby changed me. In a matter of weeks, the baby became the most important thing in my life. At night she slept on my stomach. At first, I was afraid I might roll over and hurt her. Instead, even while sleeping, I was constantly aware of her presence. I could feel her heart beat. Unlike Charlene, I enjoyed bathing the baby and changing her diapers because as the weeks passed those chores became playtime. To see her stare back at me with her beautiful blue eyes was a joy, and each month that joy increased as she laughed and giggled. An ammonia smell permeated the house as the cloth diapers were tossed in a pail for washing. Throwaway Pampers weren't available or were too expensive. Most days I washed the cloth diapers and hung them on an outside clothesline. Charlene took her and the baby's clothes to her mother's to be washed.

After Cathy was born my life with Charlene became more bearable, but there were still conflicts. Over the next few months I came to realize Charlene had concealed a large part of her character while we were dating.

While dating her, I failed to recognized she was a chameleon. In a liberal group she portrayed herself as smart, kind, considerate, and concerned about mankind. In other words, she looked and acted like a golden girl. She was for women's rights, but in many areas, she was a bigot. She did not care about the poor, starving Armenians or cats and dogs. Privately, she was vehemently anti-Semitic. Her father, I later learned, embedded these ideas into Charlene (as did her mother). I gradually realized the tremendous influence they had on their daughter.

I tried not to criticize Charlene's behavior. I wanted her to be herself. I wanted to follow my rule: "Don't tell people what to do."

Unfortunately, she was a lousy roommate and I often felt like a martyr. It is not the large issue of love that often breaks up a marriage, but rather the little things that often destroy a relationship.

I believe then and now that Charlene's parents bestowed her with a dysfunctional belief about life. She was raised to be a princess, not a commoner who did mundane things like chores. She was meant for bigger things than cooking, washing dishes, and taking care of children. Charlene as a young woman had never done any of the basic chores around the house. She certainly never took the garbage can out to the street to be picked up.

It was difficult living with a woman who acted like a twelve-year-old and treated me like an older brother who was required to love and take care of her.

When I came home from work, I did the basic cleaning of the house. I picked up glasses, plates, and apple cores scattered around. I washed the dirty dishes, mopped and swept the floors, and cleaned the bathroom; Charlene did not even know how to put the toilet paper on the roller. The chores generally took me about an hour, but for a perfectionist like Charlene, as illustrated by her high school graduation speech travails, it would have taken a week. One time when she was watching me wash dishes she said, "You are using the wrong soap." I turned and looked at her. Her mother used ivory hand soap rather than dish soap. "Ivory is 99 percent pure soap," she said. Sure it is, I thought, but so is lye soap. I gave her the "look" that became legendary in the family. She backed out of the kitchen and left the room.

She did not know how to cook, and she did not want to learn how to cook. She snacked on cheese, nuts, fruits, whole wheat bread, yogurt, and vegetables such as carrots, celery, and tomatoes. I wasn't a gourmet cook, but I could make oatmeal, fry or boil eggs, chop up potatoes, and open a can of tuna. Still, this didn't improve things much. Trained by her mother and father, Charlene was a health food nut. She carefully read the labels on cans, refused to eat lunch meat because sodium nitrate was used as a preservative, and other foods often did not meet her standards.

Precooked frozen food was out—it was loaded with preservatives and tasted awful. Besides, there were no microwave ovens. Cheap fast-food restaurants such as McDonald's were a thing of the future. Eggs and cereal were staples in the house. When the baby arrived, we both ate more baby food than the baby.

I was a lonely man while living with Charlene. My major complaint was not her lack of enthusiasm for sex but rather her failure to display any affection toward me. If I touched her in a friendly way, tried to hold her hand, or give her a hug, she withdrew and backed away with a frown as if showing affection was anathema because I wanted to cuddle and pet her as I might a cat or dog. As with so many of her other traits, she was simply following the examples of her mother and father, who never showed any affection for each other. I never saw her parents touch or hug each other or their daughter.

In a platonic relationship, it is still easy to love someone as we love a friend, a brother, or a sister, but it is difficult to maintain that love unless it is reciprocated. You can love someone in spite of their irritating traits, but it is difficult to do for long if the love is totally unrequited.

Living with Charlene was not a bag of joy, in other words. She was one of the most self-centered people I have ever known. In her mind, she was the main actor in every scene.

Why did I stay? I loved Charlene despite her many flaws. The baby was the center of my home life, and I was not looking for a way out. I even gave up smoking because Charlene hated it and used the baby as her weapon.

A few times I became angry when Charlene ignored the baby. One afternoon when I arrived home from work, the baby was crying in the bedroom. I immediately knew she had been crying for some time. Charlene sat in the living room in an easy chair reading a book, ignoring her sobbing daughter.

"What the hell are you doing?" I snapped at her as I hurried to comfort the baby, who was around five months old. In those five months, I learned she cried for three major reasons: her diaper needed changing, she was hungry, or she was lonesome and needed to be picked up and hugged. (Her sick cry was totally different.) I discovered that day it was all three things: her diaper needed changing, she was hungry, and she threw her arms up at me to pick her up. The sobbing slowly quieted while I changed her diaper and carried her into the kitchen for a jar of baby food.

When Charlene came into the kitchen, I glanced up, controlling my anger, but she knew I was mad. When I am angry, I do not shout or stomp my feet. Inside, I become cold and hard.

Charlene recognized my look. "It is good for the baby to cry," she said. "It increases her lung capacity."

Right! And if you let them cry long enough, they stop and learn not to cry for help.

Maybe, but not my baby. I considered Charlene's actions verging on child abuse.

On another occasion, she insulted my family. At the time Uncle Bunk and his wife, Muriel, were visiting my parents. Of course, my mother talked about the baby she loved as only a new grandmother can. Bunk insisted on seeing the marvelous youngest member of the Bass family, and they jumped in his car and drove over to our house. Bunk pounded on the door. I was not home, but Charlene and Catherine were.

Charlene opened the door and stared at them.

"Can we come in and see the baby?" Ga-Ga asked.

It seemed like a normal request, and she expected Charlene to open the door and invite them inside. If it were today, Ga-Ga would have called ahead and Charlene would have been prepared. But we had no phone and internet was in the distant future.

Charlene must have been bewildered. In her entire life, her mother never invited anyone inside her house except me. Charlene had never allowed anyone in our house except her parents. Gradually, she realized she had no choice. But she had one condition: they had to remove their shoes before they entered the house.

Bunk stared at her in disbelief. It was ridiculous to expect a cowboy to remove his boots to enter a house. Cowboy boots required considerable effort to put on and equal effort to take off. To him Charlene's request was insulting. He was family, and to tell family they couldn't come into your house to see the baby or take a piss was an absolute insult.

Charlene brought the baby to the porch, handed her to Ga-Ga, and closed the door. Bunk, his wife, and my mother stayed on the porch for a few minutes admiring the baby, then Ga-Ga knocked on the door and handed the baby back to Charlene.

When my mother told me about the incident the next time I saw her, I was angry as hell. If there was a rule embedded in my mind, that rule was "Do not insult my mother." Bunk and my mother were special to me, and offending them was unacceptable.

When I came home, I sat Charlene down and explained how things were. She could pick on my father, she could argue with my brother, but she should never again disrespect my mother or Bunk. If she did, there would be some real changes around the house. For now, the rule of no shoes in the house ended.

Taken back, she said, "Okay." She did not apologize, and I knew she simply did not believe she had done anything wrong and or understand why my mother and I were so upset.

Bunk and his wife moved out of Los Angeles shortly afterwards, and I did not see him for a couple of years. The next time I saw him, the first thing I did was to apologize for Charlene's actions. He accepted and said, "That's all right, son," and gave me a hug. Family honor was important to him.

Chapter 14

Changing Jobs

In early May 1959 an opportunity arose for me to switch jobs. For months, I had been looking for a different one. The hours I worked at Logan's and the night classes I took at East L.A. Community College interfered with my new family life. I attended night school two or three times week and worked a minimum of sixty hours a week at Logan's (although my pay stub stated forty-eight—*sign it or go looking for a new job*). Two weeks before Christmas and Easter, the store stayed open from nine to nine, a workload increase of twelve hours without an increase in pay; I received a token bonus for my efforts. Before taxes, my pay was $72.50 a week. Add on the hours of travel time and its costs, and I felt used and underpaid.

The job offered no opportunity for promotion. I was nineteen years old. Even if I bought into the company propaganda, I could not become a manager until I was at least twenty-one. And I did not believe the company propaganda.

After I became assistant manager in May 1958, the company transferred a new manager to the store. About twenty-eight years old, married, and with a new baby, he willingly gave me most of the responsibility for running the store. He usually arrived at work around ten a.m. On slow days, he left me in charge during two-hour lunches before leaving the store around five o'clock. I was left to close the store. Even on busy days, he seldom waited on customers and worked as a cashier. I did the books, ordered the stock, stacked the shelves, and vacuumed the store. The manager was a friendly man, and I enjoyed working alone. I also liked having something to do to pass the time. But I was working too hard for too little money.

A bigger problem loomed. The manager continuously "borrowed" money from the store. He was not embezzling, at least in the traditional sense of the term. Each time he signed a form showing he had taken an advance on his pay, and I placed the form in the books. He explained that the move to California cost more than he expected, and he temporarily needed the money for his family. Few people had credit cards back in the day; the store's cash was his only easily accessible choice, if you can call it that.

One day in early March I arrived at 8:30 a.m. to open the store, only to find the district manager from Dallas waiting outside examining the shoes on display in the windows. I had met him several times over the years. I talked to him for a few minutes and he complimented the window displays. I opened the door and waited for him to enter. As he came inside, he examined the interior and appeared pleased. For the next two hours, I waited on customers. As time passed, I saw the district manager frown, look at his watch, and continue to wait for the manager to appear. At eleven o'clock, the manager finally arrived. He had been up all night with a sick baby and had overslept, he said. The two went to lunch and appeared in good spirits when they returned.

Then problems arose. The district manager went carefully over the books, and when he had a question, he called me over to explain a certain entry. When he reached the pay receipts, he saw the manager had taken $350 in advance pay. He exploded. The store was not a bank.

Was this embezzlement? Well, within twenty-four hours, the manager had borrowed enough money from relatives and friends to replace the $350. The books were now in order.

Two weeks later the district manager returned with the vice president to audit the books and put the manager on the carpet. Meanwhile, I took care of customers as I did on any normal day. Late in the afternoon, the district manager came over to compliment me. He knew

I had been doing most of the work. The manager had explained his family problems, and the company was retaining him. I knew the manager's days were numbered, and possibly mine as well. I decided to take my week of available vacation in early May because an opportunity arose for me to make some money on a side job.

Charlene had recently informed me that the business where her father worked was desperately looking for help. After I expressed interest in it, her father offered to arrange a trial week with his boss. The pay was $2.50 an hour, considerably more than I was making at Logan's.

The job was at Vega's Granite and Monument Company in East Los Angeles. Charles Evans, Charlene's father, was the company's master stencil cutter. The company cut and delivered two to three hundred tombstones each week to several Catholic cemeteries in Los Angeles. The business included a granite quarry that provided the stone for the grave markers.

Old Man Vega was the sole owner. He migrated to the United States from Spain sometime in the early 1900s and busted his butt all his life. He was in his late sixties, stocky in build, and one of the hardest workers I've ever encountered. In the years I worked for him, he seldom missed a day. The business was his life, and he had succeeded and was a wealthy man, the patriarch of his family. Joe Vega, the old man's only son, was around forty years old and had worked in the business all his life as well. He was friendly, more like a fellow worker than one of the bosses because his father never relinquished any real power. Joe was the crew boss but had no power in hiring or firing. Joe had a wife and two daughters his father loved, but Joe was not happy in his role, which often required him to work six days a week. Joe understood the workers, and like us, would have preferred being at the beach on hot summer days in Southern California. He stayed for his future inheritance. His father expected him to remain on the job, and when he died, run the business.

Unfortunately for Joe, he would not be the sole owner. He had two older sisters who never worked a day in their lives. Old Man Vega pampered the family and was generous with his money, buying Joe and his sisters homes, cars, and televisions. There was also Aunt Marie, the old man's sister. Around sixty years old, Marie was the office manager. She never married and lived with the old man, who treated her as a partner.

The stencil cutters were the heart of the company. They worked in a gigantic metal shed on Whittier Boulevard in East Los Angeles. The shed was open at the back and front and stretched a city block in length and a half a block in width. The roof was forty to fifty feet high to accommodate the flatbed trailers that brought the stone from the quarry for polishing and cutting. The front portion of the shed was the stencil cutters' area, sheltered from the rain but not the winter cold or summer heat.

The old man spent most days in the shed, where the product was produced. He closely observed the six stencil cutters. He was from the old school: He wanted the men to work hard, but equally important—and this is one of the reasons I respected him—he wanted high quality. If you did a job to his satisfaction, he grunted and went about his business, but when you made a mistake, he barked loud enough for everyone to hear his displeasure.

Even today, many people visualize a stonecutter as someone who hovers over his work for hours using a hand chisel to carve the designs and letters with an artisan's skill. But by 1959, hand chiseling had not been used for many years except in rare cases. It slowly disappeared in the early 1900s when steam-powered pneumatic tools were developed.

In the late 1920s, techniques used in shaded glass production replaced pneumatic chisels. In the glory days of the "fabulous" 1920s, shaded glass windows and doors became a fad in expensive hotels, restaurants, and theaters. Even today, if you watch movies made in the 1930s, you will see shaded glass in scenes shot in fancy hotels and restaurants.

Shaded glass was made using a sandblaster and rubber stencils. Stencil cutters poured a specially developed rubber onto the glass, and when the rubber cooled, they drew elaborate designs on it. Then they cut the design in the rubber and removed the parts to be sandblasted. The thicker the rubber, the deeper the sand could cut into the glass.

This is where my father-in-law comes into the picture. Monument companies quickly realized the same technique could be used to carve stone as well as shaded glass. They hired master cutters from glass companies, and these cutters drew and cut design patterns for gravestones. Through the years, monument companies were able to offer hundreds of designs to customers. Charles Evans was a former glass cutter who cut the master patterns for Vega's. Vega admired good artisans, and Evans was his master cutter. He was especially in demand when a customer wanted something unique.

My week at Vega's involved helping the cutters. Memorial Day was only a few weeks away, and many gravestones needed to be cut. Speed was important, but like I said, for Vega quality was just as much a priority. I lifted stones onto the cutters' desks and brought them the rolls of rubber needed to cover the stone. Once they were cut and picked, I helped place the stones on a carriage and roll them onto tracks leading into the sandblast room. After blasting, I rolled the carriage out and carried the stones to a cleaning area to remove the rubber and clean the stones. Then I helped lift them onto the trailer of a flatbed truck that delivered the markers to the cemeteries for placement. I also helped the sandblaster—that week it was Joe—reload sand into the hopper. By the end of the week, I was sandblasting when Joe needed to do other work. Six cutters worked on headstones of different sizes. My father-in-law worked primarily on the large monuments that needed his craftsmanship.

The place was busy. In the far back, I heard trucks bring large slabs of stone to the wire diamond saw that polished and cut the markers to size. Near the front was an air-pressure tank and an enclosed sandblast room. Hundreds of unlettered grave markers stacked by size and color surrounded the six stencil cutters' desks.

Although it was hard, I enjoyed working with my hands, and it was something different from working in a shoe store for three years. That week I worked forty-eight hours and earned $120 compared to the $72.50 I made at Logan's (and many more unpaid hours I put in). I worked hard for the week, and Vega noted I did not stand around doing nothing nor did I keep disappearing to the bathroom. My size was perhaps my major liability. I was five-foot-nine and weighed 140 pounds, and some stones were too heavy for me to lift. My greatest asset was Charles Evans, my father-in-law.

Vega offered me a job. He needed a sandblaster who was willing to help do other tasks. He also wanted something from me I did not expect and that would end up costing me hundreds of dollars over the next three years: he wanted me to bring Evans to work.

Vega considered Evans his most important worker, but he had a problem. Evans only came to work when he needed money or felt he had nothing better to do. He often worked only two days a week, and some weeks he did not come to work even once. Even on days he worked, he always came in late, a trait he passed on to his daughter. Vega fired him many times, but Evans didn't care. He preferred cutting stone for small, independent dealers, and a number of other small monument companies used him for piece work. He liked to take his time with monuments, and would work for an hour, sit down, have a drink, and talk philosophy with the dealer. Since they paid him by the piece, they weren't in a hurry. But he wasn't cheap, and they paid him more for a couple of days' work than Vega paid him for a week's.

Vega invariably hired Evans back, usually at a higher salary. At the time, Evans charged him $5.50 an hour; Vega paid his other stencil cutters $3.50 an hour. Vega put up with Evans's behavior because he truly respected his artistic abilities. Most stencil cutters took their job to be a job. They were slow and never learned the finer skills of stencil cutting; as a result, most turned out mediocre work. Evans was different. He was a perfectionist and expected to be treated as a craftsman. Vega used him for difficult jobs. Evans might take hours to draw a design, but when he began to cut the stencil, he was the fastest cutter in the business. As my mentor, he often spoke with disdain about the common cutter who took a couple of hours to cut a stone he could do in thirty minutes. He proclaimed a slow cutter was a lousy cutter of letters and designs. He believed all cuts in the rubber needed to be made with a smooth stroke with no pauses. "Hackers" made stop-and-go cuts that showed up after sandblasting. Take your time on design, he counseled, but once you begin, keep your knives sharp and your hands moving. Even with his speed, Evans seldom finished a monument fast. He would cut a rose in the stencil, pick out the rubber, and stand back to evaluate his work. If the cut passed inspection, he continued.

When Evans cut headstones using common patterns, he loafed along. He cut a line or two, then paused to sharpen his knives, tell a story, or perhaps go to the bathroom, stopping to talk to other workers along the way. His habits irritated Vega, but Evans still managed to cut twice as many headstones as the other cutters and at a higher quality.

When Vega made me the job offer, I barely knew Evans. Though Charlene and I had been married for ten months, we seldom saw her father. We ate dinner at her parents' house once a week, and Inez always cooked a pot roast with fresh vegetables, but Charlie was seldom home. He wandered the city at night dropping into various diners, pool halls, and bars and got into arguments with the other customers. He was not a heavy drinker nor a woman-chaser. He was a talker. He gladly allowed anyone to buy him a drink but never reciprocated. If anything, he was more frugal than his daughter.

Gradually, it became obvious to me that Charlene was very much like her father. Both were perfectionists who believed they were smarter than even the smartest people in the country. He was always cold, and in the winter, wore several layers of clothes. Sometimes he wore the same clothes for weeks, yet did not come off as homeless; he looked like a working man, an honorable term to him. He took a bath perhaps every six months, yet he never smelled nor looked dirty. He did shave every few days. He was a fanatic about the ingredients in his food and often grumbled about how big business was poisoning the American people with the additives, such as sodium nitrite and sugar, they put in grocery store food. Fresh fruit and vegetables, eggs, plain yogurt, and whole wheat bread constituted a large part of his diet. He was a stocky man, about 'five feet, 'ten inches tall, and very strong.

His biggest character flaw was he was a talker, a lecturer who indulged in topics that bored most people to tears. Discourses on his favorite topics, philosophy, economics, psychology, and politics, spewed from his mouth as he quoted obscure sources to prove he was right. Sometimes he harped on the same subject for days. According to Evans, his father was a wealthy lawyer in upper New York state who sent his sons to expensive prep schools in New England. His father wanted him to go to Harvard, but Evans refused. His father got him an appointment to West Point, but Evans refused to go to the academy. He left home and worked at various jobs, from lumberjacking in Maine to working at an oil field in Texas. He arrived in Los Angeles in the late 1920s. Naturally, I didn't believe most of his tall tales, but I figured some were true. Which ones? I don't know.

Not knowing what I was getting into, I accepted Vega's offer, but I had conditions of my own, which he readily accepted. I wanted to give the manager at Logan's a week's notice along with a promise to help him if he had trouble with the books or displays. I did not feel I owed any loyalty to Logan's as a company, but I felt I owed the manager that personal consideration. Over the years the company executives preached that loyalty and hard work guaranteed promotion, but in reality, loyalty worked only for the company, not the employees. During my time I had seen several good managers replaced.

My second condition for accepting a job at Vega's was that on nights I had classes at East L.A. Community College I would not work past five o'clock. Old Man Vega nodded to this, although it was obvious he didn't fully understand. He had absolutely no interest in intellectual topics and couldn't image why any working man needed any education beyond the twelfth grade. His life revolved around his business and family. I was different. As far back as I could remember, I had dreamed of going to college. My life revolved around getting an education and taking care of my daughter and Charlene.

Honoring my agreement with Vega, on my first day of work I went first to Evans's to pick him up. What happened next would be repeated many times over the next three years.'

I knocked on the back door at 7:00 a.m. The family never entered through the front, because the living room was crammed with hundreds of boxes. We were due at work at eight.

Inez opened the door and let me into the kitchen. She seldom said anything except hello, and this day was no exception. She was listening to the news on the radio. Evans did not own a television set, as he considered TVs to be propaganda machines that indoctrinated the masses to accept the oppressions of giant corporations and big government. Invariably he would cite George Orwell's *1984* or quote Eugene Debs.

Evans was asleep on the floor under the small kitchen table, fully clothed and without a pillow or blanket. I looked at Inez, who simply shrugged and took a sip of tea. She gave me no advice during the hour that I tried to get Evans off the kitchen floor. She never smiled or told me anything about her daily routine. I assume that before I came on the scene, she simply ignored Evans as he snored away.

I soon found out why. He simply refused to move until I pestered him for at least forty minutes. I went over to him and shook his shoulder. He opened his eyes, and I said it was time to go to work. He nodded but did not move. I repeated my actions every five minutes for thirty minutes before he groaned and sat up.

"Get me a cup of tea," he said to Inez. She complied. She had accepted her life with Evans.

"Cook me six eggs, some toast, and bring me a cup of yogurt."

He rose, got into a chair, and nodded for me to sit down. I looked at my watch: 8:15.

Every day it took an hour or two to get him ready to go to work. I was working for Vega, but he did not pay me for the time I spent coaxing Evans to come to work. Evans, though, was not concerned about the money. Or, really, any money at all. Whenever he was paid, he threw his checks in a drawer, and Inez cashed them at the grocery store when they needed money. He usually had two or three hundred dollars in his pocket and six to eight weeks of checks in the drawer. The pocket money lasted him months.

We rode racing bikes to work, which was about five miles away. Evans had a 1950 Dodge, but he rarely used it. He did not have a driver's license or insurance. "Hell," he would say, "when I was young, we never had such things." He refused to get either because he believed big government and big corporations were exploiting the working man.

Riding a bicycle in Los Angeles was often dangerous. Because of this, we detoured through neighborhood roads and finally arrived at work around 9:30 a.m. Old Man Vega never said a word about our being late. When I came to work alone, Vega made no comment on my arrival, assuming (correctly) that Evans had disappeared for the time being. Vega knew the score.

My main job at Vega's was as a sandblaster. Within a month, I learned the ins and outs of the job but disliked sandblasting. It's the dirtiest job in the monument business. I always showered and changed my clothes when I came home from work. I had no intention of remaining a sandblaster. Stencil cutters made more money, had more respect, and certainly had a less physical job. Vega allowed me to take a stone and a roll of rubber home. If I wanted to be a stencil cutter, I had to learn on my own.

That's not completely true. Working on the job gave me many opportunities to observe the cutters. I also had Evans, who enjoyed teaching the subtler aspects of stencil cutting. After work we sometimes went to one of his independent dealers to cut a stone or monument. He took his time and talked about stencil cutting. His first rule: take care of your tools. He showed me how to sharpen the knives so they were razor sharp and how to use the various measuring and drawing tools. Evans made his own knives from high-quality steel while the other cutters used steel-handled commercial knives such as X-'Actos. Evans spit on such knives. *His* knives had wooden handles and looked much like pencils with a slightly larger circumference. While the commercial knives' blades were sharp on one side, Evans's were sharp on both sides, allowing him to cut in both directions without stopping the knife's movement. His knives cut through the rubber as if it were butter. The other cutters used dull blades and applied much more pressure to cut the rubber. As a result, they could not achieve a smooth stroke when cutting designs like roses. His second rule was to never allow anyone, even the boss, borrow your tools.

Evans helped me make my first knives, taught me how to sharpen them, told me the basic principles of stencil cutting, and left me alone to practice after work or on weekends. He looked at my practice cuts and made suggestions. Within two months, I was cutting simple stones when there was a pause in sandblasting. Within a year I was, except for Evans, the best and fastest cutter at Vega's. Despite that fact, I had two jobs: stencil cutter and relief sandblaster. Vega never raised my salary, but I did not complain because I had more important problems than money.

After sandblasting all day I would come home from work dirty. When Cathy became a toddler she waited at the door for me, jumping into my arms screaming "Daddy! Daddy!" and getting almost as dirty as I was in the process. I would pick her up and carry her to the shower, disrobing both of us in the bathroom. This became an afterwork ritual and something I looked forward to each day.

One time I was standing with my back to the door waiting for the water to heat up when I felt something hit my naked back—wham! Charlene had struck me hard with an open palm. Luckily she jumped back, because when I whipped around, I would have decked her. If I had hit her, it would not have been intentional. My natural reaction when attacked from behind was to strike back. Remember my brother and his split lip.

I glared at her, and she backed out of the bathroom, obviously scared. Although a mild-mannered man, I knew I had a temper deep down that could explode. I believed violent anger was a weakness, not a strength.

After Cathy and I showered and I cleaned up, I went to talk to Charlene in the kitchen. "Why?" I asked.

Simple, she explained. When I came home, she was sitting in the chair in the living room reading a book, and I had ignored her.

"You care more about the baby than me," she said, pouting.

I did not take her in my arms and comfort her. Instead I just stood there, shocked. Of course I cared about and loved the baby more than I loved her. I assumed she felt the same way. Her jealousy seemed insane to me.

Much later in life I realized that Charlene and I had very different views on relationships. She was comfortable with constant confrontation and arguments. I never saw Inez and Evans fighting, but I must conclude they shouted at each other, and occasionally, Evans popped her in the mouth. Charlene wanted an aggressive male who took command while she fought to take control. In sex, she wanted someone who dominated. I was not an aggressive male. I preferred the soft, gentle approach that proved impossible with her.

As for her aversion to kissing, she once went a couple of months spitting in a jar because she believed even her saliva might make her sick. This reminded me of Grandma Bell and her tobacco habits. On the rare occasions we had sex, she kept her nightshirt on because she was cold and simply lay on her back, expecting me to take charge. I never saw her naked, never gave her a back rub, never saw or touched her breasts. Considering her many sexual adventures before and after our marriage, I must conclude the blame for our basically nonexistent sex life lay as much with me as with her.

It didn't take long for life to throw me another curveball, and this one hit me in the face.

Chapter 15

Married Life: Part II

After I went to work for Vega's Granite and Monument Company marriage life improved, apart from the slapping incident, for a few months. I had more time to spend with the baby and Charlene. We often went for long walks, pushing the baby carriage down to the local parks on Saturdays to feed the ducks.

In the fall of 1959, I enrolled in two evening classes at East L.A. Community College, and to my surprise, Charlene insisted on taking the courses with me. We dropped the baby off at Inez's around 5:30 p.m. and walked the two miles to campus every Tuesday and Thursday. We were lucky in our class choices and had two excellent teachers. One was a philosophy class that Charlene loved. We read and discussed Greek and Roman philosophers such as Socrates, Aristotle, and Augustine. The other class, on editing, was taught by an attractive young woman not much older than us. She required weekly essays of three to five hundred words. The class began with thirty students and quickly dropped to twenty. I turned in my essays each week; Charlene turned in a few but ended up taking an incomplete for the class. Her excuse was that she also was enrolled in three day classes, and thus, was a full-time student.

My dream was to be a writer, and the course helped me understand the difficult task ahead of me. To Charlene's irritation, the teacher took a special interest in me. Each week she discussed with the class the most common mistakes in writing. During the last hour she called a few students over to her desk to discuss their essays. Each week she called me up as her last student for the evening and spent extra time with me. She encouraged me, but as a good editor does, pointed out my mistakes.

Charlene was jealous. She was convinced the teacher had a crush on me. I smiled but knew in reality the teacher believed I had possibilities but needed to improve. She was right. My failures as a writer have always haunted me, and I have read many books on style and grammar in attempt to improve myself. Unfortunately, my brain is a sieve.

Somewhat related, after I quit Logan's Charlene pleaded with me to grow a beard. I liked the idea. The image reminded me of the Bass family members who came to my mother's bathroom party. After years of wearing jackets and ties for work, I liked wearing jeans, work shoes, and plaid shirts. Much later, I realized Charlene wanted me to grow a beard because she considered me a handsome young man with blue eyes, long eyelashes, and dimples. She thought a beard would deter most young women from flirting with me, and she was right.

I received an A in both classes. I was extremely pleased. In 1959, few if any colleges in the country pampered students. At East L.A. Community College, if a student's GPA dropped below 2.00, they were put on probation and ousted after two semesters. Seats were limited, and colleges were crowded. To put it more crudely, it was "shit or get off the pot." Between 1959 and 1980, no student I knew earned a 4.00 GPA. A 3.00 was an amazing accomplishment. At the time, professors did not award plus grades. A's earned four points, B's got three, C's got two, and D's got one. Most teachers applied the bell curve and no more than three to five students in a class of twenty-five received an A.

Two or three nights a week, I went to school. Charlene took most of her courses during the day. The courses I took focused on the basic requirements for an associate of arts degree, with course credits transferable to Cal State Los Angeles to obtain a bachelor of arts. A good grade point average was essential, as a 2.5 average was necessary to guarantee a seat at Cal State. The baby boom generation was overwhelming the system, and most teachers were tough graders. If a student flunked out, three people applied for the seat.

By 1961, the Vietnam War was on the horizon and many young males attended college to avoid the draft. Few students achieved a GPA better than 3.0, but mine hovered around 3.4. I had always been a good student, and I excelled at East L.A. Community College, which had many fine tenured teachers in history, literature, and the social sciences. The most difficult part of staying in school was persevering through bad times, particularly when financial or family problems arose.

On Saturday afternoons I cycled over to my parents and picked up one of their cars to bring Cathy to their house for a sleepover. Ga-Ga and Granddaddy loved Cathy. If something prevented a Saturday night sleepover, they moaned and groaned. In return, I got use of the car, and Charlene and I went out to eat, to the movies, or to a museum or a lecture, much as we had done when we dated. We had no sexual relations. She was still "recovering" from childbirth and breastfeeding the baby. Those pennies stayed in the jar.

The grand event in the fall of 1959 was my brother's marriage to a young woman of Mexican descent. I had not seen much of him in over a year, but at that point he made twice my salary as the ace salesman at Regal's Shoe Store in Hollywood. His fiancée, Tina, wanted a "real" wedding at the local Catholic church with all the pomp and ceremony. My brother invited me and Charlene to the wedding and reception where family and friends would celebrate the marriage. Formal dress, a jacket and tie, was requested. Food and beverages would be served plus a band for dancing.

I had a beard and I loved the freedom of not having to dress up for my job. At the time, beards were not common, and many people associated a man with long hair and a beard with being a left-wing radical. I wore working man's clothes, and many times people in passing cars who saw me yelled out, "Go to Cuba you Commie bastard!" My father was not thrilled with the attention. He asked me to come over after dark, or least come in the back door so the neighbors would not see me. I smiled and agreed. For the next fifty years, I occasionally grew a beard but usually shaved after six months. Students and teachers often did not recognize me after this.

The idea of going to a fancy wedding reception was inconceivable to me. I did not dance, drink, or speak Spanish. "Congratulations," I said, "but no thanks." I understood the social aspect and handed Corky, aka Charlie, an envelope with money as my wedding gift. My brother smiled—he was sure I wouldn't come even before he offered the invitation. Charlene was different. She wanted to go to the reception and was angry I hadn't consulted her, which surprised me. In retrospect, I obviously did not understand women. Charlene pouted.

On the day of the wedding, without dressing up or shaving my beard, I went to the church by myself and sat in the back pew. Relatives of the bride packed the front pews. My mother and father were in the front with them. The opulent church, with its stained-glass windows, impressive altar, and other props added a certain dignity to the wedding. As the ceremony ended, I moved outside and stood with a group throwing rice on the couple as they exited the church. I nodded to my brother as he passed, and he nodded back, knowing I wished him well. The couple continued down the steps to where my father waited with an opened door to his new 1959 Chevy Impala, green with gigantic fins. The couple were off on their honeymoon. I slipped away without saying hello to my parents.

Within five years, my brother had three children, all girls, and was left wondering what had happened. His dream of owning his own shoe store withered away because of the burden of supporting a family.

When Charlene suggested having another child, I responded with a loud "no." The three of us were all I could afford if I wanted to achieve my dream of a college education, my ticket to getting off the bottom. Until she agreed, I was not going to have unprotected sex—though we had sex so seldom it probably wasn't a threat that mattered. Or maybe it was? Remember my "one-shot" experience.

By the fall of 1959, I had adjusted to married life. Outside work and school, the baby was the center of my life. Most parents will understand the feeling of love that develops when you can see pure happiness in a baby's eyes. A giggle is worth a thousand words. And, it got better and better with each passing month. When she screamed "Daddy! Daddy!" and jumped into my arms when I came home from work, I felt a joy I had never experienced before. Well, maybe since my dog Butch.

Charlene and I fell into a pattern of behavior that, although not ideal, was tolerable. I realized Charlene was not my "perfect" roommate, but many times I enjoyed her company. Our sex life remained nonexistent. She said I snored and she couldn't get to sleep, so I moved to a cot in the living room. And I did snore, as did my father, mother, and brother. I remembered times my father snored so loud no one in the house could sleep.

In the spring of 1960, I enrolled in four evening courses at East L.A. as I slowly accumulated credits toward my associates of arts degree. Charlene was also taking a night course, and after each of our classes we met at the library and walked home together. She was usually late, but one night I waited for an hour after our classes had ended. She said she had to drop a book off at the library or had been talking with other students in her class. I remember feeling something was wrong. My instincts turned out to be right.

In early June 1960, Charlene informed me she planned to go camping with her mother. "It's a tradition," she said. Apparently, every year of her childhood when school ended, Inez and Charlene spent three weeks living in a tent in one of the campgrounds in the San Bernardino Mountains near Big Bear Lake, located around seventy-five miles northeast of Montebello. From home it was a thirty-five-minute drive on a four-lane road to the city of San Bernardino. It took another hour up a winding mountain road to the Big Bear campsites. Wealthy movie stars had built homes around Big Bear Lake and skied in the area in the winter. In the summer, they went to the mountains to get away from the heat down below. Many Hollywood movies were filmed up there, including *Daniel Boone*, *Old Yeller*, *Paint Your Wagon*, and a ton of classic Westerns.

I thought Charlene's decision to go on a camping trip for three weeks was unreasonable. Camping out in a tent for three weeks would be roughing it. Besides, who would take care of the baby while she and Inez were on their trip?

"I'll take the baby with us," she said.

Roughing it in a tent in a mountain campground for three weeks with a baby seemed irrational to me. Cathy was only fourteen months old. Although partially potty trained, she needed her diapers changed occasionally. She ate solid food but also bottled baby food. Having the baby stay in a tent in the mountains where food was prepared over a small camp stove and water was available only at pumps scattered around the grounds *was not* a practical idea. I knew Charlene, Inez, and her father had the habit of wearing the same clothes for a couple weeks and would have little inclination to walk to the laundry room over a half mile from their tent. I visualized the baby wandering around in dirty diapers and the same clothes for three weeks. Campers shared showers and bathrooms, but by this point I knew the Evanses seldom took baths or showers. How would they keep the baby clean? "Whore's baths," my mother said.

I could not understand why Charlene wanted to spend three weeks living in a tent in the mountains. My goal in life was to escape poverty, not live as the homeless lived. Today, I cringe when I see middle-class men and women wearing worn-out jeans with holes in the knees. When I was a boy, I wore patched jeans and torn tennis shoes out of necessity, not as a fashion statement. I think the rich are patronizing the poor.

Charlene insisted the camping trip would be good for the baby. Besides, if she left the baby home, who would take care of her? My mother offered a compromise: She would take her two-week vacation time from work, and Cathy could stay with her. She and Dad would be thrilled to have the baby for two weeks.

Charlene and Inez went to the mountains. They agreed I could pick up the baby after one week. On the following Sunday, I borrowed my father's car and drove two hours to pick up Cathy.

When I arrived, the grounds were as primitive as I expected. Charlene insisted I stay for a few hours to explore the area. It was a hot day. I carried Cathy as we hiked around a large campground surrounded by tall pine trees. The lake was a few hundred yards away. With hundreds of camping sites, campers had worn away the grass, and the common areas were hard-packed dirt. The air smelled of pine, dust, and charcoal fires. Dressed in blue jeans, the heat quickly tired me. Many years would pass before I wore shorts and sandals. Eventually we found some lawn chairs to sit in as Cathy crawled and walked tentatively around the tent.

Suddenly, she screamed out in pain. She had turned over a jug and spilled some of the liquid in her eyes.

I jumped up and ran to her. The bottle's label showed me she had gotten bleach in her eyes. I grabbed her and dashed over a hundred yards to reach a water pump to wash out her eyes. She cried hysterically all the way. I placed her head under the pump spout, and with my other hand, pumped frantically. I was afraid my baby had been blinded, or at least had damaged her eyes. I wet the bottom of my shirt and gently swabbed her eyes. She quit crying and hugged me tightly as she sobbed. There was no damage to her eyes.

It angered me that Charlene and Inez had not been more careful. Babies get into things. Charlene shrugged off my anger. Things happen when you camp out, she said. Later, when she retold the story, she said I had overreacted. Her punch line: "I never saw Ken run so fast. He usually moves in slow gear."

The drive out of the mountains scared me. Seatbelts and single car seats in front were things of the future. I kept one hand on the baby as I drove the winding, two-lane road down the mountain. My tension lessened when I reached the flatland that would take us the forty miles to Mother's house. For the next two weeks, Mom, Cathy, and Dad had a great time. When Bunk and Muriel came over to play dominoes, he grabbed Cathy and lifted her high and slowly lowered her so he could lick her face. She giggled. She hovered around the table as the grown-ups played.

In the summer I enrolled in an evening public speaking class. I enjoyed the class but only made a B. Although a full-time student during the spring and fall semesters, Charlene decided after coming home from the mountains not to take any summer classes. Instead, she opted to do something more fun. She enrolled in a six-week evening course on polishing small stones at a technical school in Whittier, about twenty miles east of Montebello. Her love of polished stones came from her father, and we seldom took a walk where she did not pick up a stone and proclaim, "If this stone were polished it would be a lovely piece of jewelry." She had a friend who was taking the course and was willing to pick her up in East L.A. and bring her home after the class ended.

I accepted her decision. I was not Charlene's gatekeeper, and she did not need to ask permission. I was too naïve to ask who her friend was. Truthfully, it never occurred to me.

One night after school I arrived at Inez's house around 10:00 p.m. She was taking care of the baby. Charlene, however, was not waiting for me. She finally came in the back door around 11:30. I was irritated but not worried. One of Charlene's most annoying traits was that she was always, and I mean always, late. As we walked the six blocks home, with me pushing the baby carriage, I told her an hour and a half with her mother was not my idea of fun, particularly when I was tired from a full day's work and my night class. Charlene explained. The polishing course only lasted six weeks, and the students were staying late to work on their projects. She suggested that for the next few weeks I go straight home from school. She and Cathy would sleep over at her mother's. I could see Cathy when I came over to pick up Evans for work. Great idea, I thought.

There was a wrinkle, to put it mildly.

Two weeks later I arrived at her mother's house at 7:00 a.m. to pick up Evans. Inez opened the back door, and as usual Evans was asleep on the kitchen floor near the table. Cathy was asleep in the baby carriage. I looked at Inez and asked, "Charlene still in bed?"

Inez took a sip of her tea but said nothing, so I began the daily process of getting Evans off the floor as Inez fried six eggs. Around 8:30, Charlene came charging in the back door. Inez stayed at the stove, showing no interest.

"Have a late night?" I asked. Even for naïve old me, it was obvious she had just arrived home.

Charlene nodded with a broad grin. "I had a fantastic time!" she declared, bubbly and acting as if staying out all night was normal behavior for a new mother.

I took her arm and said, "Outside. We need to talk."

In the driveway, I turned to her and said, "Okay, what's going on?"

Looking me in the eyes, she said, "I've taken a lover. I knew you would understand."

I stared at her, my mind blank. Was she kidding? Several seconds passed before I said, "A lover?"

"Yes," she said, smiling broadly, proud of herself.

I felt like I was in a French movie. The cuckolded male is always the last to know.

For a few seconds I continued to stare at her in disbelief. I shook my head and said, "No." Staring some more, I shook my head again, turned, got on my bike and went to work. To hell with Evans.

All day long, I thought of what Charlene had said. It was difficult for me to accept she was "fucking" another man. Harder still to believe that she thought I would accept the situation.

Partly angry and partly raging with self-pity, I felt like a martyr who had fallen into a fantasy world. The thoughts of her betrayal crippled my ego and depressed me. I believed I had been a good husband. In my mind, the sexless marriage had not been my choice but hers. She never gave me any encouragement and withdrew every time I touched her. I had never seen her naked; she always wore long nightshirts to bed "to keep warm," she said.

I thought she loved me and just had little interest in sex. Was it my fault? I recognized my thoughts as part of a rejection syndrome. It took many years before I accepted the fact that some of the fault was mine.

The question was, should I leave or should I stay?

The obvious answer was *leave, you fool*. On the other side was Cathy. Could I move out without the baby? Could I take care of a baby by myself? *Yes* and *no*, all day long. It was a long day of introspection. As I rode my bike home, I made my decision.

Charlene was waiting for me. She sat at the kitchen table and knew I was about to tell her my decision. It was an emotional scene. Wisely, she had left Cathy at her mother's.

My response to the situation was simple: "Him or me!"

She cried as I made it clear that if I stayed there could be no outside boyfriends. She admitted she had been seeing him for a few weeks. She did not apologize and obviously believed she had done nothing wrong. Crying again, she added, "I don't want you to leave me."

"Go back to your mother's and think it over tonight," I said. "I'll talk to you in the morning."

Then I went to school.

The next morning, she waited for me outside Inez's door at seven. She said she called her friend last night and told him she could not see him anymore. She would not be going to the stone polishing class.

I nodded. I took her at her word she had ended the relationship. To repeat, I was not her gatekeeper. Naïve? You bet!

For the next few months, she pouted, acting like a child denied her ice cream. We did not talk about the issue and several times she spent her nights at Inez's. She was always there when I arrived in the morning. I continued to take Cathy to my parents on Saturdays, but I told them nothing about my marriage problems.

Six months later, in January 1961, Charlene dropped a bomb. "I'm pregnant," she announced.

Not with my child. We had not had sex in months.

She admitted she had never stopped seeing her "lover." He acknowledged the child was his, but absolutely refused to allow Charlene to move in with him and broke off the relationship.

"What now, brown cow?"

We negotiated. Though the child was not mine, the idea of blaming a baby for its predicament never occurred to me. But living together would be impossible. Being lonely when you are alone is painful, but even more painful is being lonely when you are living with someone. After a few weeks, I decided to move out of the apartment but agreed to keep paying the rent, providing money for necessities, as well as pay the doctor's bill for the new baby.

Thanks to Charlene's frugality, during our time living together we actually saved money. But at this point even our savings were stretched. I needed to find a cheap place near work, so I settled on a room in a trailer park with a small galley kitchen and a toilet. The unit was old but clean. It had a two-burner stove, a small refrigerator, and a bed with an uncomfortable mattress. A few worn plastic chairs completed the furniture set. The showers were in the center of the complex used by a dozen units. To shower, I gathered up a bar of soap, a towel, and clean clothes and walked about fifty yards. During the six months I lived there, I never saw another tenant. Living by myself was easier, although it was the loneliest time of my life.

I continued to pick up Evans for work during the few weeks I still lived with a pregnant Charlene. Whenever Inez opened the kitchen door, she said, "Hi," then disappeared with her teacup like always. Her loyalty was to her daughter, not me or even Evans. During those weeks, she did not cook breakfast. If Evans was home, he was asleep on the kitchen floor. If he refused to get moving, I got on my bicycle and left. I was not paid to bring him to work, and it cost me money to drag him out. When I arrived at work at nine o'clock without Evans, Vega looked at me and shrugged. He had known Evans for thirty years. But as my skills improved on the job, he accepted I was no longer Evans's butler. When I moved to the trailer park, I quit picking up Evans.

Charlene gave birth to her second child, a girl named Susan, in August 1961. A few weeks later she admitted she had kept in contact with her boyfriend, Darrell, throughout her pregnancy. After he saw the baby, he had a change of heart and accepted her constant pleas to move in with him.

I agreed to pay Charlene's rent for two more months as she arranged to move in with Darrell. I also agreed to give her $50 a month in child support for Cathy. That does not seem like much today, but in 1961, money had a higher value. The amount increased over the years. To my irritation, after two months she had not moved out of the apartment. I told her Darrell could pay for the next month. She was out in days.

After I stopped going to Inez's to pick up Evans, I made more money at Vega's. I enjoyed the job because I learned new skills and knowledge I could not have picked up at school. Over my life, I have learned as much about life and people at work as I have reading books and attending classes. I knew early on that to achieve independence, a person needed money to survive. That meant mowing lawns, caddying, or any better-paying job. I learned that working hard and trying to do my best job was more satisfying than loafing. Hard work usually helped you keep a job and made the time pass quicker. As I mentioned earlier, even today it irritates me when upper-middle-class people say, "Money is not the most important thing in life." If you are poor, money *is* the most important thing in life—it is how you and your family survive.

After eighteen months at Vega's, I transitioned from being a sandblaster and helper to an apprentice stencil cutter. By the August of 1961, I was the best and fastest cutter at Vega's, often cutting twice as many stones per day as the other cutters. As my skills improved, I took on monuments Vega usually reserved for Evans. The monuments required some design work and some duplication of older markers; the request to have a monument like "my dear old grandmother's" was common. Although I was now a master cutter, Vega continued to pay me $2.50 an hour while he paid the other cutters $3.50 and Evans even more. I expected Vega to raise my pay, but pride prevented me from asking him about it.

I saw Evans at work two or three times a week. He rode into the yard on his bicycle, and we said "Good morning"—or often, "Good afternoon"—but never anything about Charlene and me. We were polite. I was not mad at him, and he was not mad at me. The situation was still awkward.

When Charlene drove away with Darrell and the baby, I felt relieved to be out of a bad relationship. Of course, mothers never disappear. On the first Saturday night after the split, I went to the local tobacco store and bought three good cigars and two packs of Camels. I smoked the cigars in a state of pure pleasure at a local bar where I played several games of pool and drank a couple of beers. I loved smoking over the years, including English Ovals, the strongest cigarettes on the market, and, off and on for many years, a pipe. I promised myself not to give up smoking again unless *I* decided to, not because some "friend" wanted me to quit. I would also not sleep on the floor or take my shoes off to enter my own house, nor read the ingredients on a box of cereal before I chose one.

I shaved my beard. But over the next fifty years, I grew it back many times. In the late sixties and early seventies, as the hippie movement exploded, long hair and beards were popular among college students and teachers who opposed the Vietnam War. I was not a hippie—I was a serious student, did not use drugs, never demonstrated against the war, or went to "wild" parties. But because I was interested in U.S. diplomacy in Asia, I joined the American-Asia Society in 1962, and they did oppose the war. Initially the beards were dark brown and kept relatively short. In my forties, they were reddish with streaks of brown and gray. When I was in my early sixties, my beard—the last one I had—came in white. My friends identified me as "the short, bearded, skinny Santa Claus." Eventually I shaved the white beard but kept the moustache.

I seldom saw Darrell, and even after Charlene moved in with him, he constantly avoided me. On the rare occasions I talked to him, he seemed to be a nice fellow. I had no axe to grind with him; Charlene was the one who betrayed me, not him. He was around thirty-five years old, 'six feet, two" inches tall, and was slim and rather attractive. He drove a VW Beatle and was a messenger for a company whose name I never learned and didn't care to. He was paid well; money was no real problem. He rented a three-bedroom house on the east edge of Montebello and bought Charlene a used car.

I informed Charlene I would pick Cathy up at her mother's every Friday afternoon and keep her until Sunday afternoon. I had not told my parents of my marriage problems, but somehow, they knew a split had occurred. My plan was to stay at their place Friday and Saturday nights so my mother could help me with the baby. When my parents learned of the arrangement, they were delighted. Through the nine months of Charlene's pregnancy, Cathy had often stayed with my parents on the weekends. If there was anyone my parents truly loved, it was Cathy. In many ways, she had become the center of their lives. For the next six years, I spent most of my weekends with her.

As time passed, Susan, the new baby, joined us. She was a lovely little girl but shy. Mine or not, I adopted her in my mind. I could not say no when she called me Daddy and wanted to come along. When I picked them up after work on Friday afternoons, they came running out of the house, shouting "Daddy! Daddy!" Cathy would jump into my arms while Sue stood back. I would put Cathy down and hug

Susan. They fought over who would sit in the front seat next to me and giggled as I drove away.

"What first?" I would ask.

They would both scream out, "Burger King!"

Charlene did not cook and had a habit of forgetting to feed the kids when involved in some project or reading a book. The kids said Grandma Inez was starving them to death. Well, not exactly. As you recall, Inez, Evans, and Charlene thought processed foods destroyed people's health. Rice, yogurt, cheese, and lentil bean soup were good. Ice cream was bad. Not exactly an eating philosophy guaranteed to please little kids.

Perhaps they were right, but I was raised in a family that ate fried food, Wonder Bread, and drank Cokes as well as beer and whiskey.

I would take the kids to Burger King, and they would stuff themselves with burgers, French fries, and milk shakes. Charlene said nothing about the trips but when she occasionally joined us, she ate the burgers and fries and drank a milkshake.

Next, we would pick up Mom from work, around six o'clock. Then it was Dad and Ga-Ga's time with the kids. They fed them, played cards, and watched TV. I carefully tried to protect them from my father's alpha behavior. He assumed, much like Evans and Charlene, that he was smarter than all other human beings, particularly when he was drunk. Occasionally I had a reasonable conversation with him in the early morning hours before breakfast. He had his first drink before sunrise and sipped whiskey most of the day. He saved his heavy drinking for the late afternoons and early evenings. He usually stumbled off to bed around ten o'clock.

Whoopee! The kids were now in charge of the TV. The sound of "Daddy!" echoed in my ears all evening long. I enjoyed teasing them, but eventually, I rolled over on the pullout couch, or divan, as my mother and father called it, and placed a pillow over my head as they watched various silly programs. Charlene did not allow a TV in her house—today, I know she was frightened she might become a binge-watcher.

On Saturday mornings, I rose early to take Mother to work so I could use her car. I usually stopped for a drive-through breakfast before returning home. Normally Dad cooked breakfast for the girls while I had another cup of coffee. He cooked a traditional Oklahoma breakfast: eggs fried in bacon fat, Wonder Bread or pancakes, home fries, flour gravy, and plenty of jelly and jam.

After breakfast, I took the girls to local parks with ponds, and we spent the morning feeding the ducks and driving to spots they wanted to see. I fed them giant burgers and fries for lunch. Then I took them to a theater, always one with a double feature and cartoons. Naturally, I gave each a dollar to buy popcorn, candy, or a soft drink. Susan, as I had, wanted to buy her own treats. The Carnation Ice Cream Shop became their favorite stop after the movies. Cathy was like my brother—I couldn't let her cut the cake because she would always take the bigger piece. By five o'clock we were back at Safeway to pick up my mother.

After we got home, I did not stay for dinner. I seldom ate with my parents, and instead took the opportunity to have some time away from the kids after a hectic day. I did not lie to them, instead informing them if I didn't get some alone time, I would turn into an evil villain. Around six o'clock, I took off to eat at a local bar, drink a beer, and play a few games of pool. I returned to my parents' house around ten, and the three of us played games with the grandparents until they went to bed. Then we pulled out the couch bed, and I let the kids watch TV most of the night. They were with Daddy now and did not have to obey Charlene's rules.

Darrell remained with Charlene for about fourteen months before he split. The kids told me they constantly hissed and yelled at each other. Occasionally, Charlene physically attacked him. Both were extremely jealous and accused each other of cheating. Thankfully, Darrell did not disappear from Susan's life.

Charlene's parents moved into her house in Montebello and brought all their old junk along with them. Inez took care of the children while Charlene went to school or off on a wild adventure, disappearing for days. Evans paid the rent. The house quickly became a hoarder's paradise with most rooms and the two-car garage crammed full of "valuables." Inez's kitchen was the exception. If an appliance broke, they ignored it; if the plumbing backed up, they turned off the water; if the roof leaked, they put out buckets. They knew if the landlord ever saw the mess, they could be ejected. No one except family, a group that included me and Darrell, was allowed in the house. I continued to pick up the kids on Friday afternoons, but I seldom saw Charlene or Evans.

※

During the weeks when I had no classes, I became a wanderer. Happy to be alone, I seldom talked to anyone. I rode empty buses around the city late at night, reading books and staring out the window watching the world go by. One time, I took a train to San Francisco, walked around the downtown area, and returned to the station to take the train home. Twelve hours. It was a two-book trip.

Part of this was driven by my need to deeply analyze how my character and behavior contributed to the failure of my marriage. For the first few months, I suffered from rejection syndrome. Maybe if I had done this or that, I thought, she might have loved me more.

Ha!

As I continued to review my life with Charlene, I realized the first thing I needed to accept was that I had gotten involved with a woman who was totally different from me in temperament and character. Enamored with her intellect and cultural knowledge, I had failed to recognize her as a self-centered narcissist.

Slowly, I realized our characters did not match. I was a good, kind, gentle person with a great deal of empathy for others. I was not an ideal mate for many women, even those who proclaimed they were looking for a man like me.

Many women are attracted to the "stud," the confident, aggressive male who takes charge—in my mother's words, "a feisty man." The macho male is often surrounded by a circle of female friends eager to become his mate. Many women prefer a good fighter rather than a man who sits and takes it. They prefer a man who fights the banker, the lawyer, and the candlestick maker. He is the boss in the family.

I do not want to be a macho man, but I accept no other boss but me for me. My absolute rule is: "Do not tell me what to do. Ask me politely—and remember to say thank you." I take advice, but I make my own decisions. My second rule is reciprocity, i.e., I try to follow the above rule myself when dealing with others.

I like kind, considerate people and expect those around me to be kind and generous. Some people consider kindness to be a character flaw—a trait of a loser who lives to be taken advantage of. Givers give; takers take. Takers believe a person who picks up the check is a damn fool.

I respect people who stand up for family and friends, but I never forget the basic rule of life is survival. I do not walk away from my duty to fight my own fights, but I do not assume the obligation to fight all comers.

I have been a damn fool many times, but I learned over the years to avoid takers. When I become friendly with an acquaintance, I often pay for the first few beers, but a person who does not reciprocate is crossed off my list as a future friend. Over the years I have learned to be careful. When I accurately recognize a "taker," I feel lucky. Charlene was a taker who took advantage of my character, but I learned my lesson. Unfortunately, it is a lesson I had to relearn dozens of times.

Gradually, I took a more charitable view of Charlene. Perhaps I was also at fault. Perhaps Charlene was not the only one with sexual preferences. Perhaps from her perspective, I was the one with the problem. Perhaps Charlene wanted a man who would fight with her. Shouting was not part of my character, but I have known many marriages where verbal sparring was an integral part of the relationship.

I lived with a woman I thought I loved. When I discovered she was fucking another man, or men, I did not fight to keep her. My response was to accept the situation. I always assumed if I had to fight for a woman's love, she was not a woman I wanted to love.

What went wrong?

There were many signals indicating Charlene was different from me, times when I should have thrown up my hands and walked away. But "I was one and twenty, no use to talk to me," as Kipling delightfully noted.

A big signal: Charlene had no girlfriends. She attended group meetings, but she never stopped for coffee with any woman. She did not go to the movies or shop with anyone except her mother. And over the years I associated with her, she had no women friends. She's now eighty, and her daughters are the only women in her life.

She also had few social skills. One example is how she treated my parents the first time we went to their house for dinner. She barely talked to them, acting as if knowing a couple of hicks from Oklahoma was beneath her dignity. She did not help my mother in the kitchen nor did she set the table or help wash the dishes. Instead, she sat in front of the TV all evening. When we met other friends of mine, such as the manager of the shoe store and his wife and child, she acted the same way. I remember thinking that maybe she was not very accomplished in the social arena and was simply uncomfortable. I failed to recognize her thoughts and actions revolved around her and what she wanted. She had little empathy for anyone. But when she wanted to, she could mesmerize almost anyone.

Another signal: In the first two months of our relationship, she never introduced me to her mother and father. When I finally visited her house, I saw tons of boxes crammed into their living room. I knew they were hoarders. It never occurred to me Charlene was also a hoarder.

And the list goes on. During our courtship, there were dozens of such signals. For some reason, I did not notice them. Charlene did not hide herself—I was willfully blindfolded. Thus, I admit my misery was my own damn fault.

As I examined my marriage over the decades that followed, I slowly learned my lessons. I swore any serious involvement with any woman (or any friendly acquaintances regardless of sex) would be with a kind and considerate person. I decided I did not want to become involved with a woman, even an "intelligent woman," who wanted to boss me around. They wouldn't have a superior attitude toward me, nor would I to them. The fight should not be between lovers; the fight should be with the outside world. "Us against them," not "us against us."

I did not want a woman who is a lousy roommate. I wanted someone who likes an organized, clean house, and does her share of the mundane chores.

I did not want to become involved with a woman who dreams of having children. One or two was enough of a drain on my emotions (and pocketbook).

I did not wish to become involved with a woman who didn't work. I believe each person must contribute in order to buy the toys so desperately desired in modern life. "Must-haves" extend to eternity, even if often classified as necessities, from cars to computers to cell phones to a college education. *Want that?* Great—earn it. Paying your own way gives a person independence and prevents Type A personalities from dominating the household. If someone pisses me off, I told myself, I can and will leave. I can take care of myself.

Before my marriage to Charlene, I liked intelligent, confident, good-looking girls. It never occurred to me that my mate would not also be a kind and considerate person who would enjoy being touched as much as I enjoy touching. When a cat meows for affection, my heart sings.

Chapter 16

Master Stencil Cutter

This lonely period lasted for five or six years. But despite the ups and downs in my personal life, I always attended school with a determination few could match. I rarely skipped a class—or work. My troubles with romance aside, I was still learning other important life lessons.

In the spring of 1962, I began looking for another job. An obvious option was the other major gravestone company in Los Angeles, Pacific Stone & Monument, which made markers for most of the city's Protestant cemeteries. I heard they were looking for stencil cutters, so I called and arranged for a job interview. I agreed to work a (paid) day to illustrate my skills.

Pacific Stone & Monument was a conglomerate that provided granite, marble, and gravel for construction and other applications. They owned about forty acres in an industrial zone near Alhambra with various yards for different purposes. The gravestone business occupied about five acres and had a separate entrance. All the gravestones came pre-cut and polished.

The administrative buildings gave the appearance of an enlarged, semi-permanent construction site: several old, wooden, single-storied buildings linked together by a deck. The buildings housed the paper pushers from several company divisions.

The foreman met me in the driveway at nine a.m. and escorted me to one of the buildings. Having arrived in a reception area, we passed two secretaries to reach the manager's office. The manager rose, shook hands, and we sat down. Like most administrators, he wore dress clothes; his white shirt had a plastic pen holder, and a jacket draped over the back of his desk chair. He had no need to impress me, though. This was a business relationship, boss to worker, nothing personal.

I came dressed in working man's clothes: blue jeans, a flannel shirt, and work shoes. I had my tools in a carry box. The foreman was dressed in his work clothes.

The manager interviewed me much as he would interview someone for a clerk's job. "How many years of experience do you have?" "Why do you want to change jobs?" etc. I had been through the dance before but this time I was not applying for a clerk's job. There were few master stencil cutters in L.A., and I knew it. I was now a tradesman in a select group, with the same skill level as bricklayers, plumbers, painters, and electricians. I felt my craft could feed me anywhere in the country for the rest of my life. And, in the end, the foreman would decide whether I got the job.

We agreed on a salary of $3.50 an hour, a dollar more than I was making at Vega's. The additional money was important but I had conditions. I was still chasing my dream of getting a college education. Through all the emotional turmoil in my personal life, I still managed to take two or three courses every semester for four years, and I expected to get my AA in in June 1962 and transfer the credits to Cal State. The money from this job meant I could work part-time, go to school full-time, and cover tuition, books, and child support. I guaranteed the manager if I were hired, I would work twenty-five to thirty hours a week. But I would have to pick the hours to fit my class schedules. When needed, I would work Saturdays. Side benefits? Not expected and not mentioned.

To my surprise, they agreed to my terms. The manager informed me three of their current cutters went to college part-time, and their "golden boy," Johnny, had the same agreement. Eventually I agreed to work Monday, Wednesday, and Friday from 1:30 to 5 p.m., and Tuesday and Thursday from 8 a.m. to 5 p.m. Since I punched a timeclock, I could come late if necessary.

Even with the agreement in place, getting the job depended on my skill as a stencil cutter. Around 9:45, the foreman escorted me from the manager's officer to where the stencil cutters worked. We crossed two to three acres of barren yard; stones and construction vehicles were scattered around the area. The stencil room was part of large metal shed about two hundred yards wide and a hundred yards deep. Under the metal roof, several hundred polished headstones were stacked in piles according to size and color. Several dozen bags of silica sand were piled near the sandblasting shed. The stencil room was enclosed in the rear of the larger shed. Unlike at Vega's, the room was heated and had window air conditioners for the hot summer months in L.A.

The stencil room was large, perhaps 1,000 square feet. There were five stencil drawing tables used as cutting desks. A raised metal track with rollers allowed stones to be rolled into the room from outside and distributed to the cutters. The layout section stretched the width of the room, along a wall where the stones were taped and stamped with patterns and lettering. Letters from old printing presses were laid out here. The letters were copied onto strips of carbon paper about 6 inches wide and then transferred to the stencil. The letters came in sizes of three-quarters of an inch and two inches, and included Roman and Modern styles. At Vega's the cutter taped and laid out his own stones, but here the foreman taped the stones, stamped the pattern on the tape as well as the appropriate letters, and sent the stone down the rollers to a stencil cutter. The process of laying out each stone took about fifteen minutes. Once the stencil cutter finished a stone, he placed it back on the rollers and shoved it down the track toward the sandblaster's shed.

Two stencil cutters were at work, both young men who were about twenty-five years old. One cutter was out sick, the foreman said with a sneer, making it obvious the man had skipped many days of work.

Johnny, the golden boy, was away serving six months in the air force reserve to avoid the draft. The fear of being drafted for Vietnam was in the air. As a father and soon-to-be full-time college student, it was not something I had to worry about. John, as he preferred to be called, was apparently around twenty-four and also a part-time student. He had begun working at Pacific while he was in high school.

The cherry on top was that Cassidy had trained him. At the mention of this name, my ears perked up. Evans, notorious for criticizing other stencil cutters, praised Cassidy as among the best. He and Evans were part of the small group of cutters who came from the glass shading business and considered themselves artisans. The two had worked together in the glass industry and introduced the sandblasting technique to the monument business. Cassidy had cut Pacific's master patterns as Evans had cut Vega's.

When I met John several months later, I realized the foreman's praise was justified. He was a happy, confident young man from a middle-class family. He had no intention of being a stencil cutter the rest of his life, and in that trait, we were compatible. He lived with his parents in an upscale suburb in Alhambra. His apartment was a separate suite which included a bathroom and huge walk-in closet. He was obviously a good roommate. His parents wanted him to stay in the house until he graduated and started his own family. In my opinion, Johnny deserved all the praise heaped on him. He treated everyone at work as if they were special. He often went to the main office to tease the secretaries, and he was a favorite of the "boss man." He attended the University of Southern California, but he was in no hurry to graduate. He was in the midst of what he considered his fun years. With plenty of money in his pocket, he drove a new Mustang.

We shook hands when he returned from the air force reserve. He asked with a grin, "Is it true you worked with Evans?" Apparently Cassidy had described Evans as the only other artisan cutter in the Los Angeles area. Go figure. As time passed, John and I came to consider each other equals as stencil cutters. I was better at academics, but he had more impressive social skills.

On my trial day, I shocked the foreman and the other two cutters. When it was time to start, the foreman proudly showed me John's cutting desk, assuming I'd want to sit there. It had the best light and was near the windows, air conditioners, and heating vents.

Instead I selected the most isolated desk. It had a metal rolling track in front of it, and another one directly behind. The fluorescent lighting, though, was excellent. From my traveling toolbox, I retrieved a half dozen knives, sharpening stones, and several measuring devices used in the trade. The other cutters relied on company knives and tools, but I owned mine. When I occasionally worked for small monument companies on weekends, I needed my tools, but the work was not reliable.

A headstone came down the rollers to my station, and I lifted it off the tracks and placed it on my desk. The foreman had laid out the stencil with a normal headstone pattern and lettering. I had cut a hundred comparable stones at Vega's, and for me, it was a boring gravestone to cut. Although anyone can cut stencil, a professional cutter is comparable to a professional house painter. All a cutter or a painter has to do is cut along the lines. Easy? No. What I could do in an hour would take most people a day, and my cuts would be vastly superior and sharper. Speed was the secret of being a good cutter.

I worked at my normal speed. Forty-five minutes later, I placed the stone on the roller tracks and pushed it toward the stone-blasting shed.

The foreman came over, looked at my work, and nodded his approval. The other stonecutters stopped their work and looked over at me. Another stone came down the track, and I finished it in forty-five minutes. The other two cutters were still working on their first stone.

"Can you cut block lettering?" the foreman asked.

I nodded.

It took him ten minutes to bring in a granite stone about twice the size of a normal headstone. After putting on the tape and tapping on the pattern, he shoved the stone down to me.

The design was of a Bible, with the book's spine separating the layout into two equal sides. This was a double marker: one side for the husband, the other for the wife. Each side had three lines. The first was the "Beloved" line (e.g., "Beloved Husband & Father"), made up of letters three-quarters of an inch high; the second was the name line (e.g., "Charles W. Young"), one-and-a-quarter inches high; the third was the date line (e.g., "1910-1962"). Additionally, the letters were cut on a slant to conform to the look of an open Bible.

The problem for most cutters was that there were no letters stamped on the stencil. Knowing how to work with block letters was a basic skill of master stencil cutters who copied different styles from old gravestones. The letters, not restricted by any printer capability, could be any size or width. The average cutter used a compass and divider to lay out letters. Some then used a pencil to draw them in.

I looked at the stone and got to work. I blocked the letters on the stencil then free cut them. I was the fastest and best block letter cutter in L.A., even faster than Evans, who had taught me. Evans was slower because he never stayed at his station for an hour to finish any cut. I would find this also to be true of John.

I finished the Bible cut in one hour, pulled it off my desk, and put it on the rollers.

Everything in the shop came to a halt. The foreman had given me the Bible stone because most cutters took three or four hours to make the cuts it required. When the company was short-handed, it often took two or three weeks before there was open time for block-lettered stones.

Over the next six hours, I cut more stone than the other two cutters combined. In the next four years, I never slowed down. I needed the job, and as always, time went faster when I worked steadily.

I took the job and gave Old Man Vega a week's notice. His response, controlled anger, did not surprise me. His life revolved around his business and family. His workers were part of his greater family, and from his point of view, I was being disloyal. "Work hard for the good of family and business" was his motto. Although he knew I was going to school, he assumed his company was more important than my dream.

"Why?" he asked. I told him I would get paid $3.50 an hour and would be able to choose my own hours. I did not tell him of my family problems. That was none of his business.

"Hell, son," he said, 'I would have given you all that. Even more, if you had asked."

Yeah, sure. I knew the old man would expect me to skip classes or drop out of college for the good of his business. As for the money, he had just admitted to underpaying me a dollar an hour for over a year. My loyalty was not to him but to me. Leaving Vega's also helped me escape from an awkward situation with my former father-in-law.

At Pacific Monument, unlike at Vega's, I cut the same designs and lettering day after day. The only way to control the boredom was to work hard. The faster I worked, the quicker the day passed. This irritated the other cutters, who took long bathroom breaks or simply stopped working to bullshit when the foreman left, as he often did. Even when present, the foreman allowed the cutters to loaf rather than work. I kept him busy shoving new markers down for me to cut. The days still dragged on, and I began to proclaim that "trained monkeys" could do the job. I missed the days at Vega's when I occasionally worked on projects normally reserved for Evans. I wanted to work on large monuments where the design and lettering had to be laid out on heavy rubber stencil. At Pacific, I felt less like a craftsman and more like a robot. I felt like a master carpenter condemned to make the same twenty coffee tables all his life. "Let me make a few chairs, please," he'd beg.

I stayed on the job because stencil cutting paid more money than selling shoes and gave me more leverage with management. I was a trained craftsman. Money is money, and you work for it. The job paid for my college education and provided enough money for child support.

The other stencil cutters also often irritated me. I liked them, but they were young men who were in "good-time" mode, not survival mode, like I was. After work on Fridays, we cashed our checks at a crowded blue-collar bar. It was a noisy place with at least a hundred men celebrating the end of the workweek. The long bar had forty stools for drinkers. A dozen tables were in front of the bar for those eating, and in the back, six coin-operated pool tables. I had a good time playing 8 ball on the smaller tables and having a couple beers with the boys. Chums? Perhaps, but more like friendly acquaintances.

The three other cutters were all young men from middle-class families, still single and living with their parents. All were occasional college students who expected to return to school sometime in the future. They enjoyed having spending money in their pockets, drove nice cars, and partied hard on the weekends. Each considered stencil cutting merely a stopover job. On weekends, they searched for girls, drank a few beers, and looked for a good time. Their antics around the pool table made me laugh simply because they were juvenile—not annoying but the shouting and posturing of barroom humor.

Johnny was the leader of the group and jazzed things up with his constant teasing. I admired him for his abilities as well as his good humor. He enjoyed his bachelor years before he settled down.

Ten years later, he owned a construction company and was married with two kids. He invited me to his house for lunch and insisted I come with him and fly in his Piper Cub, as he had a pilot's license. I enjoyed the flight, but he scared me when he cut the motor at 5,000 feet to prove the plane would glide rather than fall out of the air if the motor failed. John was still Johnny.

Jim Friend, one of the other cutters, was in his mid-twenties. He looked like a guard or tackle on a college football team. To his dismay, he was going bald in front. He had a calm personality, and although he participated in the poolroom antics, he was an easygoing man. I felt he was an honorable person and considered him a friendly acquaintance.

Then, there was my nemesis: Pete Peterman. He was a bantam fighting rooster much like the ones in our back pastures when I lived on I Street in Lawton. He was around five feet, six inches tall, with blond hair, a pleasant face, and a lean, muscular body. I am sure many girls found his physique impressive.

Unfortunately, his social and political views were the absolute opposite of mine. I never try to convert the unconvertible. On the other hand, Pete talked and talked while we worked. His conservative German parents pounded chauvinistic views into his head, and he willingly spit them back out to anyone within earshot. All people on social welfare were lazy bums; all races were inferior to Caucasians; and Germans were socially, intellectually, and physically superior to the Irish, more intelligent than the clannish Jews, and better lovers than Frenchmen. He bragged about his barroom fistfights, attacked the Kennedys and Johnson, and favored bombing Russia. Joe McCarthy was his hero.

For fun, John egged him on, particularly when Pete bragged about his beautiful girlfriend.

Day after day, Pete talked. Occasionally I felt the need to respond, but mostly I ignored him. I developed a partial solution—meditation. Charlene had exposed me to Buddhism, and I retained my interest over the next few years as I learned the art of mediation. I could not chant the Lotus Sutra, but I knew vibrating sounds help black out sound as well as thought. Meditation is the art of achieving silence. I quietly hummed "hummmmmm" to give myself a break in the stencil room. When necessary, I hummed louder and louder to drive Pete out of my mind.

The first time my humming grew to massive decibel levels, all work in the shop stopped—and Pete shut-up.

"Kenny, what in the hell are you doing?" the foreman shouted.

I stopped humming, looked at him and others in the shop.

"I am drowning Pete's voice out of my mind. Otherwise, I might turn around and pop him in the head."

Silence. I returned to work. A few minutes passed. Pete started talking again, and I started humming.

I sincerely hoped my six-year-old daughter never got involved with such an opinionated man. (She did—and I reminded her to hum silently when he talked.)

It is difficult to hum all day. Occasionally, I turned around and snapped out a rejoinder. Pete grinned. He loved to piss me off, the person who seldom displayed any temper.

One day something happened that gagged Pete for a few days. He dated the same girl for months, and each day he told us over and over again about how beautiful she was, how great she was in bed, and how smart she was. He showed us pictures of a beautiful, tall, blonde-haired woman. "And she's German," he said, proudly.

There is only so much bullshit I can take. I turned around one day and said, "Pete, you know she wipes her ass just like the rest of us?"

Pete sputtered, anger spreading across his face. Apparently she *didn't* go to the bathroom like the rest of us. Ignoring him, I turned around and got back to work. I expected Pete to call me an asshole for the next hour and threaten to beat the shit out of me after work.

I didn't get what I expected but neither did Pete. Without saying a word, he stood and walked over to the shop's coffee pot, one of those big old metal pots that brewed twelve cups. I did not notice him.

"Wham!" He threw the coffee pot, hitting me in the back of the head.

Remember my rule: "Don't attack me or surprise me by hitting me from behind."

Without a thought, I leaped over the railing separating our stations and charged toward my attacker.

I was five-nine, weighed 140 pounds, and was twenty-four years old. Pete was five-six, weighed 130 pounds, and was also twenty-four.

He backed away, suddenly scared with what he had done. John grabbed him and looked at me, requesting with his eyes that I back off. Fortunately, the thirty seconds I required to return to normal had passed. I become calm and formal in tense situations.

I looked at Pete, nodded okay, turned around and went back to work. Today, I wished I had said, "Sorry Pete, my remark was inappropriate." I said nothing, but I knew it was my fault. My mother would have loved it. "Feisty," she would have said. Fortunately, over the next fifty years no one else attacked me from behind.

For the next few days, Pete and I were polite, ignoring what had happened. On Friday, we cashed our checks, played pool, and had a few beers. Within a couple of weeks, Pete was back to talking and I was back to humming.

Over the next few years, Pacific lived up to their promises. As long as I informed them, I could choose my hours, and if necessary, take a day, a week, or even a month off.

My work life was stable. Other issues, though, were banging on my door.

Chapter 17

The Yo-Yo Years

After living six months in a trailer park, in June 1961 I moved to an unfurnished second-floor apartment. It was near the corner of Whittier and Atlantic, two of the busiest commercial streets in East Los Angeles. I chose it for its convenience; I could take a bus to work, and another bus to school. It was unfurnished except for a stove and refrigerator. The price was sixty dollars a month and included utilities except the telephone. Rent was due once a month with no lease agreement. This was usual in East L.A. Most landlords did not make tenants sign a year's lease, require first and last month's rent, or a security deposit.

To find low-cost furniture I searched the bulletin boards at nearby supermarkets and scrambled around at yard sales. At one of them I bought a desk, chest of drawers, a table, and a bed set with a good mattress. The items were inexpensive but of good quality. If I could have predicted the future, I would have slept on the floor and ate standing up.

I also bought my first car. Manufactured in Britain in 1947, it was a cheap copy of a Morris Minor. The small engine took a half mile to get up to fifty-five miles per hour and its top speed was around sixty. When I drove on the freeways, the situation could be scary. The upholstery was relatively new, and the gearshift was five on the floor. The turn signals were manual—i.e., to indicate a right turn, I raised a hand lever, and a little arrow popped out on the right fender to signal "right turn"; another lever signaled left turns. I used hand signals instead, a not-uncommon practice then. I had a love-hate relationship with the car. Like the VW Beetle of later years, there were many minor things that failed, although I could make some repairs myself. Why did I buy the car? It was $250, a price I could afford. And it lasted over two years.

During my marriage problems, I seldom saw my brother. He had recently quit his job at the Sacramento location of Regal's Shoe Company and moved back to Los Angeles. During the three years he lived in Sacramento, his wife, Tina, begged him to get a job in L.A., where her family lived. He finally gave in and obtained an assistant manager's position at a retail outlet of the Brown Shoe Company in a new mall in Lakewood. Downtown retail stores were closing as national chains moved to the new shopping centers in the suburbs where parking was free. With interstate highways slowly growing, many exits had gigantic malls that squeezed out many local and downtown businesses.

My brother was having money problems. With a wife and two young children and a third on the way, his salary was not covering his expenses. Housing was more expensive in Lakewood than in Sacramento. He expected to become the store manager in three to four months and a raise along with it. He did not ask me for money, though. Instead, he asked, "How much is your rent?"

"$60."

"Great!" he said. "Just about how much I need." He wanted me to move in with his family for three or four months to help cover his expenses.

Inconvenient? Damn right. Lakewood was thirty miles from both my work and East L.A. Community College.

Reluctantly, I agreed. He had rented a house with two bedrooms and two baths. He and Tina used one bedroom, and his two young daughters, one still in diapers, lived in the other bedroom. I moved my bed, chest, and clothes into the detached garage and shared a bathroom near the back door of the house. For all this I was paying $50; the other $10 went toward extra gas money for my car. Three months seemed like a long time. I seldom saw my brother because he worked sixty hours a week, but I did see Tina, pregnant but still pretty, although hassled by two young daughters hanging onto her skirt.

I did something unusual that fall semester: I enrolled in one course at East L.A. and two courses at Long Beach Community College, which was closer to Lakewood. The credits were transferable. Long Beach's campus buildings were traditional and better-maintained than the temporary buildings at East L.A. The first class was on British literature, from Chaucer to Shakespeare. I liked the course and enjoyed the change of atmosphere. The second class was on Greek and Roman architecture.

In early December, after my brother got his promotion and raise, I said *adios* to living in a garage and driving thirty miles to work in a car that could barely reach 60 mph. I found another apartment in Montebello. It was a studio apartment built over a garage with a large walk-in closet. For the next seven months, I enjoyed the comfort, quiet, and solitude it provided.

Although I saw my parents almost every week, we never talked about financial or personal problems. I would hug my mother, and then she would immediately turn her attention on Cathy. I never talked to my father. I just nodded. He continued to think of me as a young boy who did not have the fighting spirit of Young family men. I was his "wimpy, educated idiot." (Remember, my portrait did not hang above the couch in the living room.) I heard his criticism, but long ago I lost any desire to gain my father's approval, so I just tuned him out. More bluntly, I did not really give a shit what he thought. But he was still my father, so I tried to be polite. I seldom argued with him.

Over the years, my parents moved many times, usually for the same reason: My father was an alcoholic who got into horrendous arguments with the neighbors. "Get your damn car out of my parking place!" he shouted. "Turn down that shitty music!" "Are you too stupid to hit the garbage pail, you asshole"?" He was so obnoxious that within six months none of the neighbors talked to him. Then, my parents would move.

One weekend, my mother pulled me aside. "Son," she said, "I need your help."

"Okay," I responded. "Any way I can."

"I need you to move in with us for a few months," she said.

I looked at my mother as if she were crazy. "Move in with you and Dad?" I asked, shaking my head.

My father had lost his job. His work as bartender-manager at a bar on the outskirts of Pasadena had come to an end after eight years. He often bragged about the money he made there. One Saturday night I picked him up at the bar at 3 a.m. when his car broke down. The bar was huge, with several pool tables, a jukebox, and a stage for live music on the weekends. Hamburgers and hotdogs with French fries were the normal meals. It was a bar where working men came to cash their paychecks, a place where good old boys played 8 ball and had a few beers, or, if you were a hardcore drinker, numerous shots of cheap whiskey. Only wives and good old girls were welcome. It wasn't a pickup place. That night when I arrived, a couple of older men were drinking at the bar. Dad did not have a closing time for his cronies.

My brother visited more often. "Perfect place for Dad. He's in charge, and he enjoys that role." With a gleam of pride in his eyes, my brother recounted how our father had broken the nose of a loudmouth braggart during one of his visits. According to Corky, Dad's technique was to throw the first blow. Swinging a billy club or blackjack, he cracked the loudmouth upside the head. "Hell," he said to my brother, who looked down at the man on the floor. "One blow is enough. Ain't no bother after that." Dad also kept a sawed-off shotgun under the bar. My brother hinted that Dad skimmed money. He winked when he said it, but I believe he admired Dad for his initiative.

Moving back in with my father was a hard decision, but my mother needed my help. My father had lost his job four months earlier. They never mentioned this development when I brought Cathy over for the weekend. Why did he lose it? I never asked, but it was serious enough to prevent him from getting another job as a bartender. For the rest of his life he held part-time jobs, from taxicab driver to driving an ice cream truck through neighborhoods ringing his bell and shouting out to kids, "Come and get your ice cream!" Mostly he drank, and Mother earned the money for the family. She seldom bemoaned the situation or said a negative word about Dad.

About three months before he was fired, my parents had moved to a large house near his job. Mother had to drive farther to work, but this did not disturb my father, of course. They signed a year's lease with a month's rent as a security deposit. The rent was $150 a month. The house was in a nice neighborhood, had three bedrooms, two and a half baths, and gigantic dining and living rooms. The floors were varnished hardwood planks, and the moldings were stained, not painted. The kitchen was dated but better and larger than the kitchens in other places my parents had lived. In the rear was an old double-car garage and a sizeable backyard.

Mother said the lease ended in about four months. It would help if I moved in and paid $60 a month in rent. She must have been talking to my brother. This time, though, I was not going to live in the garage. Mom showed me the master bedroom with its own bathroom, walk-in closet, and separate entrance. The room was larger than my entire apartment. The house was farther from my job and school, but I decided I had no choice.

The four months were less stressful than I expected. When I was home, I stayed in my room most of the time. I read assigned books, wrote papers on my portable Remington, and studied for tests. I attended school full-time and worked thirty hours a week. I did not watch TV, ate alone in my room. and cleaned up after myself, which included washing my own clothes. Dad strutted around the house in his underwear. Mom and I sometimes took walks around the neighborhood in the late afternoons. And Cathy, often with Susan, was there on weekends.

I moved out of Mom's house in early January 1963 to a place that became my home for three years. It was a small, unfurnished room attached to a garage behind a two-story white colonial house on a lovely tree-lined street in Alhambra. The owners lived in the house, but I rarely saw them. I spent many afternoons in the backyard under a shade tree reading books. The location was ideal. The room was about a mile to Pacific and a mile in the opposite direction to Cal State's campus. When I did not have a car, I walked to school because the campus was on a high hill, unusual in L.A., and the bike ride was harder than the walk.

The room was built to rent out to Cal State students. It did not have a kitchen, but there was a small bathroom with a shower and a bifold closet for my clothes. I already had the bed, desk, and chest of drawers. The rent was only $25 a month, including utilities and local phone calls.

Free at last! With newfound passion, I began to chase my dream of becoming a scholar.

Chapter 18

My Dream World

My dream world was college.

I had dreamed of obtaining a college education since I was in junior high, and I felt taking a break from school for any reason could lead to a slow withdrawal. I did not want to mow lawns, pick peaches, sell shoes, or cut stencils for the rest of my life.

Through elementary, middle, and high school, I was an excellent student. Perhaps not the most intelligent one, but I worked hard and enjoyed learning. Education was my way off the bottom, a way to maintain my dignity. If I got a BA, I would be a success in life even if I did not improve my economic situation. A college degree meant I accomplished something no one else in my extended family had achieved.

This dream world lasted from the fall of 1958 to June 1966. But it began with some bumps. Before I learned Charlene was pregnant with Catherine, I had enrolled in a course on reading and comprehension at East L.A. While I was adjusting to my marriage, though, I did not devote enough time to the course and made a C (community colleges did not give out plus and minus grades). Disappointed, I decided not to take a course in the spring of the following year, given all the hassles that come with a new baby, due in April. That summer, however, I took another course, and in the fall of 1959, three night courses, making A's in all three. In the spring of 1960, I felt life was settled enough that I could take four night courses. Although I made three As and one B, the four courses, in addition to my work commitments, stretched my relationship with Charlene. It was during that semester she started her affair with Darrell.

Despite the trials and tribulations of my married life, over the next two years I averaged three courses a semester and one summer course. In the spring of 1962, I took my final two courses at East L.A. and applied for graduation.

While I was applying, an assistant registrar pulled my records and examined them. Suddenly she said, "Oh! Oh!" Then she stood up from her chair. "I will be right back."

Had I miscalculated my earned credits? Would I be denied graduation? Thirty minutes passed before she returned to the office. She sat in her chair, fumbled with a few papers, then said, "We have a problem."

I nodded, dreading the worst. She was a nice lady who seemed concerned about my situation.

Finally, she laid it on me: "Last week we submitted the graduation program to the printer, and your name cannot be added to the list now."

"Does that mean I can't graduate?"

"No. It means your name will not be in the program for your friends and family to see."

I breathed in relief. I had no intention of even going to graduation. Wearing a gown, sitting in a hot auditorium, and listening to speeches loaded with platitudes again was not my idea of fun. Since my name was Young, I certainly did not wish to stand in an alphabetized line as three or four hundred students walked across the stage ahead of me to receive diplomas. I had not told my parents or brother of my pending graduation. "Big deal," my Dad would have said.

"There is another problem," said the assistant registrar, concern in her voice. "I just checked with the registrar and we examined your transcripts."

I nodded. Here it comes.

"You can't be valedictorian. Another student's name is in the printed program and is scheduled to speak. The program can't be changed."

"What?"

"As you know, this is the last week to register for June graduation. A staff member jumped the gun and sent the program to the printer last week."

"What?" I still didn't understand her point, but she explained: When she examined my grades, she noticed that my GPA was higher than the student named in the program as the valedictorian. But it couldn't be changed.

Even back in the day, it seemed inconceivable a 3.5 GPA was the highest in East L.A. Community College's class of June 1962. The teachers were demanding and hard graders, but East L.A. had a student body of about 20,000. How many were graduating with an associate of arts degree? I had no idea.

The assistant registrar suggested I delay and instead apply for a February 1963 graduation, where I would be valedictorian.

Not me, my friend. I realized valedictorian sounds nice, but for me it wouldn't change anything. I never applied for scholarships, which weren't awarded to part-time students anyway. I was twenty-two years old, married with a child, and from a working-class background. I was just lucky to live in California. Tuition at community and state colleges was not overwhelming. Most semesters, I paid more for textbooks and supplies than tuition. I could not afford a private, prestigious university—nor a state university, if I were graduating community college today. Point being, being valedictorian was nice but not that nice.

That summer I enrolled in a night course at Cal State L.A. taught by Professor Milton Meyer. Over the next few years he became my adviser, and his courses on Southeast Asia and China stimulated my interest in the area. The first course of his I took was on traditional China from the Ch'in dynasty (221 BC–206 BC) to the Ch'ing dynasty (1644–1911). For the first time, I was exposed to Chinese philosophies (Taoism, Legalism, and Confucianism). Professor Meyer was a sound teacher, a Yale graduate who had once been in the State Department, and the author of several textbooks on China, India, Japan, and Southeast Asia. He did not waste my time, and over three years I took nearly every course he taught at Cal State on Asian societies.

Switching jobs from Vega's to Pacific allowed me to attend Cal State full-time. Every year over the next three years, I took four courses in the fall, four in the spring, and two summer courses. I had discovered history was easier for me than algebra or chemistry, so I decided to major in it, specializing in U.S. history.

⁕

Over the years, whenever I mention I was a history major, many people groan. They hated history in middle school and high school. The teachers and textbooks were boring, and all the tests required memorization. Can you name all the presidents from George Washington to Donald Trump? Do you know George Clinton and the Erie Canal, Henry Clay, Daniel Webster, John Calhoun, William Sherman, or William Jennings Bryan? And why should you care? It's seems like irrelevant information in the modern world.

My interest in U.S. history began in the seventh and eighth grade when I was fortunate to have two good history teachers who emphasized knowing rather than memorization. I did not have another good history teacher until I was a senior in high school.

Administrators believed anyone could teach U.S. history, and as a result, many of my teachers were notoriously unprepared. Often, they were gym teachers required to teach one or two academic courses. Their knowledge of U.S. history was atrocious—I knew more history then them, with one exception. They taught the textbook, using publishers' discussion guides and test questions. They seldom required or recommended any other books. The mantra was "don't think, just memorize" for the upcoming state and national tests.

Boring!

I read the textbooks and memorized the facts. I also read dozens of biographies ranging from Alexander Hamilton to Andrew Jackson to Civil War generals such as Sherman and Grant.

All fields of study require memorization of basic knowledge. How do you know nine times nine is eighty-one? You memorized it. Science, math, and language courses all require memorization. Unfortunately, textbooks destroy students' interest not only in history but in all fields of study. Nevertheless, I discovered history was easier for me than algebra or chemistry formulas. So, I decided to pursue it.

Another response I get when I mention I was a history major in college is an assumption I have expert knowledge in all fields, from United States history through Greek, Roman, European, British, Russian, and sometimes Middle Eastern and Asian history. I certainly know more about Roman, Russian, British, and European history than the average person, but scholars specialize from the broad to the miniscule.

Another question I get is why anyone opts to major in history at the university level. So you know about Hamilton, Aristotle, and Catherine the Great—how does it put money in your pocket? "Go into the technical and scientific areas," I've heard said hundreds of times. Scholars specializing in literature face the same accusatory question.

For me, even today, this is false reasoning. I did not go to college simply to make money. I also wanted to *understand* things; I wanted to read and study great literature and historical events. Each person develops talents, and mine was history. I did not want to be a medical doctor, and I was not fond of advanced mathematics, which eliminated many other fields. I also knew something that is still true today: every Ivy League university and many other universities emphasize knowledge of history, literature, and philosophy for a bachelor's degree. Specialization occurs at the graduate level.

Back in the day, the major did not matter. Obtaining a BA was the end goal. A person who demonstrated the dedication and perseverance to finish college was admired. The courses, except at "Gentlemen's C" colleges, were difficult, and there were far fewer college graduates as a percentage of the population. The big boom, where a third of the population attended college, had not yet reached full force.

A bachelor of arts degree opens doors to companies who have trainee programs, and over the years, the degree generally becomes more valuable than a technical degree. Today, if your undergraduate degree is in computer science, or some other hot technological area, it's likely your beginning salary will greatly exceed the salary of an assistant administrator in the government or business. But if you want to rise in the ranks, a history or literature major is likely to find more success. The techno-craftsman is often frozen in place.

Few companies promote technicians, whether they are computer experts or medical experts, to executive administrative positions. In a dinner meeting with the CEO, they might ask, "What do you think about George Kennan's Containment theory? Did it eventually lead to the Vietnam War?" "Have you read Machiavelli?" "Was Alexander Hamilton really that important in American history?" "FDR started all this social welfare benefit shit, don't you think?" "Teddy was a damn fine president, unlike that weak-kneed Carter, don't you think?" "I hate James Joyce. How about you?"

No one knows everything, but if a candidate for a senior executive job recognizes none of these people, would you consider him qualified for the job? And the list goes on, from Hannibal to Caesar to Justinian to MacArthur to Eisenhower to Churchill and beyond.

Techno-craftsmen are notorious for producing reports the average CEO cannot understand or implement. Give me a history or English major who knows enough about clarity and grammar mechanics to rewrite the report so it is understandable.

From elementary school through community college, I learned the basics in my fields of history and literature with an emphasis on U.S. history. Yes, I can name every president of the United States and discuss the Civil War and the Great Depression among the thousands of other events I memorized. Those were my apprentice years as an amateur historian. They laid the groundwork for my future study.

I enjoyed several of my professors at East L.A., but the school was a feeder community college for Cal State. Accordingly, East L.A. concentrated on the "core" curriculum, and I took many classes outside my fields of interest. I often made A's and B's simply through hard work and rote memorization.

Cal State L.A. was a gigantic school, even back in 1962, with over 30,000 students and an excellent history department. Nearly all the professors had PhDs and were tenured. Several had published scholarly books and articles and had national reputations.

History textbooks had not stimulated my love of history. "Regular" books had. From the Carnegie Library in Lawton through community college I read biographies and accounts of great events in history. I loved small history.

Small history is the true heart and joy of history. At Cal State I was exposed to small history in the classroom. The classes no longer required textbooks covering hundreds of years. Now, professors covered smaller time periods. Class sizes were limited to twenty-five students. Typical U.S. history courses had titles like "The Federalist Era, 1787 to 1801"; "Jefferson to Monroe, 1801 to 1825"; "The Coming of the Civil War, 1820 to 1861"; "The Civil War"; and so on, through to modern times. Professors assigned several books in each course, concentrating on specific topics: "The Constitutional Convention"; "The Federalist Papers"; "Alien and Sedition Acts"; "Lewis and Clark"; "The Era of Good Feelings"; and the like. Several books were required to be read as well as a "professionally" researched and carefully written term paper with extensive footnotes.

The Cal State History Department required a major to take at least ten upper-level history courses. Several of the upper-class courses emphasized research methods and in-depth research. There were a large variety of courses. American history classes dominated, with European history a close second, followed by courses on Russia, China, Japan, India, Southeast Asia, the Middle East, and Latin America. Beyond the ten required courses, the department recommended majors take as many additional history courses as possible, with a sprinkling of classes in related areas such as literature, considered by most historians to be a subset of history.

Cal State initiated my education as a scholar, and I jumped in with a passion. A diligent student, I normally ranked among the top three or four students in every history class. The History Department maintained high standards, and the competition was intense. There were no easy classes. As in high school, many professors graded on a bell curve, and in a class of twenty-five, the maximum number of As was usually three. At Cal State, the professors could give plus grades, and thus with an A-minus included the total might be five or six. Professors were not required to give any A's, so the number could also be much lower. Undergraduates had to maintain a GPA of 2.00. If a student's grade point average dropped below 2.00 for two semesters, they were denied admission—i.e., kicked out of school. At the graduate level, no grade below a B would be credited toward the degree. Many students switched majors as they looked for easier classes.

All history majors took several required U.S. history classes, but each student selected one other area to specialize in. My major was in U.S. history, and I specialized in Asian history courses within this field, taking classes on China, Japan, India, and Southeast Asia. This led to Professor Meyer becoming my adviser, and under his guidance I slowly developed a sub-specialty: American diplomacy in Asia with an emphasis on U.S. military actions, such as the U.S colonialization of the Philippines, 1898 to 1946; the Boxer Rebellion in China; WWII in the Pacific, India, and China; the Korean War; and the escalating U.S. action in Vietnam.

※

During the three years I attended classes at Cal State, every Friday afternoon I diligently picked up Cathy, and Susan if she was available. She often remained with her "other" father. Like always, we stayed Friday and Saturday nights at Ga-Ga and Granddaddy's. On occasions when I could not bring Cathy over, I heard groans from Cathy, my father, and my mother.

At this point my father drove a taxicab a few days a week, and my mother remained a meat wrapper at Safeway. Our conversations avoided any mention of Charlene, money, my job, or school.

Shortly after I received my BA in June 1964, Dad again intervened in my life. One Sunday afternoon just before I left to return Cathy to Inez's house, Dad took me aside. He wanted a favor.

Right!

"Here comes a scam," I thought. I waited silently for him to explain.

"I have cancer," he said, speaking softly so my mother could not hear him. "I want to go back home to Lawton to see my brothers before I die."

I did not know what to say. I nodded, wondering if he was telling the truth. He was a heavy smoker. Was it lung cancer? He was also a heavy drinker. Was it cirrhosis of the liver? I waited for him to explain, feeling more dread than sorrow. My father had hustled me so many times, and I had vowed to never let him hustle me again.

He continued. "Your mother and I are planning to drive to Lawton in a couple of weeks." He did not elaborate on the type of cancer he had.

I nodded.

Then he asked for the favor. "Son, I need you to come with us to help me drive. It's a long, tiring trip, and I am not well enough to do all the driving myself."

Going to Lawton was not on my agenda. I did not want to take two weeks off without pay, and I did not want to go to Lawton. After ten years, I had lost contact with all my friends in Lawton, and the older relatives were minor parts of my childhood. My father had asked my brother, but Corky couldn't afford to take time off from his job. With three kids to support, he needed his weekly paycheck.

I looked at him, scam or not, and saw only one possible answer: "Okay, Dad."

He was my father, and if he were really dying, I owed him. I loved him, but I didn't always like him. He was further down my list, but he was also Cathy's grandfather.

The next day I told my foreman my father was ill and I needed two weeks off to take him home to Lawton, Oklahoma. Because of my employment agreement, I was not asking—I was informing him I would not be at work for two weeks. As had happened before, the foreman simply said, "I'll tell the office. Give me the dates."

The trip was as bad as I thought it would be. Dad seldom allowed me to drive, and when he did it was only on deserted sections with no traffic. Even then, he barked instructions: "Pass that damn car!" "You're too close to the center line." "Speed it up, you're driving too slow." After a couple of hours, he demanded we stop and change drivers.

I pulled over and let him drive. He drove fast, tailgated cars, passed in no-passing lanes, and cursed the other drivers. It was just like old times. I insisted Mom sit in the front passenger seat while Dad drove. I hummed in the back seat.

He stopped only for gas, food, and whiskey. I paid for the gas, the food, and two motel rooms during our one-night stop. The idea of spending the night in the same room with Dad horrified me.

He refused to stop when either Mom or I needed to use a restroom. If it was to piss, he pulled onto the shoulder of the road. We were Okies, and Mom was not shy about jumping out of the car and running into a field to do her business. If you needed to shit, you were in deep trouble. We knew when Dad stopped for gas we better run to the bathroom.

When we arrived in Lawton, we stayed with Aunt Hester and Uncle Ted. Aunt Hazel came over most evenings and I enjoyed visiting with my favorite relatives still living in Lawton. My parents visited Dad's brothers Hoot and Curly while I remained with Ted. We then drove to Wichita Falls, and visited Uncle Bill, still a deputy sheriff, and his family for a couple of days. I stayed with the family for a few hours before renting a motel room. Except for being a prisoner for forty-eight hours in the car with my Dad, I enjoyed the trip.

A few weeks after we returned to L.A., I discovered Dad's scam: getting me to pay for the trip. A dermatologist, I learned, had recently removed "potentially" cancerous spots off Dad's face. I talked to my mother. She said she agreed to the trip only because I said I would come along. The idea of spending forty-eight hours in the car with Dad didn't appeal to her, but she enjoyed the visit with her sisters in Lawton.

Dad had flimflammed me again.

⁂

Years later, Bunk regaled me with a few incidents from when he was a teenager and he and Mom took car trips with Dad. As he did with me (and everyone else), Dad always refused to stop except to get gas or another bottle of whiskey. Bunk said he and Toad often begged him to stop so they could use the bathroom, but Dad always ignored them. If Bunk pissed his pants, Dad thought it was funny.'

From 1958 to 1965, I seldom saw Bunk because I was dealing with my family problems and trying to navigate school and work. In those years, he made a good living in Los Angeles as a welder. My parents, however, stayed in close contact with him and his wife, Muriel, a kind woman who looked like a matronly grandmother—pleasingly plump.

Because of her personality, she was a delight to be around. She was ten years older than Bunk, the same age as my mother, and much like Mom, she quilted, crocheted, and preferred home cooking to restaurants. Bunk and Muriel played cards at least once a month with Mom and Dad; the Basses and Youngs loved cards and dominoes. They played for nickels and dimes and all four of them were good players. When Cathy stayed over, Bunk played with her. She loved Bunk. He was the playful uncle who had been a real cowboy. Although he never rode a horse again after his work on the ranch, he still wore cowboy boots and a cowboy hat when out on the town.

Around 1965, Bunk and his wife, Muriel, left Los Angeles and moved to Spokane.

"Why did you move?" I later asked him. He had a good job, had saved money all his life, and Muriel's grown children from a previous marriage were out of the house.

"We went up to Spokane to see the kids," he explained. "We loved the area, and Muriel missed the kids. On our return back to L.A., we stopped around midnight at a scenic overpass in the Sierra Nevada Mountains and looked down on Los Angeles. The city was covered with smog while the stars filled the night sky at the mountain overpass." Right then, they decided to move from L.A. to Spokane where Bunk continued to work as a welder. On the side, he bought small houses, refurbished them, and rented them out. He did not become wealthy, but he made enough to live a comfortable life.

A few years later, they moved near Moses Lake, a small town about a hundred miles northeast of Spokane. The high desert around Moses Lake reminded Bunk of Oklahoma. The farms had plentiful water from the Columbia River, the air was pure, and there were no traffic jams, even during rush hours. He worked as a maintenance manager at a potato-processing plant. His team repaired everything that broke in the huge, multiple-building complex. He owned a nice house, an RV, and a new truck. After he retired around 1990, every winter he and Muriel drove the RV to New Mexico or Arizona and remained there for three months. He was comfortable but never forgot the hardships he went through during the Depression and World War II, and the years he spent in the air force.

But back to my father and memorable car trips. In the early 1970s, Mom and Dad visited Bunk and Muriel for two weeks. Bunk welcomed their visit. He loved Mom and Dad. Muriel was thrilled to see Milly (or Toad, as Bunk still called Mom). They went sightseeing and played cards or dominoes at night. Every few days, Bunk drove to Moses Lake so Dad could buy his whiskey. Moses Lake was fifteen miles away over country roads.

During one of those whiskey trips they climbed into Bunk's car, and about ten minutes into the trip he heard my father groaning. Bunk glanced over at him.

"Stop at the next gas station. I need to go to the bathroom," said Dad.

Bunk nodded.

About ten minutes later, Bunk passed the first gas station.

"Goddamnit, Bunk," my father shouted. "I need a bathroom. Turn around and go back."

Bunk glanced back at Dad. "Charlie, that gas station does not have a bathroom."

As he told the story, Bunk winked at me and continued on. "Hell, Charlie never stopped for me." Besides, Moses Lake was less than ten minutes away, with several gas stations with modern facilities.

"Well," Bunk continued, "when I stopped at the next station, I expected Charlie to jump out of his seat and run like hell to the bathroom. I looked over at him, and Charlie was shoved back in his seat looking at the headliner."

"What's up, Charlie?" Bunk asked. "This station has a nice bathroom."

Dad looked over, obviously miserable.

"Too late," he said. "I already shit my pants."

Now, you have to understand that for me this was one of Bunk's funniest stories. Dad deserved it, and Bunk got his revenge. Me too—at least I never shit my pants.

Chapter 19

Looking for a Job

During my years at East L. A. and Cal State, I had no social life outside the family. I made no friends at school, never attended a single party, and never went out to dinner or to movies with other students. I worked, went to school, studied, and socialized with the kids on weekends—that was it. College was not a time for partying for me. Working as a stencil cutter and dealing with my family problems constantly reminded me that school was not a game. I could not afford to fail if I wanted to get off the bottom. I had no support system; no one was going to take care of me but me. Occasionally, I played pool with my work "buddies" at the bar where we cashed our checks, and rarely, played in one of their poker games. But usually I went alone to restaurants, movies, plays, lectures, art exhibitions, and libraries. I joined no clubs and did not participate in any college events. I took Cathy and Susan to the movies on Saturdays.

Mostly, I was a loner. I was not looking for companionship. The "good old fraternity boys" bored me, and the few women I dated were looking for a relationship leading up to a boyfriend to a husband and then to a father. Being bitten once was enough for me.

Was I lonely? Yes and no. I was not sad nor was I depressed. Was I happy? I accepted my life, but happiness had nothing to do with it.

I was working hard to achieve my goals, and I was happy with myself because of that.

In many ways, I remember little about the mundane aspects of my life in those years. I lived in a single room with a shower but no television, refrigerator, or stove. Microwave ovens were still twenty years away. What about food? Don't remember much. I must have eaten at the college cafeteria on many occasions. I do remember there was a supermarket less than two blocks from my room, and I stopped there often to buy food for my dinner and breakfast. I probably had ice in a small cooler with milk for my coffee. I went to fast-food outlets on weekends to buy the kids burgers and fries.

Transportation was a constant problem. When my car needed major repairs, I sold it to a junkyard for peanuts. For almost a year, I had no car. Finally, I bought a ten-year-old Oldsmobile with 100,000 miles for $300. It drove beautifully, but after twelve months, a front-right axle rod broke and a mechanic wanted a $175 to replace it. After taxes, that was two weeks' pay. And for a car that had cost me less than twice that amount. I decided to park the car near my parents' house and ride a bicycle until I had the spare money to fix it. Six months later, it was still sitting there, and Dad insisted I move it. I decided it wasn't worth fixing and to call a junker. Bunk heard of my plan and offered to take the car off my hands. I simply gave it to him. He repaired the car and drove it for seventy thousand more miles. He occasionally teased me about the great deal he got.

If I needed a car, I took a bus to my parents. They had two cars, and remember, they loaned me one from Friday afternoon to Sunday afternoon. On Sundays, after taking Cathy home, I went to the laundromat, always a boring, dismal place.

After obtaining my BA in June of 1964, I looked for a professional job (that is, non-stencil cutting) while taking graduate classes. If I found a good job, perhaps I would continue taking night courses. If I did not find a job before I got my master's, I had another plan in mind.

I did not want a job with local businesses that were too small to help me achieve my long-range goal of financial independence. I also did not want to work at a gigantic corporation. The image of being "the man in the gray flannel suit" was worse than the image of being a lifelong stencil cutter. I believed then, and I believe now, that large multinational corporations dehumanize their lower-level executives, who take the blame for any mistakes. Then and now, the "robber barons" have never been my heroes—they are my villains in history. Mankind has fought constantly to curtail the greed of the upper half percent.

I wanted a position with the government—federal, state, or local. Any job. I knew the upper half percent—the robber barons—also controlled the government. However, whether military or civilian, most government employees rise in the ranks from privates to noncoms to officers (or whatever their civilian equivalents are). Lieutenants rose through the ranks to become generals. I hoped to get a trainee job, something low on the organization chart, but I believed I had the talent and work ethic to move up the ladder over the years. I wanted to be a second lieutenant, not a private. Officer material.

I quickly learned federal government jobs required written tests as the second step after filling out pages of forms. College graduates generally took tests for executive assistant positions. Two months passed before I learned I had easily passed the tests. My name was put on several lists for federal jobs, but the process was slow. Two months passed before I received a letter for the first of several preliminary committee interviews. Another two months passed before a second interview, and weeks passed waiting for the committees to act. I took the State Department Foreign Service Exam, learning later that it was a fool's errand. The State Department was an exclusive club for graduates of Ivy League universities, candidates with wealthy parents who sent their children to exclusive prep schools when they were twelve years old. By the time they graduated from Harvard, Yale, or one of the other Ivy League universities, they knew all the proper social graces. As the author David Halberstam noted, they considered themselves to be "the best and the brightest." Perhaps they were, but their fathers were the hogs, and through their wealth had many contacts to guarantee that their sons and daughters (mostly sons) had an opportunity to prove they were superior. "The best and the brightest" of middle- and working-class families seldom had such opportunities.

I took tests to be a state trooper, city policeman, and city fireman. The same procedures applied: you fill out pages of papers, take tests, and wait a few weeks for the results; then wait another few weeks to be called for an interview; and then wait another few weeks as the committees met and made decisions. During one interview I had at a police department, an official admitted I scored the highest possible grade on the written tests. Unfortunately, he said, when I received an MA, I would be overqualified for the job. A fire department official, although impressed with my credentials, said, "Son, I'm afraid you can't pass the physical." I was too small—five-nine and 140 pounds.

I learned the most from an interview at the International Division of Bank of America. The interview had been difficult to arrange, and I had high hopes. It was a dream job for me. Bank of America had branches in most of the Southeast Asian countries I studied in college: the Philippines, Singapore, Indonesia, and Thailand. I assumed it would take years of training before I went to any exotic places, but I dreamed of a different world opening for me.

I did not get the job. I did not even get a second interview. I got a "Dear John" letter, i.e., a form rejection letter. Only years later did I understand why. In some important ways, I am a slow learner. I forgot to remember my brother's rules for applying for a job: know your stock (gotcha), and be on your best behavior—be nice to customers and bosses (gotcha). But I forgot to remember the very first rule: dress for the job.

When I went to my interview at Bank of America, I wore the same dress clothes I wore as a shoe clerk six year earlier: a nice blue blazer, button-down white shirt, nice tie, and polished dress shoes. The officer who interviewed me was among the aforementioned "best and the brightest." He wore a three-hundred-dollar tailored suit with two-hundred-dollar shoes. His fingernails were manicured. My reaction was to silently admire his appearance, hoping someday to have the money to dress as well.

My clothes told him I was not "suited" for the job—I was a shoe clerk. He rejected my job application. I was out of my league.

I kept on the job search as I continued my studies at Cal State for a master of arts degree. Graduate classes were primarily reading seminars. Professors assigned six to ten books to be discussed and tested in class. They also required us to complete minor research papers or bibliographical reviews of a specified set of books. A typical prompt went like this: "Select a subject, read five or more of the listed books on the topic, and write 1,000 to 5,000 words comparing the books." The classes were small, and we met three hours a week for fifteen weeks in small conference rooms. The required books were reviewed and discussed in class. The professors asked questions and every student was required to participate. Lovely small history. In the final few weeks, students presented part of their bibliographical review paper orally.

Four courses required major research papers of up to thirty pages with at least 70 percent of the footnotes coming from primary sources. Students met with the professor during the first two weeks of the course, selected or were assigned topics, and were set free to research and write the papers, due before the end of the twelfth week. One of the papers would form the foundation for each student's MA thesis.

As impressive as it was, Cal State had a major deficiency—its library was inadequate for doing high-quality research, and at that time, of course, there was no internet. Fortunately, all upperclassmen and graduate students had access to the library at the University of California at Los Angeles (UCLA), one of the great libraries in the country. I spent many days and nights there and produced several quality papers for my BA and particularly for my MA.

After I finished all the required coursework for an MA, only the "orals" remained. A committee of four professors quizzed me on basic historical knowledge about the United States, Asia, Europe, and Russia. I made A's in all their classes, a good enough performance to be asked to grade undergrad papers for two of the professors.

I received my MA in June 1965. The master of arts degree was more prestigious in 1965 than it is today. Throughout the United States, community colleges and small state colleges were exploding in size. The war in Vietnam was constantly in the news, and college students received deferments. The demand for college seats escalated rapidly and thousands of young males scrambled for admittance. But before this, few people had MAs.

A 'master's degree was the minimum requirement for college teachers. In small colleges, there were openings for recent MAs to teach lower-level courses in all fields. Recent PhDs were scarce, and few accepted jobs at smaller colleges.

College teacher was the ideal job for me. It was way to continue my education and earn money at the same time. After some research, I applied to six small state colleges. Each was located within sixty miles of a major university that offered PhDs in American diplomacy in Asia. If I got a job, I would be hired at the lowest level, as an instructor. I had no intention of taking any job just to remain on the bottom. To succeed in the profession, I knew I needed a PhD (thus the importance of the school's location).

I chose colleges near New York City, Boston, Syracuse, and Madison, Wisconsin, and in the first week of January 1966, I sent out six resumes (or in today's terminology, curriculum vitae) along with letters of recommendation from several professors at Cal State and my college transcripts. Outlining my education, I listed the areas where my knowledge was strongest. In American history, I could teach the common required courses: (1) U.S. History, Colonial Era to 1865; and (2) U.S. History, 1865 to 1960—basic requirements in every college in the United States. I was also capable of teaching upper-level U.S. history classes: (1) the Constitutional Convention and the Federalist Era; (2) Jefferson to John Quincy Adams, 1801 to 1825; (3) and almost any period from 1896 to 1960.

I had an advantage. My strongest area was U.S. wars in Asia, which included the Vietnam War, now all over the news. Few Americans knew anything about Vietnam, Cambodia, and Laos. Dien Bien Phu had tickled the world briefly in 1954, but few Americans had heard of Ho Chi Minh or General Giáp. No one paid much attention until the Buddhist burnings in Saigon in 1963 and the assassination of Ngo Dinh Diem. Even then, the events passed quickly. As a graduate student, though, I had studied Vietnam extensively.

Within three weeks I got six responses, something that would be considered a miracle in modern times. Four were personalized rejection letters. Two said they were not hiring, and two explained they were hiring only those with a PhD or candidates writing their dissertations. Cal State had the same requirement. The other two responses, one from Danbury State College in Connecticut, about sixty miles north of New York City, and one from Stout State University in Menomonie, Wisconsin, a small town an hour east of Minneapolis, were positive.

I called and wrote them immediately. Both schools wanted to interview me in March; I agreed on March 9 for Danbury State and March 16 for the Stout State. I assumed they were serious because they were asking me to come thousands of miles for the interviews.

I decided I would travel to Connecticut first and then Wisconsin, leaving on March 1 for the cross-country trip. Pacific Stone & Monument granted my request for three weeks off (without pay) beginning on February 26, giving me time to pack and get ready. I wanted to take my time and make the trip educational as well as practical. I had lived my life in two places, Oklahoma and Southern California, and I wanted to get to know more of the country. Only from the movies did I have any images of New England and Wisconsin. Airline tickets were beyond my budget, but Greyhound offered a practical alternative, a deal I could not refuse: ninety-nine bucks for a ninety-day pass to travel on Greyhound buses anywhere in the United States. Thus, a round trip ticket allowed me to take any route, any time within ninety days.

I bought a ticket and reserved a seat on a bus leaving Los Angeles and arriving in New York City. The trip would take four days and three nights. I boarded the bus with several hundred dollars in cash and traveler's checks. Credit cards were available but not widely used; I did not get my first one for another ten years. I made no other travel arrangements beyond buying my bus ticket. The bus trip seemed like a good idea, but after four days and three nights, it felt like a never-ending journey. The bus stopped every two hundred miles for gas and to give the passengers a chance to eat, use the restroom, and stretch their legs. I stared at the terrain, slept, and read books, magazines, and newspapers—as Somerset Maugham advised, "Take books when you travel."

At night it was difficult to read, and I engaged in casual conversations with a few of my new traveling companions. Every four to five hundred miles the bus stopped at a depot to change drivers, let passengers off, and take new ones aboard. A few were going all the way to New York City like me. When I tired of reading during the day, I stared out the window at the landscape. The first couple of days, the landscape looked much like Southern California as we passed through semiarid areas to the middle Plains states before we hit St. Louis. After crossing the Mississippi River, the terrain became more interesting, changing from dull brown to green fields and eventually trees. In the mountains, a dusting of snow was on the ground.

The bus arrived at Union Station in New York City in the late afternoon of March 5. My interview was not until the ninth, so I had three days and two nights to explore the city.

After retrieving my bag from the curb, I went to the information desk, picked a couple pamphlets off the rack that listed nearby hotels, and selected one in my price range within walking distance. The hotel was old and destined to be torn down in the next few years. I booked the room for two nights. From my room on the twelfth floor, I looked down on the crowds near Broadway and Forty-Second Street, the theater district. My room was bare-bones, relatively acceptable, and the right price.

I spent the first night and the next day exploring the area. Tourists packed the streets. As I walked away from Times Square, the streets became less crowded. People went about their business and the tone was less frantic. It reminded me of my Logan's days when I walked the nights away in downtown L.A.

The next day I walked the streets near Central Park. The atmosphere was like a movie image of happy New York. There were expensive hotels and horse-drawn carriages for more well-heeled tourists.

The following morning, I checked out of the hotel and carried my bag to Union Station, where I placed it in a locker. Only two buses were scheduled to go to Danbury each day. One was at 8 a.m. and arrived in Danbury around 11:30; the other left at 5 p.m. and arrived at 8:30. I opted for the late bus and spent another day in the city. I did not ride the subway because I was afraid I might get lost. I walked and occasionally rode the bus a few blocks.

As scheduled, the Danbury bus left Union Station at five. It stopped several times to let passengers off before reaching White Plains. White Plains to Danbury was an hour's ride with no stops and few passengers. The topography changed to rolling hills as we entered two-lane highways heading into the hinterland where there were no freeways and a few small towns. Finally we arrived in Danbury. There was no bus station; the trip ended at a small strip mall on the outskirts of town.

The lights in the parking lot were on, but the stores were closed. The place was deserted. And it was cold. I was glad I had an overcoat. In the parking lot, several pyramids of snow rose fifteen-to-twenty feet high. I had never seen so much snow.

Fortunately, a taxi driver was on duty and drove me to the only motel in town. The college had made a reservation for me for two nights. The motel was in the center of downtown Danbury. The main street stretched six to twelve blocks. The stores were dark, and the few blinking streetlights in the cold night made me think of Edgar Allan Poe. The locally owned motel was clean and located less than a mile from the college.

I arrived a day early for a reason: I wanted to see the town and college campus. If I took the job, was this the type of place I could live in for five to ten years?

As I walked down Main Street early the next morning, the town pleased me. The streets and sidewalls were clear of snow. The car traffic was light and the stores were just opening for business. There were no boarded-up stores. Only a couple of the retail stores were national chains. Shoe stores, clothing stores, a local department store, restaurants, and several banks lined the main street. Danbury, with a population of around 40,000, was a quaint New England town.

From the early 1800s, Danbury was known as "Hat City." Many famous brands, such as Stetson, made their hats in Danbury. In the 1950s, sales of men's dress hats declined dramatically, and the factories slowly disappeared. Danbury had a few rough years, but in the mid-50s it recovered from the collapse of its textile industry, transforming into the region's shopping center. With the nearest big city at least an hour away, it served as a magnet for people in the surrounding small towns of Bethel, Ridgefield, Newtown, and Redding.

There was also a federal prison on the city's edge that owned several hundred acres of land. It was famous in the area as a "country club" prison, its inmates convicted of nonviolent crimes; many were wealthy businessmen caught with their hands in the cookie jar. Their easy time meant easy income for the town.

Danbury State College was the economic foundation of the town. Founded sometime around 1901, the school has had many names over the decades: Danbury Normal School, Danbury State College, Western Connecticut State College, and finally, Western Connecticut State University, which it now remains. The campus buildings varied from those built in the college's early years to more modern dormitories and classroom buildings. When I was there construction was underway to expand the cafeteria and the student union, located near an imposing main administrative building whose three floors comprised the original school building. The college grounds expanded out several acres. The neighborhoods surrounding the campus were mostly old colonial-style homes rising two to four floors and were built long before the automobile ruled the suburbs. The apartments were rented at reasonable rates to students and poorer families. They reminded me of the houses surrounding USC in Los Angeles, or today, homes in New Haven near Yale University.

On the morning of March 9, I walked the mile to the school while light snow was falling. I was again glad I had an overcoat. I arrived on the steps of the administration building at 8:45 a.m. An older gentleman quickly came over to greet me even though I was fifteen minutes early.

"Mr. Young?" he asked. I nodded.

He held out his hand and said, "I'm Professor Truman Warner, the chairman of the History and Social Science Department. I have been looking forward to meeting you."

"Thank you," I said as I shook his hand. He motioned me to walk with him to White Hall, where the department's tenured members were waiting to interview me. Professor Warner sported a short gray goatee and was easily six feet, five inches tall, dressed casually wearing a gray jacket with a matching tie under an unbuttoned overcoat. He had been at Danbury State for twenty-five years, serving in many capacities, from administrator to teacher. His field was anthropology with a special interest in Japan. He was around fifty-five with a friendly smile. I learned later he was intensely involved with his students and was particularly influential with the administration. I mentioned my interest in the Russo-Japanese and the Sino-Japanese Wars, but before we could get too involved, we reached White Hall and entered the faculty lounge used for interviews.

Three other professors waited for us to remove our topcoats before we joined their group sitting around a conference table. Professor Warner introduced the other members of the hiring committee—Professors Fryer, Godward, and Roman. They dressed much like me, in dress jackets or suits with ties. I did not feel out of place. One taught European history, one taught political science, and one taught sociology. All were full professors with PhDs who had been at the school over fifteen years. The other eleven members of the department were assistant professors; four had tenure. The remaining seven were untenured assistant professors hired over the past five years. The department was still expanding, and there were openings for three historians and one anthropologist for the fall semester.

The interviewers were polite and quickly made me comfortable. They began with questions about Cal State. Consulting my transcripts, they asked about the coursework, i.e., my knowledge of the subject matter, and I answered easily. After years of study at a good university, I knew I could teach U.S. history at the college level. The interviewers shifted their questions to the war in Vietnam and the situation in East and Southeast Asia. I am sure my knowledge of China, Vietnam, and Indonesia impressed them, especially Professor Warner, who was looking for a colleague interested in Asia. I do not like to use the word "expert" unless the audience is identified. If discussing the Constitution to a college audience, I am an expert; if speaking at a history conference, I am merely a student of the Constitution.

Professor Warner reminded me that if I were hired, my rank would be instructor. To become an assistant professor an MA needed a minimum of three years of teaching experience. The department could not guarantee promotions or tenure, but if a teacher did a good job, it was likely they would keep their position.

After the interview, Professor Warner escorted me back to the administration building for an interview with President Ruth Haas and Gertrude Braun, the dean of faculty. They had led the college for two decades and were close friends of Professor Warner. President Haas interviewed all the candidates, asking them one prime question: why Danbury State College?

Naturally, I expected such a question and gave a truthful answer: I wanted to be close enough to a city with a university so I could pursue a doctorate.

After I mentioned this, the interview changed directions.

All three assured me the college did everything possible to help their teachers obtain a PhD. Each also offered advice on the university I might attend. President Haas recommended the University of Connecticut, about two to three hours north of Danbury. Dean Braun thought New York University offered the best afternoon and evening programs for getting a PhD.

Professor Warner recommended Columbia University in New York City. To my surprise, I learned Warner did not have a doctorate. His rank as full professor was due to his years as a dean. As the school expanded, he returned to teaching and became the chairman of the History and Social Science Department. He had completed his classwork at Columbia University, and after several years of research, was almost finished with his dissertation. He expected to receive his ED within a year.

After the meeting concluded, Professor Warner shook my hand on the steps of the administration building. He informed me the department planned to make a decision within three weeks. As I walked back to my motel along the snow-cleared streets, I thought to myself that the interview had gone well.

Back in New York City, I caught a Greyhound bus to Chicago,

where I transferred to a bus headed for Stout State University in Menomonie, Wisconsin. The twelve-hour trip is a blur in my memory except for a major problem. When I arrived in Menomonie, a small town an hour east of Minneapolis, my bag had disappeared. The porter must have misplaced it during my change of buses in Chicago. The agent assured me the bag would arrive within twenty-four hours.

As a naïve, first-time traveler, I had made a stupid mistake—I had not packed a carry-on bag. I had no clean clothes, toothbrush, or razor. Fortunately, though, I had traveler's checks, and I was able to register at the only motel near the bus depot. I bought the bare necessities at a Dollar General precursor on the highway. There was a Waffle House next to the motel.

Problem solved, right? I called the History Department at Stout State, explained my problem, and delayed the interviews for two days. Well, three days later, my bag was still missing. I went to the interview in my blue jeans—certainly not proper dress for the job.

The college was not much different than Danbury State, and the professors who interviewed me asked almost the same questions. They were equally encouraging about my hope of entering the doctoral program at the University of Minnesota in Minneapolis.

After the interview, I did not meet the school's president or the dean of faculty. Instead, the chairman took me for a car ride. A rapidly expanding campus surrounded attractive core buildings. He drove me to Menomonie's small business district, explaining that for major items, people went to Eau Claire or the Twin Cities. The business district was about two blocks long, with a bookstore, a hardware store, a department store, several restaurants, a supermarket, and a couple of gas stations. The town was quaint but served the basic needs of the students and the small surrounding population.

As I walked down main street, I noticed something strange. The parking meters were different from any I had ever seen. Electrical cords stuck out of them for no apparent reason.

"What are the cords for"? I asked.

I received a scary answer. Those weren't parking meters, but heating boxes. When farmers came to town in the winter, they put a couple of quarters in the meter, opened the hood of their car or truck, pulled the electrical cables from the box, and plugged them into a heater in the engine compartment.

"It gets that cold in the winter?" I asked. It was plenty cold in mid-March, about 30 degrees in the afternoon, but certainly not subzero. My guide informed me that in the winter, car owners actually removed their batteries and took them inside the house—even from vehicles parked in garages—to keep them from freezing.

When I returned to the motel my bag had arrived at last. The next morning, I caught a bus for home. As we reached Minneapolis, a blizzard struck and stranded the bus for two days. I checked into a cheap hotel near the bus station. The bathroom was down the hall, but the room was better than waiting forty-eight hours in the bus depot.

After a three-week trip I was back at work at Pacific Stone & Monument. Two weeks later I received a rejection letter from Stout State. *Sorry, thanks for applying for the job.* Naturally, the rejection was a downer. The possibility that I might be a stencil cutter for another year loomed.

A week later, Danbury State's letter arrived. The school offered me a position as an instructor at $8,000 per year, a little less than what I made at Pacific when I worked full-time. I accepted at once, thrilled that I had only four more months until my career as a stencil cutter ended. To my delight, the next week I received another letter from Stout State. The position I applied for had reopened and they were offering me the job—a boost to my ego. I wrote a polite "No, but thank you for asking" letter.

Time to prepare for my move to Danbury, Connecticut.

Chapter 20

To Danbury

I was elated when I got the letter from Danbury State. A couple of weeks later, I received a packet of forms from the college administration. I filled them out and requested Cal State send my transcripts and proof of my degrees.

Professor Warner informed me which four courses I was scheduled to teach in the fall semester of 1966: two classes on the U.S. from the Colonial period to 1865 and two classes on Southeast Asia. The courses were part of the core curriculum and open to all students, from freshmen to seniors. Twenty-five to forty students were expected to enroll in each class, for a total of a hundred to 160 students in my four classes. In preparation, the department wanted me to submit several items by June 1: a three-to-five-page synopsis, or outline, for each course, and a list of required books for each class (to be bought by students at the college bookstore). I sent the material to Warner in early May.

Now the work began. A three-credit college semester course is forty classroom hours. Day classes on a Monday-Wednesday-Friday schedule were usually hour-long sessions; Tuesday-Thursday classes were one and a half hours; and late-afternoon and evening classes were three hours. I needed around thirty-four hours of lectures for each course. The other six would be devoted to a midterm test, book tests, discussion, and a final. I planned on being primarily a lecture teacher, and I intended to be a good one.

The classes on U.S. history were relatively easy to prepare. I pulled my old course notes out of the filing cabinet and books off the shelf to begin. I had taken many courses on U.S. history, obviously, although I was weak on the Colonial period, including the Revolutionary War.

As a student, I disliked basic survey courses. This meant that as a college "professor" I intended to teach without slavishly trying to cover every aspect of U.S. history in the time period I was assigned. It was impossible to teach enjoyable history for an era that encompassed two or three centuries, much less four. To get around this, I planned to briefly touch on the high points, then center in on a few subjects I knew in depth, such as the Constitutional Convention and Federalist period, from 1787 to1801, with a special emphasis on Hamilton, Jefferson, and Adams.

The course on Southeast Asian Culture was more difficult to prepare. Most students, then and today, could not name or find on a map the nine major countries in Southeast Asia: Vietnam, Cambodia, Laos, Thailand (Siam), and Myanmar (Burma), plus the island states of the Philippines, Indonesia, and Malaysia, and the city-state of Singapore. No one-semester course could possibly cover such a huge area. In my first semester, in September 1966, I decided to concentrate on Vietnam and Indonesia, the hot topics in the news. Over the years, each of the other countries became hot topics in turn, and thus became subjects in class (e.g., in 1970, after the overthrow of Sihanouk and the rise of the Khmer Rouge, Cambodia was all over the news—and a topic of my class discussion).

I took walks in the evenings, talking myself through the lectures. As a student, I considered a teacher to be good if he knew his subject matter and did not constantly refer to his notes. I was not a fan of discussion classes—I went to school to gain knowledge from the professor, not my peers. The only good discussion classes in my opinion were reading classes where the professor gave book tests and asked questions in the class to guarantee students read the book. After my first year as a teacher, I never required a textbook or a book I had not enjoyed reading myself. I did not ask students to agree with the book but wanted to expose them to the most readable publications in my fields of study. Reading dull academic books and journal articles was my chore, not theirs.

I firmly believed lectures should be so enjoyable students would want to learn more about the subjects after I taught them. If a teacher can't make the Constitutional Convention so interesting that students want to hear more, the teacher is doing something wrong. The teacher is the author, the director, and the actor on stage. As a student, nothing irritated me more than professors who came unprepared, often bored me, and wasted my time.

⁂

The most difficult part of accepting a job 3,000 miles across the country was abandoning my family, primarily meaning my mother, Cathy, and Susan. I loved my mother, and over the years she had come to depend on me for emotional support. I loved my seven-year old daughter and her five-year old sister, yet I was willing to leave them in the hands of Charlene and her mother Inez.

Selfish? Definitely.

My mother, although saddened, understood my decision. Cathy and Susan did not initially understand, but over the years, my love and financial support for them has never been questioned.

I needed to get away from Charlene and her constant demands for emotional support. Although we had split in early 1961, she believed I owed her my love as her "best" friend. In the following five years, she went through five or six "lovers," and each time she came to me for comfort, a shoulder to cry on. Because of Cathy and Susan, I could not break off our relationship for good. For her part, Charlene assumed being their mother secured her a special place in my life.

If I wanted to achieve my goals, I had to make this move. After my years of sacrifice, the job in Connecticut was my reward, and truly my opportunity to pursue my dream of achieving financial and emotional independence.

Money was an added concern. Although my reserves were not

depleted, my earlier trip had dented them. To recharge my finances, I worked forty hours a week at Pacific from April to August. The pay was $3.50 an hour with no benefits. If I got sick, I was not paid. But the pay was good, about three times minimum wage, and I made extra money doing piece work for a few smaller monument companies. I charged five to ten dollars to cut a headstone, and twenty to thirty to lay out and cut a monument. The owners were delighted, since at this point I was among the three best cutters in Los Angeles. I was also more dependable and much faster than the other two (one of them being Evans). I could cut simple markers at a rate of two per hour; more complicated monuments took two to four hours. For these jobs I was paid two to three times as much as I made at Pacific. But I stayed with them because the smaller companies' jobs were unpredictable. With the two jobs combined, I made about $200 a week before taxes. Slowly over the summer, my reserves increased to about $2,000.

I needed a reliable car to take me cross-country, hopefully one that would last for four or five years in Connecticut; it could not be another rust bucket. After searching used car lots for six weeks, I decided to buy a five-year-old Nash Rambler station wagon with 40,000 miles on the odometer. I took the car to a mechanic who certified it was in excellent shape with a good engine, new brakes, and new tires.

The price for the car was $800. I put down three hundred and applied for a car loan. This was a first for me; I had never borrowed money before. To my surprise, the loan needed a cosigner who had held a steady job for at least two years.

With confidence, I asked my mother to cosign. The thought she might refuse never occurred to me. Although I was the second son, she loved me, partially because for years I had been a buffer between the demands of the two alpha males in the family. My father was vehemently against her cosigning the $500 loan. He pointed out if I did not repay it, she would be stuck with the debt.

I was the most dependable member of the family. It was a small amount of money, and I seldom asked any favors of the family. During the hard times when my father was in prison, I contributed money to the family. And while I was in high school, he chiseled more than $500 out of me. And yet he was still against the loan.

Over the years my mother found it difficult to disobey my father's wishes. He had convinced her he was wiser and far smarter than her. He was the boss in charge, and she had to obey him as she had obeyed him for thirty years.

This was the painful part for me. I thought I had asked for a minor favor from my mother. She knew I would never fail to pay off the loan. But my father's attitude placed her in an awful position. What's more, he had not worked full-time in years. The little money he earned he spent on booze. My mother's salary paid the bills.

She signed the loan. I wished I had paid cash for the car—I had the money but hoarded it for unexpected expenses during my move. To this day, I feel guilty for asking her. I loved my mother and never wanted to make trouble for her.

My mother only told me about my father's opposition several years after his death. When I learned about it, my attitude toward him hardened. His stance drove a stake through any lingering guilt I felt for my lack of filial piety toward him in his later years. I disliked the man. Rather than treating me as his son—even his second son—he treated me as just another relative asking for money.

Adding insult to injury, two years before my request my father persuaded Mother to withdraw $5,000 from her retirement fund so my brother could open a shoe store. His dream in life was to own a business.

$5,000 was a lot of money in 1964—multiply it by seven or eight to come up with the current-day value. My father badgered her for weeks until she reluctantly agreed to lend my brother the money.

My brother was my father's son, and I was the distant relative. I loved my brother and praised my mother for helping him. But my father's actions toward me left a bitter taste when I found out about them.

※

I left Los Angeles in the afternoon of the second Sunday in August with my station wagon packed full of books, notes, clothes, and miscellaneous items such as my portable Remington typewriter. I opted for a northern route that skirted the major cities. Big cities did not interest me—I was leaving a big city. I wanted to see the small towns. And I wanted to take my time. On my earlier trip, I mostly saw truck stops and bus depots. When I neared the Great Lakes, I planned to take side roads through northern New York to Danbury. I estimated the trip would take about fifteen days at my slow pace, timing my arrival for August 25, a week before I was to report to Danbury State.

The first four or five hundred miles were though the hot desert to Las Vegas. Like most cars on the road, my station wagon had no air-conditioning. I reached Las Vegas in the early evening and stopped to eat. At that time Vegas was only a small city rather than the gambling Disney World of today. Around 9 p.m. I continued, stopping through the night only for gas, coffee, and to use the restroom. Around one o'clock the next afternoon, I stopped in a small town about two hundred miles west of Denver. I rented a motel room, had an early dinner, and was soon asleep. I got up early, had breakfast, and continued over the mountains to Denver.

As I neared Denver, a gauge showed the car was overheating. I stopped at the first service station I passed. Back then nearly all gas stations had service bays, not convenience stores, and they fixed flat tires, changed the oil, and did minor repairs. The service station attendant smiled when I told him my radiator was overheating. "Just come over the mountains?" he asked with a grin. The higher altitude, he explained, often caused cars to overheat. He poured a sealant into the radiator. "Probably work," he said. "If it doesn't, you'll need a new radiator."

I returned to the road and headed toward Topeka. I stopped every two hours to cool the engine and refill the radiator. When I was near Topeka, I finally accepted that I would have to pay for the radiator to be repaired. I stopped at a service station to ask if a radiator shop was nearby. The attendant directed me two miles down a highway lined with businesses including several restaurants and gas stations.

The radiator shop had a half dozen cars in the parking lot waiting for repairs. A manager came out to check my car. "This damn sealant seldom works," he said as he withdrew his finger from the leaking radiator water. "Needs a new radiator."

Installed, the radiator would cost $100. Even worse, it would be three days before the shop could do it. I reluctantly agreed, signed the order, and gave the keys to the repairman, who recommended a motel a couple blocks away. Grabbing my bag, a few books, and my lecture notes, I walked to the motel, hoping my other possessions were safe in my car.

Over the next three nights I reread books, analyzed my lectures, and thought about my future. If there was a television in the room, I never turned it on. Although I had some nervous anticipation about teaching, I was confident I could do the job. A host of things could threaten my job after my year's contract expired. But I was confident that in the worst case I could survive and take care of myself. I was accustomed to being alone.

After retrieving my car, my cash reserves were down from $1,700 to around $1,200. I still had ten more days before reaching Danbury. I headed for Cleveland and reached the outskirts of the city two days later. After Cleveland, I skirted Buffalo and headed up to the shores of Lake Ontario west of Rochester, New York. At the time, the interstate highway system was still under development, and state highways were often the main roads between the larger cities, resulting in more scenic routes. The countryside was lush with farmers' fields, lakes, streams, and forests. The uncrowded roads passed through picturesque small towns. Two days later, I reached Syracuse. The next morning, I detoured to drive through Cornell University's campus in Ithaca. I had often dreamed of going to Cornell because it had an excellent faculty specializing in Southeast Asia, perhaps the best in the United States and superior to those at Yale, Harvard, and Stanford. Of course, it was beyond my means. From Ithaca, I drove all day, passing Albany that night and continuing down Route 7 to Danbury.

I arrived in Danbury around 4 a.m., pulled into the railroad station's downtown parking lot, and went to sleep. I woke up around 6. I had a week before the first faculty meeting of the fall semester.

I drove down a deserted Main Street, through the business district and past the motel. On the outskirts of town, I stopped to buy gas, purchase a map of the area, and get advice on a place to eat breakfast.

Although I had spent time in Danbury during my earlier visit, I obviously did not know the area intimately.

Over breakfast, I examined the map and discovered the roads out of Danbury went to several small towns within fifteen miles including Bethel, Newtown, New Milford, Redding, and Ridgefield. After breakfast, I drove to the college and explored the side streets in the town's older residential section. I noted again that many houses had been converted into small apartments. Widening my circle, I discovered a new shopping center on the edge of town.

A large supermarket anchored one end of the center. My experience in Los Angeles taught me that when searching for an apartment, the ideal place to start was with the bulletin boards at supermarkets. My hunch was right: ads for four apartments were posted. I copied the addresses and phone numbers and returned to my car and examined the map.

I needed a place relatively close to the college. The apartment had to be furnished. And I did not want to be in an apartment complex where upper-class students shared rented rooms. I felt I needed to maintain a distance from students, and the image of wild parties certainly did not appeal to me.

I eliminated one rental because it was too far from school. I easily found a public telephone where I could inquire about the others. The second place was a two-bedroom unfurnished apartment priced at $250 a month—too much money, too much room, too little (no) furniture. I decided to visit the third place, which turned out to be in a rundown section of town. That's not all that was rundown in the shabby second-floor apartment; the furniture reminded me of my place in the trailer park in L.A. The only thing appealing about it was the price, $60 a month.

The last place seemed ideal. A studio apartment over a two-car garage with a separate entrance, it was on the outskirts of town but only two miles from the college. I approached it via a gravel driveway that curved up two hundred yards to a large ranch style–house. It was surrounded by fields where a few cows and horses grazed, and in the distance was a large barn. The queen-size bed was new, and the other furniture, from lamps to a writing desk, was tasteful. A large walk-in closet was attached to a tiled bathroom with a tub and shower. After living four years in a one-room apartment without a bathtub, this was high-class. The kitchen, decked out with new appliances, opened to a living area with a small table.

The problem was the price of $125 a month—slightly beyond my budget. I asked the owner if I could rent the apartment for ten months. When I explained I would be teaching at the college, he understood why I wanted to rent for ten months rather than for a year. He had rented the apartment to other "visiting professors" over the years. He said he would be delighted to have me as a tenant. He wanted my first month's rent plus a $100 security deposit that would be returned at the end of the lease if there was no damage. I accepted.

At this point my reserve fund had dwindled down to $800. I did not have weeks to look for a place to live, and I was confident $800 was enough money to last me at least two months until I received my first paycheck. So, I paid the money and moved into my new, plush apartment at once. After returning from the grocery store, I sat in front of the windows and enjoyed watching the cows in the pasture and the sunset. I was content.

That settled, it was time to get to work.

Chapter 21

Danbury State:
Settling in

In preparation for the first day of class, the next morning I drove down several side roads looking for the easiest routes to the college. I also needed to scout the campus: Where is the college bookstore? Are the books I ordered in stock? Where is the faculty cafeteria? Where is the library? Where is my office? Where do I obtain school supplies? Where are the mimeograph machines, staple guns, and paper? Where are my classrooms?

I parked in the faculty lot next to White Hall and went to the History and Social Science Department's main offices. On my way in I passed two secretaries working in an outer office. The door to Professor Warner's private office was open. He waved me in, shook my hand, and motioned me to a chair in front of his desk. Books and papers spilled out of crammed bookcases that covered three walls. The other wall had windows providing some natural light.

His overstuffed office hinted at Warner's deep commitment to teaching and the college. Indeed, Warner proved to be an excellent chairman who was always available for advice and help with any problem. The school was his life, and he was a devoted teacher.

After a few minutes of pleasantries, we got down to business.

Warner informed me the new faculty did not have private offices. He apologized. The college was expanding rapidly as it prepared for the tsunami of freshmen from the baby boomer generation, he said, and construction and remodeling had fallen behind schedule. The solution: new faculty were given a large group office space that covered half the basement of White Hall. As we walked to the office area, Warner handed me a campus map and told me the secretaries would show me to the department's storage room and mimeograph room.

The "junior faculty office" area was gigantic, around 200 feet in length and 100 feet wide. Thirty metal desks lined the walls, each contained within in a small cubicle created by six-foot-high, two-foot-wide metal bookcases. The center of the large room was free of desks and chairs, giving the cubicles some measure of privacy. A desk chair, a guest chair, and a four-drawer metal filing cabinet were stationed in each cubicle. Although the space lacked the privacy consulting with students often required, Warner noted an advantage to the arrangement: the open office made it easier for the new faculty to share their experiences on and off campus. At any rate, he said that during the day the room was normally half empty because of differing class schedules. My desk was next to the other new members in my department.

"If you need any more help," Warner instructed as he left, "just come see me." Professor Warner always honored that promise, and he is a man I respected then and still do today.

After the tour I made several trips to my car to retrieve my books, typewriter, and papers. I spent the next several hours getting supplies and typing up two syllabi on mimeograph sheets, one for my two classes on Southeast Asia and the other for my two classes on U.S. History from the Colonial Era to 1865. Syllabi are short course outlines passed out to students at the beginning of a semester. Each was around four pages and included the requirements for the courses and a brief topical outline of each lecture. I needed eighty copies of each syllabi.

At the time, "Xeroxing" was not an option, and cutting mimeograph sheets took a while. Each sheet demanded perfect typing, and the ink-backed paper stained the hands and clothes blue. Once typed, a sheet went through a hand-cranked mimeograph machine that copied the stenciled paper on blank sheets. The mimeograph ink lasted for about eighty copies before it slowly faded away. When this process was complete, I collated the sheets and stapled them together for class distribution. I spent the next few days at school with one side trip to New York City.

The first Wednesday in September, all of Danbury State's faculty and administrators were summoned for a general meeting. First, though, I reported to a History and Social Science Department gathering in the faculty lounge in White Hall. The department had fifteen members, five of us new faculty: a social science teacher, an anthropologist, and three historians, including myself. After we settled into the easy chairs and sofas scattered around the room, Warner introduced the new members. A few minutes of socializing followed, and then Warner guided a discussion on topics ranging from department goals and deadlines to the library's new hours.

After an hour, we followed Warner to a small auditorium in another building. Around 125 members of the faculty and administrators were slowly filling the space, talking and shouting out greetings.

President Haas, Dean Braun, and several other deans addressed the assembly. To my surprise, the senior faculty members took an active part in the event. Several stood and suggested changes or offered opinions.

Two hours passed. This was but a taste of the future. Over the years, I learned that many academics love meetings and airing their opinions vigorously. In committees I served on that first year, hours were spent debating minor issues as all members of the committee presented their opinions.

After the meeting ended, President Hass invited all of the faculty members to the cafeteria for lunch. I went, sat at a table, listened to others talk, and after an hour, slipped out and went home. I preferred being alone to being surrounded by a large group engaging in social talk. The situation reminded me of history conferences where I knew no one. A little socializing is nice; too much is simply a bore.

Another social event awaited three nights later. In his role as chairman of the department, Professor Warner held a party for the faculty members and their wives at his house before the beginning of the fall semester. Professor Warner lived in a two-story colonial on three acres in the nicest section of town. The furniture was antique, and handcrafted wall-to-ceiling bookcases lined several rooms. Paintings hung throughout the house. Warner was a bachelor who had created an oasis for his intellectual interests and friends. He had a housekeeper, but he had prepared all the appetizers. Attendees gathered in the kitchen as well as a large, glassed-in sunroom with a view of a well-kept lawn and the trees behind his house.

While munching on the snacks and drinking wine, beer, or mixed drinks, we talked about life at the college. The senior professors dominated the conversation, informing new faculty about the ins and outs of Danbury State. Most thought it was an excellent small college. All the teachers in the department were men. The wives collected in separate groups to talk about children, shopping, and books. I was polite, smiling and nodding but saying little as I nursed a glass of wine. Apart from Warner, I was the only bachelor in the group.

I had found myself in a whole new world, one I knew only from the movies and books. The people around me came from middle-class families. Many of the men wore expensive sports jackets, without ties, and their wives wore equally proper casual outfits displaying their jewelry. I wore my old blue blazer with the silk lining stapled to keep it attached to the coat. I was not embarrassed; my clothes fit the lowly rank of instructor. But I realized I needed some new clothes to fit my new role.

At the time male college teachers wore jackets with ties when at school. People from Yale and other extremely prestigious schools often wore a blue blazer with khaki pants and mahogany wing-tipped shoes. I owned two jackets, many white dress shirts, three ties, and one pair of dress shoes. Three months passed before I could afford to slowly expand my wardrobe. Years passed before I dressed as well as most of my colleagues.

As I listened to the conversations around me that night, I heard words I seldom spoke and others I knew only from reading. One woman stumped me. "My grandchild is the most precocious six-year-old" in her entire family of precocious children, she proudly proclaimed. "Precocious?" I looked it up when I got back to my apartment and realized my daughter was the only member of my family who fit the definition.

The incident inspired me to start a running list of words. I divided it into three categories: words I couldn't pronounce, words I had trouble spelling, and words I seldom used. "Esoteric" is an example of a word I seldom used, but when I learned the term I read and heard it often. As I collected words I had problems spelling and pronouncing, I was once again reminded of the liability of sight-reading compared to phonetics.

※

Outsiders often think teachers have cushy jobs, working only ten months a year with dozens of paid vacation days. Many people believe university teachers have the easiest job in the universe, particularly full professors. The reality is a lot different. As an instructor, I taught four classes on Monday, Wednesday, and Friday for a total of twelve hours per week in the classroom. Committee and department meetings and office hours took up another twelve-plus hours.

On top of that, I spent hundreds of hours every semester preparing lectures, grading tests, correcting written assignments, and reading scholarly books. Much of a good teacher's work is done at home. And early-career professors who teach a full load of classes aren't exactly raking it in. For many years I taught split semesters and summer classes because I needed the money.

When classes began, I was nervous but prepared. Over the years that feeling never left me on the first day. The tasks on that hectic day are as familiar to students as they are to me: filling out attendance cards, passing out course outlines, talking about the required books, pointing out test dates, and reviewing teaching methods. I explained I was a lecture teacher, and students were expected to attend, listen, and take notes.

What was the class like when I got down to business? Any student could ask a question any time—they just had to raise their hand. I liked questions, but only if they were related to the topic. Midterm and final tests were based on the lectures. I seldom called roll simply because students who skipped classes did poorly on midterms and often dropped the class, making attendance-counting unnecessary. I did not expect agreement on the essays; I expected proof that the students attended classes and listened to what I had to say. I gave separate book tests that abided the same promise: if students read the book, they would be able to answer any question I asked.

As the semester progressed, I spent hours revising my notes, grading tests, and reading new books for potential use in future classes. Remember my motto: I should come to class so prepared that only an occasional glance at my notes is necessary. A good lecture is a well-prepared speech that captures an audience, a speech that changes when new ideas pop into the brain. Was I a great teacher that first semester? No, but I was a competent teacher, and after a few weeks I improved.

For me and most of the other professors I worked with, teaching was only a part of the job. A professor is supposed to be an authority in his field (remember my definition of "expert"). Outside of class, I spent most of my time trying to become a good teacher and scholar. Slowly over the years, I think I became both.

Chapter 22

New York University:
The First Year

When I started taking classes at East Los Angeles Community College in the fall of 1958, I had no idea teachers were ranked according to their degrees as well as their teaching experience. Students knew some teachers had PhDs while many others held only master's degrees. Some were full time, and some taught only one or two courses as adjuncts. But to show appropriate respect, students addressed all teachers as "professor" even though many were simply "instructors." When I went to Cal State, I irritated my adviser, Milton Meyer, when I addressed him as "Dr. Meyer." He corrected me, saying, "Professor Meyer, please." There are many teachers with PhDs who are assistant or associate professors. Only a few, those with many scholarly publications under their belt or longevity, achieve the highest rank, professor. Thus, a full professor always outranked a mere PhD, much less someone with just a master's—like I had.

At Danbury State, I was a mere instructor. My tenure and promotions depended on my obtaining a PhD as well as publishing scholarly articles or books. I accepted this and vowed to rise to the challenge. If I was going to make university teaching my career, I had no intention of remaining at the bottom, or anywhere close to it. The very lowest-level college instructors were part-time adjuncts, often high school teachers, who taught many of the night and summer school courses. I did not want that life.

This hierarchy was upended in the 1970s and '80s when cost-conscious accountants argued that colleges could save money using adjuncts for day courses (that is, ordinary college classes). Adjunct pay was much lower than what a full-time teacher received, plus adjuncts received no pensions, no health care, and no guarantee of continued employment. College administrators also liked adjuncts because they were controllable, i.e., could be fired at the drop of a hat. On the other hand, it was difficult to fire a full-time tenured teacher that the administration deemed a pain in the ass. Tenure guaranteed academic freedom, within certain bounds.

So, if I wanted to get ahead, I would need that PhD. And sooner rather than later, given the slow but steady transition of faculties from majority-professor to majority-adjunct. I would have to outrun this trend before the market for full-time professors all but shriveled, as it largely has today.

As I mentioned earlier, one of my big attractions to teaching at Danbury State was that several universities with excellent PhD programs were within commuting distance. During my job interview in President Haas's office, the administration encouraged me to go for the PhD and even promised to help me arrange my teaching schedule so that I'd have time to work on it (assuming I got the job). Yale was in New Haven, thirty miles from Danbury—but an hour's drive on country roads. The University of Connecticut, in Storrs, was about eighty miles northeast, but at the time the drive from Danbury was over three hours. New York City, sixty miles south of Danbury, had several universities including Columbia University and New York University (NYU).

In the summer of 1966, while preparing for my move to Danbury, I wrote several universities in the area requesting information on their History Department's PhD program. In a polite response, Yale explained that PhD candidates had to attend the university full time for a least one year to be accepted into their program. They encouraged all candidates to remain on campus as teaching assistants while writing their dissertations, which usually took several years. The cost and conditions of this arrangement were impossible for me, so I quickly ruled it out.

Columbia and NYU seemed more promising. They offered late-afternoon and evening classes for PhD candidates, and both had respected professors teaching courses in my area of expertise, Southeast Asia. And faculty I respected at Danbury State were affiliated with both schools: Warner was finishing up his work for an EdD at Columbia, and Dean Braun had a PhD from NYU.

Both schools sent me catalogs describing their requirements for entry into their history PhD programs and the courses they offered in the fall semester of 1966. The requirements at the two universities were comparable: (1) ten to fifteen graduate courses beyond the master's level; (2) written and oral exams to test your knowledge in areas of concentration; (3) the ability to read two foreign languages; (4) and the completion and acceptance of a dissertation.

I selected NYU because it offered more graduate classes in the late afternoon and early evening. They did this because many ambitious men and women in New York wanted the prestige of a graduate degree from NYU to improve their chances of promotion (although few had any intention of teaching at any level), and this schedule gave them the flexibility to attend. Another reason was the cost. Columbia was more expensive than NYU, although the price of the latter still shocked me.

Be that as it may, I decided it was worth it. I sent in my application and requested Cal State send my transcripts. NYU accepted my application, and in July, before leaving L.A., I sent the school a check and enrolled in one evening course for the upcoming fall semester.

The week before classes began at Danbury State, I went to see Professor Warner to talk about logistics. He graciously spent a couple of hours with me, guiding me on the best methods of getting into and around New York City. He often drove when he traveled to Columbia, but the trip took over an hour and half each way and parking was costly. The nearest freeway was the Saw Mill River Parkway about thirty-five minutes south of Danbury. Carpooling with him was impossible; he was nearing the end of his dissertation and went to Columbia only occasionally to consult with his adviser.

The other option, recommended by Warner, was to drive to Brewster, New York, about twenty miles west of Danbury, and catch a train to the city. Brewster was the last stop on the commuter line that ran as an express train from Grand Central Station in Manhattan to White Plains and then became a "local" for the final thirty miles, stopping at about ten small stations before reaching Brewster. From 5 a.m. until midnight, trains ran from Brewster to New York City. During rush hours in the morning and afternoon, the trains ran every thirty minutes. After 9 p.m., they ran hourly. The price was $3.50 each way, but a packet of ten tickets cost about $30 (although the price increased rapidly over the next few years).

I took Professor's Warner's advice and drove to Brewster around 11 a.m. on a Thursday. I was able to park near the train station this time, but as more people moved to the area, it became impossible. I bought a round-trip ticket and picked up a schedule. The train pulled six passenger cars that were nearly empty when I boarded but gradually filled up with passengers in each of the stations we passed through. By the time we arrived in White Plains, the cars were crowded.

The train arrived at Grand Central around 1 p.m. One way to describe Grand Central is "massive"—with dozens of tracks and gates sprawled out underneath the terminal. After leaving the lower area, passengers streamed into the famous Main Concourse. It was gigantic, at least the size of two football fields, with a ceiling that rose four or five stories. One area had over a hundred long wooden benches for passengers waiting for their trains. A row of tickets booths lined one wall, and above the booths a gigantic electrical board displayed the gates of arriving and departing trains. Hundreds of storage lockers were in another area, and public phone booths lined another wall. Retail shops were open along several corridors leading out to the streets. An escalator took passengers up to an exit on Madison Avenue.

As I arrived in the concourse hundreds of passengers hurried past me to stairways leading down to multiple subway lines. I followed them. Lines formed in front of token booths. After inserting a token,

I passed through the turnstile into a wide, well-lit area with food and coffee stands and novelty shops. The shops looked as if they had opened decades ago. Each subway line had double tracks for uptown, downtown, and crosstown destinations. Crowds waited on platforms as trains rumbled in and out, shaking the area with their noise. Each train pulled twelve to sixteen passenger cars, a few decorated with graffiti. When the train stopped, passengers rushed out, and new passengers shuffled aboard in equal haste.

This was a new world for me. Although Warner had instructed me what line to take to NYU, I was lost for several minutes before I found the right platform for trains going downtown to Fourteenth Street. When I got off, I had to walk several blocks to Washington Square Park, the university's "campus." A concrete jungle of high-rise buildings surrounded the park; they made up the university's dormitories, administrative offices, student classrooms, and faculty offices. Paved pathways with benches crisscrossed the park. Students, beatniks, and beggars sat on the benches or walked on the paths or grass. Trees and monuments were abundant. People surrounded several concrete chessboards near a park exit to Greenwich Village, watching players compete intensely.

When I located the registrar's office, they provided me with a campus map. I wandered around and finally found the building housing the classroom for my first course. I also went to the university's bookstore and library. Neither impressed me; there were many better bookstores and specialized libraries scattered around Manhattan, including the magnificent New York Public Library on Forty-Second Street. I used these libraries on occasion, although I used the ones at Yale, which were closer to home, more often.

When I returned to Grand Central at six o'clock, the station was a crowded madhouse. It was rush hour, and the cars of the train to Brewster were packed. Many people stood in the aisles until passengers got off thirty minutes later in White Plains. Passengers thinned out to a few dozen per car before the train reached Brewster.

My next trip was to New Haven. In our discussions, Professor Warner mentioned that he often visited Yale's Sterling Library to do research for his dissertation. Sterling was one of the great research libraries in the United States, and Yale graciously gave stack privileges to the faculties of Connecticut's state colleges. The right extended to several of the university's primary document libraries, which housed original government documents and primary sources related to specialized topics (for example, religion in New England from the seventeenth to the twentieth century).

The week after my first visit to NYU, I drove the mountain road that curved from Danbury to Newtown through Darien to New Haven. It was a slow, scenic thirty-mile drive. It took forty-five to sixty minutes.

Yale is on the edge of downtown New Haven and located in a neighborhood full of old three-to-four-story colonial houses with some in desperate need of refurbishing. Many were fraternity houses where upper classmen lived. I parked three or four blocks from Yale's campus and walked down a street lined with restaurants, clothing stores, and most important, Yale's excellent bookstore.

Sterling Library faced Yale's Common, a three-to-four-acre field with well-maintained grass. Dozens of students were playing football and frisbee while many others sat on benches reading and talking. Stone steps led up fifty to sixty feet to the library's massive main doors. Inside the entrance area, a three-story-high ceiling stretched a hundred yards to the library's checkout desks. The center corridor led past the wooden card catalog racks lining the sides. They indexed the volumes, over a million in total, housed in the eleven or twelve floors of the library. To the left of the checkout station was a reference room larger than the entire library at Danbury State. The UCLA Library I had used for research was impressive, sure, but Yale's Sterling Library was breathtaking.

I applied for a card. An assistant librarian escorted me to a private office for an interview with a senior librarian who treated me as a colleague rather than a student. She handed me forms requiring the signatures of my department chairman and the dean of faculty at Danbury State and issued me a temporary stack pass, a privilege not even given to Yale undergraduates. The pass allowed me to go to the stacks on every floor, each containing thousands of books and study carrels for graduate students. Unfortunately, the card did not allow me to check out books, but a few months later I discovered that the federal government had awarded Yale a grant to buy and house books and microfilms on Asian countries, with the requirement that the university guarantee checkout privileges for researchers from most universities in the United States. In other words, I was in. Over the next few years, I spent hundreds of hours prowling through the stacks and the basement's microfilm section as well as checking out hundreds of books.

My evaluation of NYU is not nearly as glowing as my feeling for Yale. For one, the number of graduate students attending NYU's late-afternoon and evening classes was massive, which made it hard to participate and get know my instructors. Many graduate classes were open to MA candidates and often enrolled as many as forty students; some required courses had as many as seventy. Classes open only to PhD candidates seldom exceeded fifteen students and were taught by tenured full professors. All were reading seminars.

Some of these upper-level classes required bibliographical essays meant to illustrate your research and writing skills and impress a professor into becoming your dissertation adviser. Using the Sterling Library at Yale, I researched and wrote a dozen papers over the next four years. Some formed the basis of my dissertation, and a few would later be published in scholarly journals (see Appendix). Without Yale, I could never have become a first-class scholar. My deep connection with the university almost became formalized many years later, when Jonathan Spence, a longtime Yale professor and one of the best of America's China experts, offered me a position as a one-semester teaching assistant. Unfortunately, Danbury State (by then Western Connecticut University) refused to grant me a sabbatical, and I was forced to decline the offer to my great disappointment.

Nevertheless, going to school in New York City provided me with many cultural opportunities I could not have gotten elsewhere. I explored many of its museums, such as the Metropolitan Museum of Art, which I visited dozens of times. The Guggenheim was a major disappointment and deserved only an occasional visit. When my budget allowed, I went to Broadway plays or artistic productions at Carnegie Hall. Usually, I went to less expensive off-Broadway plays.

Although my activities in the city expanded my horizons, I formed no friendships at NYU. My social life at Danbury State was more extensive but limited primarily to school functions. As a young college teacher, I could have easily formed new friendships, but I did not. I simply had no time for friends or lovers. I attended the History and Social Science Department's required annual party but declined other dinner or party invitations. All of my colleagues were married, and their social lives revolved around their families and other teachers who were going through the same stage of life. I was a loner, and social skills did not come easy to me; if I were in prison, I suspect I would opt for solitary confinement over sharing dorm rooms and meals. I went alone to school plays, public university lectures, movies, and restaurants. I socialized with colleagues at college functions, such as school plays or guest lectures, and occasionally saw colleagues in local restaurants or in the lobby of the Candlewood Theater, a nearby playhouse that featured first class off-Broadway plays. Apart from these few outings I was focused on one thing: work. I did not own a television and could not tell you who played in the World Series from 1966 to 1970.

My romantic life sputtered on and off. Over the next few years I dated several single faculty members or women I met at social functions. Most were five to fifteen years older than I was. Most had been through the wringer, like me, in previous relationships. I made it plain that I was not looking for a serious relationship, and my time was strictly limited. When they were not involved with someone else, they often called to see if I was available for dinner or a movie. We never went to parties and I knew none of their friends.

I quickly learned that women—at least the ones in my life—wanted an intimate friendship that leads to marriage. I had just escaped from a narcissistic woman and did not want a "relationship," whatever its guise. I had neither the time nor the money to date two or three nights a week. Long conversations on the telephone took up too much time, and if the call was long-distance, as many calls were back then, the rates were a minor fortune. I seldom called L.A. and wrote only a few letters to my mother and Cathy.

Lonely? No. I was busy.

When I left Los Angeles for Connecticut, I firmly believed it was my ticket to getting off the bottom. I loved my mother, brother, Cathy, and Susan, but the need to take care of myself (and by extension, them) trumped every other consideration.

Yet, it was on my shoulders to maintain contact. Each month I sent child support checks to Charlene. In a different envelope, I included a brief letter to the girls.

I also wrote my mother, but she didn't reply for several months. Finally, I complained. She wrote back that she was embarrassed. She had a third-grade education and, of course, her spelling was atrocious. She spelled words as she pronounced them in her Oklahoma accent; to decipher them, I read her letter out loud. I smiled because it sounded just like Toad. The letter made me happy.

Shortly thereafter, I received a letter from my father. In a two-page note, he criticized me for "making" mom write the letter. His penmanship was vastly superior to mine, and the spelling was perfect. He said Mom had spent days writing her letter, and in the future, I should call her rather than demand a letter.

Long-distance calls were beyond my income at that time. I resolved the situation by simply writing fewer letters. Occasionally, Mom responded, but not often. I thanked her for her letters, and I told her I didn't care if she couldn't spell. I was also a poor speller because I did not understand phonetics. I still have a hell of time spelling, I said, and her love warmed my heart.

In August of 1967, after teaching two summer courses, I scheduled a trip to Los Angeles for a three-week visit with the family. Before leaving Danbury, I moved to a new place downtown. It was a third-floor walk-up with old furniture and kitchen appliances, but it was neat and clean, and no students rented any of the other three apartments in the building. The rent was $55 a month, less than half the cost of my old place. I lived there for the next four years. Being able to walk to school and living near streets that were plowed first after snowstorms were the big advantages of downtown living.

I packed a bag for the trip, and then, for the first time in my life, I flew on an airplane. At the time people dressed up for flights, and I wore a jacket and tie. Air travel had fewer hassles back in the day. There were no ticket lines, no security checkpoints, no drug-sniffing dogs, and no baggage fees.

When I got to the airport, I checked my bag but kept a small carry-on for emergencies. I had learned my lesson after that fateful bus trip to Menomonie.

The plane was not crowded; there were lots of vacant seats and plentiful empty overhead storage bins. The seats were comfortable. Once in flight, cigarette smokers lit up. The few nonsmokers on the plane sat in a small reserved section, and no one complained about the smoke in the cabin. By modern standards, the crew pampered the passengers. Breakfast, lunch, and soft drinks were included in the ticket. There was no onboard entertainment except for a few newspapers and magazines. After lunch, stewardesses distributed pillows and blankets for those wishing to nap. Naturally, I carried two books to read on the flight.

I landed in Los Angeles in the early afternoon with one heavy suitcase and a small overnight bag. Although my father drove a taxicab, it never occurred to me to ask him to pick me up. (Apparently it also never occurred to him to offer.) Over the next ten years, whenever I visited, he never offered me a ride to or from the airport. Like always, he treated me as if I were a nephew, not his son.

I hopped a bus that took me to downtown L.A., its only stop the Biltmore Hotel. The ride took about forty minutes. Getting off the bus, I lugged my bags eight to ten blocks to the city's bus depot. Because of my work at Logan's, I knew the area. I caught a bus to Montebello in East L.A. My parents still lived in the same one-bedroom apartment. This was uncharacteristic of them; in future years, they would change addresses a half dozen times. I arrived around five o'clock, four hours after I had gotten off the plane.

I intended to sleep on their couch for three weeks. I also expected to use one of their cars during my stay.

I assumed my parents would be happy to see me. According to my mother, my visit was the highlight of her year. My father acknowledged me with a nod. Even if he didn't care all that much about my arrival, he was happy with the prospect of seeing Cathy more often. Because he loved Cathy, I ignored his nonchalant attitude toward me.

To her credit, during my stay Charlene allowed me to pick up Cathy most afternoons and keep her overnight at my parents' on weekends, just like the old days. Susan joined us when not with her "other" father. When Charlene moved in with Darrell, Susan's biological father, she was less than a month old. Charlene and Darrell separated after two years, but he remained in the picture. Ga-Ga adopted her as one of her grandchildren.

My father was not as kind. "Why should we take care of another man's child?" he demanded to know. The answer was, if he did not accept Susan, I would not bring Cathy over. Susan was a lovely child, and I refused to hurt her feelings. In my way, I loved her. Admittedly, not as much as I loved Cathy. I did not have the opportunity to bond with her when she was a baby—I never changed her diapers, gave her a bath, or fed her as I had done with Cathy.

My father loved Cathy perhaps more than he loved Corky, no small feat. When Corky married Tina, a beautiful woman but a third-generation Mexican American, my father was not thrilled. When Tina visited with their three daughters, my mother treated them like the grandchildren they were. My father, however, dismissed the kids as "those damn Mexicans." For good reason, Tina intensely disliked him and visited as seldom as possible. Every visit ended with the two of them shouting at each other. Mom and Corky were caught in between.

When I visited Los Angeles Susan called me "Daddy" and acted as if she were my second daughter, even though she had another father she referred to the same way. But despite our mutual love for each other, she kept her feelings inside and often seemed distant. While Cathy always jumped into my lap, I had to initiate hugs with Susan. When they were young children, I protected Susan from Cathy's constant bullying, both physically and mentally. When I was not around, Cathy picked on Susan as my brother picked on me when I was a young boy. I shrugged off his physical and verbal attacks, but Susan was more sensitive. Her feelings were hurt when Cathy hit her or called her stupid.

Still, she loved Cathy as I loved Corky, and I loved being together with both girls.

The girls slept with me on the pullout couch. They watched TV as I fell asleep listening to their happy giggles through a pillow I held over my head. I got up with my mother and talked over a cup of coffee before driving her to work so I could use her car. The girls were still asleep on the couch, and my father, who was usually not working, cooked the girls breakfast while I was gone.

Mom still worked at Safeway as a meat wrapper. In the late afternoon, we picked her up. We always came early and went inside to wave at her. She was pleased and introduced us to other employees with pride in her voice. She bragged about her son who was a college "professor," and showed off her beautiful granddaughters who looked like her.

I often went to see my brother and his family during visits home. When Corky was working, I took Cathy, Susan, and Tina and her girls (Cindy, Carrie, and Evonne) to drive-in movies. Dozens of drive-ins had family rates and playgrounds, and even cheap popcorn. Cartoons were shown before the double feature and between movie breaks the kids ran over to the snack bar to buy a bucket of popcorn to add to the drinks and snacks Tina packed.

On those nights, my father generously allowed me to drive his "big" car, but for him, it was part of a game. While I visited, he never put gas in his car, and after each outing, he expected me to return the car with a full tank. On the days I was alone, I walked, rode buses, or took my mother to work and used her car. On principle, I seldom ate at my parents' house, and I never ate a meal my father cooked or sat at the table in his presence. Cathy and Susan consumed a massive amount of food there on the weekends. I bought groceries and beer for my mother.

Near the end of my trip my mother took a week's vacation. While she was off doing something, Dad informed me they were going to drive over to Bakersfield to see his sister Nadine and he wanted the girls and me to accompany them.

Sounded like a bad idea. I started shaking my head. The idea of riding with my father for three or four hours each way over the mountains and through the desert to Bakersfield and back to L.A. in the heat of August did not appeal to me.

"Car's got air-conditioning," Dad said. "And I know a new route that'll get us there in three hours. Nadine says we can stay with her for the night. We will come back tomorrow in the evening." Apparently, Nadine was getting a divorce and had been feeling lonely since her three girls, Susan, Imogene, and Norma, had married and moved to Los Angeles.

Mother wanted company. "Besides, Kenny," she said, "the trip will give me more time with you and the girls."

The girls wanted to go. I said okay.

After two and a half hours, we were over the Sierra Nevada Mountains and in a semiarid landscape that stretched for miles. Dad turned off on a side road he proclaimed to be a shortcut to Bakersfield. The road had no gravel shoulders but was well maintained. Every few miles, we passed small pit stops with a service station, restaurant, and sometimes a rundown motel.

From the backseat, I noticed the car's temperature gauge indicated the engine was overheating.

"Happens all the time," Dad said. "Damn radiator's thermometer is just stuck. Don't mean shit." Dad was half-drunk, and in this state he drove full speed ahead. The alpha male at work: as always, he cursed the other "stupid" drivers, exceeded the speed limit, and tailgated cars, often honking or flashing his lights as he passed in no-passing lanes. No stopping for bathrooms and thermometers, either. He passed two gas stations as Mom and I begged him to stop.

I often wondered how my father avoided getting a DUI ticket. Normally, Dad sipped his whiskey and maintained a buzz while driving. Back in the day, when the police stopped drivers, there were no breathalyzers or drug-testing equipment. Officers determined whether a driver was drunk the old-fashioned way: by demanding you touch your nose with your eyes closed, walk a straight line for ten or fifteen yards, stand on one foot, and engage in rational conversation. The officer decided if the driver was impaired. Dad easily passed the physical tests and convinced the officers he was sober as he played his "good old boy" character. Besides, in Oklahoma he knew all the officers, and as a taxicab driver in L.A. he was on speaking terms with many patrol officers. I guess that's how he avoided those DUIs.

We waited for the inevitable to happen. I never argued with Dad. What's the sense? If I disagreed, I suffered for a half hour listening to his opinions and proclamations that I was stupid for not agreeing with him or not following his suggestions. "An educated idiot," he would snort. Why become an underpaid teacher when I could earn thousands more working for a giant bureaucratic multinational corporation? I would detest such a job. Not, of course, that he cared.

Thirty minutes after we asked Dad to stop, steam started blowing out of the front of the car; within five miles, the engine stopped. We got out of the hot car and sat on the shady side of it.

Dad waved down a car and asked the driver to tell the next service station to send a tow truck. We waited for two hours. Fortunately, Mom had brought some sodas and beer in an ice cooler. The girls and I drink sodas, Mom drank the beer, and Dad had his bottle of Jack Daniel's or Old Crow.

Forced to wait around for the car to get fixed, we stayed two nights in a cheap motel with a black and white TV and just three channels. We ate at the greasy spoon restaurant on the premises and bought snacks in the motel's small convenience store. (Young girls eat a lot of snacks.) To the girls' delight, the motel had a well-maintained swimming pool. I sat outside reading (of course I had brought a book) and watching the girls. Fortunately for Dad, the store also carried alcohol, and he stocked up on Old Crow for himself and beer for my mother. We did not see my parents much during this detour. We never made it to Aunt Nadine's house.

I swore I would never take another trip with my dad, even one down to a local grocery store. Only later in life did I realize Dad believed he was doing me and the girls a favor for inviting us on his trip to Aunt Nadine's. I also realized taking your family, including young daughters, on a road trip with a semi-drunk driver was insane, but so was the rest of society. At the time drunk driving was lightly enforced and treated as a mere misdemeanor unless an accident occurred.

Eventually, however, my father's bad habits caught up with him. Sometime in the early 1970s, Dad lost his driver's license. For the rest of his life he seldom had a job, living his last days as an alcoholic.

Two days later I flew back to New York City and my new life at Danbury State College.

CHAPTER 23

THE PHD:
TRIALS AND TRIBULATIONS

When I returned to Connecticut in late August of 1967, I was determined to retain my job at Danbury. I had enjoyed teaching during my first year, and I wanted to improve my skills and my knowledge in my fields of study. At this point I had saved enough money by teaching summer courses to take three courses at NYU in pursuit of my PhD, a degree essential to guaranteeing tenure and promotion in my new career.

I knew obtaining a PhD was difficult. At dozens of universities throughout the United States, several thousand students were in PhD programs, but only a few hundred achieved their goal each year. For me, the difficulty was not in maintaining a 3.0 grade point average in graduate courses. With one exception, over the next three years I did exceptional work in my classes at NYU, particularly in my primary field of United States diplomacy in East and Southeast Asia. PhD programs had hurdles beyond core course work. One problem in particular loomed for me: the foreign languages requirements. Languages were my worst subject. Despite my best efforts, I just could not learn phonetics. I took a Chinese-language course but discovered it was impossible, as was Japanese, Thai, Burmese, Indonesian, and Filipino. The Chinese class had thirty students, and to learn the language I would have needed to spend thousands of dollars on private tutors. There were no computer programs to help me if I tried to learn the language on my own.

I could not become an expert on China, Japan, or Vietnam, but I could become an expert on U.S. military and diplomatic relations with them and other countries in East and Southeast Asia. I decided to concentrate on two countries where language would not be a major problem, Burma and the Philippines.

I selected Burma for two reasons. One, my adviser at NYU was Professor Frank N. Trager, a well-known scholar on U.S.–Burmese relations. Two, from the mid-nineteenth century to the end of World War II, Burma was part of the British Empire. This aligned with my main areas of interest, British and American military operations in Burma during World War II, particularly the actions of General Joseph Stilwell and General Claire Chennault (see articles in Appendix).

I also wanted to study U.S. military actions in the Philippines from 1898 to 1946. The United States acquired the Philippines in 1899 after the Spanish–American War. Over the following decades, the Filipinos rebelled against United States colonialization and fought for independence. When Japan attacked the Philippines in December 1941 shortly after Pearl Harbor, the commander of U.S. Army Forces in the Far East, General Douglas MacArthur, fled the Philippines for Australia but vowed to return. His character became part of American folklore. I selected Spanish, the lingua franca of the Philippines for much of the nineteenth century, as one of my foreign languages.

Because of the Vietnam War, I selected French as the second foreign language. Vietnam had been part of French Indochina until 1954. In 1967 the war in Vietnam was escalating and becoming a major focus of attention.

Although I had two years of Spanish in high school and a year of French in junior college under my belt, I was never able to speak either language. Language courses were a farce in the United States. The cause was not always bad teachers. They had an impossible job. My language courses had thirty to forty students in classes that met five hours a week. Under these conditions, no one could teach forty students to read or speak fluent Spanish or French in a year. That said, my high school, Garfield High, had many students who spoke Spanish, and I remembered some of the basic words.

I studied hard for two years to gain an elementary ability to read both Spanish and French. Fortunately, I only needed to be able to read Spanish and French (as opposed to speaking) and show it by taking the "Princeton Language Tests" designed to prove a student at least knew the 1,000 most commonly used words in a language. To determine this, it asked students to translate five printed pages in two hours and answer a hundred multiple choice questions. The thinking was that while searching through primary sources in a library in Madrid or Paris, a scholar only needed to know enough Spanish or French to determine how important a document was after reading a few lines. Students could use a dictionary for the exams, but they still had to have a core base of knowledge. Looking up every word was impractical if they expected to finish translating a five-page document in two hours. For example, if you're reading something in English but don't know the word "esoteric," you can look it up in the dictionary. But knowing this definition can't help you if you do not know the most common English words and tenses of verbs such as "to be, to have, to take, to eat"; conjunctions such as "and, or, but"; or articles such as "the, a, an."

I took the Spanish exam in early 1968 and passed easily. I studied French for another year. In the spring of 1969, I barely passed the French test.

In my mind, the foreign languages requirement for my PhD were simply obligations. I did not intend to use and never did use Spanish or French in my research. Over my career I examined thousands of primary documents and books written by American and British diplomats, soldiers, and scholars. My interest was U.S. Diplomacy in Asia, not Chinese, Japanese, Vietnamese, Filipino, or Burmese actions and motivations. To understand "the enemy's" side, I read hundreds of books about these countries by scholars who wrote in English, but unlike many scholars today, I did not go native and write articles supporting the opposing side and attacking the United States. I admit, though, if I spoke and read Vietnamese or Japanese, I might have been more empathetic to their causes. Instead, I wanted to know why we fought in Vietnam, not why the Vietminh and Viet Cong fought for their freedom. I opposed the war in Vietnam not to "save" the Vietnamese, but because I believed the U.S. intervention was stupid and poorly planned.

※

My first misstep at NYU occurred in the spring of 1968 when I took a U.S. history course titled "FDR to JFK" (i.e., March 1933 to November 1963). As a PhD candidate, the course was an elective for me, simply one of several U.S. history courses I could have taken to fulfill the needed credits for the PhD. But it was a required course for NYU's master's degree in history.

When I entered the classroom the first night of class, I was shocked. The students' desks stretched sixty feet to the rear of the room, which was perhaps eighty feet wide. It was huge, a double-sized classroom with over seventy students settling into seats. A teacher's desk was positioned up front on a raised platform. I had never taken a graduate course with more than twenty-five students.

I was also disappointed when I discovered the teacher was an adjunct rather than an associate or full professor, as in most graduate-level classes. He had a PhD and had published a book on U.S. history from 1901 to 1960, but from my point of view he was not a professional historian. He was employed in a totally different field, and no doubt wanted the job for the prestige he would receive at parties when he revealed he was an adjunct professor at NYU. His life did not revolve around teaching and trying to become a scholar. I assumed, however, he at least knew more than I did on some topics, since he had written a book. I hoped he was a good public speaker.

My worst fears were quickly confirmed. He sat at his raised desk, pulled out several three-by-five index cards from a metal box, and waited for the seventy students to settle down. A graduate assistant stood behind him.

After putting on his glasses, he pulled a card from the stack, and without looking up, began to read the course requirements. His book, a scaled-down textbook covering sixty years of recent U.S. history, was required, he said. I had read a few chapters before class. It was relatively well written, but it was still a textbook. Besides reading his book, each student was required to read and write a bibliographical review article on at least three books on a single topic. The only test he would give was a final.

Okay, I thought. I had been through these kinds of courses for years. Boring but relatively easy. How wrong I was.

The teacher was among the worst I'd ever encountered in higher education. In every class he just sat at his desk and read the index cards. His "lectures" were chapters from his book, sections covering the stock market crash in 1929 and the beginning of the Depression. He was a slow reader. After a boring fourteen weeks, he reached December 7, 1941, the attack on Pearl Harbor.

The other two courses I took that semester, open only to PhD candidates, were a huge contrast. Both were taught by Professor Frank Trager, my mentor. One course was on Southeast Asia. My cup of tea. It required reading seven books for group discussions in class. There were only fifteen students in the class, and Trager quizzed us constantly on the books and suggested others we should read. The second course, a seminar with only ten students, required a major research paper. It was to be twenty-five to thirty pages with at least 60 percent of the references drawn from primary sources. For the first two weeks we met as a class to present the outlines of our paper topics. After a break we reconvened to turn in our papers, and then spent the final three weeks discussing them.

I went to the U.S. history class each week, but instead of taking notes I simply opened the book and read the chapter the teacher read aloud to seventy extremely bored students. I wrote the required term paper. The course was boring, but the requirements were considerably less demanding than those in the other courses I had that semester. I thought it would be a cakewalk. It wasn't—because of three mistakes I made.

The teacher presented a list of topics for a bibliographical review paper that fell within the years 1901 to 1963, the period covered in his book. I choose the presidential election of 1912. With its three candidates Theodore Roosevelt, Woodrow Wilson, and William Taft, it was one of the most important presidential elections in U.S. history. I read five books on the election and carefully reviewed and compared the books. I never took the easy way on required papers. Unlike many students, I did not examine ten to twelve reviews of the books and paraphrase their conclusions. I read the books, intent on learning as a scholar is intended to learn. But I should have read books on the election of 1960—I had already read several on it, including Theodore White's *The Making of a President: 1960,* published in 1961.

My second mistake was even more damaging. As I well knew, when a teacher assigned his own book, he expected you to read it carefully, ideally twice, while you took extensive notes. Stupid me. Hell, in class the instructor stopped at Pearl Harbor—and so did I. I never read his entire book. Hello, stupid!

Third, and, perhaps most important, I got angry during the final exam. And my behavior backfired.

The exam had five questions; the student had to select three. One was on Hoover and another on FDR. The other three questions were on the Eisenhower administration. I answered the questions on Hoover and FDR, but I refused to answer a third question. Instead, I angrily wrote out four bluebook pages criticizing the teacher, his method of teaching, and asking questions never discussed in class. I slammed the bluebook on the desk of the graduate assistant monitoring the test and left.

Why? I really don't know. Occasionally my emotions triumph over my normal rational behavior.

As I left the building and headed for the subway, I stopped, suddenly realizing I had made a stupid mistake. A *truly* stupid mistake. I knew the graduate assistant would grade the papers and the final exam, and I knew what my grades would be: an A-minus or B-plus on the two essays I completed, and an F on the one I did not, equaling a C. Add an A-minus on my bibliographical paper. Tally everything up and my course grade would be a C-plus: the kiss of death for a PhD candidate.

"Shit," I kept muttering all the way to the subway and then all the way home on the train. I hit myself in the head several times. "Stupid." I taught U.S. history courses at Danbury State and had lived through the Eisenhower years. I could have answered the questions with ease, although perhaps not at an A level, but certainly well enough for a B.

Why did I crack? After all these years, I still don't know. The test and the class simply violated every principal I held dear as a teacher.

A PhD candidate received *no* credit for a C-plus. I had to take another course in U.S. history. I selected a course covering one of my favorite periods in U.S. history, 1787 to 1824. The class had only twenty-five students, an excellent teacher, and the normal requirements for graduate classes: several good books and a quality research paper. I made an A-minus and later published the paper (see Appendix).

In the spring of 1969, I finished all the courses I needed for my PhD. But there were two huge tasks still ahead: an oral exam and writing a dissertation.

The oral exams were given before a PhD candidate could submit an official dissertation topic. The exams consisted of four full professors quizzing the candidate for up to three hours. A major part of a full professor's job was participating in orals for PhD candidates, since a department's reputation depended on putting out qualified PhDs who were experts in their fields. If a candidate failed the orals, they had to take more courses to close the obvious gaps in their knowledge. If they failed the orals a second time, the candidate was out of the program.

The doctorate program at NYU required candidates to specialize. I continued my focus on U.S. history with a specialization in U.S. diplomacy in East and Southeast Asia.

When I arrived in the History Department's conference room for my orals, four professors sat behind a huge polished desk. Escorted to a comfortable chair, I sat down in front of them. Although I knew all the professors, they introduced themselves formally and announced their areas of specialization. Two taught U.S. history, one taught courses on China, and the other one, Trager, taught courses on Southeast Asia.

I had an advantage over many PhD candidates. I had been teaching comparable courses at Danbury State (around this time renamed Western Connecticut State College), and after each semester I rewrote my lectures to include the facts and ideas I had learned at NYU. In the process, I discovered that presenting these ideas to my classes made me understand my subject matter better—a common experience for any teacher worth their salt. You must know your material to entice your audience to listen. Teaching taught me to organize and explain the stories I taught my students.

Examining my transcript at my orals, the professors specializing in U.S. history took the lead asking questions, sometimes interrupting me to say "That's good" or "Let's go on to the next question." If I did not know an answer to a question, such as "How many U.S. delegates were at the Versailles Peace Conference?" I said "I don't know" but named President Wilson and the other major figures at the conference. They asked questions on the Boxer Rebellion, the Russo-Japanese War, the Filipino insurgency, MacArthur, and the Korean War—all my specialties. It was obvious I knew more about these topics than they did—which was exactly what they wanted to hear.

After an hour, they turned the questions over to Professor Trager, my mentor, and Professor Tan. Although I had earned two As and two B-plusses in Professor Tan's courses on China, he was not happy with one of my papers, on Nationalist Chinese troops in northern Burma after World War II. Coincidentally, the paper became the basis of my dissertation.

The topic is obscure but was significant at the time. In 1949, the Chinese Communist Party ousted Nationalist leader Ch'iang K'ai-shek, who escaped to Taiwan. Thousands of soldiers in the Kuomintang (Nationalist) Army were trapped in China's interior and fled south into northern Burma. The generals survived with U.S. support and became the opium warlords in the Golden Triangle.

Professor Tan was a Nationalist, and he disliked any criticism of Ch'iang. My paper linking Kuomintang generals in northern Burma to the opium trade was blasphemy to him. Although he knew my concentration was the U.S. and Southeast Asia, not China, he centered his questions on the millions of overseas Chinese who lived in Malaysia, Singapore, and Indonesia and dominated the urban economies of the three nations. Tan kept asking more detailed questions on economic issues, and several times I answered "I don't know." Finally, Professor Trager jumped in and said, "Damn it Tan, *I* don't know the answer to most of those questions." The questioning quickly stopped.

When it was over, I was sent to wait outside the room while the panel deliberated. I waited for thirty minutes before Professor Trager came out to shake my hand. Three of the professors had passed me with honors, he said; Tan reluctantly made it unanimous. He couldn't afford to alienate Trager, who might in turn reject one of Tan's future candidates. Mentors do help.

Passing my orals meant I could submit my topic for my dissertation, the final and most difficult part of obtaining a PhD.

⁂

Great intellect is not needed to obtain a PhD. Over the years I have known professors who were boring and ignorant in areas outside their specialization. The main traits a PhD candidate needs are diligence and perseverance. A bachelor's degree requires the same traits, but graduate courses demanded thousands of hours of research in addition to hundreds of hours of class attendance. As mentioned earlier, each year thousands of students drop out of their PhD programs. Some don't finish their coursework, and many don't take their oral examinations, but the biggest hurdle is the dissertation.

The dissertation requires extensive research using every available resource. A synopsis of twenty or more pages, including a substantial list of your secondary and primary sources, is submitted to a professor who agrees to be your adviser. After recommending revisions, he submits the synopsis to the appropriate department committee. They generally approve it but recommend other sources to be considered.

When I was in grad school, candidates had seven years to finish a dissertation after they passed their orals, though extensions were commonly granted. For his part, Trager, my dissertation adviser, did not want semester-by-semester updates. When he returned my synopsis, he said, "Come back and see me when you finish." *Goodbye, so long, see you later.* I understood. Dissertations are generally boring, extensively footnoted academic papers four or five hundred pages long. Reading one chapter-by-chapter over a seven-year period sounds like hell to me.

Professor Trager was not my guardian. He would not call or contact me. I would write the dissertation, submit it, and he would edit and advise. That's it. Except for the Ivy League schools such as Yale and Harvard, who used PhD candidates to teach lower-level courses and saw their adviser often, Trager's policy was normal.

Thousands never finished their dissertations and became known as ABDs: "all but dissertation." I knew the statistics and was determined not to become one. When I enrolled in my PhD program in the fall of 1966, I recognized that finishing a dissertation was the longest and hardest part of the PhD process, and from day one I searched for a good topic to spend my days, weeks, and nights with. In the fall of 1967, I selected as my topic U.S. aid to the Chinese Nationalist Army in northern Burma. They provided opium to the CIA, who in turn distributed it in Vietnam to obtain information from the Triads. From that point on, as I researched other papers during my coursework, I also researched my dissertation. When I passed my orals in June 1969, I already had over two hundred pages written and had completed about 80 percent of my research.

I delivered my first draft to Professor Trager in December 1969. The dissertation was four hundred pages; a quarter of them were footnotes and the bibliography. Three weeks later he returned the manuscript with his suggestions for additional research and other revisions. The revisions took three months. Trager accepted my next draft of the dissertation and turned it over to the appropriate committee. In late March, it was approved.[2] I applied for graduation and received my

---

[2] My dissertation is something I would *not* recommend reading. I wrote it as an exercise to fulfill a requirement. Ivy League schools often publish their PhD dissertations, and a few even become classics. But most dissertations do not receive such acclaim. There are several reasons dissertations at Ivy League universities are superior. While they're working toward their PhD, candidates serve as teaching assistants and are in constant contact with their professors. They are under observation by many mentors, not just a single person. Also, Ivy League PhD candidates have the contacts to obtain unbelievable funding for their projects. Here's a personal example: Two years after my dissertation was accepted, Alfred

degree in June 1970. Western Connecticut State University, promoted me to assistant professor and granted me tenure.

For the rest of my life I considered obtaining a PhD my greatest achievement—me, a poor boy from Oklahoma. I had achieved my dream. I had a career I loved and security from poverty. I could take care of myself.

I was thirty years old. Of course, my work was not done. I had more to learn and more dreams to chase. "What now, brown cow?" Could I jump over the moon?

W. McCoy, a PhD candidate at Yale, published *The Politics of Heroin* in Southeast Asia. The book covers the CIA's involvement in drug trafficking in Vietnam, and the chapters on the Kuomintang in northern Burma are vastly, and I mean vastly, superior to those in my dissertation. The book is truly a classic in the field. Why? McCoy, with the help of research assistants, spent thousands of (funded) dollars on trips to Burma, Thailand, Vietnam, and Laos. Money, mentors, and Ivy League contacts meant research grants. Yes, who you know is very important!

Looking back, I wish I had written my dissertation on Adoniram Judson, the first U.S. missionary in Burma, who lived there from 1812 to 1850 (see the articles listed in the Appendix for more on him). Another possibility was the Filipino insurrection from 1899 to 1901 (see the book on Arthur MacArthur listed in the Appendix for more information).

CHAPTER 24

WOODBURY:

LIFE AFTER PHD

When I received my PhD, I felt a huge sense of relief. After years of hard work I had finally achieved my academic goal. For the rest of my life, regardless of future failures, I could always refer to myself as Dr. Young.

I did not consider myself smarter than my brother or mother but simply more educated. I will always remember I was once a poor boy from Oklahoma, and I don't believe I could forget this if I tried.

In my thirty years as a professor, I met and associated with many colleagues who came from "good" families and considered themselves to be among the best and the brightest. Some came from wealthy, or at least well-to-do, homes, and several went to prestigious prep schools where they received an education superior to most colleges. They learned to read and speak Latin and French. They read "the Hundred Greatest Books," recited poetry, expounded on philosophers, and discussed the best English, French, Russian, and American novels. They participated in sports available only in elite schools such as rowing, polo, and cricket. Superior to all others, they entered prestigious universities in the United States like Harvard, Yale, Princeton, and Stanford.

Throughout my career and life, the condescending attitude of graduates of prep schools and Ivy League universities irritated me. I accept the fact they were wealthier than me, had a stronger classical education, knew French and Latin, played tennis and golf, and had accomplished mentors throughout their lives of wealth and special privileges.

Yes, money and connections do make a difference. I envied their wealth, admired their educational backgrounds, and wished I had the inside contacts that aided their success in life.

But all those things did not make them smarter than me.

I have the working man's attitude.

Reading Latin or James Joyce, loving opera or ballet, playing polo or golf was a waste of time in the working man's world. It would not put a dime in the pocket of a plumber, a waitress, or an "associate" at big-box stores. The middle class and the wealthy generally consider manual workers beneath them, not only in money but in terms of culture and politics. "If those idiots had any brains, they would get off the bottom. They are lazy and dumb and always looking for a handout," the thinking often goes. Of course, it's only partially true. From the poor to the extremely rich, in every class, there are lazy and dumb shits.

The average working man or woman does not trust the government, and they fight hard to survive without going on welfare or begging for a handout. The working man honors the motto: "Take care of yourself, your family, and help friends in need." They believe you *cannot* depend on a government controlled by the true middle class—the top 30 percent—or the true upper class, the top 10 percent.

Many wealthy people do not understand the motto "Take care of yourself." From way up high on the food chain, they actually believe that "money is not everything in life." Well, it is if you don't have any. Then it's the most important thing in life.

The wealthy pay lip service to the knowledge a worker accumulates while raising a family and scratching out a living. A waiter may like their work, or they may hate it, but their motivation always boils down to the need to take care of themselves and those around them. First-class airplane tickets, hotels, or expensive clothes are not within their reach. Having food and a roof over their heads are more essential than polo or playing golf.

I never forgot these lessons, which I learned during my own life. After I received my PhD, I vowed to treat people as equals whether they were rich or poor, college-educated or educated in the school of hard knocks. Smart is smart. And work is work. Different knowledge for different folks.

When meeting people, I do not introduce myself as "Professor Young." I do not dominate conversations about history, literature, U.S. politics, or foreign affairs. I usually shift the conversation to topics where I am not the expert. I ask my companions about their jobs and activities they enjoy. Being a college professor did not mean I was automatically smarter. If they were good plumbers, waiters, or accountants, I had much to learn from them. Of course, there are as many dumb plumbers as dumb professors. Degrees don't count.

❧

I thought of switching jobs to a state university closer to Los Angeles and my family. When I accepted the job at Danbury State in 1966, jobs were available at many colleges for PhDs with four years of teaching experience. I wasn't thrilled with the thought of leaving the university, but I felt an obligation to try to obtain a job closer to Los Angeles so I could see Cathy, Susan, and my mother more often.

I had no wish to live in a large city, particularly one like Los Angeles or Dallas, which were surrounded by flat, semiarid countryside. I loved the mountains, lakes, and rivers surrounding Danbury. The plush green trees and flowers in the spring through fall were delightful. The town was small and retained some of its old New England charm. But guilt is a strong motivator.

After NYU notified me in March 1970 that I had earned my PhD, I sent out a few inquiry letters with a short curriculum vita to state universities in Central and Northern California and coastal Oregon and Washington. Within a few weeks, I received polite letters informing me budget cuts prevented them from hiring new teachers. The country was in a recession and remained in trouble economically through much of the 1970s. Adjunct teachers now taught many college courses to reduce costs.

To my surprise, I felt relieved. Like I said, I liked living in the Danbury area. The place suited my personality, and it was a place I could pursue my dream of becoming a good teacher and scholar in my field. I enjoyed teaching at Western Connecticut, too. Students came from backgrounds comparable to mine, and the best had the potential to excel and achieve their goals. The school was small and more intimate than big colleges like Cal State.

My promotion to assistant professor with tenure ensured my position was secure, and with hard work future promotions were possible. Although the pay was only $10,000 a year, even less after taxes, it was enough for me. The job came with perks such as full medical coverage and a pension. And the icing on the cake: Danbury was close to New Haven, New York City, Hartford, and Boston.

Since I planned to remain at Western Connecticut for a few years, I thought it was time to stop living like a poor graduate student. I was usually frugal with money. I spent it on tuition, books, research trips, trips to California, child support, and occasional dates. Somehow, I had saved about $2,500. But my car, the old Nash, was no longer dependable, and I wanted a new one. So I violated my rule not to borrow money for things I wanted, not needed.

I bought a 1970 VW Beetle, a rational selection that cost $1,600. I put down $600 and took out a two-year, $1,000 bank loan. I spent an additional $400 dollars on new suits, dress shirts, shoes, and other clothing. My reserve was down to $1,500.

I wasn't done. For almost four years I lived in a third-floor one-bedroom walk-up apartment in downtown Danbury. The apartment had several assets and several liabilities. It was close to the college and most important, the rent was $65 a month including utilities. The liabilities: it was on the third floor. Going up and down the stairs carrying groceries or books or garbage bags gets old after four years. It was an old apartment with small closets and a tiny kitchen with an antique stove and a small fridge. A small toilet was enclosed in a closet-like room, and a separate closet held the bathtub. No shower. Living downtown was convenient for work but made having an active social life more difficult. The stores in downtown Danbury closed at 6 p.m. although a few restaurants stayed open until 10.

In June of 1971, I decided to move. But first I had to do my due diligence.

With my new Beetle I started exploring the region, traveling north up I-84, the newly built interstate highway. Construction ended forty miles north of Danbury near Waterbury, a small city slowly dying as copper and textile factories closed. I-84 stimulated new hope for Waterbury since the new highway was slated to go through the city's downtown. In a few years, I-84 became the main highway from New York City to Hartford to Boston. But the new throughway was almost empty of traffic in June 1971. Several small towns were located along the route including Newtown, Sandy Hook, and Woodbury.

When I got off the interstate and headed to Woodbury, the road passed farm fields and a few developments before reaching a small downtown area. Traveling west of town, I discovered two relatively modern two-story redbrick buildings, each containing twenty-four "garden" apartments with a parking lot for a hundred or so cars. The upper-floor apartments rented for $200 a month; the basement apartments rented for $150. Utilities not included.

The debate: was a basement apartment in Woodbury three times better than my $65 place in Danbury? The emotional answer was yes. The apartment was new, with a large bedroom, a walk-in closet, and a bathroom with a sink, tub, and shower. It was twenty minutes to school but it was also only twenty minutes to Waterbury, a city with a modern mall and movie theaters. The prospect of being able to explore Waterbury and the surrounding towns without constantly bumping into students was another advantage.

I followed my emotions and signed the lease. Naturally, I needed new furniture, and I took out another $1,000 two-year bank loan. Within a few months, I realized I had overextended myself. I consolidated the loans, making the monthly payment lower, and paid off the loan in eighteen months using money I made teaching four summer classes. From this point on, I stayed within my budget, and in two years my reserve funds rose to $5,000.

Woodbury became my den, a place with bookcases and paintings covering the walls. As always, I had no TV. I read books, prepared lectures, and wrote academic articles and my first (unsuccessful) novel. I remained a loner with few friends. I went to school plays, the movies, and university lectures. On holiday breaks, I took car trips on state roads through small towns in Vermont. I was happy with my life.

But, as always, the times were "a-changin'." I was in my early thirties and still had much to learn. My education wasn't over.

Chapter 25
Midge & Me

After my bad experience with Charlene, I avoided any serious involvement with women. I did not date for over two years after our separation. Slowly, however, I realized the life of a monk did not suit me and tentatively dated several women, but I carefully avoided making any commitments.

When I took the job at Danbury State, I was busy pursuing my education, and as a teacher and scholar spent most of my time researching and preparing lectures for my classes. I had many acquaintances but no friends other than a fellow History and Social Science Department faculty member named David Detzer, who started teaching at Danbury State the same year I did. Initially he taught European history courses and specialized in the French Revolution. A few years later, he switched to teaching U.S. history classes and slowly became an expert on the Civil War. He was as antisocial as me.

After I received my PhD and tenure and moved to Woodbury, I dated several different women but refused to become involved. I took them out to dinner, movies, and occasionally, weekend trips to Boston or Vermont. I never dated a woman I did not like, but I discovered most were quick to apply pressure to develop a more permanent relationship. As a result, I preferred dating older women who had careers and were often divorced. I refused to meet their friends and family or to establish a dating routine. Over time, most became platonic friends and called me when they were feeling lonely.

In the summer of 1972, my social life changed. That summer Cathy, now thirteen years old, visited me for three weeks. I spent all my time with her. We went to New York City and explored its museums. We took car trips around New England up to Vermont. She enjoyed the beauty of the Danbury area.

Although I did not like swimming, she did, and I took her to a small, relatively quiet "pond" that was larger than the lakes I grew up with in Oklahoma. I swam with her for a few minutes, then retreated to my beach blanket and read as I watched her play with other kids, particularly one boy who was about nine years old. She stayed in the water for an hour before the boy charged out of the water and ran toward his mother.

Cathy remained with the boy, his mother, and a male companion for at least a half hour. Finally, she came back where I lay on the blanket. She grabbed my arm, pulled me up, and insisted I go over and meet her new friends.

As we approached, I realized I knew the woman. Her name was Marjorie. She was around thirty years old, about five feet tall, weighed perhaps a hundred pounds, and wore her red hair long but tied back for swimming. She was an exceptionally pretty young woman. She had been in my Chinese Culture course a few years earlier. As a returning student, she was about five years older than most of her peers. She had dropped out of college when she married and had a son. After her marriage failed, she went back to school. She sat in the back of my class wearing sunglasses and never said a word. I noticed her because on the first book test and on the midterm, she made As. Remember—I paid attention to my best students. After she graduated, I ran into her on a couple of occasions in local restaurants. We had simply said hello and moved on.

"Hello, Dr. Young," she said.

"Hi. Nice to see you again, Marjorie."

"Midge," she corrected. "Everyone calls me Midge."

I nodded.

The man with her, who I assumed was her boyfriend, was over six feet tall and towered over her as well as most men. His hair was blond, short and choppy. He was in excellent shape. His name was Ted. After she introduced her son, Jimmy, he quickly ran back to the pond with Cathy following him.

I sat down with Midge and Ted. She told me she was now a middle school English teacher—seventh grade—in Bethel, a small town bordering Danbury. I sat with her and Ted for a few minutes, then returned to my blanket.

On the ride home, and for the next few days, Cathy kept repeating how great Midge was. "Why don't you date someone like her?" she asked.

Cathy had met my current part-time girlfriend, Jan, and I interpreted her remarks as a judgment. Hey, my "girlfriend" was perhaps not an ideal partner but she was perfect for my sex life and wanted to avoid entangling commitments, which was good enough. She was smart, educated, and *Playboy* beautiful. Her flaws were that she wanted to be in control and demanded we dine at the best restaurants. Dinner always included the perfect bottle of wine. She dressed the part, wearing expensive but tasteful clothes. Practical women were more my style, with their blue jeans and down-to-earth personality.

We were not in an exclusive relationship. I took her out to dinner perhaps once every couple of weeks, and I knew from experience I would see her less frequently in the next few months.

Around this time two members of the History and Social Science Department had, after many years, finally obtained their PhDs. One was a woman anthropologist, about forty-five years old, and the other was an economist around sixty.

Since I now had a nice apartment in Woodbury, I gave a party, unusual for me, to celebrate their accomplishments. I invited four or five colleagues from my department and their wives, and asked Jan to be my date. I also invited five former students including Midge. I had listened to my daughter, and Midge was on my mind. But I assumed she was in a relationship. When I learned her boyfriend was not Ted but another student named George, a history major at Western Connecticut, I extended my party invitation to include him. I had already invited his department's adviser, Professor Roman, who taught Russian and Eastern European history courses. George had not taken any of my courses.

Midge sounded as if she wanted to come but later called me to say George felt awkward about attending a professor's party. They didn't come.

A few months later, I called Midge and asked her out to dinner. With a little hesitation, she agreed to meet at a nice restaurant. During dinner she told me she had stopped seeing George a few weeks earlier. I also had stopped seeing Jan, who had moved on to another boyfriend.

I enjoyed Midge's company. She was a beautiful woman, smart, and down-to-earth. We went dinner two or three times in the first month. I warned her of my devotion to my job, and that I was often busy doing research and writing scholarly articles and a novel that took up much of my time (see Appendix).

She nodded. She wanted the relationship to develop slowly. Like me, she had been burned in an earlier relationship that turned sour. Were we who we proclaimed to be? Could she be another Charlene in disguise? Could I be another "Harry" (her ex-husband)? With all of this in mind, we were careful not to make any quick moves.

I gradually learned she was a kind, considerate friend, a good mother, a devoted daughter to her parents, and nice to her older sister. Although she readily expressed her opinions, she was easygoing and empathetic. She was smart, pretty, and had a job—she was not looking for a sugar daddy. She worked hard to be a good middle school English teacher, preparing class instructions, grading tests and book reports, correcting essays, and reading teenage-level books to select for her classes. If I said I was too busy to see her, she understood, because sometimes she was too busy to see me.

She wanted me to get acquainted with Jimmy. Normally, this would have been a warning sign for me, an indication that she wanted more than a casual boyfriend. But she needed me to recognize she came as package deal, with friends, family, a nine-year-old boy, and a crazy

Siamese cat named Sonia. If Jimmy did not like me, or the converse was true, my relationship with her would end.

Jimmy was small for his age, shy, and stayed away from guests, retreating to his own room whenever possible. He thought, I expect, that I disapproved of him and was afraid if I became part of the family, I might try to correct his behavior and punish him if he did not obey me. Perhaps he was also afraid I would steal his mother's love.

Midge suggested I take Jimmy bowling. At times I wish I were Mark Twain. "What?" he would say. "Take a wimpy, insecure boy bowling?"

Truthfully, I was already fond of the boy.

Bowling is not my favorite sport. It was popular in the early 1970s, but leagues dominated the alleys in the evenings. Over the years, I occasionally played a game or two in the late afternoons at deserted alleys simply to pass the time. I never bowled enough to be good at the sport, probably because it bored me. Usually, my score ranged from 120 to 160.

When we went out to bowl, Jimmy acted as if he were being punished rather than being pampered by his mother's new boyfriend. He answered my questions with a curt "yes" or "no" and no further comment. I quickly realized Jimmy did not like playing games with adults. His favorite pastime was watching TV. He never played organized sports, and certainly was not interested in bowling. During the afternoon, he rarely spoke. After taking him for ice cream, I returned him to his mother.

Over the next few months, I learned he had few friends and hated school because the other children teased him. He did as little homework as possible, but Midge helped him with his lessons almost every night.

Slowly, I became friends with the boy. He had many positive traits including a love for cats, comic books, and music. Soon, when the three of us went to the movies, he wanted to sit in the middle. I fondly remember that when we went for walks, he squirmed between us. Midge and I grabbed his hands and swung him down the path.

By the spring of 1974, six months after we had started dating, I was seeing Midge twice a week. One night she cooked dinner, or the three of us went to a local diner and to the movies. Jimmy refused to conform to table manners at home. He usually picked up his food with his hands and rarely used a knife or fork. Midge tried to teach him proper table etiquette, but he ignored her directions. At the diner, he ordered hot dogs and fries, consumed the food rapidly, and quickly became bored. His mother enjoyed lingering over a cup of tea and talking. Jimmy fidgeted. The solution was to bring comic books for him to read.

Jimmy's table manners did not bother me. I was an Okie. When I was sixteen, I did not know why anyone needed two forks to eat dinner, nor did I know you could bake potatoes or broil steaks. In Mom's house, fried food was the norm, with mashed potatoes reserved for Sundays. People grow up. Jimmy's worst habit was his refusal to pick up his messes. He expected his mother to do all the housework, but in my mind, that was her problem.

Gradually we had become a couple. We socialized with her friends, going with them to the theater, small parties, and movies, or playing volleyball together. I even spent a couple of weekends with her parents, where I naturally slept on the couch.

In June 1974 my father called. He and mother were going on a trip to Lawton to visit relatives. He wanted to take Cathy and suggested I might meet them in Lawton. Charlene told Cathy she could not go unless Susan was invited. Dad agreed reluctantly.

"No way"," said Susan.

"Hurray," I thought. Ga-Ga loved Susan but Dad thought she was a nuisance and seldom paid her any attention. His attitude irritated me, but changing his behavior was impossible. To make her feel better, on many occasions I comforted her and reminded her of my love.

After Susan learned that I planned to meet the family in Lawton, she agreed to the trip. I am sure the idea of spending three days and two nights on the road with my father did not appeal to Susan or Cathy, but the prospect of seeing me won out.

Since my relationship with Midge was becoming serious, I invited her to come with me. We drove from Danbury to Lawton in August, a truly hot time of year, in my VW Beetle without AC. The three-day trip was a test for both of us. We would learn if we were truly compatible.

An example: Somewhere in southern Kansas on a well-maintained but lightly traveled two-lane highway we got a flat tire. There was not a house in sight for many miles, and only an occasional car passed us on the highway. I had changed many tires in my life of driving old cars, but this time it took fifteen minutes to unload the trunk, remove the spare, and jack up the vehicle. I had trouble getting the flat tire off the rim; one of the nuts was frozen. After another fifteen minutes, I was still working on the frozen nut in the hot afternoon sun.

A good old boy in a pickup pulled up, rolled down his passenger window, and asked, "Need any help, son?"

I looked up, stood, and wiped my hands on a rag. "No sir," I said. "Thank you, kindly."

He nodded and drove away.

It took me fifteen more minutes to change the tire.

Much later, when Midge told the story at parties, she informed my friends she thought I was crazy for not accepting the good old boy's help. "A man offered to help," she said, "and what do you think Ken said?"

"Thanks, but no thanks," my friends shouted out and laughed.

"We could have sat there for hours," Midge said. "But that's Ken."

Why did I say no thanks? The man in the truck understood. I thought I could take care of the problem, and it was my job to change the tire, not his. I appreciated that he stopped, though.

The guiding rule in my life, "Take care of yourself," hadn't changed (and I doubt it ever will). It is extremely difficult for me to accept favors from anyone. If I'm truly in need, I will ask for help but there is a principle I follow. If someone does me a favor, I never forget the reciprocal agreement—I must return the favor. "Truly in need" is an admittedly difficult thing to define. Asking the man to help me change the tire would have been convenient, but I did not really need any help. If the man had stepped out of the truck and asked, "Do you want some help?" I might have said yes. When I tried to explain this to Midge, she laughed and accepted me as I was, although over the years she has often shaken her head or sometimes rolled her eyes.

When we arrived in Lawton, we stopped at a downtown hotel that in my youth was the best place in town. By August 1974 its glory days were over, but it still had a restaurant, swimming pool on the roof, and large rooms with two double beds.

Mom and Dad had arrived in town a day before with the girls and were staying with Aunt Hester, one of Mother's sisters, and Uncle Ted. In 1953 when my father's legal problems began, Uncle Ted and Aunt Hester offered to adopt me. They were some of my favorite relatives.

When Midge and I arrived, the girls ran out of Uncle Ted's house to greet us and danced around in delight. I grasped Susan's hand, and Midge hugged Cathy, who remembered her from the swimming pond. The girls wanted to leave immediately and go to the hotel.

When we entered the house, I nodded at my father, hugged Mom, and waited for Aunt Hester to come over and hug me. Although years earlier Hester had been pleasantly plump, she was now chubby. I had not seen her in ten years, but I had fond memories of her. I then went over to Uncle Ted and shook his hand. He had always been overweight but was now obese. Near his chair was a pile of appetizers, and in his hand was a bottle of beer. He clearly still enjoyed good food and his homebrewed beer. Several peppy, lovable, pedigreed bulldogs stood up next to him hoping for attention. I remembered Uncle Ted as the only relative who saw me play baseball in my youth. He always wanted me to stay overnight when I visited, and he taught me how to use a few of the many tools in his gigantic work shed. I enjoyed my time with him.

Although the girls desperately wanted to go to the hotel, social rules dictated that we remain for supper. Midge help set the table and listened to the talk. When asked to share a few stories about our relationship, Midge recalled how Cathy had played a role. The family liked her because she came from a family much like the Bass-Young family. Midge and Mom jumped up to help Aunt Hester while I entertained the girls. Dad and Uncle Ted talked about the old days.

We left around eight o'clock and headed back to the hotel with the girls. The night was warm. Crickets covered the buildings in downtown Lawton; they must have numbered in the millions. They covered the hotel up to the fourth floor. Even I had never seen so many crickets before. We were on the twelfth floor and still found a few in our room.

The kids recounted the horrors of their trip with Dad. We stayed up until well after midnight.

"Bed time," I said.

Within minutes, I brushed my teeth, changed into my pajamas, and jumped in bed. Midge and the girls remained in the bathroom for ages. I could hear them talking and playfully teasing each other.

Finally, they returned to the room, and after a few minutes, actually got into bed. I turned off the lights and finally stretched out into a sleeping position next to Midge.

Then the talking began. Every few minutes I found myself saying, "Let's get some sleep" or "Dream time, girls. Shut-up and go to sleep."

"I can't," Susan said. "I keep having this bad dream where a witch is beating me."

"I used to have a dream like that," I said. "Susan, as you are falling to sleep, visualize you are 'Superwoman.' In my dreams as Superman, I could even beat up my brother."

Susan giggled and Cathy moaned. We all knew Cathy was in for a beating that tonight.

I fell asleep listening to Midge and Cathy talking about how dreams often scared them as well.

The next few days revolved around the girls. The days were hot, and in the afternoons, we swam in the pool on the hotel roof. One day we went to the campgrounds in the Wichita Mountains for a family reunion. Several members of the Bass and Young families came out to say hello to Charlie and Toad. I told Midge and the girls how I learned to swim in one of the nearby lakes.

Two cousins, the sons of one of my father's brothers, came over and sat down to talk. They had played with me on Taft's football team in the Pop Warner junior league. Billy Ross, who played right tackle on the team, was also in some of my junior high classes. Huey (Hubert) was a couple of years younger. Unlike Billy, Huey did not weigh enough to play on the line. He was one of the ends who seldom played because in Coach Waco's words, "Hubert, you're a wiseass. Set down and shut-up." When I met them twenty years later, Billy remained the quiet, chubby one, and Hubert remained a skinny wiseass.

"Ken played football?" Midge asked.

Wiseass Herbert talked about our year of football when I was the team's quarterback. "Yeah. Kenny was a bigshot then," he said in a resentful tone.

A couple of days later, Midge and I drove leisurely back to Danbury, enjoying each other's company.

Next winter Midge and I bought a house and moved in together. We didn't get married. Both of us were on probation, and if things didn't work out, there would be no need for a divorce. Either had the right to terminate the relationship at will.

My words of wisdom: "It wouldn't work." I hoped I was wrong.

Chapter 26

Skyline Drive &
Living Together

We bought a two-story New England colonial–style house about two miles from downtown Danbury. Built in the early 1950s, it was in a development of twenty or thirty homes built with the same plans. Our house, however, had several advantages over the others. It was located on a quarter-acre lot on a corner where the development began, which meant I could drive home without seeing the other cookie-cutter houses. Two large oak trees shaded the front yard and provided privacy from the road. Beyond the modest backyard, a hill rose gradually for a quarter mile; the grade meant no new houses could be built on the property. Trees covered the hill, and we could not see a comparable development above us. In front of the house, the land beyond the road dropped off steeply. A twenty-acre watershed covered in trees provided us a view south toward downtown Danbury. On summer evenings we often heard cars racing on a track over five miles south. In the fall, we could see the lights of the state fair near the track. It was a big deal. Schools closed, even Western Connecticut, so the students could attend the fair.

We bought the home in the spring of 1975 for around $49,000. It had four bedrooms, two baths, a workroom in a partially finished basement, and an attached one-car garage. We took out a $40,000 bank loan with an interest rate of 9.5 percent. Our combined salaries covered the loan, and for a few years we carefully stayed within budget as we remodeled the house. Midge and I were teachers, and our annual raises failed to keep up with the high inflation of the 1970s and early 80s.

The house had fewer perks than today's homes. Although it had more modern luxuries than the houses of my youth, it was still twenty-something years old. In the kitchen the cabinets were made of finished plywood and only a small table could fit. There was no dining room.

The house needed maintenance and updates. It needed to be painted inside and out, the bathrooms needed to be retiled, the kitchen and bedrooms needed more storage space, and electrical and plumbing problems needed addressing.

I knew I could do most repairs around the house. I had worked odd jobs in my youth, and as a stencil cutter, I developed a craftsman's mentality. What I did not know, I could learn. Over the next few years, I collected and read many handyman books.

I had another asset, too, though it was often a liability. Midge's mother and father moved within a mile of our house. Once a week, we had dinner and played cards with them. Both parents were retired. Her seventy-five-year-old father, Mac, was bored, and he came over several times a week and taught me how to be a handyman, fixing plumbing and electrical problems, tiling, chopping wood, and building bookcases. He was a bigoted, cantankerous old man, but he treated me special—much like a sergeant-major might treat a colonel.

Mac had lived an adventurous life. He ran away from home when he was fifteen or sixteen. In 1919, he enlisted in the army. After basic training, he joined a cavalry unit assigned to patrol the border between Texas and Mexico. For two years, he rode horses along the border. He did not reenlist but instead joined the navy for three years. Afterwards, in his twenties, he and a few buddies drove across the country from New York City to California. Good roads only existed near the bigger cities, and the car often broke down. Returning to New York, he got work near Brewster, a small town about sixty miles north of New York City where I used to park my car before riding into the city. He married

Althea, nicknamed Tee. A few years later, they moved to Vero Beach, Florida, where his older brother owned a real estate agency.

Mac bought a taxicab company and had two children, Marcia in 1939 and Marjorie (Midge) in 1943. His business boomed during World War II and he bought some land. At to end of the war, Tee and the kids left Mac in Florida and moved back to Brewster. She hated Florida and its hot, humid summer months; at the time, only the extremely wealthy had air-conditioning.

When Tee refused to return to Florida, Mac moved back to New York, got a job in a factory working in the maintenance department, and bought a small house in Carmel, a tiny one-horse town about ten miles from Brewster.

Mac was a hard worker and disliked corrupt unions and workers who loafed all day but were paid the same salary as the hardworking nonunion men. He disliked FDR for his populism. He thought Italians, Jews, and "Negroes" were trying to take over the country. Mac was an alpha male, the patriarch of the family who thought he was the boss.

Tee considered him a bully and a bore. He couldn't understand her desire to send her daughters to college. "Costs a lot of money," he said to her. "They'll get married and have kids. Don't need a college education for that."

A few years later, Tee found a job as a clerk and later became the office manager at a publisher's office for a national magazine that paid her more money over the years than Mac earned. She did not give him a dime. She saved the money for the girls' college education, purchased pretty clothes for her daughters, and bought quality furniture and trinkets for her house. She seemed to exasperate Mac. To relax, he read Westerns and spy novels. "She reads those damn women's books," he said, in amazement.

Mac was a bigot, but I have lived around many bigots so it didn't faze me much. I heard the same nonsense when I worked in Oklahoma and California where many workers believed the government favored Jews, black people, and Mexican immigrants. People on welfare were just "lazy bastards." I long ago realized that arguing with "sergeant-majors" is a waste of time. Their opinions are carved in stone.

Fortunately, Mac never talked to me about his social or religious views. He thought of me as a "liberal" university professor. He placed me in the same category as medical doctors, bankers, admirals, and generals. As far as social status went, I was a lieutenant colonel and outranked him. Sergeants may disagree with lieutenants, but they never talk back to a colonel whether he is right or wrong. Conversely, sergeants do give advice, and smart colonels listen.

Mac's handyman experience reached back sixty years to the Model T days. He could repair copper plumbing, install new electrical wiring, cultivate a garden, chop down trees, and split firewood. A fisherman and hunter, he slaughtered his chickens and drowned unwanted puppies until his daughters cried and promised to find the puppies homes—and they did.

Over the next few years I learned many things from Mac. He enjoyed working around the house. At seventy-five, he was stronger than me, and many times worked me under the table. Sometimes I regretted following his advice, like the time he ordered a cord of firewood. At the time a cord of split wood cost $125 and an unsplit cord was $75. Naturally, Mac ordered the unsplit cord to save money. We spent several afternoons until sunset splitting our haul. After the third day, my back and arms hurt so much I put down the axe in the late afternoon and said, "Enough." Mac continued splitting the wood until the sun disappeared. After that experience, I admired his hard work but never ordered unsplit firewood again.

Mac gave me tools as gifts and helped me refinish the basement. First, we organized the workshop. I painted it, put in pegboard to hold my tools, and built various cabinet drawers and shelves to hold miscellaneous items, from screws to electrical outlets.

Restless, Mac often came to the house offering his help when I was working in my office. He never understood why I spent so much time preparing my lectures, reading history books, and researching and writing scholarly articles. He knew the rule: Do not disturb me when I am in my office, but he returned day after day hoping I had a home-repair project for him to work on. A great nuisance in a writer's life is constant interruptions.

Mac taught me many things, but a major problem with alpha males is that they seldom listen or seek advice. Mac refused to read any handyman books or even assembly instructions. "Hell, I know how to do that," was his usual response to any issue. I gradually learned that his solution to many problems came from the Depression-era axiom to "Make do with what you got, and that's good enough." *Hello, Grandpa Long.*

Mac taught me to save screws, and anything else that later might prove useful. I followed his example and became a hoarder of spare parts. If an electrical outlet needed replacing, and we saved an old outlet, he used it. It did not matter to him that the outlet was black and all other ones in the room were white. If it works, it's good enough. If a cabinet in the kitchen had a loose screw, get one from the jars in the basement. It will do even if it doesn't match the other hinge screws.

One day Mac bought a small table saw for me and put it together while I was at work. When I arrived home, he hustled me to the basement workshop to see it. As I admired the saw, Mac cut several two-by-fours to illustrate how it worked. I praised him. And then I noticed six screws of various sizes on the work counter.

"What are these?" I asked as I picked up the screws.

He took them from my hand and tossed them in one of the screw drawers. "Damn fools included too many screws," he said.

After he left, I examined the saw's tabletop. It was not level. I picked up the directions and carefully read them. I discovered that Mac had put several screws in the wrong spot. It was clear that he never read the directions. He didn't need any advice from paper pushers on how to put something together, including a damn table saw. The problem was, if a table saw is not level, it is useless—that is, if you need precise cuts. I spent that night taking the saw apart and putting it back together with the directions. I needed all the screws. I never told Mac about this. At any rate, I used the saw extensively over the next twenty years to build cabinets and bookcases.

In the first few years we lived in the house I worked with Mac quite a bit, but I often had to veto his tendency to make do. We repainted the inside of the house, scraped and repainted the outside, retiled the bathrooms, put in an attic fan, and converted the single-car garage into a dining room with a brick fireplace. I actually enjoyed the work because it was a break from my main job of improving my knowledge as a scholar and a teacher.

Along with helping us on many projects, Midge planted flowers along a rock wall which separated the front yard from the two streets bordering our property. The wall resembled the walls built by farmers in the Colonial era. Connecticut's land is fertile, but the soil is full of rocks which the farmers dug up while plowing their fields. Stacked rock walls separated the farmer's fields. In the summer, tourists flocked to the Danbury area to enjoy the lakes and the beautiful countryside. People often stopped and praised Midge's flowers and admired her garden that provided us with vegetables in the summer and fall.

Over the years, the house and yard demanded constant attention but repairs and renovation always took a back seat to my academic and scholarly work. Except, of course, for emergency repairs such as a leaking roof or a flooded basement.

※

Our social life revolved around Midge's parents and her friends. We entertained guests in our new dining room and hosted family reunions that included her parents, her sister and her husband, and their six kids from two different marriages. On Thanksgiving, Christmas, and Easter, the house was crowded.

Midge's mother needed lots of attention. She lived with a man she disliked and had no other friends. Midge visited her several times a week, and Tee looked forward to Friday nights, when we came over for dinner and three hours of pinochle. She and Mac couldn't be partners. Mac yelled at her when they lost, and she smiled, happy at his frustration. Both were good players, but Midge and I took turns being Mac's partner. On other nights, Mac watched TV and Tee read a book, sipping scotch until she went to bed tipsy.

Mac had achieved the working man's dream, and like many working men, had no interest in upper-class culture. His idea of wealth was a new car every three years, a house with a garden, and a boat for fishing. Museums, operas, ballets, or plays did not interest him. A wife should cook, clean the house, and take care of children. He never talked about religion or any philosophical concepts. "How many angels can stand on the head of a pin?" Mac's answer: "Who gives a shit. Stupid question." A better one: "How much tile do you need to redo the bathroom?" Mac was a practical man, not a dreamer. He was a cowboy who wanted to be a rancher. He was not a preacher or a scholar. He was a bossy, bigoted working man much like Archie Bunker in *All in the Family*.

Tee had taste; Mac did not. She worked to create a nice home for her daughters. She never took Mac's advice on furniture, paint color, or decor. When she said she wanted her kitchen remodeled, Mac, the handyman, said, "I'll do it," and Tee shuddered. Mac's vision of a kitchen was practical: buy some two-by-fours and a few sheets of finished plywood and put in open shelves for dishes and storage. She hired a carpenter who installed knotty pine cabinets.

Over the years, Tee treated me special. She saw me as a gentleman and thought I was the ideal husband for her daughter. She always hoped her daughters would marry educated men, and a university professor is by definition well educated. I learned that when talking to Midge or others, she referred to me "Kenny Baby." An excellent typist, she typed out one of my fiction manuscripts that remains unpublished.

When I moved in with Midge, an obvious concern presented itself: How would I treat my new stepson? Jimmy was twelve years old and never knew his father, who had basically deserted Midge when he was two.

Hey, shit happens in life. My philosophy was to love Jim, not judge him. Over the years, I certainly gave him advice, but I always told him he did not have to take it. It was his decision. My advice to him was the same that I gave to myself—i.e., take care of yourself; no one else is responsible for you but you. Also, there should be reciprocity in all relations—return kindness with kindness. If I had to tell him to do something important, I always explained that if he didn't, "you will irritate your mother." He often didn't follow my advice, leading to arguments with her.

His mother remained the prime disciplinarian, and she worried about Jimmy. He didn't have good table manners; he did not do his homework; he had too few friends—as most mothers know, the list was endless. My wisdom told me to sympathize but avoid injecting myself into the fights. Just love her and the boy.

I agreed that Jimmy watched too much TV. He bitched because the TV was black and white, and he desperately wanted a color set to watch his favorite programs, like *Star Trek*. I often heard him pounding the top of the TV hoping to break it so we would replace it with a color set. Color TVs were expensive in 1975, but in 1977, we bought one. It was still the "dark" ages, though, with no remote controls, no cable, and no internet.

After three seasons *Star Trek* was canceled, shocking and outraging its loyal fans. Spock, Kirk, and company toured the country drumming up support for one more season. When it was announced they would make an appearance in New York City at a *Star Trek* convention, Jimmy begged us to take him. Midge managed to get three tickets. Sadly, the auditorium was packed to capacity when we arrived. We were refused admittance, briefly losing contact with each other in the mob. We were given passes to attend a later performance.

Jimmy was heartbroken. In hopes of compensating him, we went to see *Planet of the Apes*, the blockbuster movie of the month. For many boys it was the perfect movie, but Jimmy was so depressed we left after an hour and returned to the *Star Trek* convention. When we got there the box office informed us the actors had agreed to stay for a second audience beginning at 10:00 p.m. We entered the auditorium and easily found seats near the front. Jimmy stared at his heroes, his thrill making the hassle worth the effort.

Between the ages of twelve and fourteen Jimmy enjoyed our company, but when he was fifteen he opted out of going to restaurants or movies with us, as if he were ashamed of being seen with his parents. He also decided he wanted us to call him James, not Jimmy.

James became deeply interested in rock music, particularly Black

Sabbath and Kiss. Both, he said, were greater than the Beatles and certainly better than Paul Simon, Carole King, Frank Sinatra, and company. I smiled but believed Kiss was a flash in the pan. I showed no interest in the records he played in the game room in the basement. James dreamed of becoming a musician, and his mother bought him a guitar.

He finally made friends with two boys his age. They played pool in our basement and wanted to form a band. They played electric guitars and drums so loud it shook the whole house. Midge and I often screamed at them to turn down the volume. They'd comply, and within a few minutes would turn it up even louder. Midge encouraged Jimmy and purchased him a better guitar and amp and gifted him records. He practiced constantly, but refused to play for us. (Some forty years later, he has still never played in front of an audience.) When we were out, the boys stole a few beers but seldom drank any hard liquor in the house. This was all normal teenage behavior in my mind.

Several problems continued for as long as he lived with us. He thought it was our responsibility to clean the house, and he was a messy boy. He seldom returned his dishes to the kitchen, made messes in the bathroom, never swept or vacuumed the floors, forgot to take out the trash, seldom mowed the yard or shoveled the snow off the driveway, and assumed it was his mother's job to wash and fold his clothes.

Every Saturday there was the same fight. Jimmy's major weekend chore was to clean his room, and in the morning, his mother reminded him of it several times. "Okay, Mom," he would say, "as soon as this program is over." Six hours later, his room still untouched, the fight began. His mother dragged him into his room and helped him picked up his dirty clothes, comic books, and records scattered all over the floor.

He watched too much TV despite his mother's constant vigilance. He often crawled out of bed to watch it late into the night. His mother struggled to get him out of bed to catch the morning school bus. He hated middle and high school and often skipped school. He did not do his homework unless his mother made him. Many evenings she hovered over him at the kitchen table, helping him complete his assignments. Midge worried about his lack of interest in school. His grades were horrible, but the administration automatically passed him to the next grade. He rolled his eyes in pain and misery as he endured our constant demands for him to correct his behavior.

I was not as concerned as his mother about his Cs, Ds, Fs, and incompletes. Many teenagers hate school, pout, refuse to do household chores, and roll their eyes at their parents' advice.

In my mind, Jimmy had two traits that countered his lazy attitude about school. He enjoyed music and spent hours playing his guitar. He was also a reader and particularly enjoyed J. R. R. Tolkien books, from *The Hobbit* to *The Lord of the Rings*.

Our friends were Midge's friends. We invited them to dinner and they reciprocated. We went to restaurants, movies, and plays with them. Some of their husbands became my friends, particularly James Bradley, a retired air force major who had flown many missions over North Vietnam during the war. After retirement, he worked for a company that evaluated military weapons. Although he was an alpha male, I liked him for his feisty behavior. Fortunately, when we debated, we respected each other's opinions even when we disagreed. I sometimes felt sorry for his wife, Joan, a high school English teacher with an EdD. Joan was a smart, kind woman who loved Jim's children from a previous marriage. She could manipulate Jim but never win an argument.

The only Western Connecticut faculty we had dinner with was Arnold Brackman and his wife. Brackman was the chairman of (and only teacher in) the journalism department. He got the job through the strong support of the History and Social Science Department, where he had taught an adjunct course on Southeast Asia with my recommendation. From 1945 to the late 1960s, he was an AP correspondent in Asia. His articles often appeared in the *Christian Science Monitor*, and he wrote several books, including one on the Tokyo War Crimes Trials. Around 1975, he moved to Brookfield, Connecticut, and became a freelance writer. He usually published a new book every two years. His wife, Aggie, was a former Dutch soldier and was stationed in Indonesia after World War II. She was an excellent cook, and she and Midge talked about cooking and gardening.

I loved quizzing "Brack" about his experiences in Singapore, Indonesia, Hong Kong, and Japan and asking him about the current book he was writing. He advised me to write a book instead of the many academic articles I published. He was the pro, and I listened, but many years passed before I followed his advice. I wrote novels in my spare time, never publishing one, but I was not ready to spend years researching a history book.

I continued to spend most of my time preparing lectures, reading books, and researching and writing scholarly articles. As mentioned, working on projects around the house satisfied my need to work with my hands and relieved some of the tensions of being a scholar. A writer always faces criticism—good or bad. On home projects, I had only one critic, my wife. If we both liked my work, I did not care what others might think.

Moving in with Midge was one of the best decisions I ever made. We seldom argued, certainly never in the presence of others, and had a stability few marriages achieve. She advised me, but seldom broke the rule "Don't tell me what to do!" I likewise advised her but also conformed to the rule, rarely telling her what to do.

She respected my absolute commitment to my teaching and scholarly career. I continued going to Yale's library at least once a week and often took trips to other universities and primary source libraries all over the country, from Madison, Wisconsin, to the Library of Congress. She never questioned my need to write; instead, she encouraged me. She respected my need to improve my knowledge. I needed alone time; writing was my pain and pleasure in life. Although she was not particularly interested in my scholarly writing, we often read the same novels, philosophy and psychology books, and biographies of famous literary figures.

CHAPTER 27

LIFE IN THE HISTORY DEPARTMENT

The first summer after receiving my PhD, I took a break from academic research and reading. I allowed myself to read books I enjoyed. This included history books, particularly biographies, but mostly I read novels, sometime three or four a week. I did not own or watch television. I especially enjoyed historical novels, such as James Clavell's *Shogun*, James Michener's *Hawaii*, Herman Wouk's *Winds of War*, or C. S. Forester's *Hornblower* series. I enjoyed reading John Irving, Bernard Malamud, Joseph Heller, John Steinbeck, Ernest Hemingway, Thomas Mann, and other great authors, but also read crime and mystery books from authors such as John MacDonald, Dick Francis, and Donald Westlake. I also read science-fiction books such as Robert Heinlein's *Stranger in a Strange Land*.

In September, I returned to reading scholarly books. Even after I received my PhD, I knew I still had much to learn in my field before I could consider myself a good scholar, and as always, I continued to improve my teaching skills. As a scholar, my goal was to obtain enough knowledge in my field to advise future PhD candidates. As a "poor" boy from Oklahoma, I knew I could not contend with the scholars at the Ivy League universities, who received more support and had better libraries. I had no mentors or important contacts to smooth the way. I decided the best way to improve my knowledge and to illustrate what

I learned was by writing articles for academic journals. Doing excellent research was the only means I had to prove the merit of my articles and get them accepted for publication in prestigious journals.

While conducting research that I hoped would turn into a published academic article down the line, I spent hundreds of hours at various Yale libraries researching topics in my field of U.S. diplomacy in Asia. Asian leaders like Mao (China), Sukarno (Indonesia), Marcos (Philippines), Ngo Dinh Diem (South Vietnam), and Ho Chi Minh (North Vietnam) became as familiar to me as famous U.S. generals like Joseph Stilwell, Douglas MacArthur, and William Westmoreland, and presidents from William McKinley to Gerald Ford.

In April 1969, the *Connecticut Review* published my first article, on General James Wilkinson's involvement in the Aaron Burr conspiracy to create a new independent state in the Louisiana Territory. Burr was charged with treason in 1807, and Wilkinson was a major witness at the trial.

The following summer, *International Studies Quarterly* published my article "Neutralism in Laos and Cambodia." Prince Sihanouk's overthrow in March 1970 propelled Cambodia into the news, and my article reviewed the most important books available on Cambodia and Laos. The U.S., still deeply entrenched in the Vietnam War next door, was concerned about the influence the Pathet Lao and Khmer Rouge communist movements had in the two countries.

I continued to publish book reviews and articles, some in prestigious journals, some in journals meant only for scholars. (In the appendix I recommend a few of the more readable papers for those interested in history but not "academic" works.) My filing cabinets are full of the many articles and essays I never published, but writing them improved my understanding and teaching.

Speaking of teaching, I created and taught many different courses over the years (see the appendix for a list of those as well). The content of each course changed as I learned more, a happy result of the extensive research I conducted for the academic papers.

By 1973, the Social Science and History Department had grown to twenty members, too large for Chairman Warner to give each teacher the attention he believed they deserved. In the spring of that year he chaired a recruitment committee to find a department co-chair. He hired Dr. Herbert Janick from Fordham University as an associate professor and co-chairman. They were a delightful team.

Janick was a carbon copy of Warner. Both were involved with their students, chaired several university committees, and intimately knew many colleagues from all the various departments and administration offices. They attended school plays, ceremonial events, lectures, and football games. Both administrators, professors—including me—and students all went to Warner and Janick for advice. Over the years, they became two of my favorite colleagues.

Two years into Janick's tenure, the department separated into two departments, history (Janick) and social sciences (Warner). Although officially separated, the faculty in the two departments remained close because of the former co-chairs' friendship.

Dr. Janick remained as chairman of the department and the department's representative on many school committees for eight years. The administration even appointed him one of the school's ambassadors to the community. At school, he was on a first-name basis with the president and the deans. Because of his outside activities, he often taught only one or two courses a semester.

Janick encouraged the department to become more involved with our students. He encouraged us to give lectures to Western Connecticut's chapter of the *Phi Alpha Theta* national history honor society and write articles for *Clio*, the society's journal. We all had been members since our student days. With stately dignity, Herb periodically cornered each of us and asked with a gentle smile, "How about telling them about your research on your recent project? It's good for the students. It's the right thing to do."

The discussions changed, but Janick's core question always remained: "What's the right thing to do for the students, the college, and the department?" Often we agreed, and often we agreed to disagree, but Herb always encouraged us to remain focused on what's best for the students.

The reputation of the History Department became legendary at

Western Connecticut. I was proud to associate with faculty members who were good, or even superior, teachers, better in many ways than the professors who taught at more acclaimed universities.

The vast majority of history classes I took in middle school and high school bored me because the teachers did not know their material. Teaching with textbooks was the norm: instructors would read the textbook in class and use publisher-supplied questions for discussions and tests. While I was a university student, many of my teachers fell into the same category. A poor teacher is one who just wings it. At the university level, professors should be deeply involved in their subject matter.

It's sad but true that some of the best scholars in the world are among the worst teachers. There's no contradiction here. A good teacher knows their subject matter but also prepares their "lectures," or as I prefer to think of them, their "speeches," to capture an audience. Once engaged, students will learn a subject with enthusiasm. A boring teacher is not a good teacher.

※

In the mid-70s, as the country navigated a deep recession accompanied with high inflation (the infamous "stagflation" era), Western Connecticut's budget was cut. In response, the college administration began slowly trimming the Liberal Arts faculty. In the 1980s, administrators and IT personnel meant to help the college navigate the impending tech revolution were hired instead of teaching faculty.

As a result, the History Department slowly shrank from ten to six faculty members. Gradually, it was forced to hire more adjuncts. Although tenured full professors continued to maintain high standards, adjuncts were in a delicate situation. From the administration's point of view, being a "good" teacher had less to do with teaching quality than having a small number of withdrawals and failures in one's class. Some of the adjuncts were truly good teachers, and some were not, but none could afford to make course requirements as difficult, assign as many books, or fail as many students as tenured teachers. If an adjunct irritated the administration, they were simply replaced. Grade inflation began as quality declined. Tenured "professors" continued to teach all upper-level and graduate courses but relied on adjuncts to teach most evening freshman and sophomore courses.

Over the years, all six remaining members of the department became full professors whose qualifications equaled those of any good but small university. Although we seldom socialized outside school, I knew my colleagues well after working with them for years.

Janick resigned as chairmen in September 1980, but he remained actively involved in the university. Over my thirty years at Western Connecticut, I served under only three chairmen, each for long periods of time. First was Professor Truman Warner, a man who treated every member of the department with great dignity. Then Janick, who was much like Truman: kind, considerate, and understanding. Next came Jack Leopold, who taught Western European history with a focus on Germany. The department elected a chairman for two-year terms, and Leopold was the only person who truly wanted the job, so he was usually reelected by acclamation after each term.

Leopold had to deal with five professors who, along with himself, formed the "Fabulous Six," a group that worked together for twenty-five years. Dealing with five professors with various backgrounds required great diplomatic skill. Unlike other chairmen whose departments were often composed of non-tenured assistant professors, Jack could not threaten a member of the department. How do you threaten "full" professors, particularly ones who were highly qualified, popular teachers and widely published scholars? Although department members were often in agreement, professional attitudes varied and Leopold worked hard to keep some department meetings from bubbling over into bitter academic arguments.

I respected his work. He was a member and occasional president of the faculty Senate, and he used his position to support our department and keep everyone happy. Of course, he was not always successful in that endeavor, but the few times he had problems, he was always fair and listened to the complaints as a colleague and not a superior. I remember Jack as an organizer. He did not particularly like teaching and was happier as an administrator. He adopted a German style, advocating for more practical programs rather than Janick's more idealistic ones. In department meetings, he was all business. Although he was a colleague for twenty-five years, we were associates, not close personal friends.

The senior member of the department, Eric Roman, the expert on Eastern European countries and Russia, was a conservative, a first-class scholar, and a fine teacher. I cannot visualize him telling a student to call him Eric.

David Detzer, my only close friend in the department, and Roman disliked each other for some unknown personal reason. Detzer taught U.S. history courses and was beloved by his students. He had a flair for words and authored several scholarly books. I was the liberal and thoroughly enjoyed disagreeing with Roman. It wasn't personal—I liked him. I wanted to hear his point of view and often found myself changing my mind during meetings. Janick empathized with all schools of thought and propose a compromise. Dr. George Linabury, the Middle East scholar, seldom engaged in the debates, and seconded any Janick proposal,

Unlike at a larger university, all members of the History Department taught freshman courses as well as upper-level and graduate courses. The official name of the department was "History and Non-Western Culture," and students were required, as part of their general education requirement, to take at least two non-Western courses. These included courses on China, Japan, Southeast Asia, India, and the Middle East, but courses on Africa and Latin America were seldom taught.

For many years I taught core courses on China and Southeast Asia, i.e., Vietnam, the Philippines, Indonesia, Cambodia, Malaysia, Singapore, Thailand, and Burma. If any of these countries were in crisis, such as Vietnam, I created a separate course on that country.

My favorite course was Chinese Culture. Over the years, it became the most popular non-Western course offered at Western Connecticut. It was open to all students as an elective, and I usually taught two classes in the fall semester. I only taught one in the Spring in order to have time to teach a course on Southeast Asia, usually with an emphasis on Vietnam. Every semester I taught at least one upper-level and one graduate course.

Chinese Culture class sizes were limited to forty students and there was generally a waiting list. Although I geared the course toward freshman and sophomores, at least a quarter of the enrolled students chose the course as an elective.

I admitted my limitations upfront. My first words to the class were, "I am not a scholar on Chinese history. I do not read, write, or speak Chinese. I am a scholar on United States military actions involving China, Japan, and Southeast Asia. I was hired in 1966 to teach a course on Vietnam, primarily because of my knowledge on the political and military reasons for American involvement. To understand the war, I read and studied Vietnamese history, which was greatly influenced by Chinese culture." I made it clear to my students: I approached China from an American point of view.

My goal in class was not to bore the students while explaining the things I learned while studying Chinese culture and history. I taught what I had learned about Chinese history, from the Chou dynasty (1027 to 221 BC) to the Ch'ing dynasty (1644 to 1911), and beyond to Communist China. The emphasis was on changes in Chinese society over the years, and we touched on feudalism, Confucianism, Legalism, Taoism, Buddhism, and Maoism (check the syllabus in the appendix for more).

I did not expect my students to remember everything I taught them for a lifetime, but I do believe I enlightened them and hoped every time they saw a documentary, or movie, or read a novel on China, they would remember some of my words on Confucian, Taoism, Buddhism, and Communism. Given how important China has become on the global stage, it is nice to know more about the country than what's shown in documentaries or the movies.

Even into the 1980s, I had few friends on campus. Like me, all other members of the History Department were married, and I saw my colleagues only at department meetings and functions on campus. I did not socialize off-campus with any colleagues except David Detzer. I could not have told you much about their family lives, whether they preferred bacon and eggs for breakfast, argued with their wives, or were good fathers. Our relationships were strictly professional. Part of the reason was that offices were scattered around White Hall, the main faculty area, and in academia, friendships tend to develop with your officemates. Detzer had an office next to mine.

I only went to the faculty dining room for coffee, preferring to spend my time reviewing my notes for my next class. I seldom sat or gossiped with other faculty members. At the beginning of my career I learned quickly academia is not conflict-free. Constant complaints and fights broke out between faculty and the administration. Large issues I understood, but most of the complaints were about food in the cafeteria, parking, supplies, raises, lazy students, or stupid deans. I was happy with my job and I did not want to become a martyr. Complaining leads to discontent with your job and life.

At school I was strictly business, "Dr. Young" or "Professor" to my students and "Ken" to my colleagues. I treated faculty outside my department, administrators, office staff, and students politely and with consideration. I was at work, and my main job was being a teacher. I was not working to obtain friends. The other professors in my department felt the same.

When I walked down the hall, if I saw a faculty member from another department, I greeted with them with a "Good morning" or a nod but seldom stopped to talk. When students passed me, I looked at them, smiled, and stopped if they wanted to talk. Most simply addressed me as Dr. Young as they passed and received a nod in return. I treated department members, including office secretaries, politely as we talked "business." As a scholar, I preferred to be left alone to concentrate on my work.

Bill, an assistant professor in the Humanities Department who became a golfing friend, once told me a story that perhaps epitomized my character at school. Though he had been at Western Connecticut for many years like me, I didn't know his name until I joined the faculty golf team in 1985. When I saw Bill in the halls, he was usually in conversation with students or other faculty members and our exchanges were limited. "How are you?" "Fine, how are you?" In the faculty dining room, he always sat with friends. I gave him a nod or a "Good morning," but did not sit at his table for a chat. I always sat alone, drinking coffee and reviewing my notes for the next class.

The golf team had six to eight other faculty members, including (among others) Richie, the chairman of the Theater Department, and Hal, a former dean. I knew Hal, who was also the manager of the team, and he had asked me many times to join the team. I decided to after a close friend, James Bradley, my golfing buddy, died. Bill, I discovered, was also a member of the team.

The team played nine holes twice a month against other teams in the area. Over the next twelve years, the four of us formed a core group that played eighteen holes outside the league about twice a month.

After our games we stopped in the club's lounge for a beer and a snack. One day, in casual conversation, Bill said, "Ken, you know, I thought you were an aloof snob when I saw you in the halls at school. I felt you believed I was unimportant. You seldom even said hello."

"I never felt superior to you," I said. Maybe he felt this way because as a full professor, I outranked him on campus. Although he had taught at Western Connecticut for twenty years, he remained an assistant professor because he only had an MA.

"Well, I thought perhaps you were shy. I rejected that idea when you gave a lecture to 160 students and guests in the small auditorium. Remember?"

You bet I remembered the two weeks of preparation, writing, and rehearsing the speech. I even prepared answers for the questions I expected to get. After twenty years of teaching, I learned how to keep an audience's attention. I was the writer, the director, and the actor.

"Well," Bill said, "I was amazed. The audience remained quiet and attentive for forty-five minutes as you walked back and forth across the stage with no notes. Usually, the students were bored to death in the large classes. I never saw a more confident speaker."

I laughed. "That makes me a superior snob then?"

"Nope," Bill said. "Buy me another beer and prove you're a friendly man."

I was happy to oblige.

In the History Department, David Detzer remained my only friend. He was hired in the fall semester of 1966 as an assistant professor, the same year I was hired as an instructor. When I first saw him, I thought he was younger than me but he was actually two years older. He was of average height with a slim, athletic body. He quickly grew a beard to make himself look older. He only had an MA, but he had taught classes while he was a PhD candidate at a midwestern university. For some reason that was never explained, he dropped out of the program and applied for a job at Western Connecticut. His parents owned two large three-story colonial houses in the heart of downtown Ridgefield, where the region's wealthy lived. Although the Detzer family's money was less than most, they were still among the elite.

Detzer attended Lawrence Prep School in New Jersey from the ages of twelve to eighteen. When he graduated, he was offered admittance to Yale, Harvard, and the U.S. Naval Academy. His father was a retired navy captain, equal to a two-star major general in the army. Detzer opted for Penn State, where his girlfriend, and later wife, went to school. His major was mathematics, and he enjoyed demonstrating his superiority in statistics. In his junior year, he switched to history and quickly showed his skills as a writer. He received a BA in 1960 and remained at Penn State as a teaching assistant as he pursued his MA. With limited support from his family, he relied on his new wife to become the primary breadwinner. After obtaining his degree in 1962, he went to Northern Illinois University as a PhD candidate with a teaching fellowship. In 1963, he switched to the University of Pittsburgh. With three children, he had difficulties finishing his dissertation, and finally dropped out of the program and obtained a position at Western Connecticut as an assistant professor. He lived next door to his parents in Ridgefield.

Intellectually and socially compatible, we became friends our very first year at Western Connecticut. Like me, he did not like cocktail parties or committees, and we were both readers and enjoyed discussing historical topics. A preppy, he could be patronizing, often assuming he was smarter than me and destined for great things.

I admired his intellect and ignored his attempts to belittle my background as a poor, ignorant boy from Oklahoma. I was from the school of hard knocks, working my way off the bottom. He was from an upper-middle-class family who supported him in times of need. I knew more about the working man's world. But we both worked hard at our teaching, and he was excellent storyteller. Over the years, his reputation as a teacher grew.

When Detzer learned during our first semester at Western Connecticut that I was a PhD candidate at NYU, his competitive nature kicked in. He could not bear the thought I might earn a higher degree than someone as gifted as him. Accordingly, he enrolled in a PhD program at the University of Connecticut in Storrs, about three hours northeast of Danbury. As they did with me, the department organized his courses so he could take classes and teach simultaneously. We were best friends for four years, suffering through the same trials and tribulations in graduate school.

Unfortunately, one big area of our compatibility disappeared while Detzer was a PhD candidate. For a couple of years, we read the same novels. If he or I discovered a good book, we passed it to each other. Fiction was my relaxing time away from scholarship. One day when Detzer saw his PhD adviser, the professor asked him what books he'd been reading lately. Detzer cited several history books and a couple of recent novels he had read. The adviser expressed displeasure; as a PhD candidate, Detzer should not be spending his time reading novels. Great historians do not read novels—they spend all their time researching their area of history. Detzer stopped reading fiction.

At the time, and today still, I condemn the adviser. Everyone, no matter their station in life, should make room for fiction books.

We both received our degree in June 1970. Fulfilling the requirements for a PhD in four years was exceptionally fast. Many candidates took seven or more years, and many never finished their dissertations and became ABDs.

For ten years I considered Detzer my best friend. We had a similar sensibility. We were both ambitious. We were both basically loners who disliked the social activities many intellectuals enjoyed. We seldom drank alcohol. We were not quite pals but rather respected colleagues.

We were also different in many ways. He was extremely competitive, whether at the university, on the links, or elsewhere. After receiving our PhDs, we often played golf in our leisure time. In the beginning, he was better than me, which I did not resent. When I complimented him on his game, he brushed my compliments aside. *Of course* he won; he was better than me in all things.

Detzer hated playing with strangers, but on busy days, the pro shop teamed us up with other golfers. When this happened Detzer ignored me and socialized with the other golfers. He talked with me when I missed a shot—a top, a smother, a hook, or a slice. He gleefully pointed out to his new friends that I wasn't a great golfer.

I recognized the competitive tactic: he was bugging me to improve his chance of winning. I simply grinned at him. He would smile and return to his conversation with the other golfers. I thought the whole thing was funny. I knew he thought he was superior to me whether we competed in golf, teaching, or scholarship. He usually beat me in chess too.

I did not make comments about his bad shots or his stupid moves in chess. Detzer took criticism as a serious attack on his self-esteem. He considered himself a cultured man while I was a poor boy from Oklahoma. He enjoyed teasing me about my inability to spell or need to phonetically pronounce words I seldom used. My taste in clothes and wine were bourgeois.

As I learned the game of golf, however, he began to lose half the time we played. Eventually it became obvious I was the better player. Eventually he quit playing golf and sold me his clubs for $50, switching to tennis and badminton.

He thought he was a good pool player and challenged me to a game. I took him to play 8 ball in a working man's bar and beat him several times with ease. Thereafter, he refused to return for a rematch. He said the bar was not his "cup of tea." He hated losing, yes, but the customers in the bar scared him. He considered them crude and potentially violent. I felt right at home and called him a "preppy." He seldom thought I was funny.

I also learned from Detzer that many people who come from wealth are among the tightest people in the world. After golf, we sometimes had lunch or a drink. I usually paid. I knew Detzer thought I was naïve for letting people take advantage of me. After several years of buying him drinks and sharing my plate of wings or fries with him in the golf lounge, he invited me to dinner. We went to Ruby Tuesday, or maybe Applebee's, and he insisted it was his treat—alcoholic beverages excluded, because, in his telling, restaurants overcharged even for beer. When it came time to pay the bill, he presented a coupon for one meal, and he tipped the waitress 15 percent before taxes.

Was I offended by his behavior? No. I considered him my best friend and assumed he considered me the same. I had taken worse teasing from my brother, another alpha male, yet I loved my brother. I am sure I had traits that irritated them both.

Detzer kept a tight budget that tracked every single item he or his several wives purchased, from razor blades to lipstick. In his home, he displayed his wealth and taste. "That's a Persian rug," he might say with his nose in the air. But his office was spartan with only a metal desk and plywood bookcases.

A visit I made to his house one afternoon in the spring of 1967 sticks out in my mind. He lived in one of the three-story homes in Ridgefield owned by his parents and paid no rent. The house was large, with six bedrooms and several bathrooms, but it was also very old. His parents lived across the street, and they had begged him to return to Ridgefield so they could see their grandchildren more often. Before I left, he took me to his bedroom, saying he had something to show me. He had a closet full of expensive suits and sport jackets. He pointed out a light-blue jacket he seldom wore. He knew my budget was tight and I was short of dress clothes for school. He often teased me about my blue blazer with the lining stapled to the jacket.

He pulled the jacket off its hanger, handed it to me, and said, "Try it on."

I did. We were approximately the same size and the jacket fit.

"Like it?" he asked. "Yeah," I said. "Nice jacket." I meant it, even though the turquoise color was not my style.

"Thirty bucks," he said.

I thought he was about to give me the jacket. But I felt trapped and gave him $30, reasoning that he had probably bought it for $150, making it a bargain.

He did comparable things over the years. When he bought an expensive electric Remington desktop typewriter, I was still using my portable Remington purchased while I was in high school. "Want my old desktop Remington? Fifty bucks," he said. Same thing when he quit golf and asked if I wanted his clubs: "Fifty bucks."

He quit smoking cigarettes because they were too expensive. He wore expensive tailored clothes—no J.C. Penney's or Sear's for him, not even his casual or yard-work clothes. He drove expensive cars, but his wife cut his hair. He had no idea how to fix anything around the house although he enjoyed mowing his large yard on his lawn tractor.

He did not understand reciprocity: I would buy beers for both of us, and he never bought the next round. I gave him many things over the years. I worked on his house and even helped him move several times. When I was single, I loaned him my apartment so he could meet his girlfriends while I went away for a couple of days.

So, he was cheap. And snobby. And didn't return favors. All friends and family have quirks, and I enjoyed his company. He was a good scholar, teacher, and writer. His good traits trumped his bad. His cheapness was simply part of his character and mostly unimportant. I try not to judge a friend's behavior, as I try not to judge the weird behavior of my brother and my children. In return, I want the same consideration.

In the 1970s, I concentrated my efforts on publishing scholarly articles in a variety of journals and unpublished novels. Detzer had bigger dreams, although he never revealed them to me. He published his first book in 1977, *Thunder of Captains*, on the Korean War, and a second on the Cuban missile crisis, *The Brink*. Later he published several books on Charleston, South Carolina, and the Civil War. His books were well received, and I was pleased with his success.

I was happy with my life, and I had my own dreams to chase.

Chapter 28

Working at Being a Writer

Periodically I became weary of writing scholarly articles that often required a year of research. Many were published, but unlike many scholars I did not concentrate on one topic or country. As a result, I was not making a name for myself in any field.

My real dream was to become a fiction writer. It's not easy for me to say this. Even today I am reluctant to admit even to myself and close friends that I consider myself a writer. When asked about my profession, I always say, "I was a teacher. Writing is my hobby." I made a living as a university teacher, but deep down, I am a writer.

I dreamed of becoming a writer when I was in the ninth grade. From a young age I had been a reader, not to learn but to be entertained. By the time I was nine years old, I had read and collected hundreds of comic books.

When I was in the fifth grade at McKinley Elementary, I discovered the Carnegie Library less than three blocks from the school. I went to the library once a week and checked out four or five books at a time. My reading branched out and came to include novels with sports themes and famous frontiersmen such as Kit Carson. I moved up to Mark Twain, historical novels, and biographies. I enjoyed books where the main character, a good boy or man, triumphs over his insecurities and opposing forces. I enjoyed reading as much as I enjoyed going to the movies. As a sight-reader, I do not read words, I visualize scenes.

English courses in junior high progressed from covering the rules of grammar to reading classics. My first exposure to Shakespeare was in the ninth grade when the class read *The Merchant of Venice*. The teacher required the students to write short stories, and she read several of mine in class. I was hooked. That's when the dream took root.

I realized even then the only way I could accomplish my goal was to read extensively and continue my education. Over the years, I have read hundreds of novels and history books. I have also read dozens of books on writing and instruction guides that cover everything from the construction of sentences to the rules of grammar to the correct use of words. I still consult these books, which rest on my office bookshelves. Every serious writer has copies of Strunk and White's classic, *The Elements of Style*, and *The Chicago Manual of Style* published by the University of Chicago. No doubt, many have read Rudolf Flesch's books, such as *The Art of Readable Writing*, and *Line by Line* by Claire Kehrwald Cook. Even after sixty years of writing, grammar mistakes slip pass me. I always hope a good editor will spot those mistakes.

Grammar rules and word usage are important, but in fiction writing the most difficult thing to learn is how to plot, i.e., how to grab and keep the reader's attention. Consequently, one of my most prized possessions is a book on this topic that's long been out of print: Somerset Maugham's *Teller of Tales: A Definitive Anthology of the Short Story* (1939), which includes comments on short stories written by seventy of the all-time greats, such as Kipling, H. G. Wells, and Wodehouse. I also like Maugham's *The Summing Up at Seventy* and John McPhee's *Draft No. 4: On the Writing Process*. Another book that influenced me is John Gallishaw's *The Only Two Ways to Write a Story: A Book for Writers* (1928). Gallishaw analyzed twenty-one short stories line by line, illustrating the techniques of a number of writers including O. Henry, Charles Lamb, and John Marquand. I consider this my most important book on plotting techniques.

I also learned the major differences between academic writing and "entertaining" prose, i.e., commercial writing. Research is a prime requirement for publishing academic papers, and a certain style is essential to it. The first thing an academic editor examines is a work's bibliography and footnotes. Graduate school trained me to never use "uneducated" words in my research papers. A thesaurus was essential. Every rule of grammar needed to be obeyed; the use of adjectives, adverbs, and transitional phrases were to be avoided, i.e., never use *very*, *beautifully*, or *however*. In the text, one was commanded to avoid repeating words, remove all unnecessary words, and avoid any use of common vernacular or clichés. Hopefully, the academic paper is readable, but that is usually true only if the reader is interested in the topic. Are you interested in a well-researched article on the Sino-Indonesia Dual Nationality Treaty of 1960? I think not.

Writing for a general audience requires a different mindset. If a person is a reader, it does not mean he is interested in all topics, nor does it mean he went to graduate school. Some only read sports stories, many enjoy mystery or science-fiction, while others enjoy dieting or self-help books. The major divide is that some consider fiction a waste of time, and a few dislike categories of nonfiction books. The vast majority of readers would consider my academic articles boring and unreadable. I don't disagree—they were written for a select audience. And they were written explicitly to inform, not entertain.

When reading for pure enjoyment, nothing irritates me more than James Joyce–type books. When reading for fun, who wants to take years reading *Finnegans Wake* and constantly consulting an unabridged dictionary and other research books? Not me—there are too many other books to read. My advice to nonreaders is to discover the books on topics they enjoy, and then dive into those.

Over the years, writing techniques have changed. Fiction writers today use a more conversational style, and some grammar rules have changed and/or been relaxed. Forty years ago, most educated people said "It is I," while today "It's me" is favored by everyone except Ivy League graduates. Many rules remain. "I ain't gonna do it" is okay in private conversations but not in formal speech or writing. Editors scream for simple words. It's not just humans, either. In Microsoft Word, the grammar checker is maddening, suggesting writers avoid words with more than four syllables. "Comparable" becomes "similar, akin, equal, like, as good as." Ha! The absurd has emerged. Although all these words are good options, even Hemingway's stomach might turn at the suggestion of always using the simplest word.

I learned the rule of academic writing versus colloquial language in a graduate class at Cal State on modern American plays. It was an elective class and I enjoyed it. We read and discussed ten plays, and each student was required to read another twenty outside of class hours. Students had to write one to two paragraphs illustrating the major plot of each play. "Just write in your own words," the professor said. "Just prove you read the plays."

To me, my own words meant conversational language. At the time I was taking three graduate history courses that required considerable reading and heavily researched papers written in academic style, so this would be a big change from what I was used to.

I read the plays for fun, rapidly typed up two paragraphs on the twenty plays, and turned in a fifteen-page paper in my "own" words. I did not revise it into a second draft with more formal language. I proved I read the plays in my own way.

Bad move! No university teacher wants a paper written in Oklahoman slang. I made a B in the class. When I asked why, the teacher said my paper illustrated I was not educated. "My own words" didn't cut it, particularly for a graduate student. I never made that mistake again.

⁂

Do I enjoy writing?

The term "enjoy" carries the image of pleasure. Writing is hard work.

An analogy: If you are a cook and you bake a cake, did you enjoy the process of making the cake? If you are a cook, the answer is yes and no. When you eat a piece of the cake with ice cream, do you enjoy it? The answer again is yes and no. As the cook, you know it is a good cake, but it could have been better. You decide you'll make a few changes the next time you bake a cake.

In writing, the first draft is a painful process that involves pulling ideas from my brain during hours of sitting in my office. I know even then the process isn't ready for the oven until I go over it at least four times. Never is a manuscript finished. And often, no one reads the manuscript except me.

"If it is painful, why write?" the disciple asks.

My answer: "Ha!" It is what I do.

In my view, my sight-reading is to blame for my biggest problem as a writer. I do not read word for word—I read images. And at a very quick speed.

I seldom describe the beauty of nature, from the type of trees to the flowing streams. In my writing I describe scenes using the minimum words necessary to convey the scene and thus, my style is more "Man hit boy" than "A maniac, with a long, black beard, swung his pale oak bat and hit the small screaming boy in the head." What I read is an image of a bad man hitting a small boy with bat. If you have been reading this, I assume you noticed my tendency not to be flamboyant. The reader must interpret between the lines to conjure emotions and imagery.

Like all writers and readers, my values affect how I respond to writing. If I read a novel where the main character is an alpha man or woman, I only admire them if they are a true hero devoted to helping people, like Lee Childs's Jack Reacher, John MacDonald's Travis McGee, or Thomas Perry's Jane Whitefield. Dick Francis's mild hero characters remain my favorite—probably because I myself am mild.

The advice of most books on fiction writing is to write what you know best. The advice is often similar when it comes to academic papers. Yet, in real life, this is not enough. The "know-it-all" is the worst kind of companion. An alpha always talks about what he knows best—resulting not in a conversation but a lecture, sometimes good, sometimes unbearable. Sports lovers are often their funniest when they bore their audience with facts. Who but a golfer wants to hear about every shot in a round of golf? Or every hit in a baseball game, or touchdown in a football game? Only fans of the game.

*

I wrote several short stories over the years, and in 1972 I finished my first novel, based on my experiences playing Little League baseball. I carefully selected a half dozen publishers and an equal number of literary agents to contact. I prepared a curriculum vita: PhD from NYU, assistant professor at Western Connecticut, and a list of my scholarly publications. I included the first chapter of the book, a synopsis, and a self-addressed, stamped envelope. I received a dozen rejection form letters.

I decided it might be easier to publish an academic book in my field. So, from 1972 to 1974, I expanded on my dissertation. After two years of additional research, I sent a synopsis to publishers and agents. This time the rejection letters were polite and personal. I was naïve: no one was interested in a book tentatively titled *The United States and Burma: From Judson to U Nu*. But I was able to publish several academic articles from the book (see Appendix).

I devoted my attention to researching and publishing scholarly articles in my field, hoping that additional publication credits under my belt would improve my chances of obtaining an agent for my novels. As mentioned earlier, academic articles require intensive research and usually take a year to research and write. Though intense, the process had several beneficial results. For one, my research increased my knowledge and understanding of the subjects I taught. I constantly revised my lectures, learning to express myself using fewer academic methods, and I developed a greater sense of humor and a clearer writing style. These published articles ensured my promotions and occasionally helped me obtain fellowships and invitations to speak at conferences, which I seldom accepted.

In 1976 I was promoted to associate professor. That summer I received a grant to study Asian Philosophy at Sarah Lawrence College in New York City.

During this period, I also wrote two historical novels based on my research. One was about the CIA's use of Air America planes in Laos and Cambodia to smuggle heroin into South Vietnam. The second book, *Twice Honored*, examined U.S. military action in the Philippines and the Balangiga Massacre, when Filipino insurgents (or freedom fighters, depending on your perspective) attacked a small U.S. Army outpost on the island of Samar in September 1901, killing over sixty men and wounding another thirty. At the time, it was the highest death toll of

American troops since Custer's last stand. Neither publishers nor agents were interested. I received rejection form letters.

Over the years I've joked that I received so many rejection letters from publishers, editors, and agents I could decorate my office walls and still have paper leftover. This was not hyperbole.

Trade publishing is a mysterious world. The myth that any underprivileged person—say a poor woman, black, white, or Mexican—could write a novel or a memoir on brown paper bags from the supermarket and publish it and become a bestseller is simply bullshit. Such a book would never be looked at or published. To find success, who you know often determines if your work will be read, and—only if the book is actually good—published. Contacts don't guarantee success, but the more "right" people you know the more likely your work will be considered rather than pushed aside into a slush pile. Stephen King's experiment of writing under a different name does not prove me wrong—he still knew people, or at least who to contact.

At the time, and even today, I had trouble believing that a college professor could not get his manuscripts read by university presses or commercial publishers.

I made a fundamental mistake—something I cannot correct today. Throughout my academic career from student to full professor, I never catered to or asked favors from friends or colleagues who might have advanced my career. I never had a true mentor, because I never asked anyone for help. This was my fault. Several people could have helped me, but they never offered and I never asked. I did not join associations or committees, I seldom gave speeches at history conferences, and had no close friends who knew publishers, agents, or important scholars in my field.

Of course, I am not alone. There are hundreds of thousands of aspiring writers, and true success stories in publishing are about as common as they are for aspiring actors, musicians, and artists. Even the good ones often cannot make a living and wind up pursuing other careers. Their dreams remain, but most spend more money on their hobby than they will ever make. In desperation, many self-publish their books that are seldom reviewed or sell many copies (in my case, *Twice Honored*).

Yet, here I sit writing another book.

Chapter 29

A Fulbright Fellow

In January 1979, I applied for a Fulbright Fellowship to the Philippines. A Fulbright is a prestigious grant normally given out to PhDs with Ivy League credentials. With no prestigious mentor, I expected a rejection form letter. Instead, I was offered the top spot by the Philippines Fulbright Committee in April 1979. They were impressed with the articles I published in the *Samar-Leyte Review* (to view them, see the appendix).

Perhaps my fortunes as a scholar and writer had changed.

I accepted immediately. A Fulbright is the height of many scholars' careers. I assumed Western Connecticut would grant me a sabbatical.

I filled out the forms for a sabbatical and sent the application to the dean of faculty, also the vice president of the university. A couple of weeks later I was summoned by the dean. She greeted me and motioned for me to sit in a chair while she remained behind her desk. "Congratulations on receiving a Fulbright," she said.

"Unfortunately," she informed me, as she shuffled papers on her desk, "The last date to apply for a sabbatical was January 31."

It was mid-April, and all the sabbaticals had been awarded. "So sorry," she said. She informed me the school would gladly give me a "leave of absence" without pay.

The explanation seemed puzzling to me. In later years, I wondered if she actually knew what a Fulbright award represented for the school and me, the first professor in Western Connecticut history to obtain the award. Two years later, when the chairman of the English department received a Fulbright to live in Germany, he easily obtained a full-year sabbatical.

On the other hand, he was also co-chair of a number of committees and all the administrators knew his first name. It's quite possible that my refusal to socialize over the years proved to be a major liability—a lesson I had still not learned. Although I was an associate professor when I received the scholarship, few members of the administration knew my name. This mattered more and more. Over the thirteen years I had been at Western Connecticut, the administration had grown dramatically as had the IT department and student body. New dorms and classroom buildings were also built. The number of tenured faculty remained about the same size.

My foolish mistake was failing to participate in any administrative committees. Many of the school's deans chaired three or four committees and needed faculty members to volunteer to serve on them. Most of the faculty joined two to five committees simply to improve their chances of promotion and sabbaticals. If a faculty member did not have a PhD, the only means of promotion was seniority and "service to the college," which in Pig Latin means "service to the administration." The committees met at least twice a month and took months to make insignificant decisions. I refused to volunteer. I hated committee meetings.

The inevitable result was that few administrators knew me. In addition to the sabbatical issue, this proved to be a major problem for obtaining impressive letters of recommendations. Nothing looks better in an application than a letter of recommendation from the president of the university. My only contacts were my colleagues in the History Department.

Over the years I had many comparable rejections. In 1994, I requested a yearlong sabbatical to be an associate teacher at Yale. Each year, Yale's History Department offered positions to professors at the four Connecticut state colleges. My friend David Detzer had applied in the early 1980s, and after being accepted, obtained a sabbatical. I applied and selected professor Jonathan Spence as my sponsor. Professor Spence was one of the great American scholars on China, on the level of Arthur Waley and John Fairbank, and I had read several of his books. I felt the experience would stimulate my enthusiasm for a book I started but never finished on Chinese philosophy. Over my thirty years of teaching I spent hundreds of hours at Yale libraries, and I desperately wanted the position.

Spence offered me a position. But the selection committee for sabbaticals turned down my request. The committee awarded sabbaticals based on departments, and, I was told, the History Department had passed its quota. Again, I was told I could take a leave of absence without pay. I wanted the Yale adventure, but it was not worth a year's salary. I reluctantly told Spence I was forced to forgo his offer.

I do not blame the administrators—I blame myself. Like I said, I should have joined the committees and socialized with administrators and other professors outside my department. I never attempted to become acquainted with people in the position to help me. A major mistake in my career.

Fortunately, the Fulbright Fellowship included a stipend that was half of my normal salary. I accepted the offer. I took a leave of absence with no pay.

As part of my Fulbright work, I was asked to be the keynote speaker at the annual Philippines-American Conference in mid-December of 1979. I was also tasked with editing a book that would accompany the conference. In preparation, from April through July 1979 I researched and wrote three scholarly articles (see Appendix) on U.S. diplomacy in Asia. In August, I left for the Philippines.

When I arrived in Manila, I received a unique assignment. The other professors who received Fulbrights were assigned to teach classes at the University of the Philippines in Manila, but I became the Fulbright Association's traveling lecturer. In this role I traveled to colleges in nearly every major island and city in the Philippines including Baguio, Cebu, Tacloban, Iloilo, Zamboanga, Davao, and more. Almost everywhere I went, I spoke to faculty, small graduate classes, and sometimes to entire student bodies. Once, I was even the keynote speaker at a university graduation. On another occasion, my speech was broadcast on the local radio station.

At each stop I offered to give one of three speeches I had prepared, and the faculty chose which one. The most requested one was titled "The Vietnam Syndrome: Effects on U.S. diplomacy." At my talks to university faculties, the audience was small and spoke excellent English. The wealthy aristocracy and college teachers spoke English and Spanish and were capable of understanding political ideas like George Kennan's Containment theory, the ideological inspiration for U.S. involvement in Vietnam. But when I talked to students in Cebu, Tacloban, and Zamboanga, I quickly realized only a few students spoke English well enough to understand a lecture on this theory. I did not speak Filipino—I was a scholar on U.S. diplomacy in Asia, not a scholar specializing in the Philippines. I learned to speak slowly, often repeating myself, using hand signals and drawing illustrations on the blackboards.

Kennan argued that the world was divided into two camps: a group of communist states led by Russia, and "democratic" states led by the United States. It was a bipolar world, and if the U.S. wanted to retain its dominant position it had to oppose communism wherever it gained ground. Kennan insisted that his Containment theory applied only to Eastern Europe and the Middle East. He was ignored. His ideas led to the U.S. entering the war in Vietnam in 1954 and escalating things rapidly after 1962. From 1968 to 1973, the Vietnam War led to massive demonstrations in the United States and eventually, a major change in United States foreign policy.

After President Nixon and Secretary of State Henry Kissinger opened diplomatic relations with China in 1972, the United States finally acknowledged the world was no longer bipolar but had become multipolar. China was not a puppet of Russia but often an opponent and several military clashes occurred over border disputes. A communist Vietnam did not add to the power of either Russia or China. In fact, the Chinese and Vietnamese fought an undeclared war in 1979 over Vietnam's invasion and ouster of the Khmer Rouge in Cambodia, demonstrating that Vietnam was far from a Chinese or Russian puppet.

When the U.S. withdrew from Vietnam in 1975, U.S. policy was to avoid any military intervention that might last much longer than ninety days. This was because of our "Vietnam syndrome"—the topic of my speech. (Such reluctance to get involved in long-term military adventures remained true until September 11, 2003, when the U.S. invaded Afghanistan.) I told my audiences that the people of the United States would return to the streets if any major military operation exceeded beyond that point, particularly if the draft was still in place. My advice to the Filipino audience was to not expect ever-increasing U.S. military aid in East and Southeast Asia. It was sound advice. The U.S. shut down its two military bases in the Philippines (Subic Bay and Clark Air Base) in the 1980s.

Despite my enriching opportunities to connect with Filipino scholars and students, the fellowship had some disappointments too. At one point during my travels, the U.S. cultural affairs officer in Manila looked at my resume and realized I was not from a prestigious university. He felt my credentials were not strong enough to chair the annual Philippines-American Conference as I had been scheduled to do. In mid-December, two weeks before the conference, he informed the Philippines Fulbright Association he was bringing in a "famous" professor from Harvard to chair the conference in my place. It angered the Fulbright Association. When they informed me, they explained there was nothing they could do. The U.S. Embassy provided the funds for the conference.

Demoted from giving the keynote, I was the last speaker at the four-day conference; at that point, many attendees had departed. Additionally, the cultural affairs officer gave my room at the conference hotel to the Harvard professor and move me from a central location to the edge of the facilities. He also revoked the funding for the book I was to edit, an anthology of speeches made at the convention.

Although the incident left a bitter taste in my mouth, I did not blame the Philippines Fulbright Association. A few days after the conference, the association's director and his assistant rode with me to the airport and apologized profusely for the events, reiterating that the demotion had not been their decision. They had been humiliated as much as I was. The cultural affairs officer had castigated them for selecting me to chair the conference.

They also provided more context for what had happened. Eleven months earlier, in January 1979, the cultural affairs officer had selected a Fulbright scholar from Yale to chair the conference, but in April the professor broke his leg and withdrew. At the time the cultural affairs officer was away on leave, and the Philippines Fulbright Association was left to make the decision. They selected me over Glenn May, another Yale Fulbright scholar who had just obtained his PhD. They said they chose me because I was an associate professor with a number of publications about the Philippines under my belt. Despite my expertise, the cultural affairs officer clearly felt I wasn't qualified.

Despite the conference issue, living in the Philippines on a Fulbright Fellowship was a dream come true. I had taught courses on American policy in East and Southeast Asia countries for thirteen years, and during that time I regretted my lack of in-country experiences. I had read many books on China, Japan, and Southeast Asian countries, but I always felt I had the view of a scholar living in an ivory tower.

In 1977 Midge and I took a three-week whirlwind trip to Hong Kong, the Philippines, and Singapore, but we were tourists. We also took trips to England, Ireland, and Scotland, but it did not mean I was an expert on Great Britain or Ireland. Similarly, over the years, I have watched many foreign movies with subtitles, primarily Japanese, French, and Swedish, but that did not make me an expert on Tokyo, Paris, or Stockholm.

The Fulbright gave me priceless in-country knowledge. The Philippines is a nation composed of over 7,000 islands, and in my time there I traveled and gave speeches at colleges and universities on many islands that only a handful of Americans had ever visited, including Cebu, Leyte, Samar, Panay, and Mindanao. Most Americans just know that the island nation was a former United States colony from 1899 to 1946, and many primarily associate it with General Douglas MacArthur's famous declaration, "I shall return," after fleeing to Australia in 1942 during a Japanese assault. I lectured at Tacloban University near where he first landed in 1944 and walked on the beach fulfilling his promise. I believe my experiences in the Philippines were unique.

My five months in the Philippines made me more patriotic.

I realized I was an American, and that the United States is the only place in the world where I really belong. I was most comfortable living in my own culture. I missed the economic prosperity in most of our country, where the poor are less oppressed than the poor in the Philippines. I even missed McDonald's hamburgers!

When I say "My country right or wrong," it does not mean I give up my right to be critical of the politicians, the gigantic multinational businesses, and the fanatical believers, left or right, religious or agnostic.

While in the Philippines I realized most Filipinos felt the same loyalty to their country. It's only natural, I suppose, and many scholars and writers have examined this instinct. Journalist Keith B. Richburg offers a good illustration of how love of country ties a person to his birth nation. In his 1977 book *Out of America: A Black Man Confronts Africa*, he describes his extended trip to Africa and how it made him realize he was an American, not an African.

For most migrants, their heart remains with the old country where they were raised. But future generations, whether of Japanese, German, Russian, or Mexican descent, become Americans who love their country. American soldiers in Vietnam, regardless of race, often hated the war, but they were still loyal Americans. The country's government was wrong, but not their country.

Naturally, for me, I truly missed Midge and Jim. After I returned, I suggested to Midge we get married.

I knew the marriage would make things more painful if we split up later. But I had several scary experiences in the Philippines that made me think about our future. Incidents involving planes, boats, and insurgents made the Philippines a dangerous place, and several times during my trip I felt I could have been killed. If Midge and I stayed together as a married couple and had a happy life, it guaranteed security for Midge if I died first, as she would receive half my pension benefits.

Fortunately, I'm still alive, and we have had a happy forty-five years together.

Chapter 30

The General's General

I kept copious notes of my experiences living in the Philippines. So many, in fact, that I felt I had a book on my hands, and I turned them into a first draft of a manuscript tentatively titled *Philippine Odyssey*. The book, which was written as a travelogue, was patterned after Paul Theroux's travel books (e.g., *Riding the Iron Rooster: By Train Through China*). The manuscript was full of many fascinating stories, and I felt a publisher might be interested. When I returned to Western Connecticut in early 1980, I revised the first three chapters and sent them to a number of agents and publishers.

I received polite rejections. I was not Theroux, and the Philippines were not China. Few Americans were interested in the country. To publish such a book, I needed better credentials, like a professorship at Yale, Harvard, or Stanford. Then the book would have at least been considered. It was yet another reminder that, as always, talent is essential, but to get considered, you need to know somebody. The *Philippine Odyssey* manuscript and notes sat in a box, haunting me.

I was tired of academic writing and returned to fiction. I wrote several short stories, a play, a philosophical novel, and revised one of my old manuscripts. My results were exactly the same. The manuscripts gather dust in my filing cabinets, haunting me.

In 1984, I decided to write a biography on Lieutenant General

Arthur MacArthur, the U.S. Military Governor of the Philippines in 1900. I knew such a biography would require years of research.

"Why a biography of Arthur MacArthur?" "Why write a book on a forgotten figure in American history?"

Of course, that question was important.

I selected General Arthur MacArthur for several reasons.

The fame of his son was certainly a factor. People are very familiar with General Douglas MacArthur. They know about his importance in World War II in the Pacific, his period as SCAP (Supreme Commander of Allied Power) in occupied Japan, and his command of U.S. troops during the Korean War. Many people quote his famous lines "I shall return" and "Old soldiers never die, they just fade away" to this day. There are several excellent biographies on Douglas, including William Manchester's *American Caesar* and D. Clayton James's impressive three-volume scholarly series. I myself wrote reviews on some of Douglas's policies as SCAP in *Foreign Affairs* (see Appendix).

Douglas was a towering figure in American military history, with dozens of biographies on his exploits, but so were Lee, Grant, Sherman, Pershing, Eisenhower, Marshall, Patton, and Stilwell. None of their fathers had biographies. Maybe they should have.

Arthur MacArthur remains much less known to the average American than his son, but he had a deep influence on Douglas's character and career, a point also observed by James. And because of Douglas's fame, there was a huge archive of primary sources to draw from for a biography of his father.

Additionally, there are hundreds, if not thousands, of biographies on even less significant military leaders. In the early 1900s, Arthur was a well-known general. Before he served as the military governor of the Philippines beginning in 1900, when the islands were under U.S. martial law, he was considered a Civil War hero. When Douglas graduated from West Point in 1903, his father was the fourth-ranking general in the United States Army, and before his retirement in 1909, he was the highest ranked.

I felt many people had forgotten how important the father was to the son, not only in his career choice and promotion, but also in his character traits, like his penchant for grandiose vocabulary. There is little doubt in my mind that when Douglas ended his famous speech before Congress in 1951 with the immortal words "Old soldiers never die, they just fade away," he was thinking of his father.

It took me eight years to research and write the book. I read or skimmed hundreds of books and traveled to dozens of libraries and archives to examine primary source material. I visited most of the Civil War battle sites where Arthur fought and used my knowledge of the Philippines to explain his policies as military governor from 1900 to 1901. I asked several scholars for feedback, rewriting the manuscript after receiving their comments.

I hoped a biography on Arthur MacArthur might restore the general to his place in American history and explain the tremendous influence he had on Douglas. As a professional historian, I knew the book would be considered by many publishers who had rejected my novels without even reading them. Staying in your field seemed to be the rule in the publishing game, and a good history book had an excellent chance of selling 5,000 copies, apparently the break-even point for most publishers.

I researched various publishers and selected Westview Press, a small company in Boulder, Colorado, who was publishing a series of books on military leaders. I sent a vita and a brief summary of the book, and they responded requesting the manuscript. They offered me a contract and actually gave me a $3,000 advance. A professional editor made many corrections, spotting redundancies and inconsistencies through two more revisions. *The General's General: The Life and Times of Lt. General Arthur MacArthur* was published in the fall of 1994.

The book received excellent reviews. To see just a few of them, check on Amazon and buy a copy, digital or paperback, of the book. (See the appendix for a more in-depth summary of the book.)

The publisher hoped the book would be chosen as the History Book of the Month and went to New York City to talk to the selection committee. The committee considered the book to be an excellent biography but other good history books were also in competition; naturally, the question was which of the books would sell more copies. They decided not to pick *The General's General*, admitting economics played a small role in their decision. Biographies of "lesser-known" generals were seldom bestsellers. Apparently, I should have written another book on General Sherman, George Washington, or even Alexander Hamilton. Although I was disappointed, *The General's General* was chosen as a featured selection by the Military History Book Club. In 1995, HarperCollins published a paperback version of it.

The *Danbury News-Times* devoted a full page, about 2,000 words, to reviewing the book, and Phi Alpha Theta asked me to give a speech about it. To my surprise over 150 students, faculty, and friends attended. The size of the crowd forced a move to a larger room in the student union, and the overflow was turned away. No administrators attended, nor did any ever take note of the publicity the book accrued to the university.

The book sold around than 5,000 copies and my royalties were about $3,500. In the topsy-turvy world of book publishing, though, this could be considered a fairly successful run.

In September 1996, Paul Taylor, a senior producer of WGBH-TV (Boston's PBS affiliate) contacted me. He was writing a grant proposal for a new documentary on Douglas MacArthur and he wanted my help. A few years earlier, an excellent four-hour documentary on Douglas was shown on various PBS channels, and Taylor needed to show that he would be offering a fresh interpretation to obtain a grant. He sent me a copy of his proposal and asked for suggestions. At the time I was deeply involved in writing three articles for a new book on the Philippine insurrection (see Appendix) and teaching four classes. But I took the time to carefully read the proposal.

I suggested he create a new story called "The MacArthurs: Fathers and Sons." Judge Arthur MacArthur, Douglas's grandfather, had been an important Wisconsin Democratic politician from 1849 through the Civil War and later became an adviser to President Grant and a federal district court judge in Washington, DC, until his death in 1896. He was also a popular lecturer and author. And, of course, his son Arthur was an important military leader, as was his grandson Douglas.

Taylor wrote a new proposal incorporating my suggestions, and in the fall of 1996, he received his grant. He sent me a thank-you note saying I was the only scholar who gave him any real help. He also sent a copy of the accepted script. "Your suggestions were invaluable in helping me. You will find yourself quoted throughout [the first section]. In most cases, I've quoted your writing verbatim"," he wrote. Section one of the script "shows how Douglas's father shaped his ideas, determined his career, and was the model for his future achievements."

I am a pessimistic optimist. I didn't expect much involvement but hoped the program would follow my suggestions.

In the spring of 1997, the director of the documentary, Sarah Hoyt, contacted me. She asked me to come to Boston and assist the group. I agreed only after she accepted my terms. It was a six-hour drive from Danbury to Boston, and I needed to stay two nights in the city. Initially they offered me a $250 per diem. I didn't want the money, but I informed her I would come if she paid my hotel and travel expenses. She agreed. The hotel she selected was top-notch and near WGBH-TV studios.

I visited three different times over the next year. The first meeting was made up of roundtable discussions, and the director was delighted with my input. The second meeting included the big boss, Austin Hoyt, the producer of the documentary. The group asked me questions on Arthur but the producer seemed to be primarily interested in Douglas's role in World War II, as SCAP in Japan, his actions in the Korean War, and the conflict between him and President Truman.

The third time I went to Boston was different. I was interviewed on-camera as part of a setup scene in an impressive office with academic book-lined shelves behind me. By the questions they asked, I knew the script had changed.

In 1998 PBS broadcast the four-hour documentary with an introduction by David McCullough. My suggested revisions were ignored. I appeared for only a couple of minutes. Other scholars who refused to help write the synopsis, mostly from Ivy League universities, had extended time onscreen. Unfortunately for the audience, the new version was not as good as the earlier one, in my informed opinion.

My main thesis was ignored. Nearly a dozen biographers, even great ones like D. Clayton James and William Manchester, emphasized that Douglas's mother "Pinky" was a tremendous influence on Douglas's life. But my position was that his father was the guiding light for Douglas much as Arthur's father had been his.

I was irritated by the slights but not mad. I recognized professors or commentators associated with Ivy League schools carried more prestige than a scholar teaching at a small state university. As with my book, Western Connecticut's administrators ignored my brief two minutes of fame on national TV.

Chapter 31

Jehovah

From 1967 to 1992 I returned to L.A. every year for three weeks, usually in January. Each visit was different. In those years my parents moved often, Charlene had several "love" affairs, and Inez raised the "babies."

Charlene always acted as if she deserved my emotional support. She insisted I take her and the kids out to dinner three to four times during my visits to L.A. I agreed and was generally pleasant because she graciously allowed me to see the children, who were my constant companions while I was in L.A. I listened to Charlene's romantic and personal problems while the children were minors but gradually cut off any relationship with her in later years. Susan moved in with her biological father when she was twelve. I continued to think of her as my second daughter, but I saw her less on each trip back.

My brother fell on hard times while I was gone. He worked diligently for several years trying to make his shoe store successful but was finally forced to close. One of his greatest regrets in life was that he did not repay my mother's loan. A few weeks after his store closed, he obtained a job at Safeway as a clerk but had to move in with my parents for a few months to pay his bills. It was an awful time for him and my mother. My father was a bigot and considered black people and Mexicans to be inferior. As my brother's wife, Tina, was Mexican

American, my father treated her and her children atrociously. Tina fought back. Corky and my mother were caught in between.

Fortunately for my brother and his family, his finances improved as Safeway recognized his talents and promoted him to a department head. With improving finances, he moved his family into another rented home. Over the next twenty years he was promoted from clerk to department head to assistant manager to store manager, with the cycle restarting several times. He worked diligently, and as store manager (aka the boss) he demanded his workers show up on time and not loaf on the job. The hard workers liked him and the loafers avoided him. An excellent bookkeeper, he checked his workers as carefully as he checked his books. In the good years, he made more money than I did but usually worked sixty hours a week. He spent money on his wife, girls, and favored pastimes of craps, horseracing, and fishing. He did not rent a better house or buy new cars—such luxuries he could not afford.

Suckered into believing the company propaganda, he was convinced his hard work would lead to a promotion to district manager. His superiors applauded him for his work ethic but soon realized Charlie thought they should work as hard as he did. If he felt the home office mandated a display that was wrong for his store, he refused to implement it. When he fired an assistant manager, the district manager objected, implying the man was family. Charlie refused to rehire him— "Send the bastard to another store," he said. His superiors disliked his attitude and demoted him back to clerk. Within a year he was promoted back to assistant manager.

As his years with the company grew longer, after being busted back to clerk several times, Charlie refused all promotions—too much damn work. He remained a clerk for ten years. He joined the union, worked his shifts, came home, and ignored his job.

Charlie quickly became bored with all the free time he had on his hands. He simply could not sit around the house on his off days. He did not watch TV, was not interested in sports, was not a handyman, and was not a voracious reader. Fiction, he thought, was a waste of time.

On days off, he kept his dreams alive studying horseracing and playing simulated crap games based on casino play in Vegas. Statistics fascinated him, and he created mathematical charts on hundreds of horses and thousands of craps games. Over the years, I sat through hours watching him fill out his race cards, filing the statistics on horses on three-by-five index cards. This was long before there were computers in every house. He seldom went to the racetrack, but when he did, he usually won on the few actual races he bet. If he lost his small stake, he quit. If he won, he took Tina out to a steak dinner and slipped her a few bucks to go to Walmart. He went to Vegas occasionally. If he lost, it took the casino several hours to take his money. He admitted it was hard to know when to stop when he was winning.

I told him he had missed his vocation—he should have been an accountant. Here's a good illustration from one time when I visited him. That day he wanted to go to his bank; they had made a mistake on his statement, and he intended to show those bankers what was wrong with their books. For an hour, I sat in the waiting area as he and one of the officers went over his statement. When they rose, the officer shook Charlie's hand, thanking him for pointing out the mistake.

"What mistake?" I asked him in the car.

The bank had made a $1.35 mistake on the interest in his savings account.

"You spent an hour arguing over $1.35?" I asked in disbelief. I was tempted to hit him on the head for wasting an hour of my time.

"It's the principle," he said in his accountant's voice. "They overpaid me by $1.35."

I thought he was complaining about *missing* the $1.35. Incredible.

One dollar and thirty-five cents is not a lot of money, but if you multiple that number by millions of bank customers it added up. The bank was fortunate my brother caught their mistake.

Charlie was a happy statistician.

My brother also loved fishing. He went on trips with a friend he called "Crazy John." Charlie and John started a fishing lure business they named "Crappy John" ("crappy" referring to a fish, not the quality of the lures). As with the horses and craps, my brother studied the fishing business in California, made lists of potential retail shops that could sell them, and for a few months, Crazy John and Charlie took fishing trips to test the market for their lures. John was a well-known tournament fisherman who seldom had a full-time job, and he knew all the fishing outlet stores. Accordingly, they planned for him to be the lead salesman. My brother was the general manager and kept the books, found manufacturers to supply the product, filled the orders, and packaged and shipped the lures. It was a small business, and over the next few years they barely met expenses because when John sold the product, he drank most of the profits and deducted all his fishing expenses. John loved the bars and partied every night. After my brother retired from Safeway, he fired John, and the business made a small profit of $5,000 a year.

My father died in 1976. His drinking had escalated with each passing year, and he died of alcoholism. A quart a day does take its toll. My relationship deteriorated with my father as he descended into the later stages of alcoholism. I did not argue with him but simply nodded, knowing any rational discussion was impossible. My mother, in her quiet way, showed me she was glad to see me, and I realized she still depended on me for emotional support.

At the time of his death my parents lived in a black area in West Los Angeles. My father had been sick for the previous two years, and the doctors warned him if he did not quit drinking immediately, he was doomed. While he was ill, an older, unemployed black man lived with them and helped care for him. "Big Jim" was a kind man who had lived through hard times. He proved to be a lifesaver for my mother. When Dad died, Big Jim remained with Mom.

After couple of years a problem developed. Big Jim had kidney problems, and they were worried about medical expenses. The solution was to do something unthinkable in the prejudiced Bass family: Mom married Big Jim and placed him on her Safeway health plan. The next time I visited, Jim was on dialysis, and twice a week I took him to a clinic. He died shortly thereafter.

When I arrived for my visit in January 1980, I stayed with my mother and slept on a pullout couch. The next morning, I gave the apartment a complete cleaning from bathroom to kitchen. Her rugs always took a lot of time to vacuum. The doors, the windows, and the toilet needed some repairs too. These were all normal chores at home in Danbury.

We stayed up late the first night and talked. She told me Cathy and Susan seldom visited except when I was in town, and she only saw Corky occasionally. She was lonely. I talked to my brother, who shrugged off my concern, but he came over a couple of times over the next three weeks. Cathy became a daily visitor, but I knew in my heart she was not likely to change. She loved Ga-Ga, but she lived over an hour's drive from my mother's apartment and had her own problems.

I tried to solve Mom's loneliness. We searched for senior citizen centers, but the ones in West L.A. were in rundown shopping malls, dirty and empty when we visited.

In desperation, I went to the best used bookstore in L.A. It covered a city block with books dating back decades. It had been one of my favorite haunts when I was a student.

My mother could read, but not well enough to enjoy a book unless I found one at her reading level. Since Midge taught seventh-grade English, she knew literally hundreds of books geared to third- through ninth-grade reading levels. She gave me a list, and I found a number of books she recommended at the store. I also bought a few Westerns, some romance novels, and a couple of picture books on flowers and crocheting.

On my next visit, my mother wanted to go to the bookstore. When we got there, she bought thirty or forty cheap paperbacks. When I returned to L.A. the following year, she was out of books to read. This time she bought two cardboard boxes full of books.

Mom remained in the apartment for two years. One evening when she was returning from work in the summer of 1982, she was beaten and robbed as she entered her apartment. It left her unable to work. She applied for and received Social Security disability payments at sixty-one. She also received a pension and medical coverage from her union for twenty-eight years of working at Safeway.

At the time my brother lived in the Mexican section of East Los Angeles among Tina's family and friends. His girls had married and moved out, but one of his grandchildren, a boy about eight years old, lived with them. Charlie and Tina convinced Mom it would be safer for her to live in a small one-bedroom apartment in a complex only three blocks from them.

My brother visited mother nearly every day, and she was grateful even though Corky often irritated her. He was still an alpha male. When he came to see her, he acted as if he owned her place. He sat at the coffee table doing his books, watching TV, and ignoring her. He switched TV channels, reset the AC, and drank her beer. Although my brother smoked cigarettes and drank beer, as did my mother, both seldom drank hard liquor. I rarely saw either of them drunk. I occasionally drank a glass of cognac or a glass of beer but was basically a non-drinker.

Tina tried to be nice to Mom. She bought Mom's groceries, but to Mom's irritation, seldom bought what she put on her grocery list—not buying the coffee brand she wanted or the right soap or mop. Tina selected brands on sale and healthy foods she thought Mom should eat. "Foods I don't like," Mother moaned. "And she wouldn't buy my cigarettes or beer. Corky will, but Tina wouldn't."

Despite my Mother's complaints, my brother and Tina took care of her, and Mom's criticism was more from a place of loneliness than legitimate grievance. I will always be grateful to them for taking care of her. I occasionally suggested she come to Connecticut and live with Midge and me. She listened, thought about my offer, and told me each time she could not leave Corky all alone. He needed her, she said.

Then, around 1984, Corky, or Charlie as I called him after Dad died, did something so strange it still surprises me.

My brother became religious. A Jehovah's Witness, to be precise.

My theory is that he did this because he was bored and needed people around to improve his life. It seemed like an especially strange decision because our family had been anti-church our whole lives.

But Charlie seldom did anything halfway, be it horseracing, craps, or later, Sudoku. Just as he had studied horses and craps, he studied the Bible, and soon he was knocking on doors, usually convincing a few families to open their door and invite him inside. This is where he shined as a salesman who now sold God. As a good preacher, he followed the rules of his church. His wife enjoyed the church's social life and converted, as did his children.

Mother complained. "All Corky talks about is his damn church. I've told him a hundred times I piss on all churches, but he wouldn't stop talking about the Bible and praising the Jehovah Witnesses. I've closed the door on hundreds of Jehovah's Witnesses, but now I have to listen to religious shit from my own son"," she said.

I nodded. She and I were in total agreement on churches and preachers.

Unfortunately for my brother, his bosses at Safeway were not amused. For years he had refused promotions and worked union hours. Now he was demanding additional days off on religious holidays.

Companies have lots of tactics to force older workers to retire, and Safeway used several of them when it came to my brother. The bosses shifted his job to another Safeway store over sixty miles from his home and gave him the worst possible hours. Mission accomplished: he retired on his birthday in 1987, at the age of fifty.

With only a small union pension, he quickly had major financial problems. Though he had taken full control of the fishing lure business, his total income at this point was less than $10,000 a year. My mother helped him, but even her pension and Social Security were insufficient for a comfortable life in Los Angeles.

I went over to my brother's house one evening shortly after listening to Mom's complaints. Truthfully, I couldn't believe he had actually become a Jehovah's Witness. I'd have to see it for myself.

He lived on a side street of East L.A. near railroad tracks in a typical small two-bedroom house in a neighborhood where his wife felt most comfortable. He could barely afford the rent. Even in the ghetto, most people did not want to live next to railroad tracks where freight trains pulling sixty to eighty cars rumbled by all night long.

That evening he had guests from his church over. The women were inside the house. I hugged Tina, and she gave me a beer and sent me to a large backyard where the men were gathered around a fire burning in an old oil barrel near a picnic table. It was January, and even in

L.A., it was a cool evening. They were drinking beer and talking. My brother introduced them, prefacing each name with the title "Brother," i.e., "My Brother Ed, My Brother Tommy, My Brother Dick, and My Brother Juan." He then introduced me as his "Brother Ken."

I greeted them with a smile although my brother's introduction irritated me. These gentlemen were not members of my family, and the word "brother" was a word I used for only one man.

We stood around the fire drinking beer for a couple of hours. When a train rumbled past the house, all conversation stopped as we watched the long string of passing railroad cars.

My brother and his friends talked about why they became Jehovah's Witnesses and how it changed their lives. Of course, they hoped their tales of hard times and troubles before becoming Witnesses would impress me. They were working men with grand ambitions who failed, became drunkards, and abused their families. Although they were still poor, Jehovah had saved them and led them to become good husbands and fathers. I listened as my brother joined in citing verses from the Old and New Testaments. I smiled at him, seeing the gleam in his eyes.

When my brother became involved in betting on horse races, he wanted to talk about horses; when he became involved in craps, he talked about odds on the craps tables in Las Vegas. Now, he was involved in religion. A born salesman and preacher, he now studied his Bible and Jehovah's Witness doctrine with the same zeal.

"Are you a witness?" one of his friends asked me.

"No," I said, "I am not religious."

"Do you believe in God?"

I simply repeated myself, "I am not religious."

When I saw my brother later that week, I teased him about the incident, but also warned him not to lecture me on religion. "I am my mother's son," I said. "I do not believe in churches or preachers who damn people to hell who disagree with them."

I clarified my remarks. I don't believe there are any gods, but the great religions helped me understand the real discussion is about moral values and the meaning of life. I was raised in a Judeo-Christian society where the Ten Commandants were guidelines for living a moral life, much as the Eightfold Path in Buddhism. Unfortunately, many Jews, Catholics, Protestants, Muslims, and even Buddhists believe their way is the only true way. I told my brother the true believer who follows the moral principles of his religion is to be admired. The symbolic believer, the believer who praises the Lord on Sundays yet violates the moral principles of his church Monday through Saturday, does not have my respect. Preachers are often only symbolic believers.

My brother nodded. "I agree," he said. "But I intend to be one of the believers you admire and try my best to a follow the Word of my Lord Jehovah and my savior, Jesus Christ."

"Okay," I said. "But, and this is a big *but*."

He nodded.

"Charlie, I am an agnostic leaning toward atheism. If you want to preach the principles of the Jehovah's Witnesses, that's okay, but I will counter and compare your church's beliefs to Roman and Greek mythology, or I will attempt to convert you to Zen or Nichiren Buddhism and tell you the only true God is Amida, the compassionate Buddha."

After a brief pause, my brother said, "I agree not to preach my religion to you."

I smiled. "Good. By the way, I am your brother, not those other goofballs."

He laughed. "When you left the other night, they felt sorry for you. They said, 'Your brother has not known the pain and misery of hard times. Someday he will bow to God to help him in those times.'"

I burst into laughter and he joined me.

In the future we occasionally exchanged philosophical ideas but never attempted to convert each other. I liked it that way.

❧

Cathy and Susan became beautiful young women in their early 20s. I felt guilty when I left them in the hands of Charlene and her mother Inez in 1967, when I moved to Connecticut. I loved Cathy and adored Susan but leaving my family behind felt *essential* to achieving my struggle to get off the bottom.

As I watched them grow up, I realized the greatest influences in their earlier years were Charlene, Inez, and my mother and father. I tried not to intervene in their personal lives as they grew older. I knew they loved me, but I reminded them, "If I am a knight, my armor is rusty and I have feet of clay." I gave them advice, but always told them, "Advice is free." As was their right, they often ignored my advice.

Over the years they visited me in Connecticut from time to time, and I was always delighted to see them. On birthdays, Christmases, and Mother's Days, I always called home. I never missed a child support payment, and as the girls grew, I sent each a monthly allowance. They seldom wrote me and rarely called.

Each developed their own distinct personalities, as all children do. Charlene and Cathy often said Susan was too sensitive and "girlie." Charlene treated Cathy with more respect because both were interested in the literary giants, particularly Shakespeare and British poets such as Burns. Susan's interest was in the arts—painting, sculpture, interior decorating, and designer clothes. (Speaking of which, when it came to fashion, Charlene wasn't even in the same league as either of her daughters.) Whatever their interests, Charlene always acted as if she were the smartest person alive.

As for romantic partners, Cathy looked for a soulmate. Susan looked for a man who could provide her with a better life financially. She did not like being poor or working in low-level administrative jobs like clerking. She eventually found her prince—a chubby, balding man about five years older than her named Doran. He owned a software start-up company. He dated Susan for a couple of years, promising that as soon as his company became profitable, he would marry her. Unfortunately—from his point of view, at least—Susan got pregnant in 1988 and refused to have an abortion. He agreed to get married but opposed spending money on a fancy wedding. I sent her $1,500 so she could have a reception—about $5–$7,000 in 2020 money.

Doran's company prospered. A few years after their marriage, Susan was pregnant with her second child. Doran sold his business for millions. She never had to worry about money, and had four children, three girls and a boy. I seldom saw them. She lived in upper-middle-class luxury in Newport Beach, drove expensive cars, and sent her children to good schools. Her husband had a pilot's license and a six-seater airplane. They flew to Florida in the fall and occasionally stopped over in Danbury (and later, Asheville, North Carolina). Doran bought a small ranch in Canada and lived there most of the summer. To avoid U.S. taxes, he became a Canadian citizen. Susan retained her U.S. citizenship and preferred Newport Beach to a rural life in Canada. She disliked flying and often took the train to their Canadian ranch.

She remained in the marriage for thirty mostly unhappy years. Her husband had a fatal flaw: he considered himself superior to her in all areas, believing that he was smarter and had more common sense, and without his money Susan was nothing but poor white trash like her mother and sister. Verbal abusers are effective because there is usually an element of truth in their charges.

If Susan responded, "You are a self-centered asshole no matter how much money you have," he would have exploded in anger. Such a response was impossible for Susan, as it would be for me. My response to a bully is to walk away. Bullies seldom change their ways. No matter how much Susan hoped her husband would love her for who she was, he continued to insist she must change. He refused to appreciate her best trait: empathy. Her worst was that she expected, perhaps naively, others to have empathy for her. Like her mother, her husband had little empathy for anyone else, including Susan.

Fortunately, Susan knew she had the love of Grandpa Evans, Grandmothers Inez and Ga-Ga, Cathy, Charlene, and me. I always wished I had been the father who changed her diapers.

❧

As for Cathy: she was a beautiful, intelligent, fun-loving woman. Over the years she had many boyfriends who either respected me as her father or attempted to assert their superiority in hopes she would think I was inferior to them. If this happened, I always walked away. I loved my daughter, and the selection of a mate was her choice, not mine.

Her first true love was Kelly, a teacher at a community college in Los Angeles. His field was English literature, and he considered himself a scholar on Shakespeare. He was forty years old, closer to my age than to Cathy's. Charlene was also a lifelong lover of Shakespeare, and at her mother's insistence, Cathy read most of his plays as well other British authors. Chaucer, got you covered; Burns, got you covered. Somerset Maugham, not so much.

Cathy attended the community college where Kelly taught and loved his classes. Apparently, he was an enthusiastic lecturer, and dressed, lived, and acted as a guru for the Beatnik generation. He had long hair, listened to classical music as well as the Beatles, and smoked pot, sampled cocaine, ate mushrooms, and used LSD. His generation were often rebels who lived through assassinations, the Vietnam War, the Democratic convention in Chicago in 1968, and Watergate.

Cathy loved Kelly's free-thinking, anti-establishment attitudes, and his pure enjoyment of life. Although the relationship never became exclusive— it was the free-love era—they were together for eight years. Kelly was the editor of the college's annual literary journal, and Cathy became his assistant editor. Against my advice, Cathy remained a student at the community college, taking night courses and accumulating 124 credits. Only sixty could be transferred to four-year colleges (thus my advice).

When I came to Los Angeles one year, Cathy said she wanted me to meet Kelly. I agreed but asked my mother about him first. At Cathy's request, Mother had invited Kelly to dinner a few months earlier.

"What did you think of Cathy's new boyfriend?" I asked.

"Too old for her," Mom said, pointing out that he was fifteen years older than Cathy.

Mom admitted he was a nice enough man, but he was talkative. "He spent the whole evening talking about some damn poet. Not once did he ask me what I thought or talk about the real world."

As I learned, Kelly enjoyed talking about subjects he knew, and always redirected conversations to center on literature, particularly Shakespeare, or social topics. Mother's knowledge was in the real world of wrapping meat at Safeway, worrying about the rent, or helping Corky or Cathy with personal or financial problems. Mother did not enjoy an evening discussing Shakespeare or Martin Luther King.

Conversely, I liked Kelly. I enjoy discussing social, political, and cultural topics. I allowed Kelly to select the topics and merely joined the discussion as Cathy jumped in periodically to assert her point of view. My rule, "Do not discuss my job at social events," stood fast. I gave no lectures on Teddy Roosevelt, the Vietnam War, or Confucius. If someone wants to talk about World War II or the Vietnam War, I will be a willing listener and will express my opinions when asked. In fact, my mother, brother, Susan, and Cathy knew little about my academic life, the courses I taught, or the many scholarly articles I published. They only knew I was a college professor who taught American history.

Over the years, Kelly became part of my circle of friends, and even accompanied Cathy on one of her trips to Connecticut to visit Midge and me. When in California, I always saw Kelly several times. I often went to his "bungalow" in a low-rent neighborhood in the Valley, where we sat around smoking pot, listening to music, folk and classical, and argued over the true meaning of life.

Chapter 32

California Family Life, Cont'd

In April 1991 my brother called me with family news. My mother, who had been in declining health, had a stroke. She was out of the hospital and using a walker even in her apartment. Naturally, I was concerned, but Corky said I did not need to return immediately to L.A.

He was calling with a request. Mom wanted to visit her brother Bunk, perhaps to see him for the last time. They were the last of Joe Bass's family; her brother Red and her two sisters, Hester and Hazel, were dead. Mom knew her time was limited. She tired quickly, and unknown to the family and doctors at the time, she had colon cancer.

In my boyhood years, you may recall, Bunk was more like an older brother to me than an uncle. I always remembered the stories Bunk and Mom told me about their hard times as children. As a young girl of fifteen and a mere boy of seven, they learned Rule No. 1: Take care of yourself, particularly in hard times. Don't expect sympathy, and don't expect someone else to save you. Save yourself, save your loved ones, and then the extended family, but first and foremost take care of yourself. Listen to the problems of other people but recognize you cannot solve them.

Uncle Bunk resided on the fringes of my life for thirty years. He lived near Moses Lake, a small city in the high desert about sixty miles west of Spokane, Washington, which was over 1,300 miles from East

Los Angeles. Corky wanted me to accompany them on the trip to visit Bunk sometime during my summer vacation.

The idea of seeing Bunk again after so many years was appealing. I agreed to come in late June.

Later, I learned my brother hoped to persuade my mother to move to Washington or Oklahoma, where rent was much cheaper. They could rent a four-bedroom house with a mother-in-law apartment for half the price they paid for lousy housing in Los Angeles.

Two people vehemently opposed the idea. "Absolutely not," Mom told me when I arrived. "I am not going to live with Corky and Tina. Corky comes over, and even now, takes over my TV, drinks my beer, and talks my ear off about his damn religion. I told him a hundred times, I ain't going to attend no damn church, and don't want to listen to his preaching. He's just like your Dad—he won't shut-up."

And Tina? "Too bossy."

Tina tried to be nice, but Mom was a grouchy old woman. I think "feisty" is the best way to describe her in her later years. As always, Tina continued to buy Ga-Ga groceries that were healthier or cheaper than the ones Mom requested. For example, after her stroke the doctors placed Mom on a salt-free diet, and Tina bought unsalted butter. Mom liked Folger's coffee, and Tina bought the decaf Safeway brand. Small complaints, but Mom saw it as Tina bossing her around.

Tina was also vehemently opposed to moving out of East Los Angeles. Her three daughters lived in the area, and she took care of her only grandchild. She had family and friends in the community. My brother simply could not comprehend what life would be like—she was a third-generation Mexican American, and small towns in Washington or Oklahoma were composed mostly of whites who looked down on Mexicans much as they looked down on blacks. Such areas were foreign countries to her. Besides, Tina had no desire to share her quarters with a demanding mother-in-law. Mom was enough of a burden living a few blocks away.

When I learned of my brother's scheme, I warned him it was a pipe dream. "No way. Mom will never agree to move in with you and Tina," I said.

My brother was a better salesman when it came to the trip. Before I arrived in Los Angeles, he told Cathy of our plans, and she leaped at the chance to accompany us. Bunk was her favorite relative, and Cathy loved my mother, my brother, and me. But she also liked the idea of a two-week, expense-free vacation.

After her school closed for summer break in early July, Midge flew to San Jose, California, to see her sister who had moved there a year earlier. After visiting Bunk, I was to meet her in Portland, Oregon, for our own vacation.

My mother insisted on paying half the cost of the trip, and I paid the rest. Several years earlier, Mom had given my brother $5,000 to buy a five-year-old Lincoln Continental with low mileage. A large car, it was ideal for the sixteen- to twenty-hour trip to Moses Lake.

The trip was hard on my mother. It was difficult for her to get out of the car and eat in restaurants. We usually brought her food to the car or to the motel room she shared with my brother. Cathy and I shared another room. The first day we stopped in Fresno. In July, the desert is extremely hot and the car's AC did not work. To make matters worse, we checked into a chain hotel and discovered, after renting the rooms, that the AC was turned off. Apparently the central unit had broken after days of stress, a stretch that beat the record for consecutive hottest days in the history of Fresno.

After a miserable night in the rooms, we left early the next morning and stopped in the late afternoon when we reached a small town high in the mountains. The motel was quaint but clean. We bought food at a nearby diner and ate at a picnic table in the cool early evening and watched the sun go down.

My mother was tired but happy to be with the three people who loved her. She went to bed early. The rest of us stayed up talking and drinking beer and cognac. As tiring as the trip had been, I was happy to be with people who liked and loved me.

The next day we reached Grants Pass, Oregon. Charlie decided it would be an ideal spot to move to. The area reminded me of Connecticut. Tree-covered mountains surrounded the small city, and the countryside was a vibrant green.

We planned to stay in Grants Pass for three nights so Charlie could scout out places to live. Because my mother worried about the cost of motel rooms, Charlie chose an inexpensive motel in the downtown area that proved to be in shabby shape. After the first night, I told my brother I was moving to a better motel located on a small river. My mother wanted to remain in the original motel because she was feeling "poorly." The following day, I insisted on paying for her room and moved her to where I was staying.

For two days, my brother, Cathy, and I looked at houses to rent in the area. There were several with three or four bedrooms, two and a half baths, a garage, and a large yard in nice neighborhoods at less than the price of Mom's one-bedroom apartment in East Los Angeles.

My brother was getting excited, but again I warned him: "Mom and Tina will not move to Grants Pass." Mom had repeatedly said, "I will not live with Corky and Tina." For her to move to Grants Pass, they would need two small houses, not one large one. Equally important, before we left L.A Tina had asserted she would never move to Oregon.

Much like my father, Charlie did not listen. He believed moving a thousand miles from L.A. was the ideal solution for both Mom and his family. The weather, although cold in the winter, was better than the smog-choked summers in L.A. They could afford to live the good life in Grants Pass.

On the sixth day, we arrived at Bunk's house. The area was farm country, irrigated with groundwater produced by a nearby Colorado River dam. The eastern slopes of the Rocky Mountains were clearly visible.

As we neared Bunk's house, the area reminded me of Oklahoma. Scrub bushes and buffalo grass covered the high desert with not a tree in sight for miles. The scenery prompted Mom to tell us a story. One time her older sister Hester took a trip to western Virginia to see her daughter. On her return, Mom asked Hester how she liked the state. "Hated it. Too damn many trees. You can't see anything," said the lover of the open Plains, where the antelope play and the buffalo roam.

Bunk too was a Plainsman who disliked cities. His house was near a well-maintained country road with a few houses in the distance. He owned ten acres surrounding his house. He maintained a large yard, but left the fields uncultivated. His house was a double-wide mobile home on a concrete foundation with three bedrooms and two baths plus a porch in front and a screened-in porch in the back. There was a gigantic metal shed, much like Uncle's Ted's in Lawton, loaded with tools, a riding mower, a tractor, and his welding equipment. Although he was retired, he still took on welding jobs for farmers and agricultural factories in the area. A Ford truck, a Chevy sedan, and an RV were parked in the graveled driveway.

Bunk and Muriel greeted Mom and Cathy with hugs, and we boys hugged Muriel and shook Bunk's hand. Although older, Bunk looked much like I remembered him. Dressed in jeans and wearing cowboy boots, he was still slim with thinning red hair. Muriel looked and acted like a plump grandmother. She was kind while Bunk had a sharp sense of humor, though he always hoped for a similarly sharp retort. He simply enjoyed teasing people and expected to be teased back.

That night Charlie and I slept in the RV. The next morning, Bunk brought over a pot of coffee. He sat down at the kitchenette in the RV and motioned for us to have a seat. He wanted to talk. First, he said, "It's nice to see you boys and Cathy. I am glad you brought Toad. Our brother Red and our sisters, Hazel and Hester, are all dead now."

He paused, then came to the point. "I need to know if you boys plan to dump your mother on me."

Bunk's wife Muriel was in her early seventies, and her two children from a previous marriage lived in Spokane with their kids. They were his prime responsibilities. Toad was not his problem—our mother was our responsibility.

I was surprised Bunk was worried we might dump our mother on him. Charlie and I had no intention of abandoning Mom. None. Mom would rather die than depend on anyone but us to take care of her. She intended to die in her apartment in East Los Angeles.

I laughed. "Bunk, we know Mom is our responsibility."

What I really I wanted to say is that I had learned my lessons. In part because of Mom—and Bunk. My mother never criticized me for leaving her and Cathy when I was twenty-six years old and moving to Connecticut to pursue my goals. I had followed Rule No. 1. She believed I had done the right thing, and she was proud of me.

"Well," Bunk explained, "had to be said. Muriel is cooking breakfast. You boys come when you're ready."

Although Bunk dressed like an Oklahoma hillbilly in cowboy boots and jeans, he had no fear of the outside world. People in suits did not frighten him. Of course, outside of work he did not socialize with the "suits" and never expressed his personal views to the bosses. He controlled his temper better than Papa Joe or Red, and although he would have a beer with friends, he drank moderately. He worked hard, and if he felt he was unfairly treated, changed jobs, saved money, and fought back the hard times. He did not hunger for luxuries—if he won the lottery, I believed, he would not move into a luxurious house or buy a fancy car.

"What would you do with the money if you won a million dollars?" I asked Bunk years later after he bought a lottery ticket. "Give most of it to the kids and grandkids," he said. "I got enough."

"Would you give any to charities?" I asked. He snorted. "Might buy some Girl Scout cookies or drop a coin or two in the Salvation Army bucket at Christmas time."

He was a prideful man, and never asked the government for assistance and never lent or borrowed money from friends. He would help a friend build a barn, but he was not going to finance it. If you needed help fixing a toilet or moving your furniture, he was the friend to call, but he expected you to honor the debt if he needed help shoveling snow off his driveway. Even family should not ask for money unless it was to pay for essentials like the rent or buy groceries, in his view. He would not cosign a loan if a family member wanted to buy a house, a car, a TV, or today, a computer or iPhone.

Physically, Bunk was a smaller version of his brother Red. Their personalities, however, were quite different. Red was over six feet tall and weighed 180 pounds. His hair was cut military short, and his complexion was Swedish white. A big, strong man, Red enjoyed a good fight, carried a gun in his truck, got drunk in bars, drove like a racer, gambled, and ran a bootleg whiskey operation. He always had schemes on the edge of the law.

Bunk also kept his red hair short, was five-ten, and weighed 160 pounds. He was honest, avoided fights, and hated bullies. He would not throw the first punch, but the wise man sat down when Bunk stood up. His big brother had taught to him to fight back.

Although Bunk was not an intellectual, he was knowledgeable about the world. During two tours in the air force, he had been stationed at several bases, and lived for two years in Fairbanks, Alaska. As a civilian he had lived in Oklahoma, Washington, and California. However, he remained a "redneck" in many ways. He did not believe in welfare or gun restrictions, thought men should protect their family, and looked down on most minorities. He refused to talk to Mom while she was living with Big Jim.

His prejudice seemed strange to me. Bunk was proud of his Indian blood and suffered discrimination in Oklahoma in his youth. Indians back in the day were placed into the same category as blacks, and Mexicans, even lower than Italians or Jews. I am sure even today there is discrimination against Indians in Oklahoma, although the aforementioned order may have changed. The Bass family, of course, considered quarter-breed Indians equal to the whites and superior to all the other minorities.

Bunk would not have been a Trump supporter. He would have recognized Trump as a flimflam artist who preached fantasies, stole money from the poor, and tried to establish himself as a feudal lord. Bunk was neither a socialist nor a union man, but he had a deep hatred for the wealthy who looked down on workers. He disliked petty bosses and billionaires who stole money from the working man. He distrusted company propaganda, car salesmen, and stockbrokers. He loved his country but knew he could not trust the government or multinational corporations.

He became a reader, much as mother, late in life, and he loved Westerns and history books. When he read my books, he was intensely proud of me. He read the local newspaper but did not watch the national news on television. "Don't care much about what's going on in New York City or Washington, DC," he said. "I live in God's country to get away from big cities and big government."

After breakfast, Bunk offered to take us fishing at a small lake (more like a pond) a couple of miles from his house. Charlie and Cathy leaped at the chance. Charlie wanted to show off his fishing lures and had brought a few as gifts for Bunk. I agreed, although everyone in the family knew I did not like fishing, hunting, or camping out in the woods. Muriel and Mom waved goodbye as we left.

Everyone in the Bass family loved fishing, as did my father. When I was a boy, the family often went down to the "creek" for picnics, and spent the day drinking beer, eating, sleeping, and fishing. Boring. I always took a couple books and sat on the creek bank pretending I was fishing. I never caught a thing.

On another trip, my brother and I went fishing with my father's rabbit-hunting friends. Piled into several cars and trucks, we headed out on an overnight trip to a lake near Ardmore, Oklahoma. After setting up camp, we jumped on two rowboats and strung a thick fishing line with dozens of hooks out to the center of the lake. Then we rowed back to camp and built a large campfire. The men stayed up most of the night drinking moonshine and beer, getting rowdier with each passing hour.

At first light, we got back into the boats and dragged the line to shore. A dozen "monster-sized" fish were hooked on the line. Back on shore, they gutted the fish, sliced them into filets, and placed them in ice chests to take home.

The trip bored me. I disliked being around drunks. I was a quiet boy who preferred reading, marbles, baseball, and going to movies. Fishing did not appeal to me. I never went hunting—the blue bird and the rabbit haunt me to this day.

Over the years, I occasionally camped out during trips to save money. But I did not like setting up tents in the rain, sleeping on air mattress that inevitably went flat during the night, and getting up before dawn because the rocks under the mattress were killing me. It took a half hour just to boil water for coffee over a campfire.

As I grew older and money was not a problem, I preferred a moderately good hotel and a restaurant with hot coffee and breakfast. I have seen enough national parks, from the Great Smoky Mountains

National Park to Yellowstone, enough tourist spots, from Disney Land to Scottish Castles, and enough countries, from Scotland to Italy to the Philippines to Singapore. I would go to New Zealand if, as in *Star Trek*, Scotty beamed me there. But today I have no desire to see another airport or another city with mega-millions of people. Today, I prefer to drive slowly around the United States and stay at golf resorts near small cities rather than taking another cruise to Bermuda.

All that said, I willingly went fishing with Uncle Bunk, Charlie, and Cathy. Despite the small problems during our trip, I had enjoyed being with the people who were part of my life. When we reached the large pond, Charlie and Cathy jumped out of the truck and picked up the fishing gear supplied by Bunk from the truck bed. Cathy wore shorts while the rest of us wore jeans and long-sleeve shirts. Bunk had warned us about mosquitoes, but Cathy felt her bug repellant would keep them in check.

As Charlie and Cathy hurried off, I heard Charlie telling her they needed to select the right spot. They went about three hundred yards down the pond's bank in search of the perfect spot to throw in their lines baited with his lures. Charlie expected to catch at least a half dozen fish.

I stayed with Bunk and we moved at a more leisurely pace. Bunk picked out two rods and some bait from his metal fishing box containing line, sinkers, worms, and a few fishing flies. We moseyed down to the pond where he baited our lines with the worms. He smiled at me. "Charlie's lures won't work here," he said. "Might be good in deep lakes, rivers, or the ocean, but this is a shallow pond and most fish here are bottom-feeders."

I tossed my line in the water expecting nothing—I had never caught a fish. Within five minutes we both caught something. They were small, thin fish no more than ten inches and weighed less than eight ounces. I thought Bunk would release them back into the pond.

"No sir," he said. "Perch are small but they are good eating." Besides, he did not think of fishing as a sport. He went to catch food. In the next hour, we pulled in about two dozen of the small fish. Bunk put them into an ice bucket to take home.

As we were pulling in perch after perch, Charlie and Cathy wandered back in our direction, tossing their lines in the pond along the way. As they reached us, Bunk began packing up his gear. They had not caught a single fish.

My brother looked at the fish we caught.

"Perch," Bunk said. "Bottom-feeders. Ain't much else in this pond."

My brother's face showed his chagrin. He had fished for many types of fish on large lakes, rivers, and the ocean. He had never fished for bottom-feeders such as perch and catfish. His lures were designed for bass, trout, and even tuna, but not for bottom-feeders. Bunk had not told him because Charlie bragged so much about being one of the best fishermen in the country. Bunk considered himself a good fisherman, and any good fisherman should know how to catch bottom-feeders.

Charlie and Cathy had fished around the marshes where the mosquitoes swarmed. Charlie swatted the ones around his head. Cathy's bug spray helped some but was not strong enough protection from the swarms. The mosquitoes feasted on her, and Bunk advised her not to scratch. Despite his advice, she could not stop scratching. Drops of blood spotted her legs and arms.

We hurried back to the truck and returned to the house so Cathy could shower and put lotion on her legs and arms. After applying the lotion, Muriel and Mom put little pieces of cotton soaked in a salve on the bloody bites.

The men went to the rear of the house where Bunk had a table that he used to clean fish. Bunk gutted the tiny fish and took them to the kitchen where Muriel breaded and fried them. Charlie asserted that he knew how to catch bottom-feeders but had wanted to test his lures.

As the sun set, we moved to the front porch. After dark, thousands of twinkling stars filled the sky. It reminded me of Oklahoma and the times when my brother and I lay on sleeping quilts in the backyard on hot summer nights and counted the shooting stars. In the high desert, the summer nights were cool, and the sky, clear of clouds, was full of stars. In the distance, the lights from other houses twinkled as well. Four of us pulled out our cigarettes. I had a cognac and everyone else, except Muriel, had a beer.

That evening is embedded in my mind. We sat on the porch and listened to Bunk and Mom talk about the old times in Oklahoma. Muriel, about Mom's age, recounted her experiences on the farm in Washington. They talked about the hundreds of card and domino games they played with "Charlie (Dad) and Toad" when Cathy was a baby. "Corky" and I talked about being orange pickers and potato separators. Cathy listened in awe.

Bunk teased Cathy and Charlie about their fishing exploits. Cathy asserted she had a great time despite the mosquito bites. My brother said, "Bottom-feeders. Nobody I know has ever fished for perch."

Bunk laughed, as did my mother. "Never fished on the farm ponds in Oklahoma, like me and Toad."

Mom nodded. "Good eating fish," she said. We all agreed with her, and in the future, I often ordered fried catfish—another bottom-feeder—at restaurants.

Mom and Muriel went to bed early. The rest of us remained on the porch. Charlie defended his fishing lures, describing the fish he caught with them. Then he switched the topic to the cost of living in the Moses Lake area. Charlie learned he could buy a home like Bunk's for $50,000, or rent a place for about $250 a month. There was a familiar gleam in my brother's eyes, but I knew his dream was pie-in-the-sky. Tina would not move to Washington or Grants Pass.

While at Bunk's, I washed my clothes, and Charlie decided to do the same. I laughed at him because he did not know how to use the washer and dryer. He was sixty years old and had never done his own laundry. Nor did he know how to cook bacon and eggs. His wife did all the household chores. For the next twenty years, I teased him about his inability to wash clothes or make his own breakfast, but he never understood why I thought it was so funny.

The next day, Bunk took us sightseeing. We went to a dam on the Colorado River and later drove to a small city near the base of the Rockies where the treeline began. Charlie and I paid for lunch and dinner and also stopped at a supermarket where we bought groceries and beer. Bunk protested, but we did not want him to bear all the expenses for our visit. On July 4, we went to a local park and watched the teenage boys and girls ride horses in barrel races. In the evening, we sat on Bunk's porch and watched the fireworks.

I left Bunk's the next day in a rented car and drove to Portland to meet Midge. We spent several days exploring the coast from Oregon to Seattle before we flew home.

I truly enjoyed my time at Bunk's, and over the next fifteen years we maintained contact. I visited him several additional times in the Moses Lake area, and he and Muriel came to Connecticut for two weeks. Danbury was known as Hat City until the early 1950s, and I bought him a Stetson hat he wore on special occasions for the rest of his life. At his request, I took him to play golf. He had never played before. To my amazement, he was a natural.

Bunk was a jokester. His humor made me smile and occasionally made me giggle. His humor was much like my mother's. One time we went to the movies, and before leaving, we stopped in the men's room. It was a large, crowded bathroom with four stalls and six urinals. Five of the urinals were in use. The last urinal was open. Designed for young boys, it was a foot lower than the others. "When you got to go you got to go," Bunk said as he marched over to the small urinal and unzipped. Over his shoulder he said, "About time they built these lower ones. Tired of my pecker dropping down to the bottom into piss water." The crowd looked at him. One old man chuckled at the implications.

Six months after our trip to Bunk's, I came back to East L.A. to visit Mom. I asked if she had considered moving to Washington to be near Bunk. Her answer was of course, "No." Tina's response was an even stronger no. Corky never stopped pestering them about moving to an area less expensive than Los Angeles.

Mom was lonely and bored. I suggested she reconsider moving to Connecticut to live with me and Midge. I had made the offer before. Midge's mother had lived with us for several years, and after she died, we had a spare bedroom suite with a separate TV room.

Mom said no. She did not wish to be a burden and was determined to remain in her apartment. She felt she could not leave because Charlie needed her. Financially, this was certainly true. Mom's Social Security and pension helped pay his expenses. More important, she felt

Charlie needed her emotional support. She knew I did not need either her financial or emotional support. She had taught me to take care of myself. My brother, an alpha male, had lost his way and was doing his best to be a better person though his religion. She was not happy in her current situation, but Charlie and Tina took care of her. Truthfully, I was relieved she didn't want to leave L.A., but I felt guilty.

※

My mother died in the summer of 1992. When My father died in 1976, I did not mourn his passing and did not return to L.A. for his cremation. When my mother passed, I flew to Los Angeles to say goodbye.

By the time I reached my mother's apartment my brother had already removed most of her personal items such as photographs and financial papers. It was appropriate, since he was handling her small estate and for the past few years had been her primary caregiver, a role I was grateful he had fulfilled.

I intended to ask family members over for a wake. I cleaned the place in preparation, attacking areas that hadn't been touched for years. Then I purchased snacks, wine, beer, brandy, bourbon, and soft drinks. Cathy came, as did Susan and her husband, Doran, Charlie, and Tina and their three daughters, and Mom's one great-grandchild, a little boy. We sat around for a few hours, sipping our drinks and telling stories about Ga-Ga.

The next day, Charlie, Cathy, and I went to the funeral home for her cremation. I insisted we dress up for the occasion. Charlie and I went to a large department store and purchased matching blue blazers, pants, ties, and dress shoes. Cathy dressed accordingly. We sat silently in the viewing room as my mother was cremated. My mother would have been proud of her sons, all dressed up, and Cathy, her favorite grandchild. To my regret, I forgot to invite Susan.

After the cremation, my brother and I took a three-day driving trip north up the coast toward San Francisco. We stopped at expensive hotels with balconies overlooking the beach and ate expensive dinners. In the evening, we sat on the balconies talking about Mom and our lives.

Over the years, our roles had changed. In many ways I had become the successful one, while he lived a more modest existence. He respected my success in both my career and second marriage. It saddened me when he said he was a failure in life. I thought he had been unlucky. When our paths split, I took one path and obtained an education. His dream was to open a successful business. Yes, he had failed, but I admired him for trying. My hard work paid off, his did not. I was luckier than him, not smarter. And I owed him: he gave me $10 when I was in need, and he took care of my mother, a debt I can never repay.

❦

Whenever I first saw Cathy on my trips back to California, she reminded me of the little girl who always came running and jumped in my arms yelling out, "Daddy, Daddy!" when I came home from work. It brought me back to the days when we laughed and giggled through the showers we took together. As she grew older, she always came running to hug me, and still does.

Despite our closeness, we have very different personalities. This is to be expected, of course, but I thought she knew the first rule of life: "Take care of yourself." Only then are you truly free. Only then can you help others.

Advice can be taken or ignored. And in Cathy's case, that meant ignoring Rule No. 1, particularly when it came to relationships.

What happened?

Cathy's maternal instincts strengthened with each passing year. By the spring of 1988 they were ready to explode. Cathy was thirty years old at the time, and the baby bell had been ringing for three years. She wanted Kelly to marry her, to have an exclusive relationship and a baby or two.

"No way," was Kelly's response. He was forty-five years old, divorced from his first wife, and had a son in college. Marriage and babies were not on his agenda.

Cathy felt Kelly was her soulmate—he made her laugh, and she enjoyed talking about the arts with him. And she was always in favor of some new experience he came up with. Yet her desire to be a mother trumped her love for him. So, she gradually pulled away from Kelly and looked for a husband elsewhere.

For the next seven years Cathy went through a number of boyfriends, and as the years passed, she became more frantic. The fertility time bomb was ticking.

The first man she identified as a possible husband was British and lived in London. I have no idea how she met him, but on my trip to Los Angeles in 1989 she introduced him. He seemed like a nice guy. Cathy arranged a trip to a ski resort near Lake Tahoe and invited Susan and me to accompany them. We accepted. When we arrived, they went skiing. I did not ski, ice skate, or take walks on snow-covered paths. I had lived in Connecticut for over twenty years, and I had seen enough snow. I had plenty of books to read and enough tourists to watch and entertain me in restaurants and lounges. I got no negative vibes from Cathy's boyfriend, only slight irritations that I ignored. Cathy was thirty years old, and I refused to become involved in her decision.

Shortly after the trip, Cathy quit her job and went to London expecting a marriage proposal. After living with the man for two months, she realized his British values did not suit her. He expected a woman to stay home, clean house, cook, and take care of babies. Cleaning the house and cooking were two things Cathy refused to do. In addition, unlike Kelly, he was not much fun; he took things too seriously and disliked arguments.

She called me from London and asked if she could live with Midge, James, and me for a few weeks as she straightened out her life. After four years in the navy, James lived with us off and on. Cathy moved in with us and stayed for two months. Just like James, she watched TV late into the night, slept late, raided the kitchen for food, and waited for "the adults" to cook and clean the house.

Cathy had another potential husband in Los Angeles, and they talked on the phone for hours. After about six weeks, he agreed that if Cathy returned to Los Angeles they could live together and talk of marriage and babies.

Around nine months later, I arrived in L.A. for my annual family visit. I asked Mom about Cathy's new boyfriend, but she had not seen

Cathy for months and did not know what was happening in her life. Cathy came over the first night of my visit, and Mom was delighted. We talked for hours. I agreed to come to Cathy's house for dinner and meet her boyfriend.

The dinner was a catastrophe.

Cathy worked for days cleaning her house, but it was still in disarray. When I arrived, she was busy cooking, and I joined her and her mate in the kitchen. He was around six feet tall, weighed perhaps 180 pounds, and had the mannerisms of an accountant.

The dinner was a formal affair. I quickly realized his goal for the evening was to belittle me and prove his superiority. First, he informed me he had a master of business administration from USC. I was impressed. Along with Stanford, USC is one of the "Ivies of California." As we continued talking, he revealed his salary was probably three times the salary of an insignificant professor at a state university in Connecticut. His attitude certainly indicated he believed his MBA from USC trumped my PhD from NYU. This was no Kelly—he had no sense of humor.

During the evening I learned he was in the process of divorcing his wife and had two children. Cathy told me later he indulged the children when they stayed over, allowing them full reign of the house, and never corrected their behavior. If she complained, he defended his children and refused to discipline them.

After dinner, as they cleaned the kitchen and drank another glass of wine, I stepped outside to smoke my pipe. I took a slow walk around the neighborhood, realizing I did not like the man and thought he was a condescending asshole. I reminded myself that Cathy had the right to choose her mate, and whatever the outcome, I would continue to love her.

When I returned, we sat in the living room. Cathy and I sipped cognac she purchased specifically for me while Mr. MBA drank wine. I do not remember his name. This time the conversation was less tense and drifted from mundane topic to mundane topic.

I teased Cathy about having an exercise bike in her living room. She giggled at a private joke about it. When she lived alone in a different apartment, she had the same bike in her living room. When she pedaled, an electric motor recharged the bicycle and vibrated the seat. After I learned about this, I teased her that Midge had other uses for *her* vibrators. We both laughed, and she added, "I have a couple of those, but the bicycle is a good alternative."

Crude, you might think, for a father to talk to his daughter about such things. But I was my mother's son, and Cathy was her granddaughter. She was also Charlene's daughter, and Charlene was as crude as my mother in many ways. When out walking, if Charlene needed to piss with no bathrooms around, she moved into the bushes and squatted. She often bragged about the fact she did not wear any underclothes.

Was I shocked? No, but I was surprised. It was exactly what my mother would have done, but she would not have talked about her (lack of) underwear.

When Cathy visited me in Connecticut when she was sixteen, she told me she was sexually active.

Why did she tell me this? She knew I loved her and would not judge or lecture her. Maybe?

My response was to take her to a gynecologist for birth control pills, a thirty-minute film, and a doctor's lecture on sexually transmitted diseases. I knew the Nancy Reagan motto, "Just say no," but the promise of no sex until marriage was an impossible goal for Cathy, as it is for most people. Life's prime directive is to reproduce. And my prime directive was to protect Cathy from reproducing until she could assume responsibility for taking care of herself.

But back to our inside joke. Mr. MBA asked, "Why are you laughing? I use the bike more than she does."

At his insistence, Cathy reluctantly related the story of the bike.

Mr. MBA looked at me and snapped. "Want to know about our sex life?" Then he lectured me and Cathy for two minutes on appropriate social behavior.

Oops. Apparently I violated a rule. A father, apparently, should not even acknowledge his daughters engaged in any sexual behavior. Fat chance; I was my mother's son and Cathy was her granddaughter. My great-grandmother was an Indian squaw.

Alpha male speaks, all must listen. We had only known each other for a few hours but I already knew he wanted to prove he was smarter and more cultured than me.

I looked at my watch, rose, and said, "Time to leave."

Cathy tried to convince me to stay, and Mr. MBA stood aside and echoed her. I responded as a guest. "Thanks for the dinner, thanks for the cognac. I need to get home to check on Ga-Ga." Nice to meet to you Mr. MBA.

"Call me tomorrow," I said to Cathy as she escorted me to the door. She nodded and I left.

Around 2 a.m. she arrived at Ga-Ga's, crying and saying she was leaving him. A bad fight had erupted, and Mr. MBA hit her.

An hour later, Mr. MBA pounded on the door and shouted out, "Cathy, come out and talk to me."

Ga-Ga got out of bed, scared, and said, "Kenny, call the cops." Cathy pleaded with me not to call the police.

Reluctantly, I stepped to the door and said to Cathy, "Lock the door behind me."

Mr. MBA stepped back from the door. I heard the lock click behind me. I sat on the top step of the stoop and motioned for him to join me. I could tell he was not drunk but emotionally upset. We talked.

According to him, the second I left, Cathy started screaming at him for insulting me. He apologized, but she kept yelling and threatened to leave him. In the end, she went crazy and attacked him, and as he defended himself, he accidentally hit her in the face.

I listened to him proclaim his love for her, but he admitted they fought often. All he wanted, he said, was to talk to Cathy and tell her he was sorry.

I suggested he go home and come back in the morning. He refused, saying he was not going anywhere until he talked to Cathy.

Call the law or ask Cathy what to do?

I went back inside, locking the door behind me. Ga-Ga had gone to bed, but I was sure she was awake wishing she had a gun.

Cathy waited for me. At this point I realized she was thrilled with Mr. MBA chasing after her and proclaiming his love for her. She went home with him. Later, he told her I was a wimp that night—"He should have kicked my ass." Maybe, but he was bigger than me, and I avoid fights when possible. That's my story, and I'm sticking to it.

For the next three weeks, I saw Cathy nearly every day. Mr. MBA was not welcome at my mother's house, and I refused to see him for the rest of my visit. I also avoided discussing him. Her romantic partner was her business, and if it turned out to be Mr. MBA, I would live with the decision.

Over the next six months, their relationship ended in bitter animosity. Cathy moved out, settled into a new job, and rented a nice apartment as far from him as possible. She adopted two beautiful white cats to keep her company. She gradually recovered and began her pursuit for a new lover to marry and have the baby she desperately desired. She took our trip to Bunk's and renewed her contact with Mom until she died in 1992.

Cathy's next lover was a "cowboy." He worked on a dude ranch near Santa Barbara, and she drove four hours to be with him every weekend. When I arrived on my annual trip after they started dating, she suggested I rent a cabin at the ranch for a weekend to meet him. My brother offered to go with me, and I accepted the invite.

When I met Greg Baeder, I knew he had his orders: "Be nice to Daddy." And he was. He arranged for us stay in the best cabin at the ranch at a discounted price and informed me it included breakfast, lunch, and dinner. My brother and I did not ride horses but instead spent one day playing golf.

My impression of Greg: he was a nice young man, but I wondered how he would earn a living for a wife and child. Such a practical question. Few people seeking a mate are going to be practical, I know. But wonder is all I did; again, it was up to Cathy to pick her partner, not me.

By the time of my next visit, he had moved into Cathy's apartment. He still impressed me. He had been looking for a permanent job in the time he had been living with Cathy, but in the meantime, he worked temporary jobs and paid his share of the rent. He had talent and hooked up with a company that did children's birthday parties.

He often came home dressed as a clown. His former job titles included cowboy, soldier, restaurant manager, motorcycle repairman, bicycle repairman, and sheet metal worker. He liked working with his hands but he did not want a job repairing cars; he was looking for something different. He wanted a job doing metalwork on racing cars, and it was obvious he had the ability to do the job.

I liked him. He was not academically inclined—that is, he was not interested in poetry, the theater, or philosophy. Nevertheless, he was intelligent, and most important of all, he was kind and respected Cathy's intellectual nature. Over the years, he proved to be a dependable and admirable man. He always treated me as special because I was Cathy's dad.

Sometime in the next year, he got a job designing complicated metal parts at a Boeing aircraft facility near San Francisco. Cathy quit her job, and they moved to Guerneville, a small town twenty miles from Santa Rosa.

Greg and Cathy were different. He was a practical man and Cathy was extremely impractical. He worried about finances; she read books and talked poetry. Occasionally, Cathy worked a part-time job, but when not working, housekeeping and cooking were down on her list of things to do. She returned to college to earn her BA and loved the intellectual atmosphere. In the evenings, she enjoyed a glass of wine and dreamed of her beautiful future life with a baby. Greg worked a sixty-hour week and rarely drank.

For four years she tried unsuccessfully to get pregnant. Cathy was almost forty, and both were muttering about breaking up. She got her BA in urban studies with a minor in literature and wanted to stay in school to get an MA. Greg wanted her to get a job so he could return to college and get a degree in mechanical engineering—that had been the agreement. She procrastinated and their arguments escalated.

She was thirty-eight years old when she got pregnant in November 1998. In April 1999, they decided to get married. I was invited to the event but it was too late to attend a "shotgun" wedding. Cathy invited my brother to walk her down the aisle instead. She wanted the ceremony to take place in a local park but naturally needed money for the reception. I sent her $1,500. Susan, Doran, and their kids attended the wedding, as did Tina and Carrie (Tina and Charlie's oldest daughter), who was near the same age as Cathy. Charlene, now a sensei in the Buddhist faith, preformed the ceremonies.

Greg told me later that my brother, as the surrogate dad, took him aside and told him he better be good to Cathy. The alpha male at work. Fortunately for everyone, Greg smiled rather than popping him in the face. I grinned. "That's my brother," I said, "and I do love him."

CHAPTER 33

LOSING A FRIEND:
DETZER AND ME

Over the years, my relationship with David Detzer had changed. I married Midge. Detzer divorced his first wife, married again, then divorced his second wife and married a pretty young schoolteacher. I knew his first wife, and became a friend of his second wife, but rarely saw his third. By 1980 our friendship revolved around our jobs, and we mostly talked about our research or the books we were reading. He often asked me to support his positions in department meetings, which I did.

Several incidents over the years, however, caused our friendship to end. The first one occurred in the spring of 1990, after the Phi Alpha Theta history honor society students came to me with a challenge. Several had taken my course on Vietnam, and many had also taken courses with Detzer, who taught an upper-level history course titled "U.S. Wars in the Pacific." It covered World War II, the Korean War, and the Vietnam War. Detzer and I differed in our interpretation of the Vietnam War and why the U.S. became involved in Vietnam, and the honor society wanted us to stage a debate.

Nearly every American scholar of Southeast Asia, myself included, opposed the U.S. intervention from as early as 1956. We knew from Ch'iang's collapse in China in 1949 that the corrupt anticommunist government in Saigon was doomed. Ho Chi Minh, as Mao did earlier, was leading a nationalist revolution. American experts on China also opposed the intervention because Mao and China were never puppets of the Soviet Union, contrary to followers of Kennan's Containment theory. In 1973, when President Nixon and Secretary of State Henry Kissinger diplomatically recognized Communist China, it became obvious that the world was no longer bipolar, as visualized by the Containment theory. It was a multipolar world.

In my classes, I asserted in no uncertain terms that the United States lost the war in Vietnam. Without a doubt, using maximum firepower to destroy the Vietcong and Vietminh guaranteed failure. Fighting peasant uprisings with massive bombing was like trying to kill flies in a wheat field with a shotgun. Thousands of Americans and hundreds of thousands of Vietnamese lost their lives.

By 1969, people were demonstrating in the streets demanding the U.S. withdraw from Vietnam. Winning such a war was impossible; i.e., the United States lost the war when our final troops were withdrawn in 1975.

Detzer asserted we did not lose the war in Vietnam, but rather withdrew our troops when the fall of the South Vietnam government was no longer a threat to the security of the United States. In his telling, the U.S. had entered the war primarily to prevent the spread of Russian-Chinese power.

Detzer proclaimed in his classes that the U.S. had won the war because we prevented a communist takeover until 1975.

Detzer had accepted the Phi Alpha Theta students' request for a debate. Would I do the same?

I laughed. "You're kidding," I said.

"No," they replied. "Professor Detzer wants to prove you are wrong and he is right."

I grinned. "Sure," I said. "Sounds like fun." And I meant it. Scholarly debates among friends are the most fun thing in the academic world. Besides, I knew I would win. Even if I didn't, it was still a game of mental ping-pong. Both of us were good public speakers, but I was better in responding to questions.

I knew my friend had something up his sleeve. Remember, he was the one who quit golf when I started winning rather than be second-best. If he, a member of the Best and the Brightest Club, challenged me to a duel, he expected to win.

I later learned after the debate his confidence was based on a book he had recently published, *An Asian Tragedy: America and Vietnam*. Several weeks later, he "gave" me a copy of the book at a discounted price. It was a 145-page summary of U.S. actions in Vietnam. In it he asserted the U.S. achieved its goals in Vietnam. The book was well written. After I read it, I required it in my freshman course on Vietnam for a couple of years.

Nevertheless, it was the height of gall for Detzer to assume he knew more about the Vietnam War than I did—I had studied the topic for thirty years.

Over eighty students and faculty members attended the Detzer-Young debate on Vietnam. I tore holes through his arguments. During the question period, it was obvious I knew more about the Vietnam War than he did, and the vast majority of the audience agreed with me. What I failed to realize, though, was that from Detzer's point of view it was the final blow to our twenty-five years of friendship.

For the next five years I continued to believe Detzer was a friend, but several additional incidents drove me to reevaluate things. The next one occurred in 1992, just as I was finishing up my major scholarly work, *The General's General: The Life and Times of Lt. General Arthur MacArthur*. MacArthur was awarded the Medal of Honor for his actions as a Union soldier, and around 160 pages of the 600-page manuscript were on the Civil War. Detzer was an expert on the war, and I asked him to read and critique that section of the book. I sent other chapters to scholars specializing in later periods in MacArthur's life, from 1865 to 1909. Each responded with critical but respectful suggestions, and I appreciated their comments. I knew none of these scholars personally. They were colleagues, not friends.

After reading about seventy-five pages, Detzer returned the manuscript with several nasty comments, implying I needed to do more research and my skills as a writer were questionable. Besides, he said, he had more important work since he was involved in writing another book on Charleston and the Civil War. His begging off for time reasons could have been legitimate. He made as much money as a writer as he did a teacher.

Emotionally, I was not hurt by his comments on the manuscript because he was right: I needed to revise some of the chapters. This was the very reason I asked him to read and comment on the Civil War section. I made the corrections he suggested, but I felt his refusal to devote more time to my request was insulting. Over the previous twenty-five-years I had given him both intellectual and personal considerations on many occasions that far outranked the few favors he did for me.

I thought David was a friend—a term I never use lightly.

Detzer retired from teaching in June 1995, when he was around sixty years old. Teaching, he told me, interfered with his writing. His decision to retire was mathematical. His pension would provide 60 percent of his pre-retirement income, and if he increased the amount of time he spent writing books, his royalties would provide another 60 percent. The two combined resulted in a 20 percent raise in pay over his faculty salary. I didn't understand his figures, but he was a former math major. To my surprise, he continued to teach evening classes for less money as an adjunct. Hey, a dime is a dime. After his retirement, we occasionally met when he needed a favor. I always assumed we remained at least "friendly" acquaintances.

The next incident occurred in the spring of 1996, after the Phi Alpha Theta society, with my encouragement, asked him to give a talk on one of the battles of the Civil War. Before his speech, I took him out to dinner. The topic of our Vietnam debate came up, and he reluctantly admitted his argument that the U.S. won the war was a "little" lame.

At least a hundred people attended his speech, including all members of the History Department. Detzer, a great lecturer, kept his audience's attention for forty-five minutes. To my surprise, he belittled me several times. Although he acted as if he was merely teasing, it was payback time for my winning the Vietnam debate. To me the debate had been a friendly intellectual ping-pong game. For Detzer, I had sinned by winning a game of intellectual ping-pong in front of eighty people. He refused to answer any questions after his lecture.

There was one more incident, but I'll talk about that later.

Chapter 34

Academic Life:
Pros & Cons

After Detzer retired, I began to think about doing the same. Several colleagues who were social friends had recently died, among them Professor Truman Warner, Arnold Brackman (the chair of the Journalism Department), and Major James Bradley. The logical retirement date for me was 2002, after I turned sixty-two and could opt for Social Security payments.

Still, at the age of fifty-five, I was in my prime years as a teacher and a scholar. At least, that's what I told myself. Delusions? Perhaps.

For the time being, I decided to stick it out, but seven or eight more years seemed like a long time. I was tired, moody, and facing the reality of life.

Being a scholar and teacher is hard work. I had two dreams when I began teaching college: I wanted to become a respected scholar and a good teacher. I taught many different courses, and each demanded constant revision and research to retain my expertise. I am sure I was a respected teacher and colleague at Western Connecticut.

The General's General highlighted my accomplishments as a scholar, but I was not enthusiastic about writing another history book. I did not want to spend ten years and thousands of dollars on research. Besides, few outside scholars took notice of my work. In my mind, I was a moderate-sized fish in a tiny pond.

I considered reworking one of my novels, but placed it back in the filing cabinets—what is the sense if no one will read it? Finally, I pulled out a manuscript on Chinese philosophy from my cabinet that might have a small chance of publication. I dabbled at it in my spare time.

My pride at being a professor at Western Connecticut had declined. The administration's attitude and actions lowered the quality of the school, in my opinion, particularly in the Liberal Arts departments.

In an illustrative move, in hopes of gaining more prestige the school's name was changed from Western Connecticut State College to Western Connecticut State University in 1983, as was befitting in the age of euphemism, a time when garbage workers became "sanitation engineers." For many years, the university title meant a school that had a PhD program. But the library at Western Connecticut was inadequate for any major research by professors or graduate students, and the internet was still limited.

The administration at Western Connecticut also treated the Liberal Arts faculty, except committee members, as pampered, overpaid intellectuals who constantly caused grief because of their inflated egos. The administration paid lip service to the principles of good teaching and relied heavily on euphemism in its mission statements. In reality, they treated students and the Liberal Arts faculty simply as nuisances. The lack of administrative support toward the end of my teaching career decreased my pride in being a professor at Western Connecticut even further.

The school cut back on hiring full-time teachers for the Liberal Arts departments and hired adjuncts, often high school teachers, to teach many core courses, using tenured professors primarily to teach upper-level and graduate courses. The administration's prime concern was the budget and it wanted teachers to keep the students in their seats above all other considerations.

The administrators didn't really realize it, or didn't care, that they lowered the quality of education at the college and downgraded the cultural cachet of a university education. By tradition, a bachelor of arts degree meant the student had a well-rounded education. Core courses, packed with freshman and sophomores, provided the basics for students to expand their interest in and understanding of different ideas by exposing them to subjects taught in all the various college departments, including history, economics, philosophy, science, literature, music, and more. I believed full-time faculty, not adjuncts, should teach these courses. Apparently, I was out of touch.

Accountants had determined that the state university system could save a tremendous amount of money if the senior professors teaching in the liberal arts retired. Adjuncts and non-tenured instructors could be hired at the lowest level, saving millions. Even better, retirement benefits were paid through state coffers, not the college itself. The universities could then use the "saved" budget money to hire more administrators and IT personnel.

The accountants' argument was logical and practical and the administration at Western Connecticut (and many other colleges) embraced the plan. In the age-old dilemma over whether education is meant to teach you skills to obtain a good job or teach you skills to live a better life, the college had weighed in decisively. Why force students to study history, literature, or the arts? There's no money in reading Dante, Chaucer, or Poe. Who reads, anyway?

The state bureaucracy agreed with the university administrators that new teachers could be hired as instructors or adjuncts for a much lower cost and easily fill the positions. In April 1997, the state of Connecticut offered a buyout to faculty members with twenty-five years or more of seniority. I had taught at Western Connecticut for thirty-one years, so to sweeten the offer, the state offered to credit me three additional years of service. Each increased year my pension rose by 2 percent, meaning I would receive 68 percent of my salary along with a 3 percent COLA (cost-of-living-adjustment) clause.

Should I accept the offer?

It was difficult decision. My rational side advised remaining on the job. As a full professor, I was almost independently employed. The administration left me alone, and I taught my classes with no interference. Most of my work was done at home or at the library researching and writing scholarly articles, preparing lectures, grading tests, and reading books. I was being paid to learn. It was my dream job.

If I curtailed my research, stopped improving my lecture notes, eased up on my class requirements, and reduced the number of hours I spent grading tests and papers, it'd be a cushy job: I could work eight and a half months a year, only three days a week, required only to be on campus for twenty-four hours a week. On top of that there were six weeks off between semesters, two weeks free for Christmas and Easter, and two months off in the summer.

Rationally, I should have retained such a cushy job until I was eighty years old.

Emotionally, this arrangement was impossible for me. I could not continue to teach if I did not continue to learn. No dusty notes for me. If I did not remain a scholar, I could not remain a teacher.

Money was not part of the equation. Midge and I were in the lower-middle-class because we had two incomes. We could take trips, buy a car, help the children, and still save money.

To remove money as a potential problem in our marriage, we maintained three bank accounts: Midge's account, my account, and a joint account for household expenses. The money in our private accounts was spent without discussion. We both contributed to a joint account. (Another rule for life: "If you pay your way, no one can tell you what to do.") Because my salary was larger, I paid more into the joint account. We discussed things as equals. Midge's inheritance from her parents, part of her private accounts, had not been touched for fifteen years and grew sufficiently enough for me to say I married a wealthy woman. We both also had 401(k)s. We never argued about money.

As I was considering what to do, I learned the state of Connecticut planned to change medical coverage for state employees. In July 1997, employees would be required to contribute more money for medical coverage to help the system survive. If I retired by June 1997, the state would pay for covering Midge and me for the rest of our lives. This coverage meant potentially saving thousands of dollars.

After thirty-one years of teaching at Western Connecticut, I decided to retire in June 1997.

"Why?" Cathy asked me years later.

The decision to retire was both rational and emotional. Apart from the circumstances explained above, I can cite a half dozen reasons why. For starters, my remaining colleagues at Western Connecticut were merely "friendly acquaintances," and I had little emotional attachment to the school. With each passing year, it was harder to maintain a connection.

I didn't need the money, and if I retired, I could work on revising my old manuscripts, perhaps complete one of the books I had been working on for over ten years. I had many thick files accumulated over those years that needed second, third, and fourth drafts. Old unfinished manuscripts haunt writers. Better to burn them than leave them in my filing cabinets unfinished.

Only time would tell me if I made the right decision. I was fifty-seven years old, and for thirty-one of those years I spent studying, teaching, and writing about U.S. history from the Constitutional Convention through the Vietnam War.

Retirement was a different kind of American dream. I needed awhile to get comfortable with the idea that I was a success in our society.

Chapter 35

Life in Retirement

Shortly after my retirement, in early February 1998, I took a leisurely road trip from Danbury to Lawton. A little depressed, I wondered if I should have retired. "I used to be somebody" echoed in my ears. A retired professor, just like a retired politician, medical doctor, or plumber, is simply another person who has enough money to stop working.

I needed to get out of Danbury for a few weeks and decided to revisit the area of my youth to see how much the Lawton area had changed. Nostalgia? Perhaps. To my knowledge, all my relatives had died or left Oklahoma.

I drove west through Knoxville, Nashville, and Memphis, stopping along the way at state parks with golf courses. I was in no hurry. My first stop in Oklahoma was Ardmore, a nice city in the southeast corner near a number of lakes in what my relatives called the Piney Country. There were trees and water, unlike around Lawton, about hundred miles north.

The next day I reached Lawton.

"You can't go home again," they say. Indeed, the small city of my youth no longer existed. Downtown had been demolished and replaced with a large mall when a new interstate was built in the area. The suburbs had grown dramatically and spread out for miles, with shopping centers and housing in areas that had once been farmland. With a population of over 100,000, Lawton was the fifth-largest city in Oklahoma.

And unfortunately, it looked like most cities in the United States—interstate highways lined with Walmarts, Home Depots, McDonald's, etc. I only stayed one night, then turned around and went home.

In late March, life threw me another curve ball.

After returning from my trip, I came down with the flu and went to my doctor. I wasn't concerned but simply hoped for some medicine to relieve my chest pain. The doctor ordered X-rays, which showed a small tumor in my lungs. The biopsy proved inconclusive.

Because I had been a smoker for forty years, the doctors believed the tumor might be cancerous. I smiled at the irony—after being retired ten months I might die of cancer. They recommended the tumor be removed, a major operation. Back in the day before high-end computers and microtechnology, operations were more invasive and dangerous. The surgeon cut a fifteen-inch incision on the left side of my back, used tools to spread my ribs apart, and removed a tumor the size of a dime.

Benign. I was relieved, but it took over six months to recover physically, and even longer to recover mentally. When death knocked on my door, my days of dreaming of success as a writer were over. I was not feeling sorry for myself; I was feeling lucky. The operation drilled into me the fact I was dying. I turned to Shakespeare. Ah, he is there when you need him:

> Tomorrow, and tomorrow, and tomorrow
>
> Creeps in this petty pace from day to day
>
> To the last syllable of recorded time,
>
> And all our yesterdays have lighted fools
>
> The way to dusty death. Out, out brief candle.
>
> Life's but a walking shadow, a poor player
>
> That struts and frets his hour upon the stage
>
> And then is heard no more. It is tale
>
> Told by an idiot, full of sound and fury,
>
> Signifying nothing.

(For the record, the passage is from *Macbeth*.)

Many other philosophers, such as the fourth-century Chinese sage Chuang-tzu, echoed the same theme. Relative to the magnitude of the billions of people who have lived and died, Chuang-tzu reminds us, an individual life is no more important than a grain of sand. The question is how we spend our time while here. Each of us answers that question in different ways.

When Chuang-tzu was around eighty years old, he was working in his flower garden when a disciple came to him for advice. The disciple watched the great philosopher weed his garden, and as he watched, the disciple wondered why his mentor wasted time on such menial work as weeding a flower garden when he might die before the flowers bloomed.

Chuang-tzu paused and looked at his disciple, who asked, "Master Chuang, if you knew you were going to die tomorrow, what would you do to prepare for your death?" The Master thought for only a moment: "I would cultivate my garden," he said, and returned to tilling the ground.

My operation affected Midge. Although she was only fifty-six, she retired from her teaching job at Bethel Middle School in June 1998. She realized, as I did, our time together might be shorter than either of us had contemplated. It was time to cultivate our garden.

Danbury was a special place to us but it had two major liabilities. In the 1970s a new interstate had been built from New York City through Danbury on the way to Hartford and Boston. As a result, Danbury's population exploded. Now roughly ninety minutes from New York City and thirty minutes to White Plains, Danbury attracted international companies who set up offices in the area, and new residents' cars crowded city roads. Shopping centers appeared on the outskirts of town, and within a few years, once-rural areas became part of town.

The second liability was winter—it was cold in Danbury from November through March. Shoveling the driveway after a heavy snowstorm is a burden when you age. Midge had been born in Florida. She loved summers in Danbury but hated the winters.

So, we decided to move. Midge's parents were dead. James, her sister, and other relatives lived in Florida. We had friends in Danbury, but over the years, many had moved, died, or faded away.

I vetoed Florida. I had lived through hot summer months in Oklahoma and Los Angeles, and I had no desire to do it again in a different place. I also disliked Florida because it reminded me of Greater Los Angeles with its miles of commercial streets and the constant recurrence of the same chain stores from McDonald's to Walmart.

In April 1999, Midge and I moved near Hendersonville, North Carolina, a small town about twenty-five miles southwest of Asheville. Over the previous ten years, we had explored the area on various trips as we looked for a place to retire. Hendersonville reminded us of Danbury. I loved Danbury when it was a small town nestled in the mountains covered with trees and laced with small lakes. From April to November, Connecticut is a great place to live. Hendersonville is located in the Blue Ridge Mountains, and the spring, summer, and fall weather is perhaps superior to even Danbury, with winters that are milder and bring less snow.

We sold our house in Danbury and moved to Horse Shoe, North Carolina, an even smaller town a few miles from Hendersonville.

When I moved to North Carolina, I wrote Detzer a short note telling him I had moved to a small town south of Asheville. His response finally ended our friendship: "Good luck," he wrote. "I do not use snail mail, so don't expect a response from me in the future." And one additional snipe: "If you are moving to Asheville, you should learn to spell the name." Yep, in my note I had spelled it "Ashville," and as any preppie knows, only poorly educated people misspell words.

Ha! All contact with Detzer was thus concluded.

Despite this, my experience with him taught me an important lesson. I was not mad at him but rather irritated at myself. Over the years I had thought of only two or three people as "friends." For me, a friend is someone I stand up for during any crisis, and I assume they will support me in comparable fashion. Most people we casually call friends are merely "friendly acquaintances." I finally realized David was a friendly acquaintance, not a true friend. That it took me so long to realize this is what irritates me.

My mistake, not his. But to this day, realizing Detzer was not a true friend saddens me.

Chapter 36

Life in Horse Shoe

In my first few years in Horse Shoe, I resumed my handyman tasks developed in Danbury. I built bookcases for hundreds of books plus a separate office for my scholarly books and manuscripts. I repaired the plumbing, put in new electrical outlets, mowed the lawn, and helped weed.

I stopped drinking and smoking after my lung operation. That had not been part of my plan after retirement. I made it clear to Midge: "I am not giving up either alcohol or smoking for eternity," I told her. When I ate in restaurants, I envied those enjoying their wine, beer, and mixed drinks. On the golf courses, several players smoked, usually cigars, and I dreamed of having a good smoke.

I dabbled in rewriting the novel I first wrote in 1982 and had revised several times, about the massacre of U.S. Army troops in the Philippines

in 1901. At the time the U.S. Army was attempting to suppress Filipinos fighting for independence from U.S colonization. Defeated in several battles in 1900, the Filipinos reverted to guerrilla warfare and engaged in terror attacks on several islands in the archipelago.

To counter this the U.S. Army established hundreds of outposts on the major islands and patrolled areas where the insurgents were active. Company C, Ninth Infantry, composed of over a hundred soldiers and officers, established a post at a small, isolated "friendly" fishing village on the island of Samar several hundred miles south of Manila. In a surprise attack aided by the villagers, Filipino insurgents overran the post, slaughtering over sixty U.S. soldiers.

My novel centers around the fifty troopers who escaped in real life and the officer who led them to safety using the village fishermen's canoes. For his actions, he received his second Congressional Medal of Honor. I titled the book *Twice Honored*.

I had had enough rejection letters from agents and publishers and decided to self-publish the book.

I am a writer, not an editor or salesman. So, I looked for an editor who could also arrange for its publication. Years passed. The first candidate, who needed to research how to self-publish a book, dropped out after two years. The second took a down payment and disappeared. I finally found someone who could assist me, and the book was published. I bought fifty copies and gave them to friends and family. It is a good novel, much like the Westerns I read in my youth. Although I made no attempt to sell the book, I was pleased with it. If you look hard, you can find it on Amazon.

After almost two years of abstinence, I returned to drinking casually and smoked a pipe as I had done on many occasions. I was a moderate drinker. Every year I quit for one month to prove to myself that I could stop drinking. I did not want to become an alcoholic like my father.

After our move to Horse Shoe, we maintained contact with old friends, but we also quickly realized life can be lonely unless action is taken to find new acquaintances and friends. To find new friends, you must get out and do something. Take a part-time job or join a garden, sewing, or book club, a bowling league, tennis club, or some other active group. This gets you out of the house and provides you with opportunities to meet people. Midge and I joined the Etowah Valley Golf Club, and within weeks we had friendly acquaintances. Over the years some became close friends.

As times changed, so did I. I relaxed in my easy chair and read novels, not the great novels I read to become cultured, but simply ones that appealed to me: King, Perry, Irving, Cornwall, Marlowe, and down the line. I consumed about four novels a week, taking an occasional break to read a nonfiction book that usually took a week to digest. Occasionally, I pulled old manuscripts from my filing cabinets but always set them aside for the future.

Chapter 37

Bunk & Muriel

With everything quiet with the kids in California, in the summer of 1995 Midge and I visited Bunk and Muriel.

After my mother died, Bunk and I stayed in contact via an occasional letter or phone call. At the end of the call, he always said, "You and Midge come see us soon." Midge was all for it—she loved to travel, and wanted to meet Bunk and Muriel, who she'd heard about for so many years.

They were pleased to see us, and for a few days, we socialized as Muriel and Midge bonded. Each day, Bunk drove us around to various sights. I had seen them earlier, but Midge enjoyed the trip down to the Colorado River and a later trip to Wenatchee, a small town in the foothills near the base of the Cascades.

I was delighted to see my wife happy. After dinner, we sat around talking about our memories. Bunk brought out the family album. Going over the photographs, he discussed his life in Oklahoma. Muriel talked about their lives together, Midge talked about her parents, and I talked about Mom, Corky, and my daughters.

Bunk was proud of me. I had sent him a copy of *The General's General*. "Great book," he said. "Took me two or three weeks to read it. I enjoyed it a lot."

When I returned to Danbury, I called Bunk, thanking him for his hospitality.

A couple of years later, Bunk and Muriel visited us again in Danbury, and Midge and I acted as tour guides, escorting them from Danbury to Mystic. Danbury had long been a tourist city since it was only about two hours from New York City, but other small towns nearby were charming too, from Ridgefield to Washington, each with impeccably maintained houses dating back to Colonial times. Mystic is a tourist spot on the northeastern coast of Connecticut, about halfway between Boston and New York City. The prime attraction is the Mystic Seaport Museum that includes a nineteenth-century wooden whaling ship.

They were perfect guests. Bunk and I spent much of our time simply talking about life while Midge and Muriel bonded by cooking good dinners and talking about flowers and vegetable gardens. The TV was never turned on. Before they left, I gave Bunk a copy of the manuscript for *Twice Honored* (fourth draft), and he later called me and said he loved it. "As good as a Zane Grey book," he said. Coming from Bunk, this was high praise. He was proud of me.

Thus, Bunk's call on a November evening in 2003 didn't surprise me, but what he said did. "Son," he said, using his term of endearment for me, "I been missing you. If you want to see me, you better come soon."

Bunk was a realist. He was dying. How long had the doctors given him? "Three months, five at the most," he said.

"I'm coming," I said. "I'll call you back to tell you when."

Midge was away on a trip with her sister, or some of her old friends, and was not available for the trip to Washington.

I called Cathy and asked if she wanted to go see Bunk before he died, offering to pay her way.

She called back after talking it over with Greg. He wanted to come with their son Connor, who was four years old. I agreed to pay for a rental car and sent enough money to cover their other expenses such as motels, gas, and restaurants.

I called Bunk and gave him the date. "That's good, son. I'll be pleased to see Cathy and her son." I asked him for the name of a good motel in Moses Lake. He was relieved to hear I intended to rent rooms for Cathy et al. With other relatives expected near the same date, he did not have enough room for all of us at his house.

I flew to Spokane and drove to Moses Lake, arriving around two o'clock at the hotel where Cathy had reserved two connecting rooms. The hotel was not new, but it was well-maintained with an indoor swimming pool that I knew Connor would enjoy. A diner across the street attracted the locals as well as the hotel guests for breakfast, lunch, and dinner.

The two connected rooms were large; one had two beds for Cathy, Greg, and Connor, and the other, with only one king-size bed, felt larger. I called Bunk and told him I would be over the next day after breakfast.

Cathy and company arrived a couple of hours later and settled into their room as I played with Connor, who delighted me with his antics and desire for constant attention. I was thrilled to have a four-year-old to play with. That evening after dinner, we spent most of the time in my room as we did most evenings of our stay. I had stopped in Spokane to buy treats to munch on and beer, cognac, scotch, and vodka for the adults. Of course, Cathy had brought along goodies for the boy, who was asleep by 8 p.m. The adults stayed up until after midnight as Cathy and I told stories about Bunk and Muriel. Greg laughed and teased Cathy after I told him the fishing story about mosquitoes, perch, and Corky's fishing lures.

We arrived at Bunk and Muriel's the next morning around 9:30. The introductions and hugs all around took several minutes. Bunk's cousin Katherine and her fourteen-year-old granddaughter had been there for a week. Although Katherine introduced herself as Bunk's cousin, to him she was more like a slightly older sister. She was Aunt Hazel's daughter, the aunt who Bunk lived with as a teenager. Hazel was mom's oldest sister, a strong-willed woman that expected kids to obey, as my mom warned me when I visited her as a young boy. *Don't fuss or make a mess, or she'll pop you one.* If there was a matriarch of the Bass family it was Aunt Hazel. Bunk, Katherine, and her brother Billy Joe fought, played, and bonded in those years. Their father was a half-Choctaw Indian who drove a bus for Greyhound. He was a ghost I seldom saw, and he died before I got to know him.

Katharine, now around seventy-seven, was about three years older than Bunk, but looked younger. I had met her off and on throughout my life, but she basically remembered me only as one of Toad's kids. She remembered Corky better. She and her husband lived on a Choctaw reserve—she had some fancy name for the Choctaw community, and if you called it a "reservation" she'd jump all over you. "Isn't no damn reservation," she proclaimed. "It's the Choctaw Nation." Choctaws lived in modern houses, not tepees, and in cities with doctors, lawyers, plumbers, etc., as in most small towns in America. Her husband was a deputy sheriff for one of the ten counties controlled by the Choctaws, one of the Five Civilized Tribes (the others being the Cherokee, Chickasaw, Creek, Seminole). All of them were pushed from their homelands to Indian Territory between the 1830s and 1890s. Katherine certainly was a Bass, and she reminded me of Aunt Hazel, not in looks but in personality. Her granddaughter was a pretty teenage girl who looked like a younger Katherine because of their Indian blood, which gave them a darker look than the Swedish appearance of Aunt Hazel, Mom, Red, and Bunk.

I looked around and didn't see Bunk. "In his chair in the living room using his air machine," Katherine said. "He's been driving us nuts for days, constantly asking when's Kenny coming."

She smiled as she waved me off to the living room with Cathy and Greg following. Her granddaughter picked up Connor, and for the next few days played with him on the screened-in back porch and the backyard.

I went into the room. Bunk sat in a nice comfortable chair with prescription bottles on a nearby table. He had lost at least twenty pounds since we last saw each other and looked weary. His red hair was now light blond, thinly covering his balding head.

He started to get up, but I motioned him to stay in the chair as I came over and shook his hand. I didn't hide my shock at his appearance, and I simply whispered, "Looks like the shit has hit the fan."

He smiled and mumbled, "Damn right, son, damn right."

I sat down in a chair on his right side rather than the sizeable couch to his left. I wanted to be close enough to touch him.

He said hello to Cathy, who bent over to give him a hug. Greg shook his hand and then sat on the couch with Cathy as Katherine and Muriel came into the room and sat on the couch as well.

Then we socialized for a few minutes. Everyone avoided the obvious: we had a sick man in the room. After a few minutes Bunk finally said, "I'd like to talk to Kenny for a while." As a group, with Muriel a little slower, they rose, smiled encouragingly at Bunk, and nodded at me as they left the room.

Bunk pulled the rubber breathing tube from his nose and reached over and turned off the machine. He glanced up and saw my worried look. "Can stay off the air for an hour or two," he said as he straightened up. "Son," he said, "damn glad you came. I missed you, and the women been driving me crazy. Can't even go to the bathroom without them hovering over me."

I nodded, knowing he was saying Katherine and Muriel were worried and wanted to take care of him, but their smothering him all day long was irritating and constantly reminded him that he was dying.

I knew Bunk didn't want to talk about death and dying or his illness— topics he already thought about and didn't need to discuss anymore. He wanted to talk about his life, not his death. I knew this—I was much like him and had come prepared. I had typed up seven pages of questions. I wanted to ask him about his life as a boy and up to the present. I came with a notebook, plenty of pens, and a small tape recorder. Over the next five days, we spent most of our time in that living room as he talked about his past. Many of his stories are embedded in this book, stories of Mom, Dad, Red, Papa Joe, and down the list.

He asked Muriel to bring over the family album with photographs of the Bass family going back to the early 1900s, and family documents including birth certificates, marriage licenses, and a genealogy table dating back to the 1860s. I went to Walmart and copied most of this material.

I knew Bunk hoped that someday I would write my memoirs and

talk about the Basses as my family—I wasn't a Young, he said, but a Bass.

Every morning when I arrived, he allowed the family to come into the room and sit on the couch as I asked questions. After a few minutes, the others jumped in to tell stories about their lives. Bunk allowed them to talk for a few minutes, then inevitably became impatient and asked them to leave. "Time for me and Kenny to get to work."

We never talked about his illness. For Bunk and me, the emotion called for was not sympathy but rather respect, or, some might even say, love. I hope that when it's my turn to wander to death's door my loved ones give me the same respect I gave Bunk.

Four months later, on January 14, 2004, Bunk died. He was less than a month away from his seventh-fifth birthday.

I meant to write a short story about my uncle, but I was working on the *Twice Honored* manuscript at the time, and as new medical problems arose, the project slowly faded away.

Chapter 38

My Brother Charles

After Mom died, I visited my brother a couple of times. Each time, within minutes, it felt as if I had seen him just last week. He lived in the same house near the railroad tracks in East L.A. and continued to pester Tina about moving. Money was tight. He had inherited $20,000 from Mom's estate, but he had to dip into it every month to stay afloat. They remained in their house in east L.A., drove old cars, and had a tight budget. Why didn't he get a job? He felt his role was to support his church by preaching the gospel of Jehovah.

Charlie was miserable, but Tina was happy—for her, living near her daughters, all married, and other relatives was more important than a better house or a new car.

Their finances improved in 1999 when Charlie began to collect Social Security checks and Tina inherited about $50,000 from her mother's estate. But Charlie pointed out that their monthly income was still not enough to cover their bills, and they had to dip into her inheritance to survive. "If we move to Lawton, we can rent a house in a much better neighborhood at half the price we pay in L.A.," he told Tina.

From 1998 to 2004, I seldom saw or called my brother. I had a tumor removed in March of that year, and it took me several months to heal. In November 1998, Midge and I rented a house near Hendersonville and looked for a house in the area, finally purchasing one in March. The next few months were hectic, and involved selling our home in Danbury, moving to Horse Shoe (just outside Hendersonville), and settling into a new home.

My brother, I assume, called once in a while, and I occasionally called him. But I had lots of distractions. At our new home I was busy building bookcases, working in the yard, playing golf, taking trips back to Connecticut to see old friends, going to Florida to socialize with Midge's relatives, and visiting Northern California to see Cathy.

In November 2004, I received a "Help!" call from my brother.

Though Tina had resisted his pleas to move, Charlie kept gnawing at the bone. Remember when my Mom said, "Corky (Charlie) is just like your Dad. He never takes no for an answer. Pick, pick, until he gets his way." I would add: Cork never did things halfway—horses, craps, fishing, and Jehovah are mere illustrations of his character. The same applied when it came to moving.

Eventually Corky contacted Billy Joe Sellers, one of the few relatives still living around Lawton. Earlier in the book I mentioned Billy Joe's name in passing. He was the son of my mother's older sister Hazel. Bunk lived his teenage years with Aunt Hazel and her children, Billy Joe and his older sister Katherine. Billy Joe was like a younger brother for Bunk, and Katherine was like his slightly older sister who corrected the boys' behavior, without much success.

Billy Joe told Corky that houses in Lawton were selling for around $150,000. He'd find better bargains in Duncan, thirty miles south of Lawton, and Ardmore, around fifty miles further southeast in the Piney Country. I was familiar with Ardmore because I had stayed there overnight during my trip to Lawton after my retirement. It is a pretty, prosperous little city surrounded by rolling hills and nearby lakes. For over a century, it was a railroad stopover between Oklahoma City and Dallas. Even now, a passenger train comes through each day with freight trains dropping off goods at the many distribution branches for several national retail chains such as Best Buy. Two interstate highways pass through the city. If forced to move back to Oklahoma, I would choose Ardmore.

"How much?" my brother asked Billy Joe.

"Most of the houses are selling for between $40,000 to $180,000. Lots of good homes for $80,000 or less."

"Let's move to Duncan or Ardmore," Charlie pleaded with Tina. "No way," Tina said. And she said no again week after week for three years.

When Tina reached sixty-two in 2002, and she started receiving Social Security checks, she finally gave in. She agreed to take a scouting trip in the fall for a month to look at houses in Lawton, Duncan, and Ardmore. Thus my brother's call.

I learned about this adventure about ten days after they rented a room for a month at a motel halfway between Ardmore and Duncan. Charlie said the motel was great, and the price was also great. The motel mainly rented rooms by the month to construction crews. It was a well-maintained family motel. It was clean and the rooms were large. Breakfast and supper were available for a low price. The food was different every day for supper and was truly home-cooked.

A salesman sells you a story before he sells a product. Charlie gradually got to the point of his call: He wanted me to come to Oklahoma and help him convince Tina it was a good idea to buy a house.

I laughed. "Tina will never move to Oklahoma, Charlie. Home for her is East L.A."

"No, no, Ken," he said. "She said she would move if we could find the perfect house."

"What the hell," I thought. I was retired and it was too cold to play golf. Midge had gone to Vero Beach to visit her sister. I hadn't seen my brother in four or five years, and we seldom called each other. The internet—are you kidding? My brother was computer illiterate, and I am not exactly an expert.

I took three days to drive to Oklahoma. I wasn't in any particular hurry. When I arrived at the motel, my brother greeted me in the lobby. After I paid for a week's rent, Charlie escorted me to a two-story building about fifty or sixty yards from the main building. Parking spaces connected the two buildings and a large grassy lawn separated them.

When I agreed to come to Oklahoma, I had two conditions: I

would only stay one week; and I wanted some privacy, that is, I did not want a connecting room,

My room was perfect. It was on the second floor in a building with thirty to forty rooms, and some distance from the main building where Charlie and Tina had a room. None of the other rooms in the entire building were occupied. My room had four windows that could be opened. Both the bathroom and the bedroom were clean. There was a TV I never turned on. There was no microwave oven, no refrigerator, and no coffee pot. Hot coffee, however, was available and free in the office. A good room for the price.

After resting, I met Charlie and Tina for supper. The dining area had eight to ten tables and a small kitchen in one corner. A construction crew working near Ardmore occupied most of the rooms in the main building. A friendly bunch. Guests could take the food to their rooms, and it really was a home-cooked meal including bread and pie. Better food and half the price of Applebee's or Ruby Tuesday.

We took the dinner on paper plates to Charlie and Tina's room. After we ate, I sipped my cognac while Tina drank wine and my brother had a couple of beers. Not drunk, but mellow, we talked for four hours. Charlie was enthusiastic about moving to Ardmore, and mostly dominated the conversation. Tina interrupted several times to express her feelings, which boiled down to "I don't want to move out of East L.A." She had lived all her life there. It was home to her.

Understand, I did not come to solve their problem, I came to see them.

I love my brother and Tina is a good sister-in-law. I learned over many years, however, that my role was to listen, not advise. I understood both sides, but in my mind I felt Tina's point of view was more important than Charlie's desire to get out of East L.A. and return to the world of his youth.

For the next five days we looked at homes in and around Ardmore.

Several houses were reasonably priced ($80,000 to $110,000) and were perfect for Charlie's budget. Tina rejected every one: a new two-bedroom duplex was too small, a home near downtown on a quarter acre was too old, and a relatively new three-bedroom house on an acre in the country was too isolated—she was afraid some rednecks would break in. She had lived her life in a dangerous city and felt safer when neighbors were nearby. Besides, the idea of driving five miles to shop at Walmart was not acceptable. The small grocery store about a mile away did not suit her. And, she kept saying, "I won't move to Oklahoma unless the house is perfect." Really, in my mind, she did not intend to move to Oklahoma.

Each morning around 8 o'clock, through the window of my room, I watched Charlie walking across the parking lot with two cups of coffee.

As we sat in the chairs in my room, I asked Charlie, "Why do you want to buy a house? In East L.A., you've rented homes for years. Why not rent a house here for a year? Tina might agree to that."

The answer was obvious: If they rented a house, Charlie knew Tina would moan and groan about going back to East L.A. To her, Oklahoma was a foreign country. For Charlie, East L.A., even after fifty years, was a foreign country. He wanted to go home.

My vacation with Charlie and Tina ended the next day. I hugged them and wished them success. They still had another week to search Duncan and Lawton again.

Betcha don't know who won.

To my surprise, they bought a three-bedroom house in Duncan. Apparently, Charlie had finally found the perfect house, above their budget, but worth the price.

The first time I saw Duncan two years later, I was absolutely shocked. My reaction: "Why in the hell would anyone live in Duncan?" And over the next ten years, every time I visited, I asked the same question. Many of the stores in the old downtown were boarded up with only a few businesses surviving. The main action was on the outskirts of the old town on a busy four-lane highway. Tasteless shopping centers, including a Walmart, stretched out for a couple miles with the usual national franchises from McDonald's to Applebee's to Days Inn.

Duncan had 25,000 people. Its main employer was Halliburton, who established their headquarters in town in 1915 during Oklahoma's oil boom. Halliburton grew into a massive conglomerate and moved its headquarters to Dallas and later to Houston. Although the company maintained some services in Duncan, the population was decreasing every year, and many families lived in older, rundown sections of the city.

Charlie's house was in a moderately upscale neighborhood less than a half mile from Walmart. The homes were built in the early 1980s. Charlie's house was a two-story colonial with three bedrooms, two baths, a comfortable-sized kitchen and a dining room with a small back porch. It had an attached single-car garage with another large garage and handyman shed that they could approach from the alley behind the house. My brother's house was only two houses from the side street.

The backyard had pecan trees. In good years Charlie filled several bushel baskets during the harvest season. Charlie, Tina, and Joshua, their grandson who lived with them, picked and shelled the pecans and sold them by the pound to a business that bagged pecans for grocery stores. Naturally, every time I visited over the years, I ate a lot of pecan pie.

Seemed like a nice older house, and it was, although within minutes of my arrival, Charlie inevitably complained it was a money pit. He was not a handyman, and the "to do" list was long. He repaired a few things, but often called the electrician, plumber, and other professionals to do emergency repairs that crashed his monthly budget.

Oops! He had not budgeted in the cost of fixing and maintaining a house. The cost was always a little more than his income allowed, and they had used Tina's inheritance for their down payment. Although worried, neither he nor Tina considered obtaining a part-time job. For Charlie, preaching the beliefs of the Jehovah's Witnesses was more important.

Tina wasn't happy. She missed her daughters and called them every day. In East L.A., she was the matriarch of the family. In Duncan, she was a Mexican surrounded by a bunch of rednecks. The Jehovah's Witness church accepted them, and they had a few friendly acquaintances but no best friends in the congregation.

Chapter 39

Lonely Charlie

I am now eighty, as is Tina, and my brother is eighty-two. Their grandson Joshua, around thirty, still lives with them. Over the years I visited them, the arguments remained the same. Yet, they still love each other, and Charlie still believes he is the boss, although he often wonders if he still wants the job.

The sad part is that Charlie is now the lonely one. He sits around the house listening to his wife and grandson bitch about their lives in Duncan. Joshua is much like Charlie, and argues with his grandfather constantly, while Tina demands he take her shopping almost daily. He is no longer active in his church, does not go fishing, and sits around the house moping apart from taking Tina shopping at Walmart. Over the last few years he has been calling me about twice a month. We talk about our lives, and he sometimes keeps me on the phone for an hour. I don't mind; I feel empathy for my brother who is so lonely. On my bucket list: go visit my brother.

What will happen when he dies? Tina will probably sell the house and return to the Los Angeles area and rent or buy a house in a mobile home park outside the city close enough for her daughters to visit. Joshua will go with her.

Kenneth R. Young

Cathy and Susan

While Catherine and Susan were children, I flew from Danbury to Los Angles every year to see them, as well as my mother and my brother. During my three-week stay I spent most of my time with Cathy, and when available, Susan. It was not a perfect arrangement. For eleven months I lived 3,000 miles away, and thus I know little about my daughters' triumphs and failures, their happy times and their sad times as children. But my consistent visits for twenty years created a strong bond that endures even today.

In their younger years, I had been a "guru," but as they grew up and married and had children, I was simply a "Daddy" they saw every year or two. When their children were young, Midge and I visited them in California and played with the children. After Cathy and Greg moved to Guerneville, about sixty miles north of San Francisco, Midge and I flew to Sacramento and drove the short distance to Guerneville. Susan, who lived in Newport Beach, several hundred miles south, occasionally joined us with her four children, but not often enough for us to bond. On later visits Midge and I would fly into Reno and stay in a hotel in Lake Tahoe a couple of nights before driving down to Guerneville. One year we invited Cathy, Greg, and our grandson Connor to join us at Lake Tahoe for a family vacation. Another time, we met in Vegas and Cathy, Connor, Tina, and Carrie (one of Charlie and Tina's daughters) joined us. We went to the Grand Canyon for a couple of nights while we were there.

Cathy and her family and Susan and her family visited us several times in Connecticut and later in North Carolina. Sometimes they stayed a week, sometimes a few days, and sometimes for just one night as they passed through the area.

As the years passed, we saw less of each other. It is almost impossible to retain close contact when your children and grandchildren live 3,000 miles away. I saw Susan's four children so seldom that today I have to concentrate to remember the names of her three girls (Jennifer, Julie, and Christine) and her son (Geoffrey), who is now thirty years old. If they knocked at my door, I doubt I would recognize them. I certainly know I am a vague figure in their lives and they barely remember me.

Catherine is now sixty-one and Susan is fifty-nine. We send each other Christmas and birthday cards, call each other about every two months, and see each other every couple of years. Cathy's family, and particularly Susan's, are on the fringes of my life.

When they visit, my daughters often talk about moving to Asheville or Charlotte to be closer to Midge and me, but it's simply talk. It would be nice if my extended family lived a few miles from me, but in our modern world of great mobility, I am sure many fathers, mothers, and grandparents face the same slowly melting away of their family unit as their children have gone to live in different parts of the country.

I consider myself a good son to my mother, a good brother to Charlie, and a good husband to Midge. I grade myself lower as a father, particularly as a grandfather.

I expect some will condemn me for not being a better father and even worse grandfather. To bond with children it is necessary to be close and take care of them as they grow up. I did not have that opportunity as a grandfather. I never took care of them when they were babies, and was not around as they grew up. Now that they are grown up, it is their responsibility to take care of themselves, and it is still my job to take care of myself even at eighty.

<small>✦</small>

JAMES

Around 2008, James, who had been living in Clearwater, near Tampa, for twelve years, got a job and an apartment in the Hendersonville area. He comes over for dinner two or three nights a week, feeds the cats when we are away, helps with our computers, and shovels the snow off our long driveway.

James is an important part of my life, and over the years he has become an adopted son whom I love. In his teenage years he often ignored my advice, which was his right. He had little interest in material things and worked just enough to pay his own way. I have often said, "If you need a cat or dog sitter, James is your man." His empathy toward dogs, cats, and birds is absolutely remarkable. On the other hand, if you are a woman looking for a sugar daddy, James is not your man. If you are looking for someone to clean your house, James is not your man. I prefer the cat-lover anyway. Throughout the years, James has not changed.

Chapter 40

Midge & Me, Part II

One of the best decisions of my life was marrying Midge. We've proven to be unbelievably compatible. Over forty years we have had few major disagreements, and usually find it easy to compromise. Kindness toward each other always triumphed over anger or irritation at the minor things in life. And fortunately, we are both readers, often enjoying the same books but also reading different ones that follow our own interests.

Her passions are different than mine. She likes to take long walks through the woods, noting the different plants or landscape scenes. She enjoys working in our sizeable yard attempting to educate me, unsuccessfully, on the names of dozens of different flowers and plants. She enjoys shopping with her friends and is more social then I am.

She also likes to travel, and we went on many trips visiting my relatives in California and visiting hers in Florida. But we also journeyed, sometimes with friends, to many areas of the world, from Hong Kong to London to Rome to Acapulco. We also visited many national parks. If she made the arrangements I usually agreed to go, but there were times she traveled with her sister or girlfriends, to places like Hawaii and Cancún.

Midge remains relatively healthy and, at seventy-six, is still a beautiful woman who has maintained an exercise routine for all our years together.

Like most senior citizens, I have had periodic medical problems over the past twenty years. After my third major operation in 2010 to place stents near my heart, I slowed down and stopped being a handyman. If the kitchen sink stopped up, I did not get under the counter to unplug the stinky drainpipe. I called a plumber.

My body continued to fall apart over the next ten years, and there were even more operations, including placing stents in my legs and removing tumors in my prostate and bladder. I felt little fear of death before each operation, but after each one it took me several weeks to heal physically and mentally. For years, I required biannual CT and MRI scans. I grew to hate hospitals, and if death was again knocking on my door, I saw no reason not to enjoy life. Death had knocked on my door too many times.

My ambition slowly disappeared. I realized I was not going to fulfill my dream of being a successful fiction writer. Such ambitions seemed rather senseless when I was seventy-two. After I published *Twice Honored*, I wrote short essays and placed them in the filing cabinet. Sometimes I worked on a book on Chinese philosophy but I saw no sense in finishing the manuscript. My filing cabinets are full of unpublished manuscripts. I had had enough rejection letters in my time. I smoked my pipe, read books, and sipped cognac. Hell, somewhere it was five o'clock. I was a relatively contented man.

Gradually, over the years, I slowed down and I enjoyed my days without many worries. I leaned back and relaxed. We had parties at our house, partied at friends' houses, and often went out to nice restaurants for dinner. Over five or six hours, I drank a couple of beers and a cognac or two. I could have passed a sobriety test, but Midge usually drove home. I'd often drink two or three more cognacs before going to bed. Feeling good, enjoying life.

Bad habits have a way of escalating, and although I seldom drank before 5 p.m., I begin to drink too much. I did not notice at first, but Midge and my friends did. Fortunately, unlike my father, I was a happy drunk. I did not drink because I was sad or depressed. I drank because I enjoyed it.

Back in the Day

I quit drinking in the Spring of 2015.

Why did I stop? I realized I was following in my father's footsteps. I had promised myself I would never become an alcoholic. I was seventy-five years old and losing my balance too often, and I embarrassed my wife at social get togethers. Even happy drunks can be a pain in the ass. I began to have falls and blackouts and other medical problems that forced me to give up drinking. But I must say, I enjoyed and don't regret my drinking years.

I stopped smoking at the same time I stopped drinking, something I had vowed to never do. Why did I quit? I had trouble breathing, and equally important, I was tired of defending the habit. I loved smoking, and I promised myself when I know I have only a few months to live, I will smoke my pipe again. I still dislike zealous anti-smokers who act superior and demand no one smoke in their presence.

This I emphasize: I have not joined the anti-drinking or anti-smoking clubs. I keep wine, beer, scotch, bourbon, and cognac for guests, and wipe the dust off the bottles before they arrive. I do not mind if other people drink or smoke in my presence.

To remain a non-drinker, I began to write my memoirs. Even when I drank, I noticed I did not drink as much when I was writing. I also continued to play golf two or three times a week.

Many of my golfing friends are alphas but with attributes I respect. Usually, they are relatively prosperous conservatives, but as equals on the course, we can discuss any topic. Our conversations become debates comparable to ping-pong games, friendly interchanges of opinions, not battles where one side wins. My friends never pound the table in an effort to dominate conversations. I avoid alphas who use such tactics.

That said, I have come to appreciate certain aspects of the alphas I keep in my life. My alpha friends protect me. A mundane example: I seldom demand special attention in restaurants. If I order rye toast for breakfast and the server brings me white bread, I say nothing. My friends, though, expect good service. If they order scotch straight up, and the waiter brings scotch on the rocks, they send it back; if they order steak rare, and the waiter brings them medium-rare, they send it back. If I am with them and order a rare steak, and the waiter brings me medium, my friends look at me, smile, and then call the waiter over.

Actually, my friends treat me like their favorite uncle or grandfather. I smile and appreciate their kindness. They are wealthier, but I am "older and wiser by far"—although all of them would debate that.

Would I like a drink?

Hell yes! Would a dieter like a piece of cake with ice cream on top?

Yes, I would, but as my mother often said so elegantly, "Yeah, and people in hell want ice water."

Would I like to smoke a good cigar?

Yeah. "People in hell want ice water." And I want a cigar.

As an addict, I know I cannot smoke a single cigar or drink a glass of cognac. As most dieters know, one piece of chocolate cake leads to syrup on your pancakes. I regretted my failure to listen to Confucius, who said, "All things in moderation."

Chinese philosophy has certainly influenced many of my thoughts on the meaning of life. Alas, that is another book. If I ever finish this damn memoir, I might return to writing *Chinese Philosophy from an American's Point of View*.

Thus ends a poor boy's education.[3]

---

[3] Postscript: Initially, before I started this book, I wrote many essays on a variety of topics. As Chuang-tzu might put it, I returned to tending my garden. Some of these essays are embedded in this book. A few are included in the appendix that follows.

Appendix

I. **Essays:**
   "Why Golf?"
   "Smoking: A Sophistic Response to Anti-Smokers"
   "Computers"
   "The Robber Barons"
   "Teaching at University Level"
II. **The General's General: The Life and Times of Lt. General Arthur MacArthur: A Brief Summary**
III. **Academic Vita**
IV. **List of Publications and Partial List of Unpublished Manuscripts**
V. **Pinyin: An Academic Article**
VI. **Courses Taught**
VII. **Sample Syllabi**

I
Essays

Essay 1
WHY GOLF?

Golf became my passion in retirement. As a young boy in Lawton, I caddied at a private nine-hole golf course. Back in the day, before motorized golf carts, most players hired caddies to carry their bags. I was amazed the upper class could afford to spend so much money on the game. Only a few hundred men in town could afford membership in a country club in 1950. Before the appearance of Walmarts, small business owners were prosperous, and as today, so were lawyers, doctors, and candlestick makers. Their children went to private schools. It was when I caddied that I realized many families had a lot more money than the Basses and Youngs.

As a kid I did not dream of becoming a golfer—I dreamed of having enough money to join a country club. Caddying opened my eyes to golf, and years later when I took up the game, I knew the fundamentals. After Detzer and I received our PhDs in June of 1970, he suggested we play golf. He bought a new set of clubs. I went down to Goodwill and picked up an old set for less than ten dollars. Several clubs were missing, including the sand wedge, but I did not expect to play much. About twice a month, we went to an inexpensive nine-hole course near his home. The game was match play—score was kept only hole by hole. Looking back, I estimate I played in the mid-fifties and

David in the high forties. He picked up his ball on holes he played poorly and teased me about my nines and tens. He liked to patronize me, but I didn't care. If he couldn't win a hole, he quit. I liked winning but losing didn't bother me. I enjoy games, and when I lose, my attitude is "rack the balls" for a new game. I knew I was not a good golfer, but I enjoyed walking in the park-like atmosphere where problems faded into the background.

Although golf was only a minor pastime for me, I read golf instruction books. I found Ben Hogan's *Fundamentals of Golf* particularly useful. As my game improved, I consistently beat Detzer even with my outdated equipment. He became angry and quit the game—cost too damn much money, he said.

To my surprise, my game improved dramatically when I acquired better clubs. I played more often and joined a weekly nine-hole Western Connecticut group. My scores dropped to the mid-forties and my handicap was eighteen. For the uninitiated, a pro golfer has a handicap of zero, the average golfer has a handicap of twenty-eight, and a moderately good golfer has one between twelve and eighteen.

I enjoy golf. It fits my personality. Many golfers take constant lessons, purchase expensive golf clubs and balls, scream and curse on the golf course, and still cannot break a hundred. My personality is laid-back, and I seldom get mad. Nor have I ever thrown a club. I occasionally mutter a "bad" word that's quickly forgotten.

Golf has many assets but also a number of liabilities. The greatest liability is that it's a "snob's" game. You need money to buy the equipment, and golf courses charge too much for the average worker—bowling is more in their budget.

Golf also is a time-consuming sport. The average round (eighteen holes) usually takes from four to five hours to play. Few workers with families can afford either the time or the money to play two or three times a week.

Perhaps golf's greatest problem, though, is that so few players are able to master the game. Non-golfers watch the pros on TV and assume it is a simple game to learn—the ball isn't moving and hitting it looks as easy as T-ball, a game small children play. A beginner goes out thinking the game is easy, then discovers he can't even make contact with the ball. Nervous and insecure players quickly quit because they are so bad and embarrassed. What they fail to realize is that most golfers are constantly embarrassed on the course.

Golf is a game invented by sadistic Scotsmen and played by masochistic fools. A bad game of golf makes the player hate the game, but the addicted golfer always returns because good golf is so much fun, and golfers are generally optimistic—*today* is the day I bring my A game, they think before every new round.

To get a sense of the golfer's perspective, consider the classic tale, told a hundred different ways, about the fanatical golfer who plays nine holes every day at 8:30 a.m. with his friends. One afternoon, he comes home, removes his clubs from the car and throws them in the garbage can. Stomping into the house, he declares to his wife, "I am giving up golf. I hate the fucking game." The next day, he comes into the kitchen for lunch dressed in his golf clothes.

"Thought you gave up golf," his wife says sarcastically.

"I did," he replied. "Tee time is one o'clock." He gave it up a few hours.

(For other great golf stories, check out George Plimpton's *The Bogey Man*, published in 1968.)

Another problem with golf is that beginning players often attempt to conform absolutely to the PGA rules—no do-overs (mulligans), no kicking the ball into a better lie, no gimmies even on one-inch putts. "The rules are the rules!" proclaim the better golfers in their group. Watching bad golfers conform to the PGA rules is painful. Yes, you can pick up your ball after taking nine strokes on a par three. What most fanatical golfers refuse to admit is the rules are *PGA rules*, i.e., meant for professionals playing golf for a great deal of money.

To enjoy golf, players should join a group of friends with comparable handicaps and make up their own rules. Play for fun—that means gimme putts, winter rules that allows players to move the ball one club length even in the rough, and a double par the maximum strokes. Or play the popular game in charity tournaments—captain's choice.

Still, golf has several attributes that trump its liabilities. Good golf is fun to play. The golf course is an excellent place to make friends. Golf reveals the personalities of players better than most sports—self-centered golfers are easy to identify and avoid.

Golfers exhibit a common trait. Much like when a person has a car accident, they often look for someone or something to blame. "That damn moron pulled right in front of me." "Damn idiot had his bright lights on and blinded me." If a person drops a dish that breaks, they look for someone or something to blame. When golfers miss a shot, they look for someone or something to blame. "Will you stop talking when I'm hitting?" "Someone did not repair that divot." "Damn lawnmower destroyed my concentration." Etc.

If a golfer blames himself, he directs his anger inward, and snaps out his formal name: Harry becomes Harold, Jim becomes James, Charlie becomes Charles, Art becomes Arthur. For me, Kenny becomes Kenneth Ray, the name my mother called me when she was irritated. "Get your ass moving, Kenneth Ray," she yelled out. "I'm coming Ma," I'd say, after which she responded, "Yeah, so is Christmas."

It amuses me how many of my friends attack themselves with words far worse than they would ever allow anyone else to say to them. Usually, they berate themselves with curse words: "Shithead, keep your head down." Yes, golf is a frustrating and stressful game.

Somehow, I am afraid that my narration on what I learned playing golf might make you think all I did was play golf after I retired. The answer is, golf is a game, and I am not a golf fanatic. I do not play golf if it interferes with my family, my writing, or traveling. I continue to read an extraordinary number of books, including novels and books on history, philosophy, and even psychology. I watch golf, football, and baseball games as well as fixer-upper programs on TV as I continue to putter around the house.

Essay 2

SMOKING: A SOPHISTIC RESPONSE TO ANTI-SMOKERS

My attitude toward smoking is different from the beliefs of the vast majority of people today. As mentioned, several times, I grew up in a society that did not condemn smoking but rather considered it an acceptable habit. Every adult member in my family smoked as had their fathers, grandfathers, and great-grandfathers. In those days, the nonsmoker was as rare as the smokers of today. Cigarette companies were prime advertisers, first on radio and later on television. Their taglines were well known to everyone: "Call for Philip Morris"; "I'd walk a mile for a Camel"; "Winston tastes good like a cigarette should." The Marlboro Man was a national icon. In movies, both male and female stars smoked. Even Santa Claus and Einstein smoked.

Everyone admitted smoking was bad for your health. "Coffin nails," people said with a smile as they lit up a cigarette. Yet, in a crisis, even today, "soldiers, sailors, and tinkermen" still smoke. Apparently, cigarettes serve a purpose in emotional situations. When death stares you in the face, you are not worried about smoke. Have a glass of wine? How about a piece of cheesecake too?

Fanatical anti-smokers irritate me. Smoking is bad for the health of the smoker, but anti-smokers who believe they are on "holy ground" are obnoxious. I have the right to choose my bad habits. For some it's eating, for some it's sex, for some it's drinking, and for some it's drugs. Should the obese be forced to stop eating, alcoholics to stop drinking, and teenage sex maniacs to stop fucking? "Just say no. Sex is meant only to have children." All these habits are bad for your health. Here's one statistic that's usually ignored—there are as many former smokers in their eighties as there are nonsmokers, statistically speaking.

Many laws are passed that make the lot of the working class and poor even worse. Some are of minor importance, but even the smallest changes can hurt the poor. The crusade against smoking is a good example. It hurts the working class and the poor the most because they smoke more than the middle class and the wealthy. The crusaders knew passing an amendment outlawing smoking was impossible, so they persuaded the government to tax cigarettes out of existence. Over time the price of a pack of cigarettes exploded from twenty-five cents a pack to over ten dollars in New York City, and nationally to over five dollars. Millions of smokers making less than $30,000 a year now spend a hell of a lot of their income on heavily taxed cigarettes. "Shouldn't smoke," nonsmokers might growl. "Damn lazy bastards." To that, I quote a certain highly regarded philosopher: "Judge not lest you be judged." Have another glass of wine or another scotch on the rocks as you eat those fancy, fatty appetizers.

Essay 3
COMPUTERS

I am not proud of my lack of knowledge when it comes to new technology and constantly berate myself for my ignorance. When I retired in 1997, Blockbuster video stores still existed, and on trips people used public phones and paper maps to navigate. As public phones and the availability of paper maps disappeared, the cell phone became essential, I carried a "flip phone" that quickly became outdated but for a few years I refused to update to an iPhone. I was tired of constant changes that demanded I learn new and different ways of communicating. Checking your GPS on Google using an iPhone became the norm. Midge became the navigator. I refused to learn how to use the iPad or iPhone for taking photographs or texting. I avoided Twitter and Facebook. Although e-mail became essential for maintaining contacts, I still prefer snail mail and eye-to-eye contact over an iPhone. I seldom answer the phone and check my e-mail only once a week. When I truly want to communicate my thoughts and exchange ideas, I write letters, sometimes four or five pages long. As a historian, I wonder how documents will be viewed in the future. Unlike Franklin, Jefferson, Adams, Madison, and Monroe, and thousands of other men and women who wrote many long letters stored in archives around the country, such letters from modern leaders and scholars will not exist. It's easy to believe anything on the computer and the internet will exist forever. I still have floppy disks for the Kaypro II stored in the garage. "Betcha" can't decipher them.

Essay 4
THE ROBBER BARONS

One thing that hasn't changed in my older age are my political beliefs. My attitude toward the upper class makes many of my friends uncomfortable. Sounds like socialism.

Actually, I am a left-wing capitalist that conservatives label a socialist. I believe in the middle class. My fight is with the upper class, the top thirty percent, especially the exclusive 10 percent. Someone with a $5 million estate does not bother me; someone with a billion-dollar estate irritates me; someone with $41 billion estate is in violation of the principles of equality and decency. No one does anything in their life worth forty-one billion dollars. When a waitress is lucky to make $30,000 a year, that is greed.

I certainly admire Gates, Buffet, and company, but I am not pleased with their take. I'll give them a mere billion—interest on that amount guarantees an oligarch income of at least an easy $50,000,000 to spend each year and maintain wealth for his family for generations.

Every society from small tribes to giant empires have three classes, plus the untouchable class—the truly poor who can't, for many reasons, take care of themselves. Some are sick, some are old, some are black, some are white, and down the list. Some are simply lazy. Many are not. Governments proclaim success in eliminating poverty but poverty always prevails. Poverty creates problems—remember, survival is more important than morality. I would steal, lie, and beg to feed myself and my family if I had no choice. How about you? As my great-grandmother might have said: "This is the money hole and this is the corn hole."

※

Almost inevitably, the longer a government's reigns, the more the top 30 percent accumulate as their share of the national wealth. The people are taxed heavily, but the wealthy are taxed at a much lower rate in comparison to their income. When inflation hits, it lowers the value of the wages of the working man, and then hard times set in. And that is when the working man and some of the middle class band together to get rid of the corrupt and greedy leaders.

Demonstrations, labor strikes, and occasionally bombs explode. The government uses martial law and armed forces to protect the interests of the top 30 percent. Revolt, if successful, sees the rise of new messiahs who overthrow the government and curtail the power of the rich and pass the goods down to the working class.

Then we start again.

To illustrate my point, after the Civil War the United States blasted straight into "the Industrial Revolution" (1869 to 1900"). Railroads, factories, and financial institutions dominated the economic sector much as the technological revolution from 1980 to 2020 dominates today.

Some historians, such as Matthew Josephson, label the period from 1869 to 1901 the age of "the robber barons." For decades capitalists applauded the tactics of some of the greediest men in U.S. history. Three of these robber barons are often praised for their greatness: Rockefeller (oil), Carnegie (steel), and Morgan (finance).

These men are not heroes of mine but rather villains who accumulated billions in wealth that they refused to share with their workers for the good of the nation. When workers formed unions and demanded a better share of the profits, the "oligarchs" refused to negotiate. In my mind, these oligarchs were greedy, selfish son-of-bitches.

Strikes occurred, some erupted in bloody battles where the U.S.

National Guard and Pinkerton detectives slaughtered hundreds of men. Giant corporations, soon to be multinationals, controlled the corrupt politicians who were rewarded for their support. Populist movements erupted in the 1880s and 1890s demanding the government curtail Rockefeller and the other oligarchs. The "muckraking" press joined them. As William Jennings Bryan proclaimed in the 1896 presidential race, the wealthy were trying to crucify the people on "a cross of gold." The workers did not have "a chicken in every pot," as promised.

Then an amazing thing occurred. The children of the upper-middle-class families in the 1880s begin sending their children to private schools that emphasized philosophers, from the Greeks to the Romans to the Renaissance thinkers. They read the "classic" hundred books and beyond, literature from the *Odyssey* to Voltaire to Shakespeare to *Alice in Wonderland*. They became the educated men, the keepers of *noblesse oblige*. Honor before greed was their professed motto, and they seemed to embody the beliefs of Christopher Marlowe ("Honor is not won until some honorable deed is done") and Thomas Jefferson ("Every honest man will support honest acts to flow from honest principles"). These wealthy young men and women who did not need to work for money turned to the professions and dreamed of putting a man on the moon, discovering a cure for cancer, or improving equality within society.

Teddy Roosevelt is a good example of the mental attitude of the noblesse obligers: He was like a "bull moose" who charged in to curtail the excesses of the oligarchs, to the chagrin of Rockefeller and Morgan. "It was time to prevent the division in America between the haves and the have-nots and therefore insist on the rights and duties of all men and women" (James Chace, 1912, p. 237). Teddy used the "bully pulpit" to persuade Congress to pass laws to curtail the power of giant corporations.

The people loved Teddy and his "big stick." He became the most popular president in U.S. history. He crusaded for a powerful navy, the Panama Canal, and the creation of our national parks. In 1912, as a presidential candidate for the "Bull Moose Party," he advocated for a "square deal" for the working man. He supported "women's suffrage," "labor unions," "a Federal Reserve bank," and the direct elections of U.S. senators. Woodrow Wilson continued the trend.

During World War I the corporations regained power and used it to exploit the nation through the 1920s before the crash in 1929 and the Great Depression. Then came the new savior, Franklin Roosevelt, another card-carrying member of the noblesse obligers, who enacted "New Deal" restrictions on the wealthy, including a progressive income tax that created a boon for the working class until the 1960s, when the "military industrial complex" came to dominate the government.

Each generation believes they lived through the best of times and the worst of times. To borrow from Douglas MacArthur, history "does not die, it just fades away." When I talk to people under fifty years old, few remember Truman, McCarthyism, the demonstrations against the Vietnam War, Kent State, or My Lai. They vaguely remember Martin Luther King, Jack Kennedy, Bobby Kennedy, and President Johnson.

But the struggle never ends. The upper 30 percent grabs more than their fair share as new economic trends create another class of "robber barons." During the boom of the technological revolution, the new oligarchs have been as greedy as Rockefeller, et. al., and hundreds of new billionaires have arisen such as Jobs, Gates, and Buffet.

Capitalism is practiced throughout the world but remains an evil in dictatorial states. After a revolutionary takeover, the new regimes claim they are socialist with a central government controlled by the people. Unfortunately, the leaders usually revert to a disguised authoritarian capitalist state where the new elite become the new oligarchs.

Capitalism in a modern democratic state has its ups and downs, but the free press attempts to protect the rights guaranteed in the Constitution and the moral values of the nation. The oligarchs and multinational corporations are powerful forces in government decision-making, but all are watched closely by the press. Fortunately, the corporations are in contention with each other. "What's good for General Motors is good for the United States." There are many seats at the table from Exxon to Microsoft to Amazon.

Today and yesterday the fight goes on. The people need their fair share, and the oligarchs need to be curtailed.

Such are my beliefs. That said, I have strong feeling about many things, but I have no objections to listening to opposing arguments. I enjoy intellectual conversation that is reciprocal. For over forty years I have had a yearly subscription to *The Wall Street Journal*. I enjoy reading logical opposing articles to my ideas. They generally don't convert me, but they have often made me compromise some of my ideas. Then I sit down and pound out an essay in response. I know full well I will never mail them to the *Journal,* and even if I did, the essays would never be published. Certainly, I disagree with many of the *Journal*'s sacred cows such as its support of "trickle-down economics." The only thing I agree with are the words "trickle-down." My mind conjures up the image of my bathroom faucet dripping one tiny drop of water, drip, drip, all night long.

The big money remains at the top, and the working class, the vast majority of the people throughout the world, the families who live on $30,000 to $100,000 a year, get chicken feed while the robber barons eat the pigs. I'll maybe accept the trickle-down theory when the faucet flows a little faster—not a flood, but a slow and steady stream. Give the people a chicken rather than chicken feed. The wealthy can still eat pork.

These are some of the things I think about.

Essay 5
TEACHING AT UNIVERSITY LEVEL

Educational priorities at smaller colleges and universities have been debated for decades. Teachers who emphasize good teaching believe the value of research and publication is overrated—a teacher's time would be better spent improving courses, mentoring students, serving on committees, or working in local communities. At small colleges, teaching excellence should be the prime criteria in judging professors. A good teacher at such colleges doesn't need a PhD. As a standard, "publish or perish" should only apply in institutions that emphasize research, not teaching.

Sounds like high school to me, not higher education. And, even in high school it is difficult to determine who is a good teacher deserving promotion or tenure. College, I must add, is not high school.

Professors are supposed to be "experts" in their field. Mentoring, serving on committees, and working on local community programs, although laudable, does not relieve a professor of his obligation to maintain his expertise throughout his career.

There is no conflict between being a good scholar and a good teacher, for one supports the other. A good professor must research his theories, read extensively to support his conclusions, and develop new ideas. Sometimes that research leads to publication, but it is the research, not the publication, that is important. Thus, I think publications are important simply as direct proof that a teacher is maintaining his scholarly interests.

Good teaching is harder to evaluate than research and publications. In modern education, there is a longstanding debate over the most appropriate teaching techniques, from lectures to discussion classes to value clarification. I remain in the old school that believes the prime responsibility of a scholar, which every university professor should be, is to attempt to explain what he has learned to his students. Techniques may vary, with each teacher using the technique most suited to his (or her) personality. Since I considered myself a good public speaker, I preferred the lecture technique at the undergraduate level. At the graduate level, I opted for readings, discussions, and term papers.

II.

The General's General: The Life and Times of Lt. General Arthur MacArthur: A Brief Summary

Arthur' MacArthur's illustrious forty-six-year military career began in August of 1862, when he was seventeen years old. His father, Judge Arthur MacArthur, was an important political figure in Wisconsin and obtained for his son an appointment as Adjutant of the 24th Wisconsin Volunteers with the rank of 1st Lieutenant. During the Civil War, he fought in eighteen major battles and hundreds of skirmishes on the Western front and was cited for bravery over a dozen times and wounded on three different occasions. He was at Stones River in December 1862, at Missionary Ridge in November 1863, and with Sherman when he captured Atlanta in the summer of 1864. For his heroics at Missionary Ridge, he was awarded a Congressional Medal of Honor.

When he was twenty, he was promoted to lieutenant colonel in command of the 24th Wisconsin Regiment, making him the youngest regimental commander in the Union Army during the Civil War. He was Wisconsin's "Boy Colonel" and the state's most famous soldier. For his Civil War exploits, even if he had not later sired a very famous son, Arthur MacArthur deserved a biography.

After the Civil War, over his father's strong objections, Arthur joined the regular army. The U.S. Army rapidly shrank from over a million men to a mere 25,000 enlisted men and 2,500 officers. Officer commissions were difficult to obtain even for Civil War heroes. Except for the most famous generals, such as Grant, Sherman, and Sheridan, most officers who remained in the army accepted demotions to lower ranks. Generals became colonels and colonels became captains.

At the age of twenty-one, Arthur obtained a commission as a captain in the infantry, a rank he retained for over twenty-three years, from 1866 to 1889.

While the U.S. Cavalry spent their time chasing hostile Indians, the infantry acted as the police force and protected the workers constructing America's massive new railroad system. The infantry protected citizens living near railheads in new farm communities, cow towns, and mining camps.

During a tour of duty in New Orleans in 1875, Captain MacArthur met a young Southern belle, Mary Pinckney (Pinky) Hardy. Over the objections of her brothers who fought for the Confederacy, Captain MacArthur and Pinky married in May 1875 on the Hardy family estate in Norfolk, Virginia. Proud and strong-minded, Pinky proved a formidable ally for her husband, and a powerful influence on her children. Over the next five years, the MacArthurs had three sons: Arthur III, Malcolm, and Douglas.

Much like the period after World War I, the period after the Civil War meant that promotions in the army were slow, and only obstinance kept him in the military as he served with his wife and children on isolated frontier posts over many years from Wyoming to New Mexico to Arizona. His time was not wasted. He was an excellent trainer of men and treated them fairly. He was rated as the best infantry captain in the army, and his company had the lowest desertion rate.

Captain MacArthur read extensively during those years in "the desert."

His father, Judge MacArthur, a well-known figure in Washington,

DC, was an entertaining and witty public speaker, equal to any of his day, a time when the public honored speakers more than today. He authored eight books, illustrating his knowledge and famous sense of humor. The Judge wanted his son to be cultured and educated, and he constantly sent him books, magazines, and newspaper articles. Captain MacArthur consumed them. Reading became one of his passions for the rest of his life

Unlike his father, though, the Captain lacked a sense of humor.

Finally, after twenty-three years, in 1889 MacArthur received a promotion to major and transferred to a staff position in Washington. His father's influence certainly helped him. A few years later, he was promoted to lieutenant colonel in the Adjutant General's Department.

In 1898, when the Spanish–American War erupted, MacArthur was rapidly promoted to brigadier general and assigned to the Philippines. Troops he commanded participated in the battle for Manila in August 1898, and shortly thereafter, he was promoted to major general and given a division of over 10,000 men.

When the United States annexed the Philippines in January 1899, a major rebellion erupted. Led by Emilio Aguinaldo, the Filipinos desired independence rather than another colonial master. The war to suppress the insurrection lasted over three years and cost the U.S. more fatalities and more money than the Spanish–American war. In the first year of the rebellion, MacArthur's division did most of the fighting, and he became one of the more famous military leaders of the period. Unlike his son, he avoided the press and often praised his subordinates and recommended them for promotion.

In May 1900, the President selected MacArthur to be the U.S. military governor in the Philippines with 70,000 men under his command and ten million Filipinos under his control. His enlightened policies, both military and civilian, later served as a model for his son Douglas when he was the SCAP in Japan after WWII.

During his reign as governor, he became involved in a dispute with William Howard Taft, the major civilian politician in Manila. After a year of conflict, martial law was lifted, and Taft replaced MacArthur as governor in July 1901.

MacArthur returned to the United States, commanded several departments over the next eight years, and was promoted to lieutenant general, the highest rank in the United States Army at the time.

His fame and power were curtailed primarily by Taft, who became Secretary of War in 1903 and blocked MacArthur's appointment as chief of staff.

The general retired in 1909 and settled in Milwaukee, Wisconsin. Three years later, he died in a bizarre way. While giving a speech to the forty-seventh reunion of the 24th Wisconsin Volunteers, he had a heart attack. His death made front-page headlines throughout the nation, but within months his name was forgotten except in his beloved city of Milwaukee and among his many supporters in the U.S. Army who helped his son Douglas in his career.

The General's General received excellent reviews in a dozen journals and newspapers—only a few are mentioned on Amazon.

III

Academic Vita

Kenneth Ray Young
Professor Emeritus
Western Connecticut State University
History Department
181 White Street
Danbury, Connecticut 06810

Position:

I joined the Western Connecticut History and Social Science Department in September 1966, when I was twenty-six years old. Over the next seventeen years I was promoted through the ranks from instructor to full professor, which I became in 1983. Western Connecticut is a small state university (2,500 students and 170 faculty members) located about sixty miles north of New York City. Master's degrees are offered in a number of fields, including history.

Specialty:

American diplomacy in East and Southeast Asia, from the Spanish–American War (1898) through the Vietnam War (1975).

Degrees:

PhD, June 1970, New York University
MA, July 1965, California State University at Los Angeles
BA, June 1964, California State University at Los Angeles
AA, June 1962, East Los Angeles Community College

Courses Taught:

See attached pages.

Publications:

See attached pages.

Major Grants:

Fulbright Fellowship to the Philippines, 1979–1980; remain member of Fulbright Association, 2018
National Endowment for the Humanities (NEH), Summer Institute in International Affairs (1976), Sarah Lawrence University
Asian Institute (1963), California State University at Los Angeles

Conference Papers:

Over the years, I have spoken at a dozen regional scholarly conferences; if the details are important, I will supply a list. I consider myself to be a good public speaker.

IV
List of Publications and Partial List of Unpublished Manuscripts

Books

The General's General: The Life and Times of Lt. General Arthur MacArthur. Boulder, Colorado: Westview Press, October 1994 (400 pages, 28 photos, 11 maps, notes, and bibliography). HarperCollins paperback, 1995. Routledge edition, 2019. The book required ten years to research, write, and edit. It is my most important scholarly work.

Twice Honored. Self-published in 2012. A novel based on the Balangiga Massacre in September 1901 in the Philippines. Captain Littleton Wyler, the main character, received his second Congressional Medal of Honor for his bravery during and after the battle.

Articles and Book Reviews

The focus of my published articles, as in my academic career, is United States diplomacy in East and Southeast Asia. The types of articles vary;

some are bibliographical reviews that examined the literature on a particular topic, some are case studies that required intensive research in primary sources, and some are more philosophically oriented. The list that follows is divided by article type: case studies, bibliographical reviews, theory and opinion pieces, and book reviews. Each category is organized in reverse-chronological order. I also briefly summarize the articles and discuss the time and reason for which each article was written.

Case Studies

Four entries in *The War of 1898 and U.S. Interventions, 1898–1934: An Encyclopedia*, edited by Benjamin R. Beede. New York: Garland, 1994. 75 pages.
1. "General Arthur MacArthur and the Philippines," pp. 274–282.
2. "The Battle for Manila, August 1898," pp. 302–304.
3. "The Manila to Dagupan Railroad during the Philippine–American War," pp. 460–461.
4. "William Howard Taft and the Philippines," pp. 531–535.

This assignment was one of those "I will be honored to write a few entries along with a hundred top-name scholars in the field" situations. I accepted the assignment because I was already researching the Philippine–American War. The four articles I wrote are summaries of topics covered in *The General's General*.

"Atrocities and War Crimes: The Cases of Major Waller and General Smith," *Leyte-Samar Studies*, XII (Spring 1978), 64–77. Included in *Readings in Leyte-Samar History*, edited by Luz Vilches. Tacloban City, Philippines: Divine Word University, 1979.

"Guerrilla Warfare: Balangiga Revisited," *Leyte-Samar Studies*, XI (Spring 1977), 21–31. Also in *Readings in Leyte-Samar History* edited by Luz Vilches.

The above two articles came out of another project I was working on. Around 1975, I wrote a historical novel based on the Balangiga Massacre. In September 1901, over fifty American soldiers were killed when a band of Filipino revolutionaries attacked a small garrison at Balangiga on the island of Samar. The novel was never published, but my research resulted in two very solid articles about the atrocities committed during the war in the Philippines (above), and eventually, my interest in General Arthur MacArthur. The articles are also the reason I received a Fulbright Fellowship to the Philippines in 1979. In 2012, I self-published the novel with the title *Twice Honored*.

"The Forgotten Man: Adoniram Judson," Part I, *The Commission*, XXXVII (July 1974), 16–19; Part II, *The Commission*, XXXVII (Aug.1974), 18–21.

Judson was the first American Baptist missionary to Asia, serving in Burma (now Myanmar) from 1815 to 1845. These two articles grew out of an attempt to expand my dissertation into a book. The dissertation was on U.S. actions in Burma from 1949 to 1961; the book expanded the range to U.S.–Burmese relations from 1789 to 1961. The book was never published but several articles were.

"Harbinger to Nixon: DuBois in China," with Dan S. Green. *Negro History Bulletin*, XXV (Oct. 1972), 125–128.

The idea for this article was suggested by Dan Green, a colleague in the Western Connecticut sociology department who wrote his dissertation on DuBois. I did the research and writing, but the idea was Dan's. The article, which drew from Communist Chinese publications, describes DuBois's visit to China in 1956, long before U.S. recognition of Communist China, and the problems the visit caused for the black scholar and nationalist.

"The United States and Laos: The Kong Le Debacle," *Asian Forum*, IV (Jan.–March 1972), 22–40.

This article was written for a book to be edited by Frank N. Trager, a respected professor at New York University (and my adviser). When the project was abandoned, *Asian Forum* published the article. The topic is a military coup in Laos in 1961 that led to international complications and was a precursor to U.S. involvement in Vietnam.

"The Asia-Pacific Conference on Cambodia," *Asian Forum*, III (April–June 1971), 104–110.

When Prince Norodom Sihanouk of Cambodia was overthrown in March 1970, most Southeast Asian nations hoped the combatants could agree on a negotiated settlement. It was not obtained, but the conference where the negotiations took place, described in the article above, is important for being one of the first attempts at a diplomatic solution to problems that still faces Cambodia today.

"And Then There Was One: Yung Wing at Yale," *Connecticut Historical Society Bulletin*, XXXVI (Jan. 1971), 16–22.

While doing research at Yale on another topic, I stumbled across records of the university's first Chinese student, who attended Yale in the 1850s. The material was too good to pass up, and this article was the result.

"Sino-Indonesian Dual Nationality Treaty," *Asian Forum*, II (July–Sept. 1970), 172–182.

For years I was interested in Indonesian politics as related to the Vietnam War (Sukarno, PKI, CONEFOS, etc.). Up to 1960, Communist China proclaimed that the three million Indonesians of Chinese descent owed loyalty not only to Indonesia but also to China. This treaty tried to resolve the issue.

Bibliographical Review Articles

"The Stilwell Controversy," *Military Affairs*, XXXIX (April 1975), 66–68.

"Vinegar Joe" Stilwell, the Allied Commander of the China-India-Burma Theater during World War II, is a controversial character; renowned American journalist Theodore White described him as one of the four greatest men he ever met. This article examines the literature on Stilwell.

"Adoniram Judson and the American Missionary Movement," *Connecticut Review*, VII (April 1974), 25–34.

Judson was an American missionary in Burma from 1813 to 1850. When I began research on Judson while expanding my PhD dissertation, I was amazed to discover there were over twenty-five biographies on him. This article reviews that large body of material.

"Neutralism in Laos and Cambodia," *International Studies Quarterly*, XIV (June 1970), 219–226.

This essay examines the most important books on Cambodia at the time Sihanouk was overthrown and considers how they relate to books on Laos.

"General James Wilkinson," *Connecticut Review*, II (April 1969), 24–27.

When I taught U.S. history, I was most interested in the early Federalist era, from the Constitutional Convention through 1809. This essay is on the Aaron Burr conspiracy and General Wilkinson's involvement in it. I am fond of this article because it was my first publication.

Theory and Opinion Pieces

When I received a Fulbright Fellowship to the Philippines in 1979, part of my assignment was to deliver the keynote speech at the Third Annual Philippine–American Conference outside Manila and to edit the conference papers for a book. Although I presented two papers at the event, the publication project fell through because of a lack of funding. When I found out about this, I allowed Western Connecticut State University's Phi Alpha Theta history honor society to publish the two papers in their journal, *Clio*. Because I was so pleased with the quality of the publication, I later wrote another article for *Clio*. These three articles, all ideological opinion pieces, represent some of my best scholarly work.

"The Pinyin System: New Speak in China," *Clio* (June 1985), 12 pages.

When the United States government adopted the new Pinyin system in 1979, thus dropping the Wade-Giles method of translation of Chinese into English, it created a gigantic problem for non-area specialists. This article examines the problem and advocates for a compromise between the two systems.

"United States & the Philippines: Reagan Policy," *Clio* (Dec. 1984), 20 pages.

A critical examination of Reagan's support for the Marcos regime.

"Cycles in American Diplomacy," *Clio* (April 1982), pp. 7–16.

This article provides a theoretical analysis of U.S. foreign policy. The point of the article was to predict U.S. foreign policy in the post-Vietnam War period. The predictions proved accurate over the next nineteen years.

Book Reviews

These book reviews represent my changing scholarly interests in the 1970s. You might note I did not review books after 1979—having served my time as a junior scholar, after this point I decided not to review any more books.

"The Lost Peace: America's Search for a Negotiated Settlement of the Vietnam War by Allen E. Goodman," *American Historical Review*, LXXXII (1979), 1201–1202.

"Foreign Relations of the United States: 1949. VII: The Far East and Australasia," Part II. *American Historical Review*, LXXXI (1978), 299–300.

"The Institute of Pacific Relations: Asian Scholars and American Politics," by John H. Thomas," *Asian Profile*, VI (Feb. 1978), 95–97.

"Foreign Relations of the United States: 1949. VII: The Far East and Australasia" and "Foreign Relations of the United States: 1950. VI: East Asia and the Pacific," *American Historical Review*, LXXX (1977), 1359–1360.

"Foreign Relations of the United States: 1948. VI: The Far East and Australasia," *American Historical Review*, LXXX (June 1977), 770.

"The Last Emperor by Arnold Brackman," *Asian Affairs*, June 1977.

"Mutual Images: Essays in American-Japanese Relations edited by Akira Iriye," *Journal of Asian History*, X (1977), 93–95.

"Prisoners of Liberation by Allyn and Adele Rickett" and "Prisoner of Mao by Bao Ruo-Wang and Rudolph Chalminski," *The Journal of Criminal Law and Criminology*, LX (Summer 1975), 224–226.

"They Wouldn't Let Us Die by Stephan Rowan," *Armed Forces Journal*, CXI (July 1974), 34.

"The Politics of Heroin in Southeast Asia by Alfred McCoy," *Pacific Affairs*, XLVI (Summer 1973), 343–345.

Partial List of Unpublished Manuscripts

Only a Game (1972). Short novel on my experiences in Little League Baseball.

Helicopter to Hell (1974). A book about a U.S. soldier held prisoner for seven years in Laos.

Heaven or Hell (1982). Sci-fi book on how reincarnation works.

Chinese Philosophy from an American's Point of View—still working on it.

Addiction: A Comedy Play—or a collection of short stories on smoking cigarettes and pot and drinking whiskey. Potential titles include: "Set Them up Again Joe" and "I'm Not Obese—Just Fat."

V

PINYIN:
AN ACADEMIC ARTICLE

This article is typical of my academic writing. If you're interested in my academic exploits, you will enjoy it; if not, go read Shakespeare. It was published in *Clio*, Western Connecticut State University's Phi Alpha Theta history honor society journal, in June 1985. For twelve years, I passed out copies of the chart on the last page to students in my Chinese Culture class. I did less research on this article than most of the others I've written because I wrote it primarily for my student audience.

* *Excuse the footnote style. I wrote this article on my CP/M Kaypro, transferred it to MDOS in 1986, then to Word in 1990.*

The Pinyin System:
China's New Speak

On January 1, 1979, followed shortly by the rest of the world, the People's Republic of China, officially called Zhonghua Remin Gongheguo, adopted a new method for translating Chinese into English and other Western languages. Under the new system, called Pinyin, tremendous changes were mandated for the English spelling of Chinese words. No longer would Peking be called Peking but now was to be spelled and pronounced Beijing as it sounded in Mandarin Chinese. No longer would Teng Hsiao-p'ing be *Teng* but now was to be spelled *Deng* Xiaoping. No longer would Chou be Chou, nor Chiu be Chiu, nor Ch'iang be Ch'iang. Now, they would be respectively Zhou, Qui, and Jiang. For the non-Chinese-language scholar, it appeared as if a system of New Speak had been interjected into Chinese names. The new Pinyin System dropped the Wade-Giles System, the method used to translate Chinese into English for over a hundred years.

When Western contact was established with China in the early sixteenth century, Western observers transcribed Chinese names in a multitude of ways. Since Chinese is monosyllabic and tonal, no phonetic system provided more than an approximation to the actual pronunciation. Thus, American, British, French, Dutch, and other Western accounts of China spelled Confucius, Mencius, Shih Huang-ti, Li Po, and even China in a variety of ways. In 1867, by common agreement, English language countries adopted a system of translating Chinese into English developed by Sir Thomas Wade. [1] While a British diplomat in China, and later as the first professor of Chinese Languages at Cambridge University, Thomas Wade developed a system for approximating Chinese sounds. Admittedly inadequate, [2] it was modified in 1912 by Herbert Allen Giles who was Wade's successor of Chinese Languages at Cambridge. [3]

The Wade-Giles System of translating Chinese into English had both advantages and disadvantages. Its prime asset was it codified English translations of Mandarin Chinese and thus Tz'u Hsi was universally spelled Tz'u Hsi as Mao Tse-tung was always spelled Mao Tse-tung. Its disadvantages related to attempts to obtain precise Chinese sounds, an impossible but desired goal. [4] Many Mandarin Chinese sounds simply had no exact English counterpart. In the Wade-Giles System a number of letters were not pronounced precisely as in English. P' is pronounced p, a T' is t, a K' is k, a Ch' is ch; but, *without* the apostrophe, P is pronounced as b, T as d, K as g, and Ch as j. This double usage of Roman letters created confusion and mispronunciation. Peking was not pronounced Peking but Beijing. Teachers of Chinese studies, although irritated by the trend, became used to students referring to Taoism with a T pronunciation rather than a D, or Li Po instead of Li Bo, or Kuomintang instead of Guomindang. Teachers knew that, except for the devoted Chinese language student, "it was impossible to reproduce the exact pronunciation by the use of the Western alphabet in any form." [5]

In 1951, shortly after the Communists achieved power in China, Mao Tse-tung expressed an interest in developing a new phonetic alphabet for translating the Chinese language. Burdened with many Chinese dialects, the Communist leadership wanted to unify the nation by developing a common language based on Mandarin, or Northern Chinese. The easiest way to teach Mandarin Chinese in elementary schools, as it is the easiest way to teach any language, is through a phonetic alphabet. Calligraphy, a writing system based on symbols rather than phonetics, simply was too difficult for the masses to learn and provided no aid in pronunciation of Mandarin. The Wade-Giles System was considered inadequate. In an attempt to develop a universal means of translating Chinese into Western phonetics, a National Language Reform Committee was convened to examine the hundreds of potential techniques. Eventually, in 1958, a new system was developed for phonetic transliteration called Hanyu Pinyin. [6]

Communist China adopted the Pinyin System for its schools to aid students in learning the correct Mandarin pronunciation for all characters in Chinese calligraphy. At first glance, the Pinyin System appears to be more logical than the Wade-Giles System. Pinyin eliminated the P, T, K, and Ch problems by spelling the names more like they sounded in Mandarin Chinese. Thus, Kuomintang was spelled as Guomindang, Taoism as Daoism, and Peking as Beijing. [7] By 1963, some American University Chinese language teachers adopted the Pinyin System proclaiming it more rational and effective in teaching Chinese pronunciation than the old Wade-Giles System. [8]

Communist China continued to print its English language publications, such as the **Peking Review, China Pictorial**, and **China Reconstructs** using the Wade-Giles System but began a campaign to get the Pinyin System adopted by all nations using the Roman alphabet. When the People's Republic of China was admitted to the United Nations in 1971, government intensified its efforts to obtain an international agreement to drop the Wade-Giles System of translating Chinese in favor of the new Pinyin System.

Despite Taiwan's opposition, the United Nations Committee on Standardization of Geographical Names voted in 1977 to accept the new Pinyin spelling for all Chinese names. Communist China announced to the world that it would implement the new Pinyin spelling in all is publications and correspondence effective January 1, 1979. [9]

Shortly thereafter, President Jimmy Carter accepted Communist China's offer of reciprocal diplomatic recognition. In a burst of enthusiasm, Carter directed the State Department to adopt the Pinyin spelling system for all Chinese names since it was desired by Peking now to be called Beijing. The United States press responded by immediately adopting the Pinyin spelling of Chinese names. **The New York Times** announced it would use the Communist Chinese spelling as of March 5, 1979. The Pinyin System, the **Times** proclaimed, was superior to the Wade-Giles System because it provided a more accurate transliteration of Mandarin Chinese pronunciation. [10]

Adopting the Pinyin System appeared overwhelmingly logical. Communist China used the Pinyin System and, since China belonged to the Chinese, they had the right to spell their names, cities, and historical figures as they pleased. Besides, everyone acknowledged, the Pinyin System was more logical and rational than the old Wade-Giles System. Few observers noted that the switch required a gigantic retooling effort by the general public as well as scholars. Fewer still noted that even the Pinyin System had phonetic problems.

For scholars and the publishing world the switch to the Pinyin System was a nightmare. Conversion of names from Wade-Giles to the new Pinyin spelling generated extensive confusion as Mao Tse-tung became Mao Zedong, Chou En-lai became Zhou En-lai, Teng Hsiao-p'ing became Deng Xiaoping, Chu Chiu-pai became Qu Quibai, Ch'iang K'ai-shek became Jiang Jieshi, and Hsu Hsiang-chien became Xu Xiangqian. Communist China also simultaneously included new names for many geographical areas with Tibet, for example, becoming

Xizang, Canton becoming Guangzhou, Amoy becoming Xiamen, and so on. [11] Equally confusing was the fact that in many instances the new Pinyin spelling was as phonetically illogical as the old Wade-Giles System. In the Wade-Giles System, p was pronounced as b, t as d, ch as j, and k as g. Hence, the correct pronunciation of Peking was Beijing, of Taoism was Daoism, of Chou was Joe, and Kuomintang was Guomindang. In the Pinyin spelling there were equally irritational usages.

In Pinyin, C is pronounced as TZ, X is pronounced as Hs, Zh is pronounced as J, and Q is pronounced as Ch. Thus, Ci Xi is pronounced as Tzu Hsi, Zhou as Joe, and Qin as Chin.

Some scholars and publishers decided to ignore the new Pinyin spelling while some adopted it partially and some adopted it with slavish devotion. In 1982, three years after the official adoption of the Pinyin System, Professor John Fairbank of Harvard published a new book titled **Chinabound: A Fifty Year Memoir** in which he used the Wade-Giles spelling system and did not mention the new Pinyin spelling. Immanuel C. Y. Hsu, professor of History at the University of California at Santa Barbara, one of the world's foremost experts on China, reluctantly switched to Pinyin. In the 3rd edition of his classic, **The Rise of Modern China** (1983), Professor Hsu continued to use the Wade-Giles spelling, but in two appendices, provided conversion charts to Pinyin. In his latest book, **China Without Mao** (1983), Professor Hsu compromised. "In reference to mainland China," he used the Pinyin phonetic spelling system. For Taiwan and all overseas Chinese names, Hsu continued to use the Wade-Giles spelling. He noted an obvious loophole—Taiwan and the overseas Chinese did not adopt the Pinyin spelling.

Another loophole created even greater confusion. According to the **Beijing Review**, an official publication of the People's Republic of China, "the traditional spelling of certain historical places and persons such as Confucius and Sun Yat-sen need not be changed." [12] Apparently, each author could decide which historical places and persons would remain in the old Wade-Giles System. It is noteworthy that Dennis Bloodworth, an old China hand, insisted that the title of his new book on China be **The Messiah and the Mandarins:**

Mao Tse-tung and the Ironies of Power (1982). Bloodworth used the Wade-Giles spelling for Chou En-lai, Ch'iang K'ai-shek, Sun Yat-sen, Kuomintang, and for place names, Peking, Nanking, Chungking, Canton, and the Yangtse River. Fox Butterworth, a reporter for **The New York Times**, in **China Alive in the Bitter Sea** (1982) refused to alter four place names—Peking (Beijing), Canton (Guangzhou), Tibet (Xizang), and Mongolia (Nei Monggol)—plus retaining the traditional spelling for places and people outside Communist China such as Hong Kong (Xiang Gang) and Nationalist leaders such as Ch'iang K'ai-shek (Jiang Jieshi). Jonathan D. Spence, Professor of History at Yale University, in **The Gate of Heavenly Peace** (1981) converted nearly all Chinese historical figures from 1895 to 1980 to the Pinyin spelling. Spence made only two exceptions: Ch'iang K'ai-shek and Sun Yat-sen. W. Scott Morton, in the second edition (1982) of his **China: Its History and Culture** made no exceptions but did make a compromise by including both spellings—the text read Jiang Jieshi (Ch'iang K'ai-shek), Qu Quibai (Chu Chiu-pai), Xu Xiangqian (Hsu Hsiang-chien), Guomindang (Kuomintang), Ci Xi (T'zu Hsi), and Guangzu (Kuang Hsu). Some publishers simply provided the new spelling and ignored the old such as **Journey into China** (1982) by the National Geographical Society and **The Great Wall** (1981) published by McGraw-Hill.

Adoption of the Pinyin phonetic spelling system caused outlandish problems for teachers. From 1867 to 1979, all Chinese names in English were spelled using the Wade-Giles System. To read and understand the tens of thousands of books published on China before 1979, the student needed to know the Wade-Giles System. To read and understand contemporary publications, the student needed to know the Pinyin spelling. For China specialists, the task was formidable but most slowly accepted the new Pinyin spelling.

For the Asian area teacher, the adoption of the Pinyin System was a major irritant. Few scholars teach exclusively about one Asia country. At most U.S., colleges, and universities, the same professor teaches survey courses on Japan, China, Southeast Asia, India, and the Vietnam War. If the teacher was not a China expert but rather an expert on Japan or India or Vietnam or the Philippines, the new spelling was a chore to learn. Only a few major universities in the United States support an expert on T'ang China, or even Communist China, who teaches exclusively in that field. The new Pinyin spelling system requires other Asian specialists, even those whose treatment of China was secondary, to re-educate themselves in Chinese studies.

Re-education is often delightful, but it is no delight to be forced to "retool." As William Safire noted in **The New York Times,** (March 11, 1979), "resentment and resistance set in when language change is dictated" more by governments than rational need. Even the Renaissance man grumbles when he is forced to relearn changes dictated by new modern nations for nationalistic reasons. Name changes seems to be a favorite game: Batavia becomes Djakarta; Saigon becomes Ho Chi Minh City; Cambodia becomes Kampuchea; Ceylon changes to Sri Lanka; Burma becomes Myanmar; and the old favorite, Siam becomes Thailand.

Russell Baker, **The New York Times** (Dec. 28, 1980), declared the new Pinyin spelling was simply too much. "In the short run," Baker said, the results of the new Pinyin spelling "is to make it harder than ever to make any sense out of China." The "new spelling may approximate Chinese pronunciation slightly better than the old and… in 30 to 40 years English speakers will get used to it." But, Baker continued, "the temptation, if you figure you may not have 30 to 40 years to get used to it, is to throw up the hands and write off China as one of those things you are never going to have time to learn."

FOOTNOTES

1. Immanuel C.Y. Hsu, **The Rise of Modern China,** (N.Y.: Oxford University Press, 3rd edition, 1983), p. xviii.

2. Thomas Francis Wade, **A Progressive Course in Colloquial Chinese** (London: Trubner, 1867), page v, noted that no transliteration system of a Chinese dialect is "more than an approximation."

3. Herbert A. Giles, **A Chinese English Dictionary**, 3 Volumes (London: Quaretch, 1912).

4. All authorities agreed.

5. W. Scott Morton, **China: Its History and Culture** (N.Y.: McGraw-Hill, 1980), p. xix.

6. **Peking Review**, March 11, 1958, "Making Chinese Easier to Learn," pp. 14-16; **Peking Review**, Oct. 28, 1958, "Progress in Popularizing the Phonetic Alphabet," pp. 15-17; **Beijing Review**, August 18, 1980, "Special Feature: Language Reform," pp. 19-26.

7. For detailed pronunciation guides see: Dennis K. Yee, **Chinese Romanization: Self-Study Guide**, a Comparison of Yale and Pinyin Romanization and a Comparison of Pinyin and Wade-Giles Romanization (Honolulu: University of Hawaii, 1975); and United States, Joint Publication Research Service, No. 72501 (Dec. 26, 1978), **Handbook for Pinyin Romanization of Chinese Proper Names.**

8. See John DeFrancis, **Beginning Chinese**, New Haven: Yale University Press, 1963, p. xviii.
9. **Beijing Review**, Aug. 18, 1980, p. 24.
10. Feb. 4, 1979.
11. Conversion charts appeared everywhere. See for examples: Hsu, **Rise of Modern China**, Appendices; **Asia: The Language, Focus on Asian Studies**, I (Spring 1982), p. 39; **Beijing Review**, Aug. 18, 1980; **The New York Times**, Feb. 4, 1979.
12. **Ibid.** Aug. 18, 1980, p. 24.

Pinyin

Wade-Giles
Pronunciation Difficulties

When a letter is followed by an apostrophe ('), it is pronounced as that letter: Ch', T', P', K', etc.

When the same letter is not followed by an apostrophe ('), the letter or letters are pronounced differently:
1. Ch(j)=Chou is pronounced Joe
2. T(d)=Taoism is pronounced Daoism
3. P(b)=
4. K(j)= Peking is pronounced Beijing

Other problems include:
1. Ts(z), Tz(z)=Mao Tse-tung is Mao Zedong
2. Hs(s)
3. J(r)

II. Pinyin System
Pronunciation

Vowels and consonants are basically pronounced the same as in English with a number of major exceptions:

1. Q is pronounced as Ch: Ch'in Dynasty is spelled Qin & pronounced Chin
2. Zh is pronounced as J: Chou becomes Zhou pronounced as Joe
3. X is pronounced as Hs: Teng Hsiao-ping becomes Deng Xiaoping pronounced Deng Hsiaoping
4. C is pronounced as Z: Tzu Hsi becomes Ci Xi pronounced as Zu Si

VI

COURSES TAUGHT

Chinese Culture (every semester). Although I utilized a broadly chronological approach to examine China from prehistory to 1997, my major emphasis was on Chinese society, philosophies, and religions. Operating under the thesis that culture changes less rapidly than politics, I helped students attempt to understand the Chinese through their social and intellectual ideas. Family relationships, Confucianism, Taoism, Legalism, Buddhism, and Maoism were the many topics discussed in class. I enjoyed teaching this course. *Syllabus attached to this Appendix section.

Vietnamese Culture (varied; every semester in the 1970s to every third semester in the 1990s). Vietnamese culture formed an integral part of this course, but the major emphasis was on the Vietnam War from 1940 to 1973. American involvement and failures in Vietnam were examined within the context of both American and Vietnamese attitudes and policies. When I first taught this course in 1966, the title was Southeast Asian Cultures and included an analysis of all nine countries in the area stretching from Burma to the Philippines. Later, I broke this into two courses: The Island Nations of Southeast Asia (Indonesia, the Philippines, Singapore, and Malaysia) and Mainland Southeast Asia (Burma, Thailand, Laos, Cambodia, and Vietnam). The last incarnation, concentrating on Vietnam, still analyzed area rivalries and conflicts but ended with an evaluation of the then-current situation in Vietnam.

Revolution in China (upper-level history course, alternate semesters). This course began with the Opium War in 1839 and proceeded through the revolutionary movement in China from the T'aiping Rebellion to Mao Zedong's takeover in October 1949. I enjoyed teaching this course and believed the time period was inherently interesting. Topics included: the Western impact on traditional China; peasant rebellions and traditional society; the Boxer Rebellion; Sun Yat-sen and the Nationalist Movement; Ch'iang K'ai-shek's rise to power; Mao Zedong's concepts of guerrilla war; World War II in the Pacific; and the Chinese Civil War, 1945 to 1949.

Communist China (upper-level history, alternate years). When Mao Zedong declared the People's Republic of China in October of 1949, the new government dreamed of a utopian society of equality. It failed to achieve its grand objectives, however, partially because of a struggle between the ideological-oriented members of the Communist Party and the practical-minded members of the government. This course examined the initial dream and the squabbles that disrupted Chinese society through the 1970s, and how these internal upheavals influenced Chinese foreign policy from the Korean War through the Vietnam War. *Syllabus attached.*

The American Empire: The Spanish–American War & Its Ramifications (upper-level history, alternate years). Patriotism swept the United States when Congress declared war on Spain in April 1898. "Remember the Maine!" became the jingo of the press, and Theodore Roosevelt and Admiral Dewey became the heroes of the day. But with victory came problems as the United States ended a century of grand isolationism. Most significant was the acquisition of the Philippines, where a rebellion erupted as Aguinaldo and his followers demanded independence.

American Diplomacy in East and Southeast Asia (graduate seminar, alternate years). This was a reading seminar and lectures were used sparingly. The content varied according to the availability of certain books. Some of the subjects covered: the Philippine Revolution, 1899 to 1901; the Boxer Rebellion; World War II in the Pacific; the Chinese Civil War; the Korean War; and the Vietnam War.

Communist Revolutions in Asia (graduate seminar, alternate years). A reading seminar. The students read seven to ten books and wrote a paper on one of the Communist upheavals in Asia. Typical topics: Mao Zedong's theories of guerrilla war; the Chinese Civil War; the PKI (Indonesia); Ho Chi Minh and the Vietnamese Revolution; the Khmer Rouge; the Pathet Lao; Kim Il-sung and the Korean Revolution. *Syllabus attached.*

Occasionally Taught Courses

Senior history seminar (revolved around the Western Connecticut History Department; professors took turns—thus I taught it about every three years). As in most history departments, this senior paper course was both a joy and a pain. When I was forced to teach it, I usually enjoyed the students more than in any other class, but I also felt overworked. The course's goal was to teach the students how to research and write a thirty- to forty-page academic article. See the Pinyin article as an example of such an article, albeit in shorter form.

Japanese Culture. I reluctantly taught this course three or four times when our Japanese expert, Professor Warner, was on sabbatical or ill. My interest in Japan revolved around Oriental philosophy and culture, World War II, and the American occupation period. The students' prime interest was modern Japan's economic policies, and I spent more time explaining Japan's trading practices than discussing Zen Buddhism.

American History. From 1966 to 1980, I taught at least one survey course in American history each semester. Usually I covered United States history from 1787 to 1877. From 1982 to 1997, I occasionally taught the Federalist Period and Beyond, 1787 to 1816.

VII

Sample Syllabi

1. **Chinese Culture**. Core Course open to all; usually made up of thirty or forty students, with 60 percent freshman and sophomores. Six other courses could fulfill the requirement including Middle Eastern Culture, Japanese Culture, etc.

2. **Communist China: 1949 to Present**. Upper-level history class offered every third semester. The History Department required majors to take six upper-level history courses (and two literature or social science courses). The course was open to any upperclassmen as an elective regardless of major. Usually a class of twenty-five quickly became twenty when they saw the requirements.

3. **Communist Revolutions in Asia**. Reading seminar open to MA students from any department. Graduate-level course that continues the China theme and more; offered alternate years. The class usually began with twenty-five students and reduced to fifteen to twenty when they saw the requirements.

I included these syllabi to show how my courses became more scholarly (intellectually demanding) at each level.

I have read every book mentioned in each syllabus. Every time

I taught a course, I added and subtracted books. These syllabi were included to illustrate the typical courses I taught and the depth of my knowledge on the subjects I taught. I was a good scholar, writer, director, and speaker. I did my best not to bore the student.

Peruse—i.e., flip through—the pages until you find a topic that interests you. Maybe, someday you can ask me what I said in my course on the topic.

Glance through the other courses I taught. All have comparable syllabi.

Check the Pinyin article, above, for the spelling and pronunciation of Chinese words translated into English.

Syllabus 1

CHINESE CULTURE:
NWC-103
Spring 1997
WH 305 12-12:50

Instructor:

Professor Kenneth R. Young, Office White Hall O22, Hours: M-W-F, 10:00 to 10:50. If you really want to talk, catch me after my last class, 11-to 11:50, Monday, Wednesday or Friday. I will not wait around the office, so either make an appointment or be waiting when I come down from class.

Smoker: also check outside.

Required Books:

Mark Salzman, **Iron and Silk**, Feb. 12 (Wednesday)
Lao She, **Rickshaw**, April 4
Liu Zongren, **Two Years in the Melting Pot**, April 25
Paul Theroux, **Riding the Iron Rooster**, Extra credit at final

Tests:

Three book tests (33%) on due dates listed above; a midterm (33%) around March 14; and a final (33%) on Friday, May 16.

Course Outline

TRADITIONAL CHINA

I. Feudal Kingdoms

Shang (c.1523-1027) to Chou (BC 1027-221)
Feudalism & Warlords
Religion: Animism
Calligraphy; Transliteration; Wade-Giles; Pinyin

II. Philosophical Schools

Taoism: Lao Tzu; Chuang-tzu
Confucianism: Mencius & Hsun Tzu
Legalism: Han Fei Tzu

III. The Chin (BC221-209)

Shih Huang-ti
Li Ssu & Legalism
Economics: State ownership; farmer-soldier; taxes
Culture: book burners
Collapse: Liu P'ang

IV. The Han (BC 206 to AD 220)

Bureaucratic Government: The Structure
Emperor
Council of State

Back in the Day

Censurate Boards (Cabinet)
Provinces
Civilian Governor Military Governor
Districts

Bureaucratic Recruitment
Grades & Examinations
Contents of Examinations
"Classics":
(1) Book of Rituals; (2) Book of Changes; (3) Book of History (4) Spring & Autumn Annals; (5) Songs or Poetry

Analects
Commentaries: Mencius, Hsun Tzu, Han Fei Tzu

Traditional Society
Clan-Village-Household-individual
Collapse: The Cyclical Theory

V. Disunity & Buddhism

Six Dynasties, 220-589
Spread of Buddhism to China
Pilgrims
Theravada Buddhism: Gautama, Hinduism, reincarnation, nirvana, caste, 4 Noble Truths, 8 Fold Path, Tripitaka, Lotus Sutra
Reasons for Adoption
Mahayana: Amida; Zen; Nicheren; Meditation

VI. The T'ang

Sui, 589-618
T'ang, 618-907: The Second Empire

Arts:

Poetry—Li Po, Tu Fu
Novels: Monkey; Golden Lotus; Romance of the Three Kingdoms; Men of the Marshes
Theater: Opera; Puppets
Painting

Collapse

VII. Alternating Dynasties

Sung, 960-1260: The Barbarians; Zhong Guo; The Great Wall; Military Colonies
Mongols (Yuan), 1260-1368: Genghis Khan; Kublai Khan
Ming, 1368-1644
Manchus (Ching), 1644-1912

REVOLUTION IN CHINA

I. Impact of the West

Marco Polo
Jesuits: Mateo Ricci; 1530-1773
Era of the Trading Companies
Barbarians; Trade Concepts; Diplomatic—Cohong or Canton System
Opium War (1839-1842) Lin Tse-hsu
Treaty of Nanking: Reparation; 5% Tariff; Ports; extrality; MFN
Arrow War (1856-1860)
Treaty of Peking: diplomacy; ports; opium travel
Effects: quasi-colony; prestige; rebellion

**Course normally ends here, but if time allows

II. The Rise of Mao Zedong

Biographical Sketch
Revolutionary Times
Communism & Confucianism
Mao theories of Guerrilla Warfare: Base Camp, terror, reforms, concentric circles, the short attack
Effects on World Revolution

Syllabus 2

Upper-Level History
Spring 1994

Communist China:
1949 to Present

I. Required Readings
  Bill Holm, **Coming Home Crazy,** Feb. 11
  Nien Cheng, **Life and Death in Shanghai**, April 4
  Harrison Salisbury, **The New Emperors**, April 13
  Fox Butterfield, **China Alive in the Bitter Sea**, May 6
II. Tests
  A midterm and a final, plus four book tests. Read the books and you will be able to answer any question I ask—guaranteed.

Course Outline
1. American Images of China: Myth and Reality
2. Geography of China: Geopolitical Setting
3. Communism and the Rise of Mao Zedong
4. PRCI—The First Year: Mopping up from Tibet to Korea
5. The Korean War
6. Peaceful Coexistence: 1953 to 1957
7. Internal Socialization
8. Economic Policies: 1950 to 1957

9. The First Purge: 100 Flowers
10. The Great Leap Forward
11. (1960) Zhou & Liu: The Practical Politician
12. The Cultural Revolution
13. Diplomacy: The Super Power
14. The Counter Revolution
15. Age of Liberalization: 1978-1989
16. Population Control
17. Sino-American Relations: Ping-Pong Diplomacy
18. Tiananmen Spring: June 1989
19. And to the Present (1994): The Economic Miracle

Syllabus 2 (cont.)
Communist China
1949 to 1994
Lecture Outline

I. Introduction: American Images of China: Myth & Reality

II. Geopolitical Setting
- China Proper
- North China: The Yellow River; Beijing
- Central China: Yangtze River; Nanking; Shanghai
- South China: Canton; food & images
- Outer Regions: Manchuria; Tibet; Inner Mongolia
- Other: Taiwan; Hong Kong

III. Communism & the Rise of Mao Zedong
- Brief Historical Review: China in Chaos, 1839 to 1949
- Mao Zedong: Biographical sketch
- Maoism: rural proletariat; protracted warfare. Stages of War: base Camp; terror tactics; reforms; concentric circles; guerrilla warfare; positional warfare
- Oct. 1, 1949: The Peoples Republic
- World Revolution theory: Underdeveloped Nations of the World
- Leadership: Mao, Chou, Chu, Liu, Lin, T'eng, et.al.

IV. People's Republic of China: Mopping up from Tibet to Korea

- Military operations:
  - Tibet
  - Taiwan: Ch'iang K'ai-shek and the Kuomintang
- Domestic policies: rural areas; urban areas
- People's Trials: the classes; the techniques; the numbers

V. The Korean War
- Introduction: "Let the Dust Settle"
- Korea: historical background: Kim Il-sung, Syngman Rhee
- June 25, 1950: Why?
- U.S. Reaction:
  - The Containment Theory
- United Nations
- June to August: U.N. Defeat
- Sept. to Oct.: MacArthur, Pusan, to the Yalu; "Home by Christmas"
- China's intervention: Oct. 1950; Why?
- MacArthur's Recall; Negotiations
  - Age of Hostility

VI. Peaceful Coexistence:
- Introduction: Korea & Indochina
- Geneva Conference of 1954: Chou En-lai
- Bandung Conference: peaceful coexistence with Southeast Asian Nations

VII. Internal Socialization, 1950-1957
- *The Party*: purpose (Lenin), size, membership; Youth League, Probation
- *Prison*: thought reform
- *Social Controls*: Party line; media; mass organizations
- *Small Group:* workplace, school, home, prison meetings: study, persuasion, struggle
- *The Arts*: Social Realism

VIII. Economic Policy, 1950-1957
- Urban Areas: state factories, offices, businesses

- work, small group
- Rural Areas: mutual aid teams to cooperatives

IX. 100 Flowers Campaign & Anti-Rightest purges
- Ideological Dispute: Reds vs. Experts
  - On Contradictions; on Criticism; the Three Evils, Three-Antis and
  - Five-Anti Campaigns
- Pressure: artists, writers, teachers, editors
- Mao Takes Command: rightest purge; thought reform; work camps

X. The Great Leap Forward
- Bootstraps
- State Ownership
- Urban areas: dormitories to state factories
- Rural: to communes
- Statistics and claims
- Results: deep economic depression

XI. Chou En-lai and Liu Shao-qi Take Command
- Introduction: Failure of the Great Leap
- 1960: The Experts regain power
- Top leadership: Chou En-lai; Liu Shao-qi; Deng Xiao-ping; Lin Biao
- Mao: Symbol of the Revolution—The Great Leader

XII. The Cultural Revolution
- Introduction
- Reasons for CR: Youth; entrenched bureaucracy
- The Stimulus: The Swim
- Cultural Revolution Committees
- Red Guard
- Thought Reform Centers & Labor Camps
- Cult of the Personality
- Ninth Party Congress, April 1969

XIII. Diplomacy & The Super Powers

Syllabus 3

Fall of 1995
Graduate Reading Seminar
Communist Revolutions in Asia

I. Required Reading
   Stanley Seagrave, **The Soong Dynasty**, due Sept. 25
   Edgar Snow, **Red Star Over China**, due Oct. 9
   C.P. Fitzgerald, **The Birth of Communist China**, Oct. 16.
   Ronald H. Spector, **After Tet**, Oct 30.
   Li Zhi-sui, The **Private Life of Chairman Mao**, Nov. 20
   Le Ly Hayslip **When Heaven and Earth Change Places**, Dec. 11

   On Due Dates:

   The class begins with a twenty-minute written test on the book followed by two hours of discussion.

II. Additional Reading:
   Each student will select *two* additional books from *two* different areas from the recommended reading list, and **one week prior** to the due date, provide the class with fifteen to twenty questions on the book. The questions do not have to be grand

and glorious, but rather something of interest. See the attached sample questions on Seagrave's **The Soong Dynasty.**

III. Grades

Grades rest on six tests on the required books, oral discussions, class reports on outside readings, and a comprehensive final.

IV. This is a reading seminar. There is no term paper.

Class Schedule

1. Sept 11: Introduction & Class Requirements. Review of each of the recommended books. After a fifteen-minute break, students may select the two recommended books. You may delay until next week, but no book can be selected by two students—first come gets the book.
2. Sept. 18. Lecture Communist Theory: From Marx to Lenin The Comintern & China Chinese Revolution, 1839 to 1927
3. Sept. 25: Sterling Seagrave, **The Soong Dynasty**, twenty-minute written test, two hours of class discussion on the book
4. Oct. 2: Chinese Society & Politics circa 1930. If a student selected one of the recommended books, questions due. Discussion. If no one selected a book, I will discuss the books and fill in the gaps.
   Recommended Reading
   Arnold Brackman, **The Last Emperor**
   Andre Malraux, **Man's Fate**
   Harold Isaacs, **Tragedy of the Chinese Revolution**
   Betty Lord, **Spring Moon**
   Pearl Buck, **The Good Earth**

5. Oct. 9: Edgar Snow, **Red Star Over China,** twenty-minute written test, two hours of discussion that includes
   Recommended Readings
   Dick Wilson, **The Long March**

Chamber Johnson, **Peasant Nationalism and Communist Power**

6. Oct. 16: World War II & After. C.P. Fitzgerald, **The Birth of Communist China,** twenty-minute written test, two hours of discussion that includes
   <u>Recommended Readings</u>
   Barbara Tuchman, **Stilwell**
   Theodore White, **In Search of History**, appropriate sections
   Jerome Ch'en, **Mao and the Chinese Revolution**
   A. Doak Barnett, **China on the Eve of Communist Takeover**

7. Oct. 23: Ho Chi Minh and the Vietnamese Revolution

   Part I: to 1954

   Jean Lacouture, **Ho Chi Minh**
   Lucien Bodard, **The Quicksand War**
   Bernard Fall, **Hell in a Very Small Place**
   Jules Roy, **The Battle of Dien Bien Phu**

8. Oct. 30: Part II, Vietnam to 1973. Ronald Spector, **After Tet,** twenty- minute written test, two hours of discussion that includes
   <u>Recommended Readings</u>
   Malcolm Browne, **New Faces of the War**
   Robert Shaplen, **The Lost Revolution**
   Marguerite Higgins, **Our Vietnam Nightmare**
   Bernard Fall, **Last Reflections on the War**
   Dennis Warner, **Certain Victory**
   Stanley Karnow, **Vietnam: A History**
   Philip Caputo, **Rumor of War**
   James Risner, **The Passing of the Night**
   Stephan A. Rowan, **They Wouldn't Let Us Die**
   Nhu Tan Troung, **V.C. Memoir**

9. Nov. 6: Case Studies in Southeast Asia
   <u>Recommended Readings</u>
   Indonesia
   John Hughes, **Indonesia Upheaval**
   Movie: "Year of Living Dangerously"
   Cambodia
   Haing Ngor, **Cambodian Odyssey**
   Movie: "The Killing Fields"
   Malaysia
   Noel Barber, **War of the Running Dogs**
   Robert Thompson, **Defeating Communist Insurgency**
   Laos
   Arthur Dommen, **Conflict in Laos**
   The Philippines
   Gregg R. Jones, **Red Revolution**

10. Nov. 13: Catch Up Day: Oral reports continue
11. Nov. 20: Communists in Power. Li Zhi-sui, **The Private Life of Chairman Mao,** twenty-minute written test, two hours of discussion that includes
    <u>Recommended Readings</u>
    Bao Ruo-wang and R. Chelminski, **Prisoner of Mao**
    Allyn and Adele Rickett, **Prisoner of Liberation**
    Liang Heng and Judith Shapiro, **Son of the Revolution**
    Nien Cheng, **Life and Death in Shanghai**
    Dennis Bloodworth, **The Chinese Machiavelli**
    Dennis Bloodworth, **The Messiah and the Mandarins**

12. Nov. 27: Oral reports continue
13. Dec. 4: A Different View
    <u>Recommended Readings</u>
    Fox Butterfield, **China Alive in the Bitter Sea**
    Harrison Salisbury, **The New Emperors**
    Bill Holm, **Coming Home Crazy**

Liu Zongren, **Two Years in the Melting Pot**
Simon Leys, **Chinese Shadows**
Paul Theroux, **Riding the Iron Rooster through China**

14. Dec. 11: Communist in Power
    Le Hayslip, **When Heaven and Earth Change Places,** twenty-minute written test, two hours of discussion that includes

    Part II: Vietnam

    <u>Recommended Readings</u>
    William Broyles, **Brothers in Arms:** A Journey from war to peace

15. Dec. 18: Final Exam

Syllabus 3 (cont.)

Sample Question Set:

Sterling Seagrave
The Soong Dynasty

Names to Remember:

Joffe
Charlie Soong
Ai-ling
May-ling (Madame Ch'iang)
Ch'iang-ling (Madame Sun)
TV SoongCh'iang K'ai-shek
Claire Chennault
Henry Luce
Green Gang and its leader Big Ear Tu Yueh-sheng
Mikhail Borodin
Theodore White

Discussion Questions
On written book tests, I will list three questions. You will select one to answer.

1. Discuss the development of Shanghai after 1860.
2. Ai-ling Soong was notorious for her financial cunning, but most people were unaware that she was the chief manipulator of the family destiny. "If she had been born a man," it was said, "she would have been running China." Discuss.
3. May-ling Soong Chiang "inspired two generations of Americans." Discuss.
4. Ching-ling, Madame Sun Yat-sen, remained loyal to the ideals of her husband. Discuss.
5. Discuss TV Soong.
6. Discuss Ch'iang K'ai-shek.
7. Discuss Henry Luce of **Time.**
8. Discuss Claire Chennault.
9. "To start with, their name was not really Soong." Discuss the family of Charlie Soong and how he obtained his name.
10. Discuss Charlie Soong's experiences in the United States.
11. Discuss the influence of religion on Charlie Soong.
12. Discuss Charlie Soong as a missionary.
13. Discuss the author's opinion of Charlie Soong—was he a good man?
14. Discuss Charlie Soong and the Red Gang.
15. Discuss Charlie Soong as a publisher.
16. Discuss Charlie Soong and Sun Yat-sen.
17. Discuss the education of the Soong Sisters.
18. Evaluate Sun Yat-sen as a revolutionist and as a person.
19. Discuss the Soong sisters and Sun Yat-sen.
20. Discuss the Green Gang and its leader Big Ear Tu Yueh-sheng.
21. Discuss Ch'iang K'ai -shek and the Green Gang.
22. Discuss the personality of Chiang K'ai-shek.
23. Discuss the Canton Government of Sun Yat-sen, circa May 1922.
24. Discuss the Russian policy in China 1922 to 1927.
25. Discuss Mikhail Borodin.
26. Discuss the situation in Shanghai around March-April 1927.
27. Discuss Ch'iang Ching-kuo, son of Ch'iang K'ai-shek.

28. Discuss the politics of Ch'iang-ling and visit to Russia. Was she a communist?
29. Discuss Ai-ling, wife of Ch'iang K'ai-shek.
30. Discuss Ch'iang K'ai's devotion to the Christian faith.
31. Discuss Japan's actions in China from 1914 to 1945.,
32. Discuss the financial problems of the Nanking Republic, 1927 to 1949.
33. Discuss the opium trade in China from 1927 to 1949, i.e., discuss the drug problem.
34. Discuss the kidnapping of Ch'iang by Ch'ang Hsueh-liang in December Dec. 1936, i.e., the Sian Incident.
35. Discuss Madame Ch'iang's visit to the U.S. in late 1942 to early 1943.
36. Discuss President Roosevelt and the Ch'iang regime.

www.ingramcontent.com/pod-product-compliance
Lightning Source LLC
Chambersburg PA
CBHW021926290426
44108CB00012B/738